POLITICS, RELIGION AND SOCIETY
IN ENGLAND, 1679–1742

Queen Anne
Enamel miniature by Charles Boit. *National Portrait Gallery*

POLITICS, RELIGION AND SOCIETY IN ENGLAND

1679 – 1742

GEOFFREY HOLMES

THE HAMBLEDON PRESS

LONDON   AND   RONCEVERTE

Published by the Hambledon Press, 1986

35 Gloucester Avenue, London NW1 7AX (U.K.)

309 Greenbrier Avenue, Ronceverte
West Virginia 24970 (U.S.A.)

ISBN 0 907628 75 3 (cased)
ISBN 0 907628 76 1 (paper)

British Library Cataloguing in Publication Data

Holmes, Geoffrey, *1928-*
    politics, religion and society in England,
    1672-1742.
    1. Great Britain – History – 1660-1714
    2. Great Britain – History – George I-II 1714-1760
        I. Title
    942.06   DA435

Library of Congress Cataloging-in-Publication Data

Holmes, Geoffrey S., 1928-
    Politics, religion, and society in England, 1679-1742

    Includes index.
    1. Great Britain – Politics and government –1660-1714 –
    Addresses, essays, lectures. 2. Great Britain – Politics and
    government – 1714-1760 – Addresses, essays, lectures.
    3. England – Church history – 17th century – Addresses,
    essays, lectures. 4. England – Church history – 18th
    century – Addresses, essays, lectures. 5. England –
    Social conditions – 18th century – Addresses, essays,
    lectures. I. Title.
    DA435.H615 1986   941.07   85-30571

Printed in Great Britain by WBC Print Ltd, Bristol

CONTENTS

LIST OF ILLUSTRATIONS

PERMISSIONS

The illustrations are reproduced by the kind permission of the following: The National Portrait Gallery, London (Frontispiece, 1, 3, 4, 6); The House of Lords Record Office (2); The Ashmolean Museum, Oxford (7).

FOR BILL SPECK

INTRODUCTION

The articles, essays and lectures brought together here, along with one pamphlet, were written and published over the course of twenty years between 1962 and 1982. Warts and all, they are reproduced without major amendment, although I have taken the opportunity, occasionally, to update some bibliographical and archival information, where this could be done with minimal disturbance of the typeface. I have also altered cross-references in the notes which would otherwise have been meaningless, and changed a handful of other unhelpful references. A short postscript has been added to paper 6, to clear up an ambiguity which has long troubled me. A few manuscript collections referred to in the notes are now no longer in the locations where I originally consulted them. By far the most important migration has been that of the Blenheim MSS, cited extensively in Paper 9 and used to document important points elsewhere. They are now in the British Library, embodied in the Additional Manuscripts (61101-61710). *The Marlborough-Godolphin Correspondence,* a substantial component of the Blenheim archive, has been edited by Henry L. Snyder (3 vols, Oxford, 1975). The Nicolson diaries, which I consulted in manuscript at Tullie House, Carlisle, and cite in that form, have been published as *The London Diaries of William Nicolson, Bishop of Carlisle, 1702-1718,* ed. Clyve Jones and Geoffrey Holmes (Oxford, 1985).

The twelve pieces selected for this volume reflect, on the one hand, a continuing interest in the political life of England under the later Stuarts and early Hanoverians, which was originally focused mainly on Anne's reign but which in time extended to the whole of 'the first age of Party', from the Exclusion Crisis of 1679-81 through to the period of Walpole's administration; and, on the other hand, a developing, parallel concern with both the religious climate and the social order of the country over this same period, for their own sake as well as for their importance in conditioning political activity.

The book falls logically into two parts, equal in length. The seven papers in Part I (which are arranged chronologically) are concerned exclusively with politics or politicians. Part II, however, though containing a substantial political overspill, has other priorities. In paper 8, for

instance, I consider how the religious loyalties and animosities which
had been the cause of so much division in Early Stuart, Civil War and
Republican England — especially allegiance to the Established Church
of England, devotion to the Puritan ideal and the passionate force of
anti-Popery — remained almost as great a source of tension and political
disturbance for thirty years, at least, after the 1688 Revolution as they
had been between the Restoration and the fall of James II; and this,
despite the illegalising of Catholic monarchy by the Bill of Rights in
1689 and the institutionalising of Protestant Dissent by a Toleration
Act in the same year. Years of friction between Anglicans and non-
coformists and between High Churchmen and Low Churchmen, as well
as between Tories and Whigs, inevitably created an atmosphere that
became dangerously overcharged. Since it was rendered even more un-
stable by persisting fears for the security of the Protestant Succession,
it could hardly fail ultimately to cause a spectacular political explosion.
This explosion duly occurred in the winter of 1709-10, after a High
Anglican clergyman, Dr Henry Sacheverell, had laid and fit the fuse.[1]
Its shock waves rocked Parliament and undermined a strong and able
government. But they also disturbed the normally inert substratum of
the English political nation, provoking in the process the second worst
London riots of the 18th century; and these effects are examined in
detail in a separate study (9), in which, among other things, a social
profile of the London 'crowd' in 1710 is constructed.

A prominent subject of debate for almost twenty years has been the
growth of political stability in early-18th-century Britain.[2] And while
historians may still not entirely agree as to why this took place, nor indeed as to how far it went, or how lasting it proved, few have seriously
challenged the importance of continuing religious conflict in perpetuat-
ing the chronic instability which had beset the 17th-century political
system and constitution. Likewise, few have failed to recognize the
tranquillising effect on politics after *circa* 1720 when religion became —
partly as a result of deliberate ministerial policy — a matter of lower
parliamentary and electoral priority. The isolated eruption of the old
fears and antagonisms which occurred thereafter — as in 1736 — only
served to emphasise the political acumen of Walpole's normal Church

1. Geoffrey Holmes, *The Trial of Doctor Sacheverell* (1973). Unless otherwise stated,
    London is the place of publication of all books cited in the footnotes to this Introduction.

2. The debate was initiated in Professor Sir John Plumb's 1965 Ford Lectures, published as
    The Growth of Political Stability in England, 1675-1725 (1967).

policy, which was that *quieta non movenda.*[3]   In the present volume, besides an essay on Walpole, there are two contributions to the debate on stability. The first paper discusses a major *de*stabilising force in the situation, the influence in the years between 1679 and 1722, during which 17 General Elections were held, of an energetic electorate which was as volatile in composition as it was in conduct; and this discussion concludes by offering some explanation of when and why a body which, in its rough and ready way, had succeeded for more than half a century in broadly reflecting the National Will through the represent-atives it sent to Westminster, fell captive to a relatively small clique of Whig ruling families, who had managed by the 1720s to monopolize the influence of the Crown. The second contribution to the debate **(10)**, by examining the social context of politics between the 1680s and the Walpole era, attempts a revision of accepted orthodoxy concerning the relationship between political stability and social stability in this period. Party zeal unquestionably caused rifts within every social group, from dukes down to the humbler small farmers and artisans; and with-out doubt, too, thousands of heavily-taxed country gentlemen genuine-ly felt their status threatened by the boost which almost twenty years of war gave after 1689 to certain (mostly Whiggish) business and pro-fessional interests, and above all to the 'monied men' of the City of London. None the less, it is argued that over the same period most non-political and non-religious developments were working directly counter to those fissiparous pressures: that demographic and economic trends, for instance, together with rising living standards and rapidly improving employment opportunities imparted (for all appearances to the con-trary) an *underlying* stability to English society which helped to

3.   Walpole, like most of his Cabinet colleagues in the 1720s and 1730s, was well aware that the powerful anti-clericalism still prevalent among many Whigs, the organized pressure of Dissent for further relief, and the unabated concern of the Tories for the interests of the Established Church, remained potentially disruptive forces: which makes his temporary aberration in supporting the Mortmain and Tithes bills in 1736 all the more puzzling. See Norman Sykes, *Edmund Gibson, Bishop of London, 1669-1748* (Oxford, 1926); N.C. Hunt, *Two Early Political Associations: The Quakers and the Dissenting Deputies in the Age of sir Robert Walpole* (Oxford, 1961); Linda Colley, *In Defiance of Oligarchy: the Tory Party, 1714-60* (Cambridge, 1982), chs. 4, 8; Stephen Taylor, 'Sir Robert Walpole, the Church of England, and the Quakers Tithe Bill of 1736', *Historical Journal,* 28, 1985.
      The example of England's largest county suggests, nevertheless, that by the 1730s the iron hand of government patronage in the velvet glove of conciliation had wrought a remark-able change in the political attitudes of the parish clergy. In the 1734 shire election the parsons of Yorkshire abandoned their traditional Tory allegiance in droves, and by 1742 barely more than a quarter of the 346 who polled voted for the candidate of the 'Church Party'. J.P. Quinn, *et al.,* 'Yorkshiremen go to the polls: County contests in the early eighteenth century', *Northern History* 21, 1985, p. 173.

confine the fury of party conflict within bounds that were − or in time
became − acceptable and respectable.[4] Hence the decline of popular
radicalism for decades after 1688 and, at the other end of the spectrum,
the minimal involvement of politically proscribed members of the
English social élite in the conspiracies and rebellions of the years from
1683 to 1722, with the partial exception of the Revolution of 1688.

Two of the distinguishing features of late Stuart and early Hanoverian English society which did most to ensure that the achievement of
social stability both antedated and assisted the restoration of stability
to the political system and the constitution, were the flexibility of the
social structure and the degree of upward mobility which that structure, and the social conventions of the day, permitted. Both features
were the exception rather than the rule in contemporary Europe. Both
are touched on in paper 10, and linked with other trends of the day,
such as the significant growth of towns and the superimposition of
urban on rural or 'county' values in the century before the Industrial
Revolution. But each figures much more prominently in the two closing
studies in this collection. Many of the assumptions made for so long
about the 18th century social structure were deeply influenced by the
static view of it taken in 1696 by the pioneer statistician, Gregory King.
The celebrated social table, inserted by King into the 'Natural and
Political Observations' which he wrote in that year, ostensibly
subjecting the England of 1688 to what we should now call 'quantitative analysis', exercised until recently a mesmeric effect on historians;
and the discovery by Professor Mathias that King's only 18th-century
counterpart, Joseph Massie (1760), was also under his spell[5] made
exorcism no easier for us. Paper 11, by seeking to demonstrate that
Gregory King's 'Scheme of the income and expense of the several
families of England... for the year 1688' was largely coincidental to his
main purpose in writing his *Observations,* and that his estimates alike
for the size of social groups and for their average annual income and

---

4. It may be that a further factor was the strengthening of traditional bonds of deference at a
    time when the aristocracy was rebuilding its social and political, as well as its economic
    dominance. This is an important theme of recent work by John Cannon, *Aristocratic
    Century: the Peerage of Eighteenth Century England* (Cambridge, 1984), and J.C.D.
    Clark, *English Society, 1688-1832* (Cambridge, 1985). On the other hand, the limitations
    of 'deference' in the preservation right through to 1742 of a non-radical but vigorous
    tradition of popular politics, are revealed by H.T. Dickinson in a masterly essay, 'Popular
    Politics in the Age of Walpole', in Jeremy Black, ed., *Britain in the Age of Walpole* (1984).

5. Peter Mathias, 'The Social Structure in the Eighteenth Century: A Calculation by Joseph
    Massie', *Economic History Review,* 10, 1957.

expenditure were based on highly dubious evidence as well as shaky methodological foundations (in sharp contrast to some of his rightly-praised demographic calculations), support the conclusion that King's value to social, economic or political historians is strictly limited.[6] Furthermore, by setting some of King's more widely-used social statistics against other figures and estimates for the 17th and 18th centuries, which have stemmed from the independent work of modern scholars, it suggests a model for a pre-industrial social structure which was susceptible to organic change and receptive to the operation of mobile elements within it.

The traditional rungs of the ladder of rural society up which many ambitious and successful families had clambered to social prominence, or at least 'gentility', in the 16th and early 17th centuries (tenant farmer or freeholder − substantial yeoman − parish 'gentleman' − squire− and sometimes higher) do seem to have grown more difficult of access and more slippery between 1660 and 1750.[7] Yet this was compensated for by the fact that other avenues of mobility grew wider and attracted an increasing volume of upward traffic. Such was clearly the case with the trade and industry avenues, especially after the 'Commercial Revolution' began to gather momentum from the late 1660s onwards.[8] But even more enticing were the social opportunities presented by the remarkable expansion and diversification of the English professions from around 1680 onwards. The final contribution to this volume (12) examines this phenomenon over the following half-century, analyzing some of its causes and effects, and stressing two aspects, in particular: on the one hand, the important part played by formal

6. In an illuminating article Colin Brooks has since explained that it was an integral part of the social and political philosophy of King and of other political arithmeticians, that 'the social order had to be stabilized, if not "frozen"'. C. Brooks, 'Projecting, Political Arithmetic and the Act of 1695', *English Historical Review,* 97, 1982.

7. The evidence is not, however, overwhelmingly one-sided, as the case of Lincolnshire shows; and the opportunities denied in some areas may still have been present in others, where taxation, for example, was less burdensome and a different type of farming prevalent. E.A. Holderness, 'The English Land Market in the Eighteenth Century: The Case of Lincolnshire', *Economic History Review,* 27, 1974; cf. J.V. Beckett, 'The Pattern of Landowner-ship in England and Wales, 1660-1880',*Econ. Hist. Rev.,* 37, 1984; C.G.A. Clay,*Economic Expansion and Social Change: England 1500-1700* (Cambridge, 1984), vol. I, pp. 92-101, 158-64.

8. See, for instance, Richard Grassby, 'Social Mobility and Business Enterprise in Seventeenth-Century England', in D.H. Pennington and Keith Thomas, eds., *Puritans and Revolutionaries* (1978); Marie B. Rowlands, *Masters and Men in the West Midland Metalware Trades before the Industrial Revolution* (Manchester, 1975); also below, p. 266.

apprenticeship in the rise of the professions, especially in the development of the legal and medical professions, and the significance of that for young men of talent and good fortune from relatively disadvantaged backgrounds; and on the other hand, the exceptionally favourable climate for advancement in some professions[9] created by a quarter of a century (1689-1713) that was dominated by warfare.[10]

Politics in the years from 1679 and 1742 have intrigued modern historians, and will doubtless continue to do so, not merely because of their vigour but because of the many dimensions they present for investigation. Inevitably a number of very important facets are not explored in the papers which follow. Prominent absentees, some of which have attracted notable attention since most of my early work on politics was published in the 1960s, include the politics of the press, of the city of London and its clubs, and of Jacobitism.[11] Nor is there any hint here of the struggles in the provincial corporations either in the 1680s or thereafter.[12] Nevertheless readers of this miscellany should acquire some insight into the working of late 17th and early 18th century politics at very different levels: from the high politics of courts and ministerial power struggles (3, 6) and the propaganda and proselytising politics of the pulpits and of their Anglican and dissenting occupants (8, 9) to the grass-roots politics of the constituencies (1) and the low politics of the streets (9). Even when focusing on the par-

9. The armed services, the bureaucracy, and those branches of teaching involved in mathematical and technical instruction.

10. Cf. my *Augustan England: Professions, State and Society, 1680-1730* (1983), some of whose arguments and illustrations are, of course, anticipated in the 1979 Raleigh Lcture with which the present collection closes.

11. See, *inter alia*, J.A. Downie, *Robert Harley and the Press: Propaganda and public opinion in the age of Swift and Defoe* (Cambridge, 1979); Michael Harris, 'Print and Politics in the Age of Walpole', in Jeremy Black, ed., *Britain in the Age of Walpole* (1984); Gary S. De Krey, *A Fractured Society: The Politics of London in the First Age of Party, 1688-1715* (Oxford, 1985); H. Horwitz, ed., 'Minutes of a Whig Club, 1714-1717', in H. Horwitz, W.A. Speck and W.A. Gray, eds., *London Politics, 1713-17* (London Record Soc. Publications, vol. 17, 1981); I.G. Doolittle, 'Walpole's City Elections Act (1725)', and Nicholas Rogers, 'The City Elections Act (1725) reconsidered', *English Historical Review*, 97, 1982 and 100, 1985; Bruce Lenman, *The Jacobite Risings in Britain, 1689-1746* (1980); D. Szechi, *Jacobitism and Tory Politics, 1710-14* (Edinburgh, 1984); Eveline Cruickshanks, *Political Untouchables: the Tories and the '45* (1979), chs. 1 and 2.

12. See R.G. Pickavance, 'The English Boroughs and the King's Government: A Study of the Tory Reaction, 1681-5', Univ. of Oxford D. Phil. thesis, 1976; John Miller, 'The Crown and the Borough Charters in the Reign of Charles II', *English Historical Review*, 100, 1985; Judith J. Hurwich, '"A Fanatick Town": the Political Influence of Dissenters in Coventry, 1660-1720', *Midland History*, 4, 1977.

liamentary arena the perspective is not artificially narrow. It is doubtful whether the House of Lords has ever been more directly influential over the course of political events and fortunes than in the years between the defeat of the second Exclusion Bill in 1680 and the rise of Walpole to power in the early 1720s. The Upper House is put under the microscope here in two essays (4, 5) which illustrate how important the balance of forces in the Lords could be to the prospects, and in some cicumstances the very survival, even of a seemingly well-entrenched administration like the last Tory ministry of Queen Anne (1710-14).[13] And the same two studies – one of them written in conjunction with Clyve Jones – also reflect my interest in the serious political teething troubles of the Union of England and Scotland, established in 1707, and in the way the world of Westminster was forced to adapt itself thereafter to the replacement of the separate Parliaments of England and Scotland by the united Parliament of Great Britain.

Another revealing perspective on Westminster politics is the view from the back benches of the House of Commons. Such a view, even when taken, as it is here (2), over a period – from 1702 to 1716 – when the rivalry and struggle for supremacy between Whigs and Tories was at its most intense, reminds us that many M.P.s had other preoccupations and that there were times when these became major priorities. A tradition of 'Country' suspicion of the Court, and the associated conviction that it was the duty of independent members of Parliament to act, when it seemed necessary to do so, to preserve the purity of the constitution from taint, had taken root in Restoration Parliaments some years before the formation of the Whig and Tory parties during the Exclusion Crisis. The persistence of this Country tradition after the 1688 Revolution and the Revolution settlement, and the bipartisan coalitions which this produced from time to time against the Crown (notably in William III's reign) or against the aggrandisement of ministerial influence in the Crown's name, has been illuminated by a number of recent writings[14]. And it is in this context

13. For discussion of the problems and methods involved in the government's management of the House of Lords in these years, see my *British Politics in the Age of Anne* (1967), pp. 382-403 *passim*, and Clyve Jones, '"The Scheme Lords, the Necessitous Lords and the Scots Lords": the Earl of Oxford's management and the "Party of the Crown" in the House of Lords, 1711-14', in *idem*, ed., *Party and Management in Parliament, 1660-1784* (Leicester, 1984).

14. J.A. Downie, 'The Commission of Public Accounts and the Formation of the Country Party', *English Historical Reivew*, 91, 1976; Colin Brooks, 'The Country Persuasion and Political Responsibility in England in the 1690s', *Parliaments, Estates and Representation*, 4, 1984; David Hayton, 'The "Country" interest and the party system', in Clyve Jones,

that the study I made twenty years ago of one of the most important and persistent of Country campaigns — that designed to limit drastically the number of government office-holders allowed by law to sit in the Commons — should now be set.

A prime mover in the emergence of a 'New Country' interest in the Lower House in the early years of William III was Robert Harley, elected M.P. for Tregony in April 1689. Although elected as a Revolution Whig, Harley went on to become, first, the kingpin of the Country opposition to William and his Whig Junto ministers in the later 1690s, and then under Anne, when he served the Court for all but two of the Queen's twelve years, the acknowledged rallying point for the moderate wing of the Tories and finally head of the Queen's last ministry from 1710 to 1714. Harley, created earl of Oxford in 1711, was in many ways the most significant figure and certainly the shrewdest manipulator in politics in the first twenty-five years after the Glorious Revolution, and it was, of course, Robert Walpole who took over that mantle, wearing it a good deal more flamboyantly, over the next twenty-five years. The former was as determined an opponent of party government — or, at least, of government by party extremists — as the latter was an exultant advocate of it, a fitting chief architect of the long Whig oligarchy after 1714. It is altogether appropriate, therefore, that both these political master-craftsmen should figure prominently in the gallery of personalities assembled in this volume Walpole is the subject of a study in his own right, briefly assessing his achievements and appraising his methods (7). Harley's presence is more pervasive, especially in Part I; but in particular he is brought into the spotlight at the two most critical junctures of his career, in 1708 and 1714 (3, 6). On both occasions, Harley's distinctive concept of the proper relationship between the Crown, the parties and the administration under the post-Revolution constitution was put to a searing test. Each time, the immediate future of the two political parties and the whole complexion of the government hinged on the outcome of his relations with the Queen and with his chief rivals in the power struggle at Court: Earl Godolphin and the duke of Marlborough in 1707-8, and Henry St John, Lord Bolingbroke, from 1711 to 1714. On the other hand, as I

ed., *op. cit.* In 'Whigs and Tories dim their glories: English political parties under the first two Georges', his essay in John Cannon, ed., *The Whig Ascendancy: Colloquies on Hanoverian England* (1981), William Speck argues that '"Court" and "Country" had become more meaningful terms [than Whig and Tory] to describe the realities of English politics by 1742'. For reservations expressed about his case, see the 'Colloquy' on this essay, ed. Geoffrey Holmes, *ibid.* pp. 71-5; Linda Colley, *In Defiance of Oligarchy*, pp. 90-101.

argued in 1969 (6) and as has since been conclusively proved (see 259-60 below), Oxford's success down to the autumn of 1713 in beating off the challenge of Bolingbroke and of his full-blooded, exclusive brand of Toryism, and the long rearguard action he fought then until his fall, only a few days before Queen Anne's death, did not in themselves condemn the Tory party to the lasting inferiority it was to suffer under the first two Georges. For that, the ineptitude, misjudgments and misfortunes of the Tories themselves *after* August 1714, and the combination of ruthlessness and luck with which the Whigs exploited them, were mainly responsible[15].

15. For a brief elaboration of this point, see my review article 'Eighteenth-Century Toryism', *Historical Journal*, 26, 1982, pp. 755-60.

ACKNOWLEDGMENTS

The contents of this volume first appeared in the following publications: (1) *The Electorate and the National Will in the First Age of Party* (privately published, Lancaster, 1976, an expanded version of an inaugural lecture delivered at Lancaster University, 1975); (2) *Bulletin of the Institute of Historical Research,* 39, 1966; (3) *English Historical Review*, 80, 1965; (4) *English Historical Review,* 77, 1962; (5) *Parliamentary History,* 1, 1982; (6) G. Holmes, ed., *Britain after the Glorious Revolution 1689-1714* (1969); (7) H. van Thal, ed., *The Prime Ministers,* vol. I, 1974; (8) *Religion and Party in Late Stuart England* (Historical Association, Pamph. G86, 1975); (9) *Past and Present,* 72, 1976; (10) J. Cannon, ed., *The Whig Ascendancy: Colloquies on Hanoverian England* (1981); (11) *Transactions Royal Historical Society,* 27, 1977; (12) *The Professions and Social Change in England, 1680-1730* (1981), British Academy Raleigh Lecture, 1979.

For permission to reprint matter originally published by them, the Hambledon Press and I are indebted to Messrs Macmillan, Allen and Unwin and Edward Arnold; to the British Academy, the Royal Historical Society, the Historical Association, and the Institute of Historical Research, University of London; and to *The English Historical Review, Past and Present* and *Parliamentary History.* Professor Bill Speck and Mr Clyve Jones have most generously agreed to the inclusion in this collection of two pieces of which they were, respectively, joint authors with me; and Professor Harry Dickinson to the re-publication of the 'Colloquy' which accompanied paper 10 at the latter's first incarnation. Alasdair Hawkyard's assistance with the index is gratefully acknowledged.

November 1985   G.S.H.

PART ONE

THE ELECTORATE AND THE NATIONAL WILL

IN THE FIRST AGE OF PARTY

IF THE 'INAUGURAL LECTURE' HAS A *RATIONALE* — AND I HAVE HEARD suggestions to the contrary — it is, I suppose, as an opportunity for the incumbent to pass on some of those 'mature thoughts' of academic middle-age which professors are assumed to harbour. The subject I have chosen for this lecture is certainly one I have been thinking about, on and off, for a very long time. Whether the wine, in this case, will be mature is not for me to prophesy; but at least I can assure you the bottle is old. My initiation into historical research, twenty-five years ago, was through a study of the electioneering activities of the English peerage in the early years of the eighteenth century.

Parliamentary elections, of course, have been a national addiction of the English for at least 350 years: they have always appealed to their inbred gambling instincts. And while infinite time and money have been expended in the indulgence of this pastime, successive generations of our countrymen have bet on the outcome, and argued, rejoiced, groaned and, in more recent times, goggled over the results. This common mania, together with a resurgence of interest lately in the reform of our own electoral system will, I hope, go some way to justify choosing this subject for a public lecture.

My own renewed concern, after a gap of many years, with the electoral history of my period has been largely stimulated by a change of focus. Originally I studied those whose aim it was to influence elections; now it is those whom they sought to influence, the voters themselves, who interest me most. Over the last decade or so the behaviour of the late seventeenth- and early eighteenth-century electorate has attracted much attention: through general studies, from J. H. Plumb, William Speck and John Cannon,[1] and from students of particular areas or particular Elections.[2] And in this work

---

[1] J. H. Plumb, 'The Growth of the Electorate in England from 1600 to 1715', *Past and Present*, 45, 1969; W. A. Speck, *Tory and Whig: The Struggle in the Constituencies 1701-1715* (1970); J. Cannon, *Parliamentary Reform 1640-1832* (Cambridge, 1972); R. Sedgwick (ed.), *The History of Parliament: The House of Commons 1715-1754* (1970), i, 115-21 (Contested Elections), 189-381 (Constituencies), hereafter cited as Sedgwick. Derek Hirst's *The Representative of the People?* (Cambridge, 1975), subjecting the electorate of early Stuart England to masterly scrutiny, was published after this lecture was written.

[2] E.g. R. Hopkinson, 'Elections in Cumberland and Westmorland 1695-1723' (Univ. of Newcastle, Ph.D. thesis, 1973); W. A. Speck, 'The General Election of 1715', E[nglish] H[istorical] R[eview], 90, 1975; P. Langford, *The Excise Crisis* (Oxford, 1975), pp. 101-171 [1734 Election].

that fashionable tool the computer has at times been brought profitably into play.[3]

My debt in this lecture to all this research is indeed a heavy one. Nevertheless, by setting some recent arguments and conclusions, along with work of my own, in a particular context; by approaching the evidence with a few fresh questions in mind; most of all by relating political evidence to other species of evidence — especially demographic and social evidence of a sort which too often tends to be undervalued by political historians — in all these ways, it seemed to me, one might hope to offer something more, and something with a difference.

*   *   *

The importance of studying the English electorate in what I have called 'the first age of Party' is not hard to demonstrate.   One major reason why the political stability which had eluded England right through the seventeenth century was not achieved for over three decades after the 1688 Revolution was, self-evidently, the novel division of Parliament and of the whole political nation into parties; and the apparent powerlessness of Englishmen, for over a generation after 1688, to come to terms with the bitter rivalry of these parties and their leaders' struggle for supremacy.   But a second and equally important explanation for the acute political stresses which wracked post-Revolution England unquestionably lies in the emergence of the electorate as a decisive force in politics.

These were the two inescapable features of the political system of the day — party, and a dominant electorate.   Each had its origins before 1688, and from first to last they were closely linked.   To illuminate both the title and the time-span of my paper, may I remind you that the first genuine political parties known to historians, Whigs and Tories, took clear shape in England during the Exclusion crisis between 1679 and 1681; while the faction-based oligarchy of the eighteenth century became firmly established in the 1720s.   Now this same period of just over forty years between 1679 and the early 1720s, the period which I would call 'the first age of Party', also saw in England an astonishing number of Elections; seventeen General Elections in forty-three years, or one on average every two and a half years.   (In the next forty-three years there were six, an average of one every seven years).

[3] E.g. by Hopkinson (see n. 2): W. A. Speck and W. A. Gray, 'Computer Analysis of Poll Books: an Initial Report', B[ulletin of the] I[nstitute of] H[istorical] R[esearch], 43, 1970, and 'Londoners at the Polls under Anne and George I', *Guildhall Studies in London History*, I, 4, 1975; Speck, Gray and Hopkinson, 'Computer Analysis of Poll Books: a Further Report', *B.I.H.R.* 48, 1975.

For students of the electorate, however, it is the second half of this period, from roughly 1700 onwards, which is by far the more fruitful; and it is these years which yield a good deal of the evidence on which my paper is based. This is partly because in those two decades the general political context of the electorate's activities is more clear-cut than either before or after. There were fewer cross-currents to disturb the clear flow of its Whig and Tory loyalties. But in the main it is a simple matter of evidence. Just before, or around, 1700 three springs of evidence can begin to be tapped which are either not available at all, or only briefly available, to historians of any previous period.

One is demographic evidence; and this I shall come back to later in my paper. The second is newspaper evidence, with the London newspapers for the first time since 1681 beginning to cover certain contested elections in reports which become indispensable from 1710 onwards. And thirdly there are the poll-books, those records of all who voted in particular elections, and of how they voted. These remain a peerless source for investigating the electoral behaviour of our ancestors, right down to the introduction of the secret ballot in 1872. Yet they survive in any numbers only after 1700; for it was as late as 1696 that returning officers were first obliged by law to take a copy of the poll at elections held under their jurisdiction and produce it on request.[4] The first *printed* poll-book I know of, however, resulted not from the passing of this Act but from the ghoulish public interest two years earlier in the suicide of the member for Essex, John Honywood. After a succession of unsuccessful efforts, involving 'thrusting the rump of a turkey down his throat', forcing 'tobacco-pipe ends into his mouth' and, more conventionally, throwing himself downstairs, he finally succeeded at the fourth attempt with the help (we are told) of 'an old broken garter, fastnd . . . to the curtain rod of his bed', plus 'the assistance of the Divil, for both the garter and the curtain-rod else could not have held a quarter of his weight'.[5]

The poll-book for the resulting Essex by-election, printed in London, must have opened the eyes of many politicians to the possibilities for their own electioneering of such a mine of information; and I suspect it played its part in the proposal embodied, almost casually, in the 1696 Act. At all events, from 1698 onwards, first in a trickle, finally in a spate,[6] we have at our disposal this

---

[4] By a clause in 7 & 8 Wm. III, *c.* 25, 'An Act for the further regulating elections of members to serve in Parliament, and for preventing irregular proceedings of sheriffs, and other officers'.

[5] *The Autobiography of Sir John Bramston* (Camden Soc. 1845), pp. 377-8.

[6] By 1970 Dr. Speck had located 148 (60 for counties, 88 for boroughs) for the period Dec. 1701-1715 alone: *Tory and Whig*, pp. 132-5. In the past five years many more have come to light, even for that short period.

marvellous new source for studying the English electorate at a period of unique dominance.

* * *

Ample work has been done of late to demonstrate this dominance: to show how this rampaging electorate, for all but a few of the forty-three years from 1679 to 1722, controlled the political fortunes of the so-called governing classes, toppled, buttressed or embarrassed governments, held at times the fate of the succession, and once that of the monarchy in its hands.[7]   Likewise the main reasons for this dominance are by now, I think, generally agreed: notably, after the Revolution, the patent unwillingness of two monarchs and of some leading ministers to deploy the interest of the Crown in elections, following the scandal caused by Stuart attempts at borough manipulation in the 1680s;[8] and above all the passing of the Triennial Act, which from 1694 to 1716 put a three-year maximum on the life of Parliaments, and became the chief contributor to that frequent exercise of the voters which helped to build electoral muscle.

The principal question I want to pose in this lecture, however, has not so far been squarely confronted.   It is this:

Granted that the votes of the electors in these years were immensely influential, how accurately did these votes, and the great political changes they wrought, reflect what we should call the 'public opinion' of the day?   Was there such a thing as a National Will in the first age of Party?   And if there was, how can we possibly be sure that the votes of a small, in some ways random, section of the population was transmitting this Will into the instruments of political action at Westminster?

On the face of it, one must admit, it seems rather absurd to refer in the same breath to 'public opinion' and to an electorate which was still manifestly 'unreformed'.[9]   In the 172 years between the Restoration and the first Reform Act the representative system in England and Wales remained unchanged in its essential features: the two-member constituency norm, outside Wales; the universal forty-shilling freehold qualification for a voter in each of the 52 counties,[10] yet the utterly fortuitous distribution of seats between

[7] Even James II in the late 1680s dared not put his attempts to tame it to the test.

[8] For some of the many instances, see (for 1690) Salop R.O. Attingham MSS. 112/3: Carmarthen to [Abingdon], 15 Feb.; (for Dec. 1701) Add. MSS. [Brit. Lib.] 7074, f. 72; (for 1702) Add. MSS. 29588, ff. 47, 93; H.M.C. Cowper MSS. iii, 13-14; (for 1707-8) P.R.O. 30/24/21/141,144: Sir J. Cropley to Lord Shaftesbury, 30 Dec. 1707 (recd.), 15 Jan. 1708.

[9] E. and A. G. Porritt, The Unreformed House of Commons, i (Cambridge, 1903).

[10] Unchanged since 1430.

counties; above all the bewildering variety of franchises in the 215 cities and parliamentary boroughs. Even in 1700 these made up a mosaic of astounding intricacy, all the more surrealistic because the number of voters within boroughs of the same type of franchise could vary so enormously: there might be 40 inhabitant householders (alias 'potwallers') or 1500; 50 freemen or 2000; 60 'Scot and Lot men' (or ratepayer voters) or 6000; 40 holders of burgage tenements or nearly 300.

Such features were as much a condition of electoral politics in the first age of Party, therefore, as they were of its second age, prior to 1832: apart from the fact that the Scots arrived to add their own weird eccentricities in 1707 (I have left them out of account in this paper) the *system* — if such it can be called — remained the same. Many of the 'rotten boroughs' of later eighteenth-century notoriety already disfigured the scene in 1680 or in 1700;[11] indeed sightseers were virtually encouraged to go and gape at them by superior guide-book writers of the early part of the eighteenth century.[12] Two members were regularly returned for a huddle of decrepit little Cornish fishing villages. Dunwich, up what East coast seamen called 'a lousie creek' in Suffolk, was already confidently said to be dropping into the sea: and Defoe, on viewing it in the 1720s, was moved to recall a couplet of stunning bathos:

> By numerous examples we may see
> That towns and cities die, as well as we.[13]

At Old Sarum it was a moot point, even in Queen Anne's reign, whether there was a single farm-house there or not, and if there was, whether anyone lived in it.[14] Assuredly there was little to be expected of any 'public opinion' in, say, the Yorkshire borough of Aldborough, where Browne Willis found in 1736 'a poor village of very mean cottage houses', whose sole claim to distinction apart from the beer at the *Duke of Newcastle's Arms* was that it contributed half of the four M.P.s sent to Westminster from a single parish, which also included Boroughbridge. And if little could be expected of Aldborough, how much more could be expected of the voters of Winchelsea, where they were said in the 1720s to 'have made good cornfields of the streets', and where, John Caryll told a prospective property-buyer, 'I question not but a stranger may be chosen there

[11] Most of them already decayed at the time of their original enfranchisement· Plumb, 'Growth of the Electorate', *loc. cit.* p. 98 and n. 23.

[12] D. Defoe, *A Tour through the whole island of Great Britain* (Everyman edn.), i, 130-1, 155-6, ii, 219; J. Macky, *A Journey through England* (1714-22), i, pp. 91-2, 109-10, ii, 233-5.

[13] Defoe, *Tour*, i, 54-5.

[14] Cf. *ibid.*, i, 188 with Bodl[eian Library], MS. Willis 15, f. 82.

att any time for £300, and as the markets now run, I believ few Borroughs are cheaper'.[15]

Inevitably, then, the electioneering politicians of post-Revolution England already had to bargain for the small venal boroughs in the system, the 'whores', in the duke of Richmond's words, 'that [were] anybody's for their money':[16] Hindon, a single street of thatched houses, whose only amenities were the elm trees growing in the street, serving in wet weather in lieu of a market house; and Bramber, whose vicar, recuperating from his pastoral labours in Oxford, confessed to a friend he had no difficulty squeezing all his parishioners into a minute church only 25 feet long.[17]

Inevitably, too, there were a few of these small boroughs which had already fallen captive to some big landlord before the Revolution; so that even the storms of party failed to ruffle their placid docility. And there were others whose independence was being eroded over the next thirty years, while the party battles were actually at their height. Burgage boroughs were particularly vulnerable, provided borough mongers were prepared to pour enough money into them, as the Whig chieftain Lord Wharton — 'Honest Tom' to his friends — did at Richmond. In 1705 alone he laid out £1293 on buying just 21 of the 250 burgages in this quite populous Yorkshire borough.[18] Yorkshire indeed was peculiarly susceptible to such tactics as these. Thirsk was sewn up late in William's reign by its formidable neighbour, Sir Thomas Frankland, and its 48 burgage tenants (all their properties being incongruously confined to one street in 'Old Thirsk') were allowed no further contest after 1695.[19]

Yet, although the unreformed representative system as it operated in the first age of Party allowed no little scope for such abuses, it had its other and very different face. This face shows us, for one thing, many party strongholds in 'popular' constituencies — places which despite a lot of voters or a broad franchise, remained consistently loyal, or nearly so, to either Whigs or Tories, and quite frequently

---

[15] Bodl. MS. Willis 15, ff. 123, 128; Defoe, *Tour*, i, p. 130; Add. MSS. 28227, f. 67; Caryll to Sir Nathan Wright, draft, 8 Dec. 1708.

[16] Add. MSS. 32688, f. 46 (quoted in Sedgwick, i, 338).

[17] Bodl. MS. Willis 15, ff. 27, 62. There were barely 20 cottages in the whole of Bramber parish, and so far as John Macky could see, when he passed hastily through in 1714, scarcely one 'fit for a stable'. *Journey*, i, 108.

[18] Huntington Library, California, Stowe MSS. 'A Perticular of the Severall Burrough Houses bought by the Right Honble. the Lord Wharton at Richm[on]d . . . in order to Mr. Dunches Election in 1705'. I am obliged to Dr. John Beckett for this transcript. MS. Willis 15, f. 130, for Richmond 'borough houses' (271 out of c. 800) in the 1730s.

[19] MS. Willis 15, ff, 123. 126. Nearby Northallerton lost its last chance of independence in 1722. North Yorks. R.O. Pierse MSS. 24/4/25 (reference kindly supplied by Mr. John Quinn).

demonstrated this in a series of contests, like the town of Bedford or the county of Wiltshire. These were the rough equivalents of the 'safe seats' of our own day: there were approximately 133 such seats in 86 popular constituencies between 1702 and 1715.[20] Even more crucial to the outcome of Elections in the first age of Party were the very large group we may call the 'weathervane constituencies'. There were in Anne's reign about 69 counties and boroughs, with electorates from 10,000 down to 250, or in one or two cases a little lower, whose returns of members could be seen by contemporaries as reliable (often infallible) indicators of the way the wind of electoral opinion was veering from one Election to the next. Frequently both their seats would be equally sensitive to change; but sometimes, where there was an extremely powerful family or party hold over one seat,[21] it would be only the second seat which was volatile. In all I estimate 113 seats were at stake each Election from 1702-15 in this way, out of a total of 513.

Now it was of course in these two large groups of 'open' constituencies, with their 246 safe seats and 'weathervane' seats, that the opinions of the Augustan electorate chiefly made themselves felt. Together they probably embraced roughly ninety per cent of the whole electorate, and it was, in the end, the 'weathervane' constituencies, the most sensitive reflectors of the *electoral will* of the day, which chiefly held in their hands the fate of Whigs and Tories throughout virtually the whole period from 1679 to 1722.

*   *   *

However, this still takes us only a small part of the way towards an answer to the main question I have posed in this paper. For the *electoral will* was not necessarily the same as the *National Will*. We may agree that up to 1722 the representative system, for all its manifold faults, did by and large express the opinion of the electorate, rather than the will of the electoral manipulators. But the problem remains: did it equally reflect the opinion of the wider public?

It may be objected that 'public opinion' is an anomalous concept to apply to the seventeenth or to the eighteenth century. It is true that the phrase itself is relatively modern. Yet it is abundantly clear that thinking Englishmen of the seventeenth and eighteenth centuries were perfectly familiar with the concept of a National Will: they

---

[20] I include here constituencies where the representation was normally shared between one Whig and one Tory, either in a series of contested elections, as at Worcester or Evesham, or with little contest (e.g. Cumberland and Lancashire).

[21] E.g. that of Sir John Pakington in Worcestershire.

recognised its political validity (that is to say, that what the majority of English people desired, at this time or that, on this matter or that, was both a legitimate and a necessary concern of politicians), and they had their own vocabulary to express their notion of 'public opinion'. When they spoke of 'the temper of the people', or 'the disposition of the nation', or, as they most frequently did, of *the sense of the people*, they articulated their own mental image of the National Will. This was what Halifax meant when he claimed in 1684 that it was in acting through Parliament that an English king gave 'sanction to the united sense of the people'. It was likewise in Swift's mind when he considered in 1711 how 'the Dispositions of the People' could be most truly judged at the polls.[22]

However, the recognition that there was a National Will does not imply an automatic assumption that the peculiar methods of choosing English Parliaments allowed this Will to express itself. After the country had just experienced three Elections in two years a pamphleteer of 1681 preferred to leave this question open. 'If elections of members to serve in Parliament be the best standard to judge the disposition of the Kingdom by', he cautiously argued, 'it is not so long since we had an opportunity of feeling the pulse of the nation'.[23] On the face of it his caution seems justified. We may well wonder whether a system which for over sixty years before the first Reform Bill was to be raked with criticism could at *any* time have allowed 'the sense of the people' to make itself understood. Even the post-Revolution generation, which did (after all) take a special pride in the advance of Reason, never pretended the system was rational. And yet, criticism of the mechanics of parliamentary representation at that time was muted, and most of what there was, academic. Locke uttered some pious platitudes in 1689.[24] Toland urged the rationalisation of the electoral process in 1701: as the most maverick intellectual of his day, his support was tantamount to the kiss of death for any cause. Molesworth went on record in 1711 as believing that 'a waste or a desart has not right to be represented, nor by our original constitution was ever intended to be'.[25] And tucked away among the working notebooks of Gregory King[26] one finds a scheme for

[22] J. P. Kenyon (ed.), *Halifax: Complete Works* (1969), p. 65; *The Examiner*, No. 24, 18 Jan. 1711.

[23] Quoted in C. S. Emden, *The People and the Constitution* (2nd edn. Oxford, 1959), p. 178.

[24] Toland in *The Art of Governing by Parties*, Locke in *An Essay concerning the True Original, Extent and End of Civil Government*, ch. 13, sections 157-8.

[25] Robert Molesworth, *The Principles of a Real Whig* (1711). See H. T. Dickinson (ed.), *Politics and Literature in the Eighteenth Century* (1974), p. 27.

[26] 'A Proposition for Electing Parliamt. men'. Greater London Council, 'Burns Journal', p. 250, reproduced in P. Laslett (ed.), *The Earliest Classics: John Graunt and Gregory King* (1973).

reorganising the whole representative system, of such hair-brained ingenuity and such terrifying complexity that if it had ever been adopted the electioneering country gentleman of England would have been forced to give up in despair, and devote himself exclusively to his claret and his foxes.

As for the practical parliamentary politicians, apart from a few half-hearted moves before 1703, which we shall notice later, there is concern only with attempts to 'clean up' the existing system, through bills aimed against corruption and blatant gerrymandering.[27] I agree it is naïve to deduce from an absence of reforming ideas, or intentions, a widespread satisfaction with any institution. Men are always reluctant to reform what they have a vested interest in preserving: who should know that better than we? That the Whig oligarchs of the Walpole-Pelham age had an interest in the preservation of *their* electoral system is beyond any doubt. But I am by no means convinced that before the 1720s, in a period not of oligarchy but of frequent elections and fluctuating fortunes, the element of self-interest is anything like so obvious. It would have been no difficult matter for any Tory of Anne's reign to make a convincing case, on grounds of interest alone, for increasing county representation at the expense of small boroughs; and likewise there were quite a lot of unrepresented towns, by then noted strongholds of Dissent, which it would undoubtedly have profited the Whigs to enfranchise. Nor was '1688' yet the sacred cow it was to become by the Walpole era: it was still thought possible to tamper with the 'Revolution constitution' without sacrilege. Can it be, therefore, that the total absence of root and branch reform schemes between 1689 and 1720 ought to be taken at face value? Can it be that, despite all the flaws of which they were aware, Englishmen in the first age of Party were at bottom satisfied with the way the representative system worked in practice; above all with the way it expressed what they called 'the sense of the people'?

My main question, therefore, resolves itself into two parts: did *they* believe that this was so? And, even if they did, can *we* agree it was so?

I

First let us look at what the men of the late seventeenth century and of the eighteenth believed, or professed to believe. In 1681 when Court spokesmen in the third Exclusion Parliament opposed a Whig motion to print the Votes of the House, on the ground that this would be 'a sort of Appeal to the People', Sir Francis Winnington exclaimed: 'pray, who sent us hither? ... the

[27] G. Holmes, *British Politics in the Age of Anne* (1967), pp. 143-4.

House of Commons is by the choice of the People'.[28] The conviction that 'the whole Kingdom', or 'all the people of England' had repeatedly shown through two previous Parliaments that only Exclusion could save the nation was voiced again and again: and after the dissolution of this Oxford Parliament a Whig newswriter clinched the point. 'The general choice of the same members in the last Parliament that had served in the two former, sufficiently shews the sense of the nation'.[29]

Not impartial witnesses, perhaps? And in any event, the borough-rigging of the Stuarts after 1681 had by 1688 aroused widespread fears that the National Will could be completely distorted now by 'packed' Parliaments. The cry of the political nation in 1688, therefore, was for 'a free Parliament'; and immediately after the Revolution the elections to the Convention appeared to satisfy William of Orange that they had produced not only a free Parliament but one that was (he said) a 'true representative of the Kingdom'. Not every Tory agreed with him. Sir Robert Sawyer, very much a man of the 'right' and a long-standing opponent of any notion of popular sovereignty, challenged the Whigs to resort to a referendum or to new elections on a broader franchise, if they truly wished the settlement of the crown to have the people's endorsement; for less than a quarter of the people were represented in the present Parliament. Yet most members of the Convention, tacitly at least, accepted William's view, and that of one of his advisers who had prophesied before the elections of January 1689 the same outcome as the King, and in virtually the same words.[30]

The professions which precede elections naturally impress us more than those which follow them. And as William's reign went on, in spite of much talk of different threats to 'free elections' — from the fat purses of the 'monied men', for instance — a growing underlying confidence can be detected in the capacity of the existing system to transmit the pulse of the nation to Westminster.[31] 'Your choice now', the electors were told in 1701, 'will be the best standard by which to judge the present disposition of the Kingdom'. Thirteen

---

[28] Anchitell Grey, *Debates of the House of Commons from the Year 1667 to the Year 1694*, viii (1769), 294. Cf. Boscawen's speech, *ibid.* 293: 'the People you represent will have a true account of what you do'.

[29] *Ibid.* 313-17 *passim*; *The Impartial Protestant Mercury*, 12 May 1681 (cf. Vaughan's speech, in Grey, *Debates*, viii, 327).

[30] G. Burnet, *The History of my own Time* (Oxford, 1833), iii, 394; Grey, *Debates*, ix, 21-3; *Hardwicke State Papers* (1778), ii, 403-4; Burnet to Admiral Herbert, 25 Dec. [1688], in *E.H.R.* 1, 1886, p. 535.

[31] Likewise, growing acceptance by those to whom the pulse-beat was unwelcome that there was little, electorally, they could do about it. See Charles Montagu and Lord Somers to Shrewsbury, 11 Aug., 25 Oct. 1698: W. Coxe, *Private and Original Correspondence of Charles Talbot, Duke of Shrewsbury* (1821), p. 551, *Hardwicke State Papers*, ii, 435.

years later, when the Whigs had just recaptured the administration before the first Election of George I's reign, Atterbury reassured discouraged Tories with the reminder of 'several elections formerly, and one or two of late', where the issue had been decided by 'the temper of the people'.[32]   Above all, I have no doubt, Atterbury had in mind the epic Tory triumph of 1710.   It is worth our attention for a moment too.

In the early summer of 1710 the most powerful Whig ministry England had known since the Revolution found itself low in the esteem of a war-weary nation, and of a nation further antagonised by the notorious trial of Sacheverell.   As the Whigs faced a probable dissolution of Parliament, the duchess of Marlborough canvassed two experienced M.P.s for their views on the party's prospects.   One of them, Hugh Boscawen, was inclined to be optimistic.   Not so James Craggs.   'I think he is extremely mistaken [Craggs wrote] when he supposes that if this present Parliament be dissolved, we shall be able to deal with the adversary in the next elections.   I will be bold to foresee, as the common people are now set, they [the Tories] will get at least three for one':[33] and how right he was, in his judgment if not in his mathematics.

'*As the common people are now set*': what remarkable words — especially as they were not written for public consumption.   Craggs did not fool himself into wishfully thinking that an election held then could be decided by magnate influence, or by venal self-interest, or by the manipulations of the Crown.   Rather it would reflect the fact that, in Atterbury's words, 'the Kingdom took fire' in 1710 against the Whigs.   However, if the 1710 Election plainly mirrored 'the sense of the people', what politician could have said less, in retrospect, of that of 1715, when the boot was very much on the other foot, when the Tories were damningly tainted in popular eyes by their equivocal attitude to the Succession, and when the Whigs gained 22 county seats and lost only one.   After all, the Tories themselves had always contended that the county vote was the purest expression of public opinion.[34]

But now let us move on another twenty years or so, twenty years in which a Whig oligarchy strove with consistent government help to tame the electorate and to 'play' the system.   Paul Langford's new

[32] *The Best Choice of Parliament Men* (1701), quoted in Emden, *op. cit.* p. 178; Francis Atterbury (Bp. of Rochester), *English Advice to the Freeholders of England* (1714), repr. in *Somers Tracts* (1815), xiii, 522-41.
[33] *Private Correspondence of Sarah, Duchess of Marlborough* (1838), i, 318; 18 May 1710.
[34] W. A. Speck, 'The General Election of 1715', *E.H.R.* 90, 1975; Swift, *The Examiner*, No. 24, 18 Jan. 1711; [Abel Roper], *The Post-Boy*, Nos. 2421, 2871, 16-18 Nov. 1710, 1-3 Oct. 1713.

study of the Excise crisis of 1733[35] shows vividly that passions ran almost as high against Walpole at the 1734 Election as they had against the Whigs at the Sacheverell Election of 1710. After the Walpole government had won the Election, its supporters were treated to a King's Speech early in the new Parliament which once again smugly professed that 'the sense of the nation is best learned by the choice of their representatives'. But now these words had a hollow ring. Even before all the results were in in 1734, the opposition journal *The Craftsman*, elated by the swing against the government in the counties and large boroughs, but aware that they alone could not defeat it, had advised 'the Court-writers' to be 'so modest for the future, as not to insist on the general Sense of the People'; for as regards the Excise, 'the late Elections are sufficient to convince them that it is neither forgot nor forgiven by the Body of the Nation'. The anonymous writer of a treatise of 1747 expressed the view, now gaining in currency as the Walpole régime was perpetuated by the Pelhams, that the growth in authority, and above all in wealth and unscrupulousness in using it, of successive post-Revolution governments had at last equipped the ministers of the Crown with the power 'to subvert and destroy the honour and integrity of the popular representation'.[36]

By 1761, when one of the earliest 'radical' M.P.s, William Beckford, spoke of public opinion to the House of Commons after the Election of that year, he did not conceal his view that it was no longer reflected on the benches around him. 'When I talk of the Sense of the People [he said], I mean the middling people of England — the manufacturer, the yeoman, the merchant, the country gent[lema]n, they who bear all the heat of the day . . .';[37] and as Beckford and his associates continually stressed in the first major reform campaign in the late 1760s, many of those 'middling people', especially 'the manufacturer' and 'the merchant', could now only make their voice heard 'without doors' and no longer through the so-called 'representatives' of the people in the Commons. By 1774, although the force of this first campaign had spent itself, the time was ripe for the past and future case for reform to be classically set out by James

[35] See note 2 above.
[36] *The Craftsman*, 25 May 1734, quoted in Langford, *Excise Crisis*, p. 131; [John Campbell?], *Liberty and Right* (1747), extracts printed in Dickinson (ed.), *Politics and Literature*, pp. 115-19.
[37] Add. MSS. 38334, f. 29, 13 Nov. 1761, quoted in P. Langford, 'William Pitt and Public Opinion, 1757', *E.H.R.* 88, 1973. For a radical Whig's surprisingly conservative definition of 'the people' in the 1690s, see James Tyrrell, *Bibliotheca Politica* (1694), p. 156. For both radical and conservative definitions in the 1760s, cf. J. Viner, 'Man's Economic Status', in J. L. Clifford (ed.), *Man versus Society in Eighteenth-Century Britain* (Cambridge, 1968), p. 29.

Burgh, whose *Political Disquisitions*, in three meaty volumes, rose far above the ephemera of the Wilkites. Starting from the pure old Whig premise that 'all lawful authority, legislative, and executive, originates from the people', Burgh argued that 'when our ancestors first proposed government by representation it is certain, they intended *adequate* representation; for no other deserves the name, or answers the end'. Yet now, 'in consequence of the *inadequate* state of representation, the sense of the people may be grossly misapprehended, or misrepresented'.[38]

Both Beckford and Burgh were born before the first age of Party had run its course. But the electorate they depict for us in the '60s and '70s appears to bear small resemblance to the virile creature which swept the Whigs to defeat in 1710 and the Tories in 1715. By the 1770s the cause of electoral reform might still face sixty years of frustration. But the case for reform had been fully made out; and it was a case that could only get stronger, since in the nature of things time could only magnify the more glaring abuses its critics had exposed. Yet in 1710 or 1715, as we have seen, the case for reform — if it was put at all — was received with a deafening silence. And the acceptance by both Whigs and Tories then of the basic adequacy of the existing system is manifestly less purblind, far more confidently based, than the tortured defences of those who resisted reform after 1760.

II

And so to the second and more important part of the question I have posed in this lecture. Were the politicians, and the public, of the first age of Party justified in their complacency? Can we accept that an electorate so very different in scale and character from anything in the experience of the last ninety years can possibly have embodied 'the sense of the people' during those intoxicating years when that electorate ruled the political roost?

I want to look in the main at three aspects of the problem: (1) at the *growth* of the electorate, in relation especially to the growth of the population; (2) at the *size* of the electorate, in relation to the size of the adult population; and (3) at *who* and *where* was represented. And wherever we look we shall find, I believe, that it is in the sharp contrasts between the first and second ages of Party that the keys to our problem of the electorate and the National Will are to be found.

*   *   *

[38] [J. Burgh], *Political Disquisitions: or An Enquiry into public Errors, Defects and Abuses* (London, 1774), i, 3, 24, 27.

The view of both the size and growth of the late Stuart electorate which has been most commonly expressed by specialists on the period over the past few years, and is now becoming accepted ortho-doxy, is briefly this. It starts with what Plumb deems a 'conservative' estimate for 1689 of around 200,000 voters, and then assumes[39] that there was a growth of roughly twenty-five per cent over the next quarter of a century. The *History of Parliament*'s findings on the 1722 Election suggests the expansion went on, to the extent of several more per cent, at least until then.

What we might call the 'anchor' or 'base' figure of some 250,000 for 1715 has then been set against a population figure for the end of the 17th century, a figure based usually on Gregory King's magic five and a half millions for 1695. The moral is: that by the beginning of the Hanoverian period the electorate of the first age of Party had grown to a point at which it comprised some 4·6 per cent of the population; and in case this should seem laughably small, it has been compared, first with the situation in 1831, when it had shrunk to a minute 2·63% of a population now swollen to 13·9 millions, and secondly with the position *after* the first Reform Act, when the registers reveal 653,000 voters, a percentage of the population almost identical, at 4·7 per cent, to the 'unreformed' position of 1715.[40]

However, what really matters is what proportion not of the whole population but of the adult males in the country had the right to vote; for full adult male suffrage was as far as even the wildest mid seventeenth-century radical would have gone. My own conclusion in 1969, reached on the basis of King's extremely careful contempor-ary work on age structures, was that 250,000 voters 'included roughly one in every five adult males in the country',[41] and I commented that at least half the residue were men to whom even most of the Levellers would have denied the vote.[42] And the significance of this, bearing in mind the considerably higher ratio of adult males to the rest of the population by the early nineteenth century, is that it plainly suggests, to quote W. A. Speck, 'that the electoral system

[39] Mainly on the basis of voting figures; but cf. Speck, *Tory and Whig*, pp. 124-6.

[40] *Ibid.* pp. 16-17; Plumb, 'Growth of the Electorate', *loc. cit.* p. 111; G. S. Holmes, 'The Influence of the Peerage in English Parliamentary Elections 1702-1713' (Oxford Univ. B. Litt. thesis, 1952), p. 11 and Appx. A; Sedgwick, i, 189-381, *passim*; Cannon, *Parliamentary Reform*, pp. 41-2, 259 and Appx. 4.

[41] *Britain after the Glorious Revolution 1689-1714*, p. 12. Gregory King's estimate of 1,300,000 adult males in 1695 inspires confidence in those who have examined his working papers.

[42] But cf. Keith Thomas, 'The Levellers and the Franchise', in G. E. Aylmer (ed.), *The Interregnum* (1972), pp. 57-78.

was more representative in Anne's reign than it had ever been before, or was to be again until well into Victoria's'.[43]

Now my purpose in touching briefly on these two related questions of size and growth is not to disagree, in any fundamental way, with the broad shape of the argument I have just outlined; on the contrary I still accept its essence, and its obviously crucial relevance to my whole theme of the National Will. But, as I now see it, some of the figures which prop up the argument are based on assumptions no longer justified; and their revision has the effect of lending even greater weight than we have recently imagined possible to the case for considering the electorate of 1700 far more 'representative', in purely numerical terms, than that of, say, 1850.

One of the shakier props of recent orthodoxy concerns the size of the early eighteenth-century population. The assumption has been that it remained largely static for a quarter century after the Revolution. This assumption is frankly untenable. Recent work by historical demographers suggests there are very strong grounds indeed for believing that the population of England and Wales grew rapidly between the 1680s and 1720 — the very decades of the first age of Party — possibly from around 5·4 to roughly 6·2 millions, before it was savagely checked by two decades of 'massacre by epidemic' from 1720-40.[44] At first sight this might seem to undermine one of the very arguments I have just been outlining. But on reflection we can see that the really important question is this: how fast did the electorate grow in relation to the growth in population? We know that after 1780, when the population was climbing steeply, the electorate was only crawling slowly upwards. Professor Cannon believes it increased by about twenty per cent between 1754 and 1831, whereas the *population* at least doubled in the same period.[45] But in the first age of Party, far from lagging miserably behind population growth, it rushed well ahead of it. After all, even the twenty-five per cent growth in the electorate, 1690-1715, which has been posited, represents ten per cent per decade compared with a population growth in the same period of four per cent.

Whatever the precise figures involved — and these, as I shall hope to demonstrate, will probably never be known with any certainty — the evidence that the English electorate did grow exceedingly rapidly between the Revolution and the early 1720s is incontrovertible. There is time for only a handful of illustrations to emphasise

[43] *Tory and Whig*, p. 17.
[44] The case for growth is best argued by J. D. Chambers, *Population, Economy and Society in Pre-Industrial England* (Oxford, 1972). The figures suggested above are my own estimates.
[45] *Parliamentary Reform*, p. 42.

the way the trend went: and in order to demonstrate how it could run right across the board I have selected examples from various types of constituency.

For the counties there are, in general, only voting figures to guide us, and these, as we shall see, can conceal snares. Nevertheless there is no mistaking some of the patterns such figures reveal. Essex, into which a lot of the surplus population of London was over-spilling in the later Stuart period, provides a fine case in point. 2266 voted here in 1679. By the time of the 1694 by-election, 4076 were polling. In the 'Church in Danger' election of 1710, 5864 participated, a rise of 160 per cent in thirty years.[46] As with Essex, quite a lot of the growth which produced the large, volatile county electorates of Anne's reign had already taken place shortly before 1700;[47] but in many counties there is still an emphatic upward surge to come. The two and a half thousand Shropshire voters of 1702 had grown to around 4000 by 1722.[48] Buckinghamshire is one of a string of counties where a peak is reached either in 1705 or in 1710, both of them Elections where the cry of 'the Church in Danger' rang out more than at any other time; and one reason for the 'peaking' was an epidemic in the middle years of Anne of freehold-splitting and temporary conveyancing, supplementing the natual growth produced by a swiftly-rising population and *bona fide* purchases.[49]

And yet, the truly spectacular increases in the electorate by the early eighteenth century were taking place less in the counties than in the boroughs: especially in the large to middling inhabitant and freemen boroughs, where both population growth and pursuit of party advantage combined to swell the numbers entitled to vote. In fast-growing cities or towns of the late Stuart period, like Norwich,

[46] D. George, 'Elections and Electioneering, 1679-81', *E.H.R.* 45, 1930; 1694 P-B; 1710 P-B. Thereafter there is apparent stabilisation, even some decline in voters turning out, for many decades. Only 4683 voted in 1722 (1722 P-B), and J. Brooke, *The House of Commons 1754-1790* (Oxford, 1964) suggests 5-6000 voters in Essex by that period. *Note*: In this and all subsequent citations, *printed* poll-books of which copies are held in the Institute of Historical Research, London, are referred to simply as above, by date followed by P-B.

[47] Norfolk's active electorate hovered round the 6000 mark from 1679 right through to the 1720s. D. George, *loc. cit.*; Sedgwick, i, 289.

[48] *The Post-Boy*, No. 1125, 30 July 1702; Sedgwick, i, 308. The 2290 Middlesex voters of 1702 had grown to nearly 3000 by 1715.

[49] For Buckinghamshire, a superb run of poll-books, unbroken except for the 1704 by-election (for which, see MS. Willis 18, f. 154), enables one to trace an upswing from 2645 freeholders voting in Jan. 1701 to 4519 in 1705 and thence a slighter downswing, to 3957 in 1713. For sources see Speck, *Tory and Whig*, p. 132; Bodl., *Gough's Buckinghamshire Tracts*, vol. i, A similar pattern, with the peak varying from 1705 to 1710, is revealed by poll-books in Essex, Hampshire and Hertfordshire; also in Surrey (Add. MSS. 11571, f. 57) and Cheshire, the most chronic example of freehold manipulation in 1705.

Newcastle-on-Tyne and Liverpool, it is fair to regard much of this increase as 'natural' — for example the growth in the number of Norwich freemen voters by one thousand in the ten years from 1705 to 1715.[50] Inhabitant boroughs such as Northampton, Taunton and Bedford experienced increases of from fifty to sixty per cent in a comparable period.[51] But there was more than mere nature at work in many places; above all in freemen boroughs, where the 'manufacture' of freemen by local party bosses became one of the growth industries of the early eighteenth century. Take the case of Beverley. Attractive as it was as a place of residence for the East Riding gentry and pseudo-gentry, it did not enjoy a rise in its freemen electorate from roughly 250 in 1694 to at least 800 in 1722 for that reason alone.[52] Far less did the small cathedral city of Wells, where a Tory corporation had kept the franchise unnaturally tight, restricting the voters to a mere 60 as late as 1715, only to see a new order, through 'freemen inflation', send the number soaring to 500 by the Election of 1722.[53]

Lastly, remarkable changes took place even in small boroughs, or despite limited franchises. It has been shown how burgage-splitting doubled the electorate of Pontefract in 14 years; while in Cockermouth, through the same techniques, the electorate was trebled, so that by April 1715 the number of its burgage tenements, and electors, was estimated at thirty more than the number of houses in the town.[54] At the other end of the country, in supposedly

[50] *The Post-Man*, No. 1408, 31 May 1705; 1715 P-B. Cf. Newcastle P-Bs, 1710, 1722. The Liverpool electorate was said to have reached *c.* 1500 by 1715, though it is doubtful whether more than 800 had voted there in 1705. *The London Post*, 21 May 1705; MS. Willis 48, f. 361.

[51] E.g. for Taunton, cf. *The Post-Man*, No. 496, 2 Aug. 1698, with Sedgwick, i, 317, for 1722.

[52] On the Beverley electorate: J. Dennett (ed.), *Beverley Borough Records, 1575-1821* and K. A. MacMahon (ed.), *Beverley Corporation Minute Books* (*Yorks. Arch. Soc., Records Series*, 84, 122), esp. MacMahon, p. 190; B.L. Loan 29/237, f. 43; Sir W. St. Quintin and W. Maister to [Newcastle], 29 Nov. 1701; *The Weekly Journal*, 10 Mar. 1722; Sedgwick, i, 357-8. There were similar trends in other 'gentry towns', notably Shrewsbury, where 970 voted in 1702 and about 1900 in 1722, and Derby, where Browne Willis noted in 1716 that the freemen were 'augmented to about nine hundred' since 1710, when 659 had polled. See *The Post-Boy*, No. 1125, 30 July 1702; Sedgwick, i, 311; Derby MS. P-B, 1701 (Central Library, Derby); Derby 1710 P-B; Willis, *Notitia Parliamentaria*, ii, 229.

[53] Sedgwick, i, 318; J. Cannon, 'Polls Supplementary to the History of Parliament Volumes, 1715-90', *B.I.H.R.* 47, 1974, p. 112; *Evening Post*, 27 Mar. 1522.

[54] For Pontefract, see Speck, *Tory and Whig.* p. 15 (here the inflationary process is illuminated by a valuable series of P-Bs in the Galway MSS. [Nottingham U.L.] and the Wrightson MSS. [Leeds City Libraries, Archives Dept.]). For Cockermouth, *ibid.* and MS. Willis 48, ff. 145-6: Thos. Jefferson of Cockermouth to T. Troughear, Fellow of Queen's Coll. Oxford, 26 Apr. 1715; cf. R. Hopkinson, 'Elections in Cumberland and Westmorland', pp. 223-4, for the confused situation in Cockermouth.

dreamy Dorset, voters sprouted like mushrooms late in our period. The scot and lot men of Wareham increased from 150 in the 1690s to 700 in 1722; the ratepaying voters of Corfe Castle to about a third of the entire population of the town by 1715, through what Willis darkly called 'some late practices'; while in Weymouth and Melcombe the 200-odd freeholders of 1704 had far more than trebled by 1716.[55]

Growth there was, then; vigorous, hot-house growth; and usually where it counted most numerically. But what does it all mean in terms of the true size of the electorate by the early 1720s? I have referred to what I called the 'base-line' estimate of 250,000 voters in 1715 which could be raised to some 260,000 by 1722. Now these totals were based heavily, though not quite exclusively, on polling figures. It is only very recently that the flaws in their underlying assumptions have begun to be appreciated.[56] The truth is, they take scarcely any account of two factors utterly crucial to understanding the electorate and its workings in the first age of Party. The two factors are *turn-out* and *turn-over*. Because of this neglect, the totals we have hitherto accepted with some measure of confidence turn out to be little better than token figures; and the implications of this for any assessment of the expression of the National Will at this period are fundamental.

First, the question of turn-out. We know, of course, that the possession of the vote in the 'unreformed' system was cherished; that it was regarded as a piece of property and that the loss of the vote was seen as an infringement of property rights. This explains much of the outcry against the work of James II's 'Regulators' in 1688; this, too, is what the celebrated Aylesbury case of 1704 was largely about. But why should it be assumed that the value attached to the vote was so priceless that, unlike the vote of today's elector, it was never wasted? What logical ground can there possibly be for taking the *whole* electorate to be virtually equatable with the *voting* electorate?

After all, there were an abundance of reasons why a man might not have been able — or indeed willing — to go to the polls. In some respects the deterrents were far greater then than now. They are perhaps most evident in the case of county contests, especially in the larger counties. The weather was sometimes vile: six of the seventeen

[55] Wareham at this time was 'a neat town' but, with its silted harbour, hardly a flourishing one. Defoe, *Tour*, i, 208. For the Dorset electorates, see Willis, *Notitia Parliamentaria*, ii, 436, 488, 496-7, 533.

[56] See especially R. Hopkinson, 'Elections in Cumberland and Westmorland', p. 231. Cf. note 39 above.

elections of our period were held in mid-winter[57] (and it did sometimes rain, even then, in the summer!).   The harvest was a big
consideration: this affected four more Elections.   It was not every
yeoman who was prepared, as the Essex Whigs boasted of their
supporters in 1679, 'rather [to] trust God with their corn than trust
the Devil to chose their Parliament Men'.[58]   And for the rural voter,
spring sowing and spring fairs were as pressing as harvest.   John
Hall reminded James Grahme of Levens in May 1705 how serious
it would be if the Westmorland shire election clashed 'with the
business of the electors, that must be at Brough Fair on Thursday
in the next week, at Orton on Friday, at Appleby on Saturday and
at Appleby again on Whitsund Monday and at Penrith on Tuesday
and at Kirkby Stephen beast fair on Wednesday; but if [he added]
you think fit to defer it until Tuesday the fifth day of June then all
the fairs will be over and the electors better able to attend'.[59]   But of
course small farmers always found it difficult and costly to leave their
farms and get to the county town and back.   For forty poor freeholders from Rye in Sussex, to vote in the county election of
February 1715, held at Chichester, meant an absence of eight days
from their work.   How many would have gone at all, one wonders,
if the agent of the young earl of Clare (later the great electioneering
duke of Newcastle) had not been instructed to compensate them to
the tune of two shillings a day each, for [as his accounts put it]
'hiring people in their absence and their own loss of time'.[60]

In addition, many county elections were not for the faint-hearted.
In Wiltshire in 1705 'the proud duke' of Somerset was 'insulted in the
streets of Salisbury by the mob'; and Robert Walpole and his
supporters were pelted at the Norfolk hustings in 1710, the same
year in which Whig voters in Kent, even 'of the highest quality' had
to brave not only 'all the rude insults of the mob' but even 'letters
threatening assassination'.[61]   But a more universal, and in general
far more important deterrent for the forty-shilling freeholders were
a distant or inconvenient place of polling (there was, remember,
in general only one polling place for a whole county), combined with
bad communications and, here and there, with physical barriers of a

[57] Viz. those of Jan. 1679, 1689, 1690, Jan. 1701, Dec. 1701 and 1715.
Voters were snowed up in Westmorland in Jan. 1701 (Hopkinson, p. 209).
[58] *Essex's Excellency: or the Gallantry of the Freeholders of that County*
(London, 1679), quoted in E. Lipson, 'The elections to the Exclusion Parliaments', *E.H.R.* 28, 1913, p. 62.   Other Elections affected were 1698 and 1710,
to some extent, and 1713.   The Lancashire election of 1710 was 'accommodated'
without a poll partly because of the harvest. H.M.C. *Portland MSS.* iv, 578.
[59] Levens Hall MSS. (by courtesy of Mrs. O. R. Bagot).
[60] Add. MSS. 33058, ff. 224-8: Clare's election expenses.
[61] H.M.C. *Portland MSS.*, iv, 213; Dyer's Newsletter, 14 Oct. 1710, Brit.
Lib. Loan 29/321; *The Flying-Post*, No. 2283, 28 Oct. 1710.

kind we may find it hard to appreciate. It took very little rain, even in high summer, to turn the midlands clay of Leicestershire or Northamptonshire, or the even more execrable clay of Sussex and the Kentish Weald into a treacly mire. Not all polling places were central. Appleby was far from it, giving the voters of Kendal and particularly Grasmere wards a hard time of it over most inhospitable country. The bulk of the freeholders of Lancashire were in the south; so the expedition to Lancaster — for those in the south-west especially, over some unspeakable terrain (including the horrors of Chatmoss) — put a severe strain on party loyalty. In Sussex, Chichester was as unacceptable to the numerous eastern freeholders of a county with reputedly the worst roads in the South of England as was Lewes to the westerners.[62] All Cumberland elections save that of 1702 were held at Salkeld Yeats (or was it Gates?) near Penrith, which meant a fifty-mile journey for some voters, and as a Tory complained, only 'three or four straggling cottages, on the edge of a large moor' to greet them when, or if, they got there.[63]

York was at least reasonably central; but that was little comfort to many round Sedbergh, or even round Sheffield, Hull or Whitby. We know from the first poll-book to survive for Yorkshire, for 1708,[64] that at this contest 9141 freeholders polled. It seems a huge number by early eighteenth-century standards, even in high summer; yet in view of the fact that nearly 12,000 were to vote at a Yorkshire by-election in 1727 and almost 15,000 at the General Election of 1734, one may well wonder what proportion of Yorkshire's unquestionably great electorate those 9000 of 1708 represented. Turn-out, in such circumstances, was so unpredictable a thing. It is less surprising perhaps that only one freeholder from Bentham and one from Clapham parishes made the long trek to York that year than that, for some extraordinary reason, 52 went to the city and back again from the parish of Dent, struggling to Settle, and then on from Long Preston, over what Bishop Nicolson feelingly called '29 of the longest, and worst, miles in Yorkshire'.[65]

Apart from all the physical or occupational deterrents, there were an infinite number of personal considerations too which could cause a man to abstain (and most of these applied as much to borough as to county voters): apathy; uncertainty how to vote; *politique* considera-

---

[62] S. H. Nulle, *Thomas Pelham-Holles, Duke of Newcastle: His Early Political Career, 1693-1724* (Philadelphia, 1931), p. 32.
[63] Levens Hall MSS., Gilfred Lawson to James Grahme, 9 May 1705, quoted in Speck, *Tory and Whig*, p. 83.
[64] In York Minster Library MSS.
[65] MS. diary (Tullie House, Carlisle), vol. 8, 13 Nov. 1706. Cf. *ibid.* 6 May 1709, in *Trans. Cumb. and Westm. Antiq. and Arch. Soc.* 35, 1935, p. 95: 'From Leeds to Settle, 27 long (long) Miles'.

tions, or discouragement at the prospect of defeat;[66] absence from home; the frequent illnesses which beset all but the most blessed in constitution, from baronets to potwallers. But what kind of statistical allowance can we possibly make for such abstentions? Full lists of forty-shilling freeholders in counties at this time are almost unknown. But a careful estimate has survived for Northamptonshire in Anne's reign, not a large county, nor one with formidable physical barriers. It puts the number of feeeholders with the right to vote at 6304.[67] Yet on the basis of the voting figures at the only two county contests of the reign, in 1702 and 1705, one would have put the electorate at between 4500 and 4900. In fact, it looks as if there was something like a 72 per cent turn-out there in 1702 and only a 78 per cent turn-out in the peak-interest year of 1705. A contemporary put the turn-out in Rutland in 1713 — the tiniest county by far, which presented no physical problems at all for the great bulk of voters — at 86 per cent.[68]

My belief is that such figures were much higher than average. And one powerful reason for thinking so is a study of what we might call the 'quality' vote. Fortunately this element can be readily identified in every one of the surviving county poll-books, and it can then be checked against the virtual roll-calls of the major gentry of every county, from baronets down to esquires and the better known 'gentlemen', which are to be found in the lists of Land Tax Commissioners, printed in the Land Tax Acts of 1693 to 1722 and beyond. These lists were brought up to date every two or three years; after the late 1690s they omitted few names of any note (indeed, they are superb and almost wholly unused social, as well as political documents).[69] One such revision took place in 1710, just after the General Election of that year; and using it as a yardstick, I have checked the turn-out of the upper and middling gentry at their shire elections in several

[66] E.g. the Gloucestershire election of 1705, when Jack Howe complained of being abandoned by his 'old friends', who 'stay'd at home and kept many with them' once it was clear the tide was flowing against the Tories. Blenheim MSS. A1-20: Howe to Marlborough, 23 May (by courtesy of the duke of Marlborough).

[67] Blenheim MSS. D2-9 (Sunderland Papers).

[68] There was furious canvassing at this election. Brit. Lib. Loan 29/153: Thos. Peale to Oxford, 27 Jan., 15 July 1713. For the turn-out, Leicestershire R.O. Finch MSS. Box 4969: 'The Poll taken Sept: 9th 1713. For the Election of Knights of the Shire of Rutland', p. [15]. The number of freeholders recorded as present was 522; those absent, including 'outlyers', 82. I am grateful to Dr. W. A. Speck for supplying me with a photocopy of this poll-book.

[69] Naturally they are not flawless. The local M.P.s responsible for each revision did not always have the time, or take the trouble, to inform themselves with perfect accuracy. James Lowther complained of the Cumberland list in 1708 that 'they have put in two dead men, they have murdered the names of thirteen others ...' Cumbria R.O. (Carlisle), D/Lons/W: to Wm. Gilpin, 24 Jan. 1708. Reference kindly supplied by Dr. J. V. Beckett.

counties in that year — the men who were, of all county voters, the least affected by physical or occupational problems, with their horses, their carriages, and of course their leisure.   There is scarcely an account of a county contest in this period which omits to mention 'a good appearance of gentlemen' at the booths, and they might well account for anything from 5 per cent to 10 per cent of all the voters. And yet how assiduous were they in casting their votes?   Of the 387 'quality' of Suffolk named as Land Tax Commissioners in 1710, only 150 had voted at the election a few weeks before.[70]   Of their 405 counterparts in Hampshire a mere 121 had polled.   These, to my mind, are staggering figures, percentage turn-outs of only 39 and 30 respectively.   A mere 60 of the 348 West Riding gentry found in the Yorkshire Land Tax list of 1710, under 18 per cent, had voted in the contest of 1708 to which I have just referred.   I am not suggesting that any of these absentees on particular occasions, any more than the absent 22 or 28 per cent of Northamptonshire freeholders in 1702 or 1705, were apolitical animals; that they never voted at *any* election. Rather that they were just a tiny part of a very large army of *occasional voters*, which was a vital constituent of the Augustan electorate.[71]

One might not expect that the rate of absenteeism, or occasional voting, in the boroughs would equal that of the counties; although it is well known that mob violence in many popular boroughs — Southwark and Westminster, Coventry, Bristol and Northampton, for instance — was an even greater deterrent than in the counties.   Yet there are indications that borough turn-out, too, was far lower than has ever been realised, and that consequently a lot of figures for borough electorates, based on polls, are thoroughly misleading. The freemen boroughs are the best instruments for gauging this; because there we do have either complete lists of what was in effect the electoral roll, or many reliable contemporary estimates of numbers on the roll.   Using the London poll book for 1710, which prints the names of all the liverymen who were qualified to vote as well as those who actually did so, one finds a turn-out of slightly over 75 per cent — this, note, in the capital city at the height of the Sacheverell fever, when the citizens had had six days on which to get to the hustings.[72] Michael Mullett has done valuable work on Preston, which shows

[70] Hants 1710 P-B; Suffolk 1710 P-B (Bury St. Edmunds Pub. Lib.); *Statutes of the Realm*, ix, 309-12.
[71] See also Speck, Gray and Hopkinson, 'Further Report', *B.I.H.R.* 48, 1975, p. 84.
[72] *The Poll of the Livery-Men of the City of London, at the Election for Members of Parliament: Begun Munday, October 9th 1710, and ended the Saturday following* (London, for John Morphew, 1710).   Copies in Guildhall Library and St. John's College, Cambridge; xerox in Inst. H.R.

that although over a thousand inhabitant burgesses alone were on the roll even before the Revolution, the average number of votes recorded in the elections of 1689-1712 was only in the region of 550.[73] We are assured by Canon Stratford of Christ Church that the number of freemen entitled to vote in Oxford City by 1722 was 1200; yet the highest number who ever polled, 1701-22, seems to have been about 750; while Liverpool, a notably active and fiercely-divided city politically, may not have exceeded 70 per cent turn-out in the election of 1710 and almost certainly achieved no more than 60 per cent in 1722.[74] One can go on accumulating examples,[75] and add to them a fair number, of similar pattern, from smaller boroughs such as Helston and Launceston in Cornwall, Totness and Dartmouth in Devon.[76] But there is no need, I think, to labour the point further. There is enough evidence already to make it well-nigh certain that the nominal size of 260,000 for the electorate in 1722 is at least 25 to 30 per cent too low. Between 330,000 and 340,000, I suggest, would be a not unreasonable estimate of the true size of the electorate by that year.[77] And, even allowing for a considerable population expansion since 1690, that represents not far short of one in four of the adult males in the country.[78]

But we can also be certain of something else: that there were far more than that number, of those still alive, who had voted at earlier elections but were not qualified to vote at this. Poll book analysis[79] has revealed a truly astonishing turn-over of voters in the early eighteenth century: partly of course through death, inheritance or coming of age, but also through all manner of other causes. The most important were probably mobility, especially in the larger boroughs; thousands of freeholders selling out and others buying;

[73] M. Mullett, ' "To Dwell together in Unity": The Search for Agreement in Preston Politics, 1660-1690', *Trans. Hist. Soc. Lancs and Ches.* 125, 1975, p. 65. Henry Fleetwood was able to canvass only 425 before the 1706 by-election. Staffs R.O. Gower MSS. D. 593. P/13/10.

[74] H.M.C. *Portland MSS.* vii, 317; Bodl. MS. Carte 129, ff. 427-43; MS. Willis 48, f. 361; Sedgwick, i, 270.

[75] Derby is another case in point.

[76] For Launceston, for instance, cf. MS. Willis 5, f. 134 and Sedgwick, i, 212. There is ample scope for further work on the freeman boroughs. E.g. Hertford is superbly documented.

[77] Since this was written Derek Hirst has suggested *c.* 300,000 as the possible size of 'a hypothetical and potential electorate' before the Civil War; though at that time, as he has convincingly shown, the 'freeholder' qualification in the counties was far looser than it had become by the early 18th century. See *The Representative of the People?*, p. 105 and ch. 2 *passim*.

[78] King's age tables for the 1690s would suggest a total of 1.45 million adult males out of a poulation of approximately 6.2 millions. 340,000 electors would have been 23·45 per cent of this figure. It is worth emphasising that King regarded over half the population in his day as poor or chronically poor.

[79] See note 3 above

burgages changing hands at a rapid rate; freemen being created in blocks, and others being as arbitrarily struck off by partisan corporations; and frequent changes in many corporations themselves. And on top of all this there was, because of so many disputed franchises, until the second 'Last Determinations Act' was passed in 1729,[80] a vast 'grey area' of voters of dubious or disputed rights, all of whom had exercised these rights *at some time*, even though at any given Election they might be unable to do so.[81]   For all these reasons, there was probably an annual drop-out and renewal rate in the electorate ranging from between four and eight per cent a year in the small or small-to-medium boroughs, to very much higher rates of turnover in some of the large towns, with high mobility.[82]   Even in the burgage borough of Pontefract the rate of loss and replacement almost defies belief.   Between 1710 and 1713 the number of voters rose by just 18, from 229 to 247.   Yet the 247 includes no fewer than 105 completely new names, who had not appeared at all in the two previous contests.   By 1715 only 76 of the 264 who voted in that year, some 28 per cent, had done so a mere seven years before.

As for the counties, computer analysis of some of those with runs of poll books, such as Hampshire, has revealed a turnover in voters which Dr. Speck has rightly described as 'tremendous'.   In Bedfordshire only 1020 of the 2563 voters who turned out in 1705 were still there to poll at Bedford for knights of the shire ten years later, a phenomenal rate of renewal of about fifteen per cent per annum.   With these trends in mind, I suggest that it would be very surprising if the number of Englishmen and Welshmen who had voted at at least one election in the two decades from 1702 to 1722 did not reach, at a very conservative estimate, seven to eight hundred thousand; of whom perhaps 80,000 (that is only the roughest of guesses) had died in the interim.

*   *   *

There still remains, however, a final test that we must apply to the efficacy of the National Will in the election of Augustan

---

[80] See Cannon, *Parliamentary Reform*, p. 34.

[81] E.g. the polling of poor inhabitant householders, as well as ratepayers, at Fowey in Jan. 1701 and at Milborne Port, 'for the sake of keeping the peace', in several elections before 1702; the prolonged dispute at Reading over whether freemen were allowed to vote as well as inhabitant ratepayers; the curious convention at Clitheroe, whereby the *occupiers* of the 'voteable burgages' were allowed to vote provided the *proprietors* did not turn up to do so; etc.   Gloucs. R.O. Dyrham Park MSS. D.1799 c. 5; *Commons Journals*, xiv, 75; Sedgwick, i, 193-4; MS. Willis 48, f. 360.   In the Commons Journals alone examples are legion.

[82] Speck, *Tory and Whig*, pp. 18-19, for analysis of Bletchingley, Appleby, Horsham, Brackley, Hertford and Mitchell.

Parliaments. It is clear that, even allowing for the elements of plural and on occasion multiple voting which the old system admittedly allowed, far greater numbers were directly represented than has ever been appreciated. But we still have to ask, *who* and *where* did the system 'represent'?

I shall have to leave entirely out of this last stage of my argument any reference to the representation of 'interests', to the theory of 'virtual representation' that was the desperate resort of the system's late eighteenth- and early nineteenth-century defenders. There is no time to develop this theme here; and in any case the men of William III's reign and Queen Anne's scarcely ever bothered to apply it to their circumstances. Instead, I shall concentrate for the rest of this paper exclusively on the more sensitive question of the places that were represented.

The assumption has always been made that, in this regard, at least, the unreformed system, by its very irrationality, was inadequate and unfair: not so bad, perhaps, in late Stuart England as it later became, but in all conscience bad enough. It seems to me this assumption, too, is based on a number of very significant misunderstandings; and that unless one realises that contemporaries did not share them, it will remain hard to appreciate fully their acquiescence in the system that was an ever-present framework of their political activities.

First, let us be clear that there were two distinct sides to the representation of places. On the one hand, there is the question of whether the system gave an equitable representation to the main regions of the country, in relation to population or to wealth, and within the regions, to particular counties? On the other hand, since well over four-fifths of M.P.s sat for borough seats, there is the question: were the towns of England and Wales, by and large, equitably treated?

The answer to the first question, however one might qualify it, must be NO. Regionally the system was over-weighted in favour of two areas: the south-west, where six counties returned 148 members, because of the gross over-representation of the Cornish and Wiltshire boroughs; and the south-eastern seaboard counties of Hampshire, Sussex and Kent, with their 72 members.[83] The few writers who did try to publicise the inequities of the system in the 1690s, such as Houghton and Smart, concentrated entirely on this aspect of the problem; and even here, preoccupied as they were in the '90s with the mind-boggling cost of the first great war against Louis

---

[83] 9 southern counties—Cornwall, Devon, Somerset, Wiltshire, Gloucestershire, Dorset, Hampshire and Sussex—thus returned 220 out of the 513 English and Welsh M.P.s. The anomalous privileges still enjoyed by the Cinque Ports were a major factor in the over-representation of the south-east.

XIV, it was not the relation of seats to population but to the tax-paying contribution of the different regions which seemed to them to require attention.[84]

As to the second question, were the towns of Augustan England fairly represented, my answer to this — perverse as it may seem — is YES. By the end of the eighteenth century when industrialisation was well under way, the treatment of towns had become patently unjust. At the beginning of the century, while the first Party war still raged, I suggest that this was not the case at all. In fact, one of the principal reasons why the electorate could be identified with 'the sense of the people' at this period is that, although everyone recognised that there were about thirty so-called 'towns' which no longer had any rational claim to have their own members, it was very hard indeed in 1700 to point to more than a handful of towns with a clear-cut case to replace them.

This is unquestionably a major reason why such reform projects as were floated at the time sank like stones. William Bromley, late Speaker of the House, recalled in 1715 how 'in 1693, when the Bill was depending for disfranchising Stockbridge, the gentlemen of Hampshire were for having that borough supplied by Alresford, Alton or Basingstoke, [but] could not agree in any one of them'. All were respectable towns, but none was exceptionally thriving, and none could be proved to have been represented before. And so 'the gentlemen [writes Bromley] . . . were divided, according to their respective interests'; and Stockbridge was reprieved.[85] This little incident I find immensely illuminating; as indeed is the proposal, made in a bill of 1701 — the only general reform measure of any consequence between 1660 and the 1780s, one which would have had the effect of disfranchising thirty or so rotten boroughs — to allocate the seats concerned not to other towns but to the county hundreds in which the decayed boroughs themselves were situated.[86] The fact is, there was a general belief as late as the beginning of the eighteenth century — and the belief is crucial to our appreciation of the acceptability of the whole system at the time — that the vast majority of towns in 1700 whose population and wealth cried out for representation *were already represented*. And what is more, not-withstanding the short-lived Cromwellian precedent of enfranchising

[84] E.g. John Smart's broadsheet, *A Scheme of the Proportions the Several Counties in England paid to the Land Tax in 1693 and to the Subsidies in 1697 compared with the Number of Members they send to Parliament* (London, N.D. [?1698]).

[85] MS. Willis 48, f. 429: Bromley to Willis, 28 Feb. 1714[-15].

[86] Only part of this bill (one which aimed by various means to reduce bribery at elections) was concerned with constituency reform. N. Luttrell, *A Brief Historical Relation of State Affairs* (Oxford, 1857), v, 45; Speck, *Tory and Whig*, p. 15.

Manchester, Leeds and Halifax in the 1650s, this belief was absolutely sound.

In 1700 about 77 per cent of the people of England and Wales were still living either in hamlets and villages or in tiny market towns indistinguishable, even to contemporary eyes, from villages.[87] Outside London, of course, the proportion of country to town dwellers was very much higher still. Thinking of this in electoral terms, it will be apparent that the bulk of the voters must have resided in county constituencies and could only have aspired to vote in county elections. Now the borough electors were, it is true, far more influential than those of the counties in terms simply of the number of M.P.s they returned. And in view of this the borough electorate looks to us very small; even putting it, as I have, significantly higher by 1720 than any previously accepted figure, at over 110,000. Yet what if we set this figure against such statistics as are now available about England's urban population in 1700? In all, there were only some 32 places in the English provinces with over 5000 inhabitants in 1700,[88] only two[89] having more than 20,000. Of these 32 towns, only four were unrepresented in Parliament: Birmingham, Manchester, Leeds and Sheffield. There were perhaps a further two dozen towns with populations of between 3000 and 5000. They included cathedral cities, such as Durham and Winchester; county towns like Bedford and Derby; ports like Dover and Scarborough; manufacturing centres such as Taunton, Andover and Sudbury; resorts or thoroughfare towns such as Stamford, Preston and Bath. All these, and most of the rest in these categories, were already parliamentary boroughs. Lower still down the scale, there were a great many towns which to us would seem very small, with populations of from one thousand to two and a half thousand, but which to contemporaries were still respectable and even sizeable in a local context (we should bear in mind that they still drew the line between a 'town' and what they called a 'great town' at around 1200 inhabitants in 1700). It is only at this level, among the mass of towns with between 1000 and 2500 residents, that the number of absentees from the list of parliamentary boroughs begins to grow to significant proportions. It is here one notes the absence of Whitehaven and Falmouth; of Bolton and Blackburn; of Wakefield and Doncaster; of Sherborne and Farnham, and many others.[90] But then, the overwhelming bulk

[87] C. W. Chalklin, *The Provincial Towns of Georgian England* (1974), pp. 3-4, 16 and n. 40.
[88] To those towns of this size identified *ibid*, ch. 1, I would add Reading. I would exclude (in 1700) Northampton and Sunderland.
[89] Norwich and Bristol.
[90] Both Defoe and Macky urged the claims of Sherborne and Falmouth in the early 18th century. *Tour*, i, 217, 237; *Journey*, ii, 48, 232.

of parliamentary boroughs fell into this very same category: even nine Cornish boroughs were classed as 'great towns',[91] and several towns that were apparently in sorry decline — Bridport, with its choked-up harbour, and down-at-heel Droitwich — still contained between 1200 and 1400 inhabitants each.[92]

We can see now the scale of the problem, or rather the lack of scale. In these circumstances any significant redistribution of borough seats was out of the question. How could the claims of Farnham or Chelmsford which were without their own members be set against those of, say, Helston or Wycombe, which had them? No wonder it was a non-issue.

I have been talking about the situation in 1700. It is worth adding that by the 1730s, by which time I have suggested a recognition of the inadequacy of the electoral system to represent the National Will was taking root, the process of pre-industrial urbanisation had already advanced far enough to throw some of the relatively slight anomalies of 1700 into sharper relief. By then Birmingham's population had passed 20,000; Leeds, Manchester, Sheffield and Chatham were past 10,000, the first three well past; several other unrepresented ports and industrial towns, notably Whitehaven, Sunderland, Halifax, Wolverhampton and Frome, had grown with great rapidity in the past thirty years. The shape of things to come was by then in sight.

Now there is one sense, it is true, in which 'public opinion' in some large represented towns had no adequate outlet. Tiverton, a rare example of a large industrial centre *per se*, with eight or nine thousand inhabitants in 1700, elected its members by the votes of a restricted corporation of 24. Bath and Andover (at this time a large clothing town) committed their voting rights to similarly tiny numbers, as did Bury St. Edmunds and Salisbury. And there were other towns, too — the ports of Plymouth, Portsmouth and Poole, for instance — where although the franchise was in the freemen of the borough, admission to the freemen's roll was jealously limited.

But what is so often overlooked is that many of the rest of their inhabitants were not disfranchised, any more than the inhabitants of those scores of respectable market towns or those few growing manufacturing centres and ports that did not happen to be parliamentary boroughs, were disfranchised. It was a political fact of the first importance that, over the country as a whole, literally tens of

[91] Liskeard, Truro, Bodmin, Helston, Penryn, Saltash, St. Ives, Fowey and Launceston. Launceston was one of the least populous of the nine (MS. Willis 5, f. 134); but Celia Fiennes, visiting it in 1698, described it as 'one of the last great towns' in England. C. Morris (ed.), *The Journeys of Celia Fiennes* (1949), p. 269.

[92] MS. Willis 15, f. 97; *Notitia Parliamentaria*, ii, 462, 464.

thousands of these inhabitants did vote. They voted in *county* elections. And quite often they exercised great influence on the outcome of those elections.

Once again it is the poll-books that bring this to light, and in so doing illuminate still further the expression of the National Will in the first age of Party. Take those large towns or cities with a corporation or narrow freeman franchise. In 1710 Portsmouth, with its dockyard annexe of Portsea, despatched about 500 forty-shilling freeholders to Winchester to vote for knights of the shire; 500 out of a total of 4753. Here was the compensation for the cheating by the borough franchise of a rapidly growing population in this booming urban centre. In the same Election the corporation borough of Andover, which sent its own members to Westminster by the votes of a select 24, provided 162 county voters. Bury St. Edmunds in Suffolk, a large town but a corporation borough, in the same year supplied 282 of Suffolk's 5000 voters, only Ipswich sending more.

But these were bonuses for towns already represented. The role of the directly unrepresented towns is even more significant, if not always as impressive numerically. By far the biggest single block of freeholders in Yorkshire in 1708 came from Leeds, 194 of them. Although the West Riding was badly off for parliamentary boroughs, its unrepresented towns were a vital factor in county contests. In 1708 Sheffield (with Attercliffe) sent 86 freeholders to York, Wakefield 112, Halifax 91, Bradford 89 and Doncaster 83. And of course the *actual* electorate of these towns was in all cases much larger than the number of voters who turned out in this one year for which we happen to have detailed evidence. In South Lancashire we know that the nonconformist voters alone, from the Manchester, Bolton and Warrington regions, amounted in 1715 to 320.[93] The story is the same in the south. Luton supplied more freeholders than any town in Bedfordshire; Kingston on Thames and Croydon than any of the parliamentary boroughs of Surrey, Newbury in Berkshire more than represented Reading, itself one of the main towns in the south.[94]

Candidates and local election managers were fully alive to the crucial importance of courting the freeholders in the towns. Landlord influence in this period even in country areas has been shown to have been much exaggerated.[95] But in a lot of towns it could be discounted altogether. And taking the 'market town' as our criterion

[93] Dr. Williams's Library, MS. 34.4, pp. 58-63.
[94] Bedfordshire 1705, 1715, 1722 P-Bs; Surrey 1710 P-B (Bodl. Lib.—this version also contains votes cast for each parish and township in 1705); Berks 1727 P-B.
[95] A good example is the Derbyshire election of Dec. 1701, at which (Lord Stanhope complained) the influence of the numerous Tory gentry was overthrown 'meerly by the multitude of the rabble that came out of the Peak against' them. Chevening MSS.: to Lord Chesterfield, 20 April [1702].

at the lower level, the extent of the urban vote in county elections was always considerable, sometimes staggering. In Bedfordshire the urban vote was over twenty per cent in 1705, in Berkshire over thirty per cent in 1727, in Hertfordshire almost forty per cent in 1705.[96] In Hampshire in 1710 an astounding 2268 voters out of 4753 — very nearly half — came from cities, boroughs and market towns. And far to the north in Northumberland — where the electorate was kept under 2000 by the exclusion of the freeholders of Newcastle — Hexham, Alnwick, and North Shields together could exercise a sometimes decisive influence.[97]

Now, in the late eighteenth century, and the early nineteenth, such voting power would have been little comfort; for as is well known, there were by then so few county contests, the franchise was largely academic. But in the first age of Party these unrepresented towns not only had plenty of voters but, often enough, the chance to use them. The exceptionally high incidence of contests which marked the 17 General Elections of the first age of Party was important enough even in the parliamentary boroughs. Whereas in George III's reign borough electorates that were wholly, or all but wholly, anaesthetised littered the scene, during the post-Revolution struggle in the constituencies from 1689-1722 there were only seven boroughs out of 215 where not a single contest can be traced.[98] And the places in question were almost all negligible.[99] Even most so-called 'rotten' boroughs were hives of activity by later standards. For the uncertain favours of the inhabitants of Bramber's twenty or thirty hovels Whigs and Tories wrestled eleven times from 1689 to 1722. The famous sheep of Old Sarum had their peaceful grazing disturbed four times between 1689 and 1715. And there was actually talk of a contest in 1698 at Gatton by the Hill, that connoisseur's piece in Surrey, a ten-house hamlet which set an almost unique standard in Anne's reign of bucolic deference.[100]

[96] Herts 1705 P-B.

[97] This was clearly so in 1716, when the three towns together cast 176 Whig votes and only 115 Tory ones (1641 voted altogether). Without them, and the support of the Whig freeholders from the parliamentary borough of Morpeth, Francis Delavall would not have been elected. *The Poll-Book of the Contested Election for the County of Northumberland taken on the 2nd day of February 1715[-16]* (Newcastle upon Tyne, 1899).

[98] The exhaustive findings of Henry Horwitz on William III's reign, printed as an appendix to his forthcoming *Parliament, Policy and Politics in the Reign of William III*, now supplement what is already in print for the years 1701-22 in Speck, *Tory and Whig*, Cannon, *Parliamentary Reform* and 'Polls Supplementary', and Sedgwick, vol. I. I am much indebted to Prof. Horwitz for allowing me prior access to this information.

[99] The only exception was the Carmarthen boroughs.

[100] For the 'parliamentary tree' at Old Sarum where the handful of votes were taken, in the absence of a house, see *V.C.H. Wilts*, vi, 66-7. For the extraordinary ritual at Gatton, MS. Willis 15, ff. 6-7.

How much more important, therefore, was the contrast in the counties between the early and the later eighteenth century, since it was in the counties that two-thirds of the electorate voted. During the last sixty years or so of the eighteenth century, a combination of the crippling cost of contesting county seats, and a marked scarcity of great national issues worth letting purses for, induced a prolonged electoral coma in the great majority of English counties. But if we look back to the period between the Revolution and 1722 we are in a totally different world. Then there was only *one* English county out of the forty, Dorset, which left its freeholders completely unexercised. Devon, one must concede, was only slightly better off, with a single by-election to its credit. But these were quite exceptional cases. Very few counties experienced less than five contests between the Revolution and 1722. Many shires went quite berserk. Essex and Gloucestershire were both contested twelve times in those 33 years;[101] Gloucestershire, Middlesex and Buckinghamshire each eleven times, and Surrey ten. Suffolk, and Norfolk, Hertfordshire, Bedfordshire and Sussex were not far behind.[102] Here, then, we have a situation in which what Cannon calls the 'urban penetration' of the county electorates, its penetration by voters overwhelmingly independent of the land and, in the main, of the influence of big local landlords, was a genuine and continuing reality; not the polite fiction it so often was during the last 90 years of the unreformed system. Of all the transmitters of 'the sense of the people' in the first age of Party this was perhaps the most sensitive and the most vital.

*   *   *

I could have pursued my theme further; but I shall not try your indulgence any more. I hope, in any case, by now to have said enough to convince you — as I myself am convinced — that when Lord Delamere in 1689 reminded his fellow peers that the House of Commons of their day was indeed 'the body of the people in their representatives'[103] he was not talking idly nor indulging in a mere rhetorical flourish. He was in fact enunciating the reality of the National Will, as embodied in the electorate of the first age of Party. He was not claiming that all the people were represented in the House of Commons; that is a purely twentieth-century ideal. But he *was* saying that 'the sense of the people' was represented in the House of Commons: that was the highest eighteenth-century ideal.

[101] For the Gloucestershire by-election of March 1720, omitted from Sedgwick, *loc. cit.*, see Cannon, 'Polls Supplementary', p. 112.

[102] The freeholders of the last four were involved in eight contests, respectively, and the Suffolk voters in seven.

[103] Althorp Savile MSS., box 4 (Earl Spencer's muniments), quoted by H. Horwitz, 'Parliament and the Glorious Revolution', *B.I.H.R.* 47, 1974, p. 39.

In my view there were only three General Elections in the 43 years we have been concerned with at which this will was, up to a point, perverted. In March 1681, in 1685 and finally in 1722, in each case for different reasons, 'the sense of the people' was not so much mis-interpreted as exaggerated. In the thirty years after 1685, on the other hand, there was not one Election of the twelve fought in that period which failed to produce a House of Commons initially at least in tune with the mood of the nation at the time — whether we take as our criterion how the politicians themselves gauged that mood before and during their campaign, or how we can judge it from all the other evidence available to us.

Only in the last Election of the first age of Party, that of 1722, delayed for four years by the repeal of the Triennial Act, was a party able once again, as in 1685, to win a majority in the Commons disproportionate to its strength in the country. The electorate of 1722 was exposed to the full blast of government patronage, following a long preparatory attack by the Whig landlords on the independence of many of the smaller boroughs. Inevitably some of those 'weathervanes' I referred to at the outset had already begun to seize up. Just as 1722 marked the end of an epoch for the first political parties, so too it left the writing clearly on the wall for the great electorate of late Stuart England, not least because the major ideological issues of 1679-1715 were fast losing their relevance. Only twelve years ahead lay 1734, when (as we have already seen) Walpole lost the popular battles in the constituencies but won the war. And then in the 1741 Election — irony of ironies — Walpole was toppled, not by 'the sense of the people' (he actually did rather better in some of the counties and large boroughs than he had in 1734) but because so many of the much-despised 'closed' constituencies at last deserted him: or to put it more realistically, he had lost the support of too many of their borough patrons.

Has what I have been saying in this paper, and in particular the sting in its tail, a lesson for us, in 1975? I think it has. The lesson surely is, to beware of complacency about our representative institutions; to recognise, in the experience of the years from 1680 to 1780, the uncomfortable truth that a system which answers the true ends of representative government in one set of circumstances can become, within perhaps a very few years, grotesquely unfitted to cope with a changed set of circumstances; and to eschew that excessive veneration of the past which has always been the Englishman's favourite resort for an argument, when it has suited his convenience. 'We must never tamper with the sacred edifice of 1688', shrilled the anti-reformers of the 1780s and 90s: 'it has served our forefathers, and a new edifice will only confuse the people and produce its own far worse distortions!' Perhaps our present-day Burkes, in their self-interested complacency, could profitably remember the words of Tom Paine in the 1790s: 'The vanity and presumption of governing beyond the grave, is the most ridiculous and insolent of all tyrannies ... The Parliament or the people of 1688, or of any other period, had no more right to dispose of the people of the present day, than the Parliament or the people of the present day have to dispose of ... those who are to live a hundred or a thousand years hence. Every generation is, and must be, competent to all the purposes which its occasions require. It is the living, and not the dead, that are to be accommodated.'[104]

---

[104] Thomas Paine, *The Rights of Man* (Everyman edn., 1915), p. 12.

1. Portrait of Thomas, 1st earl and 1st marquess of Wharton (d. 1715).
The Whig chieftain and Junto lord – 'Honest Tom' to his friends – was his
party's electioneer supreme and leader of the great Whig offensive over the
Protestant Succession in 1713–14.

Sir Godfrey Kneller. *National Portrait Gallery*

2

THE ATTACK ON 'THE INFLUENCE OF THE CROWN',
1702-16 [1]

WRITING IN 1924 about the politics of the sixteen-nineties, Sir Keith
Feiling observed that 'To most men of that day the radical division still
seemed, as formerly in King Charles's time, to be that between the "country" and the "Court". But this line crossed and zigzagged with that of
Whig and Tory . . .'.[2] Most modern scholars would accept, as Feiling
himself clearly did, that by the time Queen Anne came to the throne in
March 1702 this situation had been reversed:[3] that by then the fundamental
line of demarcation in politics was the line dividing whig from tory, although
this was still traversed at times by the traditional but no longer distinct
line between the consistent supporters of Government and the 'natural',
if not habitual, pillars of Opposition. One recent authority has preferred a
circular rather than a linear representation of the major political divisions
of the early eighteenth century; visualizing what he calls 'the parties' as
being ranged round the circumference, 'from Court through Court Tory
and Country Tory to Country and so back through Country Whig and
Court Whig once again to the Court'.[4] But whatever one's geometrical
preferences may be, or for that matter one's reservations on the use of the
term 'parties' to describe the various groups involved, there is no question
that among both the whigs and the tories in the house of commons after
1702 there were still large numbers of 'country members'. An average
total in the neighbourhood of 250 in the first five parliaments elected after
Anne's accession would not be far wide of the mark.

These were, almost without exception, party men;[5] but they were also

[1] I am grateful to Mr. W. A. Speck of the University of Newcastle for his helpful
criticism and advice during the writing of this article. My colleague, Dr. A. L.
Brown, kindly read the article in typescript and it is at his suggestion that I have
tried to clarify the rather confused position with regard to the dates of the two
Regency acts of Anne's reign (see p. 54 and n. 4 below).

[2] Sir Keith Feiling, *A History of the Tory Party, 1640–1714*, p. 287.

[3] *Ibid.*, pp. 276, 353–9; though it should be remarked that Feiling also pointed
out (p. 277 and n. 1) that political observers, especially foreign observers, were
slow to recognize the change.

[4] R. Walcott, 'The idea of party in the writing of later Stuart history', *Journal
of British Studies*, i (1962), 54–61. Cf. the same author's *English Politics in the Early
Eighteenth Century* (Oxford, 1956), p. 157.

[5] The 'pure' country member, the backbencher who recognized no party allegiance, was almost unknown in the house of commons by Anne's reign. Dr. Walcott,
though allocating a segment of his theoretical circle to a group of country politicians,
distinct from Country Whigs and Country Tories, does not apparently succeed
in identifying any specimens of the breed in practice. See, e.g., his analysis of the
1705 election results, *English Politics*, p. 115n.

men whose built-in suspicion of the Court—their distrust of Government, as such—was as much a part of their political creed as their party principles, whatever these happened to be. And they were men who on certain issues, at least, would normally be found in opposition to the administration of the day, no matter what its party complexion. Compared with the great 'party matters' of Anne's day, however, these issues were relatively few in number. It may be partly accidental that of the ten house of commons' divisions in the period 1702–14 for which lists of voters are known to exist,[1] only one[2] concerned an essentially Court-Country issue, while the rest all involved in some degree whig and tory loyalties. Yet this proportion of 1 : 9 provides a rough indication, if not a precise reflection, of the decline which had overtaken the old 'country tradition', not merely since the sixteen-seventies but since the sixteen-nineties. It was a trend which lasted at least until 1722—that is, as long as politics was so largely dominated by the competition for power, or alternatively the struggle for survival, of two great parties, whig and tory.

Only in one major field in the early eighteenth century did country activity genuinely flourish, rather than stagnate or become diverted into unhealthy channels.[3] One intensely live political issue survived into the age of Anne, and beyond, into the opening years of the Hanoverian period, which consistently encouraged a combination between the independent backbenchers of both parties against the government of the day. The *Journals* of both Houses preserve a bare but impressive monument to its importance in their record of parliament's proceedings on the long succession of Place bills or 'self-denying' clauses which followed each other with inexorable regularity between 1702 and 1716. Except on the rare occasions when the country members had equally exciting game to hunt, as in the winter of 1703–4 for instance, or that of 1707–8,[4] scarcely a session went by in these fourteen years without one, and sometimes more than one, measure of this kind emerging to harass the occupants of the ministerial benches.

Place bills were, in fact, the most persistent of all major legislative projects brought forward in the first decade and a half of the eighteenth century; and for the most part they represented, as one stoutly independent whig once put it, 'a plain question between Court and Country in the House of

[1] Details will be found in W. A. Speck, 'The choice of a Speaker in 1705', *Bulletin of the Institute of Historical Research*, xxxvii (1964), 37-46.

[2] That of 18 Feb. 1706, printed by Walcott, *BIHR*, xiv, 30-3. See also A. Boyer, *The History of the Reign of Queen Anne digested into Annals* (1703–13), vii. 150–4, and p. 46 below.

[3] The work of the commissioners of public accounts from 1702 to 1704 and from 1711 to 1714 is a good example of the latter development.

[4] 1703–4 saw the attempt of the tory commissioners of accounts to fasten a charge of financial malpractice on the earl of Orford and a number of his Junto clients; in 1707–8 country energies were absorbed by a searching enquiry into the conduct of the war in Spain and also by the promotion of a bill against bribery and corruption in elections.

Commons'.[1] Their object, put at its simplest, was either wholly to eliminate or drastically to reduce the capacity of the Crown to corrupt parliament or sway its decisions through the presence of well over 100 office-holders and pensioners in the Commons.[2] It was not their purpose to ensure a 'separation of powers' between executive and legislature (for no such separation was within the bounds of possibility as long as the vast majority of the queen's cabinet and privy councillors were members of the house of lords, enjoying hereditary seats there which could not be affected by legislation); but rather, as the titles and preambles of the bills make plain, to ensure 'more free and impartial proceedings in Parliament' and to secure 'the freedom of Parliaments' from undue royal and ministerial influence. The intensity of feeling which such measures almost invariably aroused in the house of commons, especially after 1704, can only be appreciated against the background of the Spanish Succession war of 1702–13. For this war, like its predecessor in the years 1689–97, not only raised the army and navy to an unprecedented level of strength but necessitated a parallel development of the administrative machinery required both to supervise and service the armed forces and to pay for them. In consequence the number of placemen, both civil and military, who found their way into parliament rose significantly,[3] and so did public concern at the implications of this growth.

Presumably because the concrete gains achieved by the attacks on the parliamentary influence of the Crown in the years from 1702 to 1716 were not dramatic, the campaign as a whole has attracted very much less attention from political historians than it did from contemporaries; while constitutional authorities, for their part, duly record the landmark of the Regency act but little more. What is not generally realized is that on three occasions during the period, in 1706, 1712 and 1714, the country forces stood on the brink of really spectacular successes, any one of which could well have had a profound effect on the political and constitutional development of early Hanoverian Britain. For this reason alone a brief account of their activities and some reassessment of the importance of these activities appears to be called for.

Limited progress had already been made towards the restriction of 'influence' between 1694 and the death of William III. By a series of acts passed in 1694, 1700 and 1701, important groups of revenue officials, including the collectors of the land tax, the commissioners of the salt duty and the commissioners of customs and excise, though not the commissioners of the treasury, had been excluded from the Lower House. On

---

[1] Cumberland and Westmorland Record Office, Lonsdale MSS.: James Lowther (M.P. for Cumberland) to William Gilpin, 2 Feb. 1709[10].

[2] *A List of Gentlemen that are in offices, Employment etc.* (Cambridge, 1705), which was probably the most comprehensive list of placemen in the house of commons compiled during Anne's reign, estimated the number sitting in the House at the time of the dissolution of the queen's first parliament (including officers of the armed forces and a small number of pensioners) at 126.

[3] See p. 44 below.

the other hand four general 'self-denying bills' introduced between December 1692 and the spring of 1700, providing for the disqualification of all placemen without exception, had all failed, although two of the four had been passed by the Commons themselves.[1] One of these had fallen in the house of lords, which because of the high proportion of power-politicians as well as of office-holders and courtiers among its members, was to be the fatal hurdle for the great majority of measures of this kind for almost a quarter of a century after 1692; and the one general Place bill which had survived the Lords[2] had been promptly blocked by the royal veto. The year before Anne's accession, however, the country legions in the house of commons had apparently scored a signal victory, when both the Lords and the king were persuaded to accept the sweeping Place clause inserted in the Act of Settlement, a clause providing that after the Hano-verians succeeded to the throne 'no person who has an office or place of profit under the King or receives a pension from the Crown shall be capable of serving as a member of the House of Commons'.

In reality, however, the seeming triumph of 1701 was much more a party victory than a country one,[3] and as such exuded an air of impermanence almost from the start. Some of the leading champions of the 'country interest' in the sixteen-nineties, especially among the whigs who had been the chief sponsors of the original Place bills, had already begun to recognize by 1701 that the sweeping general measures conceived at a time when William III was extremely unpopular were not only impracticable—in the sense that any bill designed to take early effect had little or no chance of surmounting the twin barriers of the Lords and the veto—but also undesirable. More and more it was coming to be realized that the efficiency of the Commons themselves would be severely impaired if all lines of communication between their chamber and the king's ministers were ruthlessly severed; that the authentic information which the House needed to sustain many of its debates, especially debates on vital questions of finance, foreign policy and war policy, could only be supplied if such ministers as the chancellor of the exchequer and the treasury commissioners, the secretary at war, the treasurer of the navy, and at least some of the admiralty lords were sitting on its benches. The new trend of opinion had been indicated in 1699 when one leading Country Whig, Sir Richard On-slow, and two of the lieutenants of Robert Harley's 'New Country Party' drafted a bill to 'restrain' the number of officers sitting in the Lower

---

[1] The bill of 1695 was defeated in the Lower House. Another, introduced in the winter of 1699–1700, got as far as the committee stage but had still to be reported when parliament was prorogued. (David Hayton has recently pointed out, however, that only in this fourth and final instance was *both* total *and* permanent exclusion contemplated. See his article in *Parliaments, Estates and Representation*, 5, 1985).

[2] This was in the winter of 1693–4, after the measure had been watered down by the proviso that members who vacated their seats on accepting office should be permitted to offer themselves for re-election.

[3] A point which is emphasized in B. Kemp, *King and Commons* (1957), pp. 58-9.

House, and the bill subsequently passed the Commons though not the Lords.[1]

It seems fairly clear that, by contrast, the all-embracing Place clause of 1701 was inserted in the Act of Settlement mainly under pressure from the large tory majority in the house of commons. It was part of the tories' price for making a statutory settlement of the succession on a Protestant heir who was remote from the direct hereditary line: one of a series of provisions in the act designed to ensure that no foreign ruler should have the opportunity in future to pervert the natural course of English policy, as the tories accused William of doing.[2] And although it received uncritical support from the more dogmatic and the less perceptive Country Whigs, and was accepted with as good a grace as they could muster by the whig leaders in the house of lords, who could certainly not afford to jeopardize the act as a whole by challenging it, most whigs had no desire to see it come into force unadulterated (the more so as they anticipated that a Hanoverian successor would be favourably disposed to their own party), while some were prepared to take the first favourable opportunity of repealing it outright. Even shrewd tories were soon ready to concede that the 'limitation . . . was so absurd that the next successor might easily have got it repeald'.[3]

Such was the background against which the campaigns of Queen Anne's day against 'the influence of the Crown' took shape. The outstanding feature of these campaigns was the determination of the country members to capitalize on the Crown's acceptance of the principle of exclusion, conceded in the legislation of 1693–1701, in order to secure a measure of limitation on 'influence' which would be at once more immediate and more realistic than the dramatic but insubstantial gains embodied in the Act of Settlement. Broadly speaking there were after 1701 two feasible avenues of approach to this objective. One was to progress by a series of minor measures along the lines of the acts passed during William's reign,

---

[1] *Commons' Journals*, xii. 496, 590.

[2] These limiting conditions were first voted as resolutions of a Committee of the whole House on the Succession between 1 and 11 March 1701, before the bill itself was ever drafted. The resolution to exclude all official place-holders and pensioners from the Lower House of parliament was one of the last two to be passed (the other concerning the independence of the judiciary), immediately before the declaration in favour of the Electress Sophia of Hanover on 11 March; and although it appears to have met but little frontal opposition, it seems clear from the reports of the Prussian resident, Bonet, and even more from the accounts supplied to the States-General by l'Hermitage, that by this time many whigs who had been enthusiastic for the principle of a conditional settlement to begin with had cooled appreciably as they came to share the apprehension of some of the Junto whigs, notably Lord Spencer, that the tories were deliberately making the conditions as drastic as possible in the hope of wrecking the subsequent bill. See British Museum, Add. MS. 30000 E fos. 63, 78: Bonet to Frederick III, 4/15, 14/25 March; Add. MS. 17677 WW fos. 179–80, 183, 185, 189; l'Hermitage, 4/15, 7/18, 11/22 March.

[3] Brit. Mus., Add. MS. 4291 fos. 42–3: Charles to Henry Davenant, 22 Jan. 1705[6].

excluding specific types or groups of office-holders from the Commons. A tentative move in this direction was initiated by the whigs in December 1702, when they tried to graft on to a bill settling a revenue on the prince consort a clause disqualifying members of the prince's household from serving in the Lower House. This particular proposal found little support.[1] But the method of proceeding by selective exclusions was revived early in 1705 when two bills were simultaneously presented to the Commons. One was brought in by the whig lawyer, Peter King, and was designed to eliminate the holders of 'new' offices—those established since 6 February 1684;[2] the other was promoted by a prominent tory backbencher, Ralph Freeman, with the intention of disabling 'all persons who are entitled by their offices to receive a benefit by publick annual taxes to be granted'.[3] Erasmus Lewis, Harley's under secretary of state, suspected that both projects owed their birth 'to the resentment of some people for the miscarriage of the bill against Occasional Conformity';[4] and this was no doubt true of Freeman's bill, which had the backing of other High Church zealots like William Bromley, Charles Caesar and Arthur Annesley, and appears to have been aimed primarily against army and navy officers.[5] This may explain why it narrowly failed at the third reading,[6] while King's measure, supported by a broad spectrum of whig as well as Country Tory opinion,[7] ran into no difficulties until it reached the Lords. The peers, though they thought the proposed exclusion too sweeping, and rejected the main clause on the grounds of its 'uncertainty and absurdity', were ready to consent to 'a particular disability put on some officers by name', including the specific clause inserted by the Commons at the committee stage disqualifying officers of the Prize Office. With this vital amendment the Upper House passed the bill, despite government opposition, by forty-four votes to thirty. But the Commons would not accept any adulteration, and a measure which had by now acquired a bewildering variety of names— 'the Exclusion Bill', 'the bill of offices', 'the Prize Office bill'—accordingly dropped, to the obvious satisfaction of Lord Treasurer Godolphin.[8]

---

[1] *C.J.*, xiv. 95.

[2] I.e. 6 Feb. 1684[5], the date of Charles II's death. See *C.J.*, xiv. 482: 16 Jan. 1705.

[3] *Ibid.*, p. 480; Buckinghamshire Record Office, Claydon MSS. (microfilm): Sir Thomas Cave to Lord Fermanagh, 30 Jan. 1704[5].

[4] Brit. Mus., Add. MS. 4743 fo. 20: to Henry Davenant, Whitehall, 19 Jan. 1704[5].

[5] M.P.s who held places in the government and household and whose salaries were paid out of the Civil List, were presumably outside the scope of the bill.

[6] By 139–133. *C.J.*, xiv. 499: 27 Jan. 1705.

[7] See the names of its sponsors, *ibid.*, p. 480.

[8] *Ibid.*, p. 486; *Parliamentary History of England* (hereafter cited as *Parl. Hist.*), vi. 438 (an account based on N. Tindal, *History of England from the Revolution to the accession of King George II* [1732–51] which contains some inaccuracies); Cumb. and Westmld. Record Office, Lonsdale MSS.: J[ames] L[owther] to [Sir John Lowther], 8 Feb. 1704[5]; Brit. Mus., Loan 29/192 fo. 42: Dyer's Newsletter, 10 Feb. 1704[5] (I am grateful to the duke of Portland for permission to make use

Despite this setback in February 1705, the method of making limited exclusions by easy stages always seemed the more likely to commend itself to the house of lords. But by this time the sights of a growing number of backbench M.P.s were becoming fixed on an alternative and more ambitious solution to the problem of 'influence'. This was to provide for the continued presence in the Commons of a specified and strictly limited number of household officials and working ministers, while excluding the great bulk of minor placemen, sinecurists, pensioners and officers of the armed forces. The achievement of an unqualified, general exclusion was now scarcely within the realm of practical politics. It is true that for several years after Anne's accession not a few members still clung doggedly to the utopian ideal of a Lower House of parliament completely independent of all ties with the Court. But in practice the only *general* Place bill and Place clause mooted in the new reign (both of them, significantly, in the first four years) were the products of party manoeuvring by the tories, and were in neither case launched on a genuine 'country bottom'.

The most scandalous example of this perversion of the country ideal occurred on 23 December 1702, when Walpole's friend Sir John Holland moved for leave to introduce a Place bill, apparently with some kind of limited measure in mind,[1] and the High Tories (many of whose friends were now in office) set out to quash it by the cynical device of proposing an amendment that was calculated to make the measure wholly unacceptable. Their proposal would have provided that 'no person whatsoever, in any office or employment' should be capable of sitting not merely in the Lower House but 'in Parliament'. Having carried the amendment against the whigs by 135 votes to 80—the House was fairly thin on this last day before the Christmas recess—they then proceeded by an almost identical majority to kill the bill itself at conception.[2] The one remaining attempt, early in the next parliament, to translate the principle of total exclusion into law was ostensibly more genuine than the first, and commanded some country support from whigs as well as tories; but as it was initiated by some of the very men who had been responsible for the disreputable farce of December 1702 it was, in reality, scarcely more respectable.

It was the arrival from the house of lords of the Regency bill, providing

of this collection); Longleat MSS., Portland Papers, vol. VII fos. 38, 81 : [Godolphin] to Mr. Secretary Harley, [10] and 12 Feb. 1705 (I am indebted to the marquess of Bath for access to the Harley papers in his possession).

[1] This was the most crowded day in the session of 1702-3, in which no fewer than 4 important measures occupied the House's attention—Prince George's Settlement bill, a Land Resumption bill, the Place bill and a bill for fixing a landed qualification for membership of the Commons—and contemporary sources consequently have little to say about the substance of Holland's motion. But it seems clear from the record of the proceedings in the *Journals* that the account in *Parl. Hist.*, vi. 144 is most misleading in asserting that the original intention was to promote another Place bill.

[2] *C.J.*, xiv. 95.

new machinery to secure the succession after Anne's death, which gave the advocates of a general self-denial a last opportunity to put their case in January 1706. Clause IV of this bill authorized the continuance, for a maximum of six months after the queen's death, of the parliament which was then sitting or which had last sat, and country members assumed from this that for these six months at least the Place clause of the Act of Settlement would be *ipso facto* suspended; some clearly suspected that during this interval the lords justices, with the help of the reprieved placemen, would repeal the clause. Playing on these apprehensions to find an excuse for obstructing and perhaps defeating the whole Regency bill, the leading High Tories, again led by Ralph Freeman, moved during the committee stage on 12 January that the committee should be instructed to receive a clause effectually to secure the general exclusion provided for in 1701.[1] Court members and their friends opposed the move vehemently. Arthur Moore, an associate of Harley and St. John, complained that 'an instruction not to alter a law [was] extraordinary', and Lord Coningsby did not scruple to accuse Freeman and his colleagues of trying to insert 'some thing in the bill to destroy the Succession'.[2] Some leading Country Whigs also declared against the motion, among them Sir Richard Onslow, Robert Eyres and John Morgan of Tredegar;[3] and yet, factious as it was, it attracted enough support from the diehards on the whig back benches to make its final defeat a very narrow one.[4]

Freeman's motion of January 1706 was nevertheless the last spasm of the dying cause of total exclusion. Its defeat, together with the knowledge that the government and the whig leaders were desperately anxious to get the Regency bill through, provided the genuine supporters of a limited Place bill with the opportunity they had been waiting for. A bill aimed specifically at 'preventing too great a number of officers sitting in Parlia-ment' had been sanctioned before Christmas and given an unopposed first reading on 11 January.[5] But its supporters were under no illusions about the reception it would meet with from the peers. If parliaments were always governed by reason, Robert Eyres drily observed, the Self-Denial bill would pass, 'but reason [does] not alwaies prevail'. On the other hand, 'the Regency bil has such friends as wil see it pass with a reasonable instruc-tion'.[6] This 'reasonable instruction' which Eyres, Peter King, James Stanhope and other Country Whigs had in mind was for the insertion of a clause in the Regency bill 'explaining, regulating and altering' the Place clause of the Act of Settlement. They proposed to remove one of the main objections which the Court had brought against Freeman's clause: namely,

[1] Cambridge University Library, Add. MS. 7093 p. 72; *C.J.*, xv. 85.

[2] Camb. Univ. Libr., Add. MS. 7093 pp. 72–3.

[3] For the first two see *ibid.* pp. 73–5; Morgan was a teller against the motion when it was put to the vote.

[4] It was rejected by 156 votes to 151. *C.J.*, xv. 85.

[5] *Ibid.*, pp. 64, 84.

[6] Camb. Univ. Libr., Add. MS. 7093 p. 84.

that it would endanger rather than secure the succession by turning out of the House, as soon as the queen died, every placeman—so necessitating something like 150 by-elections, and meanwhile leaving no responsible ministers in the Commons to keep members informed on the state of the nation.[1] But at the same time they were determined to ensure that the broad principle of exclusion would not be evaded when the present reign ended. A general exclusion was wrong, King conceded, but a partial exclusion was right and necessary.[2]

So was born the notorious 'Whimsical clause'[3] which from 12 January until 19 February 1706 gave rise to the fiercest struggle between Court and Country in Anne's reign. The clause, as it finally emerged from the cauldron of the Committee of the whole House between 12 and 21 January, named a limited number of important officials who, in addition to those who held offices for life and during good behaviour, were to be permitted to retain their seats in whatever parliament assembled after Anne's death under the terms of the Regency bill, and in any subsequent parliament if re-elected. The absolute maximum number of 'officers during pleasure' who could receive this dispensation was forty; and in the existing parliament it would, in fact, have affected under thirty members.[4] All other placemen would be automatically disqualified at the end of the reign unless they resigned their seals of office within ten days of parliament's meeting.

The clause proved an instant success with the rank and file of the whig independents, some fifty of whom consolidated behind its chief sponsors, resolved to make their support for the bill as a whole conditional on acceptance of the clause by the Court. Although many of these men had by now acknowledged the futility of pressing for a general exclusion it is clear that they were truly concerned about the steady increase in the numbers of 'Queen's servants' holding seats in the Commons and that they believed it was urgently necessary to guard against any further abuse of the prerogative by the successor to the throne. Eyre's claim that 'the clause' would preserve the constitution by wresting the decisions of the House out of the hands of pensioners and vesting its future firmly in those of the

[1] *Ibid.* p. 75.
[2] *Ibid.* p. 81.
[3] See Hist. MSS. Comm., *Portland MSS.*, iv. 464: Godolphin to Harley [25 Jan. 1705], misdated 5 Dec. 1707 by the editor.
[4] The officials selected for special treatment were the treasurer, comptroller, vice-chamberlain and Cofferer of the household; the chancellor of the exchequer; two principal secretaries of state; the queen's first serjeant-at-law; the attorney- and solicitor-general; up to 5 commissioners of the treasury; the treasurer and comptroller of the navy; the chancellor of the duchy of Lancaster; the lieutenant-general of the ordnance; up to 5 general officers of the army and a similar number of admirals; and finally 'other officers, being sworn members of the Privy Council, not exceeding ten, the first sworn to be the first preferred'. *C.J.*, xv. 110. At the time the clause was drafted, however, the treasury was not in Commission, a few of the specified offices were held by peers (e.g. those of treasurer of the household and chancellor of the duchy), while the number of privy-councillor M.P.s not holding specified offices was well under the authorized ten.

Gentlemen of England made a sure appeal to their emotions, and they found it easy to agree with King when he pointed out that at the time the Act of Settlement was passed there were only 100 placemen and pensioners in the Commons, but that now, with half as many again, it was 'a fit time to dispute this moot point'. The tory backbenchers were only too willing to join forces with the Country Whigs. Sir Thomas Meeres, the veteran member for Lincoln, took the view that the House could deal with 100 courtiers well enough, but not with 150; and the firebrand Cornishman, John Manley, said of the bill: 'if there is any good in it, 'tis this clause'.[1]

The government, however, and the whig chiefs in the house of lords were very far from agreeing with Manley's viewpoint. They found themselves in much readier sympathy with the opinion of the vice-treasurer of Ireland, who had described the clause in the Commons' committee as 'a tack upon the legislature' (Walpole had already branded it in similar terms), and who believed it would necessarily obstruct if not wreck the whole bill;[2] and they were somewhat encouraged, therefore, when the Court's vote fell only twenty-three short of the opposition's in a division at the Report stage on 24 January. 'You fought it soe stoutly last night, and brought it so near', wrote Godolphin to his chief political manager in the Commons, 'that I hope the H: of Lords will be encouraged to ruffle the Clause pretty handsomly, before they meet you upon it ...'.[3] In this he was not disappointed. The Lords, while insisting on the explicit repeal rather than the vague 'regulation' of the Place clause of the 1701 Act, did not reject the new clause outright; but they did amend it out of all recognition. They went some way to meet the fears of the country members on one score—the future proliferation of offices—by agreeing to the disqualification of members appointed to 'new' offices, which they defined (unlike Peter King the previous winter) as any office 'which at any time hereafter shall be created or erected'; they also agreed to the specific exclusion of officials of the Prize Office, who had been one of the targets of King's bill of January 1705; and finally, in an effort to disarm or divide the country opposition, they conceded that the provisions of the amended clause should come into force not on the death of Anne but at the dissolution of the existing parliament.[4] These concessions, though, were nothing like enough to conciliate a country interest which had now recognized the unusual strength of its bargaining position, and the Lords' amendments were rejected in St. Stephen's chapel on 4 February by 205 votes to 183.[5]

There followed a fortnight's deadlock, marked by formal conferences in the Painted Chamber between managers appointed by the two Houses, by furious informal wrangling, and by the growing conviction among leading

[1] Camb. Univ. Libr., Add. MS. 7093 pp. 81–2, 127.

[2] *Ibid.* pp. 78, 84.

[3] Brit. Mus., Loan 29/64/16: [Godolphin] to Secretary Harley, 'Friday noon' [25 Jan. 1706?].

[4] *C.J.*, xv. 123.

[5] *Ibid.*, p. 127.

ministers that the whole bill was in acute danger. The first glimmer of hope for the Court appeared on 11 February when the Lords' reasons for continuing to insist on their original amendments to the 'Whimsical clause' were reported to the Lower House. Two of these reasons made some impression on the Country Whigs. One was the insistence on what the Lords called 'the negative method' of approach to the problem of 'influence': which was that 'there can be no safe or just way of making such alteration [in the terms of the Act of Settlement] but by naming expressly, and in certain and plain words, what officers ought to stand *excluded* from the House of Commons, and to repeal the general clause as to all others'.[1] This method, as we have seen, had been favoured by some country members in the past and had been responsible for what concrete successes they had achieved since 1694. A more powerful argument adduced by the Lords was directed against the scale of the exclusions proposed by the clause, which it was estimated would involve something like 100 by-elections at the very time when the country needed a full and strong house of commons, and when the turmoil of elections, offering 'a dangerous opportunity to all, that are disaffected, of disturbing the publick peace', was most undesirable to good whigs and supporters of the Protestant Succession.[2]

Having thus prepared the ground a little, the Junto lords, together with allies like Townshend and Cowper, sought private talks with leading Country Whigs as the best way of reaching a compromise. But progress was slow and the bargaining tough: 'I have had this morning an acct. of a long tedious meeting betwixt the heads of the Whymsicalls & some Lords of our house', the lord treasurer told Robert Harley on the 15th.

The summ of it was that they would agree to the negative method proposed by the Lords provided they might exclude severall officers besides the prize office. The Lords told them they might exclude negatively whatever they would in the next reign provided they wd. not disturb the Queen in the present reign. This obliged them to take off their masque and they fairly told them, that was doing nothing at all and they shd. be laughed at. In short, after much wrangling they agreed to some additional heads to those I mentioned last night, none very material, but some of them very foolish. The particulars I have given to Mr. Boyle[3] & Mr. Secy Hedges whom I have desired to shew them to you, & to take all of you as much pains as you can to agree this matter today, for nothing will be so uneasy to the Queen as losing this bill . . .[4]

Later the same Friday the Court managed to gain a further breathing-space for the negotiators by getting the Commons to postpone further discussion

[1] *Ibid.*, p. 141: the italics are mine. The point here was that the Commons had named only those placemen who were to be *included* in the first Hanoverian parliament. 'This method of the Lords', on the other hand (as the latter went on to explain), 'gives a fair opportunity of considering distinctly the nature of the office and weighing the reasons on both sides, before so hard a judgement is passed as that of excluding the officer from his seat in the House of Commons'.

[2] *Ibid.*

[3] Chancellor of the exchequer.

[4] Brit. Mus., Loan 29/64/3: [Godolphin] to [Harley], 'Friday at 12'.

of the Lords' amendments for an unspecified period. They did so by a majority of twenty-three in a House packed to the doors with 421 members (a fair indication of the intense excitement the affair had by now aroused); and this vote was to prove a crucial one, for it was over the subsequent weekend that the vital secessions from the Country Whig leadership were finally secured. 'Sr Ri[chard] fainted at last in the pursuit', wrote Sir John Cropley to General Stanhope, whose departure from Westminster at the height of the struggle to take ship for Spain had deprived the Whimsicals of perhaps their most persuasive champion; '& Ro. Eyres unknown
& I [inserted]
to Peter King   who stood his ground very firmly had treacherous[ly] made at my Ld Hallifaxes this bargain & in the most audacious as well as infamous manner that ever was seen in that house gave up his cause, his friends & himself . . .'.[1] On the following Monday, 18 February, the 'Whimsical clause', defended to the last by Cropley, King, Sir William Ellis and other 'patriots', finally perished by eight votes in another House of well over 400.[2]

But although the final victory clearly went to the Court, which had succeeded both in repealing the 1701 clause and in scotching an alternative which many ministerialists had prophesied would prove an intolerable 'cramp to the Prerogative',[3] it was by no means a total victory. Even a disappointed Cropley privately admitted that

we lost it very honourably & advantagiously for England, for next to the carying it [the Whimsical clause] the Crown has made the greatest concessions that ever were obtaind.[4] You know the amendments of the Lds how little they offerd, meerly a stop to a future increase & the prize office, but now they have grantd the self same bill K[ing] W[illiam] refused on the throne & the Lds once in their house & tis to commence immediately wth several other articles.[5]

To his patron, Lord Shaftesbury, Cropley supplied fuller details:

The Court yesterday proposd an expedient for a clause to commence at the end of this parliament. It excludes in this manner: no offices to be erectd for the future for members to be in; no comm of the prizes; no sub-com of the prizes; no agents of regiments; no comptrollers of the accounts of the army; no com of wine license, transports, sick & woundd; no com of the navy in the out ports; no governours nor deputy governours of the plantations; no pensions durante

---

[1] Chevening MSS.: 19 Feb. [1706]. (Transcript kindly lent by Dr. A. N. Newman.)

[2] *Ibid*. Cf. Brit. Mus., Add. MS. 4291 fo. 54.

[3] Brit. Mus., Add. MS. 4291 fo. 43: Charles to Henry Davenant, 22 Jan. 1705[6].

[4] Not every 'Whimsical' whig, it must be said, agreed with him. Thomas Johnson, for instance, wrote despondently: 'The Lords have got their end, relating to the Regency bill—the Expedient is a jest as near as I can take it'. *The Norris Papers*, ed. T. Heywood (Chetham Soc., 1846), p. 147: to Richard Norris, London, 18 Feb. 1705[6].

[5] Chevening MSS.: Cropley to Stanhope, 19 Feb.

bene placito;[1] proviso that no more persons nor commisioners shall be at any time in any office than are at present or have been.

Here comes the best. No man to take any place after his being electd a member of parliament, but accepting such a place shall make his election void . . .[2] Tis what we should last year have thought a great deal, but in exchang for our clause a very sorry matter. But our clause being in reversion and this in present makes it goe down. We shall have this good. Tis a foundation for more & I will defye any sessions to pass wthout bills & divisions agst the army & household.[3]

With this last sentiment of Cropley's Stanhope found himself in full agreement: 'if they had taken our clause and given it with a good grace', he considered, 'it might have secured the Administration under this reign from anything of that kind, whereas they have now made a substantial precedent to alter even in this reign...'.[4] These prophecies, however, were not at once realized. Country activity in the next few years was diverted into fresh channels, and there was a long lull in the campaign against 'influence' between February 1706 and the winter of 1709–10.

By that time the whigs, and especially the Junto, were firmly entrenched in office. And it was partly the extent of the Junto's domination over the house of commons, made still more complete by the exceptional discipline it exercised over its private following, and partly the disappointment of many backbenchers at the relatively slight impact which the Place clause of the Regency act appeared to have made since the dissolution in 1708,[5] which once more roused the country forces to action. The influx of Scottish members since the Union of 1707 and their general subservience to the Court, especially apparent in the session of 1708–9, had added to their anxiety. On 25 January 1710, therefore, at a time when the political world was seething with the ferment of the Sacheverell affair, Edward Wortley Montagu—who had been a tyro at the time of the struggle over 'the clause'[6] but had since emerged as a prominent figure among the Country Whigs— moved for leave to introduce a new bill 'for securing the freedom of Parliaments'. In his speech[7] he gave expression to the real concern which

[1] The first effect of these provisions, thought Charles Davenant, would be 'not very hurtfull to the Court as excluding not above 12 or 14 of the Inferior Officers'. Brit. Mus., Add. MS. 4291 fo. 54: to Henry Davenant, 22 Feb. 1705[6].

[2] Such a placeman was, of course, to be eligible for re-election. This particular provision was to place a premium in future on appointments to offices in the intervals between parliaments, for in this case the beneficiaries did not have to stand again if they were successful at the general election.

[3] Public Record Office, 30/24/20/114: [19 Feb. 1706], endorsed 'Feb. 1705–6 self-denying clause'.

[4] P.R.O., 30/24/20/113; Stanhope to [Cropley], Plymouth, 24 Feb.

[5] On 4 Feb. 1709 the Commons had appointed a committee to consider methods of making existing laws against placemen and pensioners effective. See *Parl. Hist.*, vi. 779–80.

[6] He was first elected to the Commons, as a member for Huntingdon, in 1705.

[7] This is apparently the one printed in *Parl. Hist.*, vi. 888–92. It is not attributed to Wortley Montagu but simply to an unnamed country member, but the fact that it begins 'What I rise up for is to propose a bill . . .' makes the identification fairly certain.

backbenchers on both sides still felt, justifiably or not, about the formidable power of the Court interest in the Commons.

If every gentleman's office and employment were added to his name as it is called over, every call of the House would put us on considering whether some new law is not wanting to lessen the number of such members as possess them. And I am afraid it would now appear to you that they are more numerous than ever, notwithstanding the several bills that have passed both Houses, and several others which have passed only this House; by which the sense of the Commons hath been so often declared . . .

Wortley Montagu's bill saw the 'negative method', which the Lords had approved, once more abandoned and a return made to the principle of January 1706. Indeed the bill was almost a reincarnation of the Whimsical clause, except that it was to take effect from the termination of the current parliament and that a few more exceptions were made to the general disqualification—the favoured circle being extended to include up to five admiralty commissioners, the secretary of the treasury and fourteen instead of ten general and flag officers. A few concessions were made to the Court during the bill's progress through the House; originally it was designed to allow about fifty employees of the Crown (including officers for life or by inheritance) to keep their seats, but after the Report stage on 1 February it was reported that 'they have now made it to exclude all but about threescore'.[1] Even then the government did everything in its power to destroy the bill before it came up to the Lords. This was the only Place bill in Anne's reign to be taken to a vote at every possible stage in the House. There were six major divisions in the full House between 25 January and the third reading on 4 February, and another in committee where there was a huge attendance of 417.[2] Apart from straight opposition, moreover, the Court resorted to various stratagems. James Lowther of Whitehaven, who had been elected for Cumberland with Junto support but who prided himself on not being 'tractable . . . in obeying the word of command' in the Commons, noted that 'Those that are against the Bill have try'd all ways to blog it. First they try'd to exclude all officers, then to exclude offrs. for life as wel as during pleasure, & yet always endeavour'd to throw out the whole Bill & so not exclude any'.[3] But the country interest received some formidable backing in the debates, some of it from predictable quarters like Stanhope and Sir Peter King,[4] but some from unexpected sources—from Sir Joseph Jekyll and Richard Hampden, for instance, who had normally supported the Junto line in the Commons, and from the ex-

[1] Cumb. and Westmld. Record Office, Lonsdale MSS.: James Lowther to William Gilpin, 2 Feb. 1709[10].

[2] *Ibid.*: 31 Jan. 1710; *C.J.*, xvi. 278–94 *passim*.

[3] Cumb. and Westmld. Record Office, Lonsdale MSS.: to Gilpin, 2 Feb., 8 June 1710.

[4] A. Boyer, *History of the Life and Reign of Queen Anne* (1722), p. 447; *C.J.*, xvi. 278.

Secretary Robert Harley.[1] And although its majority was gradually whittled down by persistent government canvassing (it slipped from sixty-six on 25 January down to thirty-two on the 31st and finally as low as twenty-two on the question 'that the bill do pass'[2]) it proved sufficient.

In the end, therefore, the Court was forced to fall back on the unpopular expedient of leaving the house of lords to apply the *coup de grâce*. The ministers were not kept long in suspense. The queen was persuaded to attend the first reading in the Upper House on 9 February, and after a perfunctory half-hour's debate[3] in which independent peers of both parties showed their distaste for the measure—Lord North and Grey and the earl of Scarborough both speaking against it—and Lord Wharton threw the full weight of the Junto into the government scales, the bill was refused a second reading without even the formality of a division. 'I cant but think a good many of those that were for throwing it out', observed Lowther, 'wil wish for it in a few years'.[4] But not even he can possibly have anticipated the astonishing turn of events which took place two years later.

Even in 1711 there was no more than a hint of what was to come. During the last four years of Anne the impetus of the country offensive which had been mounted in January 1710 under a whig administration was maintained equally strongly, for some time at least, under the tory ministry of Robert Harley, earl of Oxford, and in an overwhelmingly tory house of commons. In each of the four sessions between November 1710 and July 1714 a fresh Place bill was introduced, all of them more or less carbon copies of the one originally brought in by Wortley Montagu, who remained in the van of the attack right up to 1713 although by now most of his support came from the High Tory independents rather than from the attenuated ranks of the whigs. Except for this last factor[5] the pattern of the campaign of 1710–11 was much the same as that of January–February 1710. The bill itself excepted the same officers, with the negligible addition of three Scottish placemen;[6] despite the apprehensions of some country stalwarts,[7] the Court fought it rather less hard in the Commons (there were only two divisions this time instead of seven, the first of which was a token affair[8]

[1] *C.J.*, xvi. 278; *The Wentworth Papers*, ed. J. J. Cartwright (1883), p. 106; Hist. MSS. Comm., *Portland MSS.*, iv. 531: Abigail to Edward Harley, 26 Jan. 1710.

[2] The final division was 197 votes for the bill and 175 against. *C.J.*, xvi. 294.

[3] N. Luttrell, *A Brief Historical Relation of State Affairs, 1678–1714* (Oxford, 1857), vi. 544.

[4] *Lords' Journals*, xix. 62; Boyer, *Hist. of Life and Reign of Queen Anne* (1722), p. 447; Cumb. and Westmld. Record Office, Lonsdale MSS.: Lowther to Gilpin, 11 Feb.

[5] And even in Dec. 1710, according to the Hanoverian Resident, it was the whigs who 'ont porté la pomme de discorde dans la Chambre'. Staatsarchiv Hannover, Cal. Br. 24 England 99 fo. 17: Kreienberg to Hanover, London, 8/19 Dec.

[6] Viz. the lord advocate, the Lord Chief Register and the solicitor-general in Scotland. See Hist. MSS. Comm., *House of Lords MSS.*, new ser., ix. 86.

[7] Auchmar MSS.: Mungo Graham, M.P. to duke of Montrose, 7 Dec. 1710. I am grateful to the present duke for allowing me to examine the family papers for the period 1707–16 now at Auchmar, [since deposited at Register House].

[8] *Ibid.*, Graham to Montrose, 21 Dec.

while the second, at the third reading, saw the ministry decisively defeated by 235 votes to 143[1]); but it once again made an all-out effort to crush it in the Lords, and as in 1710 the bill was denied even a second reading there, receiving its quietus to the accompaniment of some barbed comment from Harley's lieutenant, Lord Poulet, on the irresponsibility of the country members.[2] Yet there was just one mildly disturbing development from the point of view of the Court. Since Anne's accession only Peter King's 'Exclusion bill' of February 1705 had received any countenance from the whig Junto.[3] But this time a few of the opposition whig peers, including some who had been adamant in the past against permitting any significant erosion of the government interest in the Lower House, forced a division; and though it was a half-hearted affair,[4] one speech, delivered by Lord Sunderland, contained behind its façade of irony a half-veiled threat that next time the Lords might not prove quite the insurmountable obstacle that they had been for so long to measures of this nature. 'The Commons', he remarked, 'have of late years sent up this Bill for form-sake, and only to throw the odium of its being lost on the House of Peers; and therefore your Lordships ought at least to give it a Second Reading, to let the Commons know that if they should send it up once more, the Lords will take them at their word, and pass it'.[5]

[1]William Salt Library, Stafford, MS. Diary of Sir Arthur Kaye, pp. 1–2, 29 Jan. 1711; Staatsarchiv Hannover, Cal. Br. 24 England 99 fo. 96: Kreienberg, 30 Jan./10 Feb.; *C.J.*, xvi. 471.
    Kaye's summary of the arguments used in the debate on the third reading is worth recording. 'The chief objections were, its lessening the interest, the power & as some improperly call'd it, the prerogative of the Crown; that it inferr'd, wt. wee ought not to suppose, the Crown & people to have different interests, as if gentlemen in places cou'd not serve both at the same time; that it wd be ill taken by the Queen that such a Bill shou'd now pass, in such a Ministry & such a Parl. wch wou'd never be allowed in the late Administration, and that it wd give the Whigs an opportunity of making their court again by opposing it here and throwing it out in another place. But those who were for it said, the Bill show'd sufficiently the respect the House bore to the Crown by allowing so many exceptions; that it cou'd be no inconvenience to it, under a good Prince, who having no other view then the true interest of the subject, wou'd not stand in need of any corrupt partie in the house, when he wou'd have the united hearts of all, nor with a good Ministry, who shou'd act upon right reason with honour & integrity, who wou'd not want to be supported; but as so great a number of people so influenced might lift their heads up against the Crown as well as against the power & prerogative of the Prince, as wee had seen in a late instance, it cou'd never be for the true interest of either to have the House liable to such corruptions . . .; and tho tis true, it wd not prevent private pensions . . . it wd at least take off part of the inconvenience, by stopping the current at least of one evill, wch at present flowed upon you in two channels'.
[2]Hist. MSS. Comm., *Portland MSS.*, iv. 657. There was a small compensation for these members later in the session when a clause was successfully inserted in the Post Office act (9 Anne, c. 11) disqualifying the joint postmasters-general forthwith from membership of the House.
[3]Brit. Mus., Loan 29/192 fo. 34: Dyer's Newsletter, 8 Feb. 1704[5].
[4]Hist. MSS. Comm., *House of Lords MSS.*, new ser., ix. 86.
[5]Boyer, *Hist. of Life and Reign of Queen Anne* (1722), p. 488.

A year later the possibility at which the junior lord of the Junto had half-jocularly hinted suddenly became a most disturbing reality. For a few days in February 1712 'the influence of the Crown' came nearer to suffering a crippling blow than at any time since Sir Edward Hussey introduced the first Self-Denying bill in 1692. There were two main causes of the crisis, one connected with the climate of opinion in the political world at large concerning the whole question of 'influence', the other bound up with the party struggle. Early in February there were signs of a striking resurgence of country antagonism towards the Court; not merely in the Commons, where a new Place bill designed to cut down the number of suspected government 'dependants' from 150 to just over 60 passed, significantly, with the minimum of opposition,[1] but in political circles generally, both in and outside Westminster. 'The scandal of corruption' had become the talking-point of the moment, and rumours circulated every day round the coffee-houses of men who 'were not only bribed for a whole session, but had new bribes for particular votes'.[2] At the same time the whigs had reached a critical stage in their great effort to overthrow the Oxford ministry by discrediting its peace policy. Their main attack had been repulsed at the beginning of January, following the block creation of twelve new peers by the queen over the Christmas recess. But they still had an outside chance of success in the house of lords, where for once the Scottish peers were wavering in their allegiance to the government; and the whigs thought that the passing of the Place bill, with all its concomitant embarrassments for the Court, might conceivably force open the door which was so nearly closed against them. To achieve it the Junto lords were now prepared, for the first time in the reign, to mortgage their own future freedom of action if necessary. For a brief while the issue hung precariously in the balance. An opposition majority of twenty-one at the second reading seemed to spell disaster for the Court and triumph at last for the untiring champions of the country interest in parliament. Oxford and his colleagues, however, whipped up every possible supporter and every available proxy in time for the meeting of the Grand Committee of the Lords on 29 February. There the prime minister planned to submit an amendment which, by making the act effective from the end of the reign instead of from the end of the existing parliament in 1713, would draw its teeth and make the Junto lords unwilling to pursue it further. The whigs fought the amendment bitterly; but at the crucial moment a number of their Scottish and tory allies deserted to the government, which carried its point in the end by seventy-five votes to seventy.[3]

February 29th 1712 represents the high-water mark of the Place campaigns of Anne's reign. Thereafter the tide ebbed steadily, at least in the

---

[1]Brit. Mus., Add. MS. 17677 FFF fo. 85: l'Hermitage to the States-General, 29 Feb./11 March 1712.

[2]G. Burnet, *A History of My Own Times* (6 vols., Oxford, 1833), vi. 113–14.

[3]Hist. MSS. Comm., *House of Lords MSS.*, new ser., ix. 202–3; Brit. Mus., Add. MS. 17677 FFF fos. 91–2; Swift, *Journal to Stella*, 29 Feb.; Burnet, vi. 114.

house of commons. Wortley Montagu's last bill, in 1713, was received with noticeably less enthusiasm, and a rather desperate attempt by the Country Whigs to force it past the Lords by 'tacking' it to the Malt Tax bill was heavily defeated.[1] After this the measure died a lingering death in the Commons. In the last parliament of the reign the withering of genuine country zeal, at a time when party issues dominated men's minds, is illustrated by the very different treatment meted out to Sir Joseph Martyn and James Murray, two members of the house of commons recently appointed Commissaries to negotiate a new trade agreement with France, compared with the fate suffered by Sir Henry Belasyse two years earlier. In each case the members concerned were tories, being judged by a predominantly tory House, and all three unquestionably held 'new' offices in the sense that those who had drafted the Place clause of the Regency bill understood that term. But while Belasyse in 1712 was unseated, Martyn and Murray were confirmed in their seats in April 1714 by what appears to have been a fairly straight party vote.[2]

It is true that in this same parliament a new Place bill was sponsored by a group of former March Club men, led by Sir Arthur Kaye. Since its promoters were all Hanoverian tories[3] neither the whigs nor the Court were prepared to antagonize them at a time when such men held the key to the political situation in the Commons, and it may well have been for this reason that the measure was allowed to go through all its stages without a single division in the Lower House, where it passed in little more than three weeks.[4] Although one observer described the 'chief design' of the new bill as being 'to prevent the sea and land officers, who take pay, from laying taxes on the subject',[5] it was in essentials almost identical to its four immediate predecessors,[6] and to judge from lack of contemporary interest

[1] *C.J.*, xvii. 308, 352, 354; Berkshire Record Office, Trumbull MSS. Alphab. Series, vol. LI: T. Bateman to Sir W. Trumbull, 15 May 1713. Even then some of the votes the 'Tackers' mustered were Scottish votes, aimed at wrecking the Malt Tax, rather than country votes directed towards furthering the Place bill. See Hist. MSS. Comm., *Polwarth MSS.*, i. 10: [G. Baillie] to [Marchmont], 16 May 1713.

[2] The majority in their favour was 189–115. See *C.J.*, xvii. 577: 19 Apr. The majority in Feb. 1712 *against* Belasyse, M.P. for Durham City, who had been appointed a commissioner to enquire into the state of the forces in the Peninsula, had been 182–99. *Ibid.*, p. 91.

A third tory member, Frederick Herne, had been appointed a Trade Commissary at the same time as Martyn and Murray. But whereas both the latter had successfully applied to their constituents for re-election in March 1714 Herne had already given up (or lost) his seat at Dartmouth before the Commons' vote on the nature of the new appointments was taken in April.

[3] Apart from Kaye they were Charles Cholmondeley, M.P. for Cheshire, Lord Downe, M.P. for Yorkshire, and Robert Heysham, M.P. for Lancaster. *C.J.*, xvii. 493. The March Club, founded in March 1712, had been patronized by tories who combined strong country principles with zeal for the legal succession.

[4] *Ibid.*, 11 March–5 Apr. 1714.

[5] Luttrell, vi. 725.

[6] Hist. MSS. Comm., *House of Lords MSS.*, new ser., x. 278.

in the measure—few political correspondents in March-April 1714 favour it with so much as a mention—its supporters anticipated no repetition of the quixotic behaviour of the Lords in 1712. Success in the Lords seemed all the less to be expected because the whig peers, following the queen's critical illness at the end of 1713, were more than ever preoccupied with securing their reversionary interest in the successor.

However, there was a last surprise in store for the country politicians. Against all expectation a number of tories, most of them Hanoverians, joined with the whig peers to support the bill. A government attempt to prevent its commitment was defeated by sixty-one votes to fifty-six on 14 April[1] and on the 17th a Court manoeuvre similar to that which had succeeded in 1712 (postponing the operation of the act until after the queen's death) was thwarted by a majority of five. Before the bill came out of the Grand Committee to receive its third reading on the same day, both sides seem to have combed the precincts of Westminster Palace for every available peer. The Court mustered five more and the opposition two; but since the Court peers carried nineteen proxies to the opposition's seventeen, the votes when the final question was put 'that the bill do pass into law' were absolutely equal.[2] '*Semper praesumitur pro negante* took place', recorded the Clerk of the House; and so, by the narrowest parliamentary margin possible, the last Place bill of Anne's reign—a bill which would have had the effect of reducing the number of placemen and serving officers in the first Hanoverian house of commons by well over half—failed. It may be that the government's escape was even more fortuitous than the mere figures suggest, for one observer maintained that 'had not one of the Bishop's been detained out of the House longer than usual by the strangury' the single extra vote which the opposition needed would actually have been secured.[3]

The final act was anti-climax. In the first parliament of George I the last of the old-style Place bills made its bow. It was brought in by Sir John Cope in June 1715, with the support of one other Country Whig and three Hanoverian tories.[4] It reached the Lords towards the end of July where almost immediately it was forgotten in the emergency of the '15 Rebellion. It was the following April before the Commons gave the peers a gentle reminder of its existence, but after receiving a second reading the bill lay on the table of the Lords for several weeks until the prorogation of parliament on 26 June quietly anaesthetized it.[5] The Commons had probably anticipated its fate, for on 25 April, when the Septennial bill was

[1] *Ibid.*

[2] 69–69.

[3] *Ibid.*, p. 279; *Wentworth Papers*, pp. 371–2: Newsletter to Lord Strafford, 20 Apr. 1714. Cf. Hist. MSS. Comm., *House of Lords MSS.*, new ser., x, intro. p. xxviii for the curious confusion over the recording of the votes in the final division in the MS. minutes of the house of lords.

[4] Thomas Onslow, Robert Heysham, Ralph Freeman and Sir Arthur Kaye. See *C.J.*, xviii. 135.

[5] *Ibid.*, pp. 135–230 *passim*, p. 418; *L.J.*, xx. 326, 337, 341.

due to be debated in committee, the country members on both sides had a final fling. They moved that the committee should 'have leave to receive a clause to disable persons from being chose members of *either House of Parliament*,[1] who have pensions during pleasure or any number of years from the Crown'. The tellers for the minority in the subsequent division— the motion was defeated by almost two to one—were the two knights of the shire for Cumberland, the tory Gilfred Lawson and our old whig acquaintance James Lowther. This time, however, the blow of defeat was softened when the ministry promptly brought in its own bill to disqualify pensioners for a term of years from sitting in the house of commons. Three days before the prorogation the Lords gave their assent to this bill[2] and in doing so, without knowing it, brought to an end a distinctive phase in the political history of the early eighteenth century.

After 1716, to quote Miss Kemp,[3] 'the period of almost annual Place Bills came to an end'; and although there were isolated periods of revival in the Walpole era, marked by further restrictive legislation in 1734 and 1742, 'the influence of the Crown' did not again become a major political issue, as opposed to a stock-in-trade of opposition debaters, until it was taken up as a battle-cry by the Rockingham whigs in the seventeen-seventies and seventeen-eighties. Moreover, the new and highly important en- croachments on 'influence' made from 1782 onwards were mostly the result of Economical Reform, a quite different approach to the problem from that envisaged by the 'patriots' of Queen Anne's reign.

What, then, did the country agitation of the early eighteenth century achieve? Most of its concrete gains were owed to the one great *coup* of the 'Whimsical Whigs'. Embodied in the Regency act of 1706, and con- firmed by a similar act passed in 1708 after the Union with Scotland,[4] they admittedly fell far short of the highest hopes of the Whimsicals. Yet they were nonetheless substantial, on paper at least. Together with the Post Office act of 1711 and the Pensions act of 1716, the legislation of 1706-8

[1] My italics.
[2] *C.J.*, xviii. 430–1, 459–60, 468.
[3] Kemp, p. 64.
[4] This act, 6 Anne c. 41, was not passed in 1707 as is commonly thought (cf. *Select Statutes, Cases and Documents, 1660–1832*, ed. Sir C. Grant Robertson (8th edn., 1947), p. 179; W. C. Costin and J. Steven Watson, *The Law and Working of the Constitution: Documents 1660–1914* (1952), i. 111). It was not introduced into the house of commons until Jan. 1708, and it is interesting that the government, afraid of making 'each paragraph liable to the disputes formerly raised, and perhaps to new cavils', at first contemplated 'an Act of Confirmation only, with no other alteration than inserting Great Britain instead of England' (J. Vernon, *Letters illustrative of the reign of William III*, ed. G. P. R. James (3 vols., 1841), iii. 305). In the event this device was not required, and the differences between the new act of 1708 and the earlier one of 1706, except for 'one or two in favour of the Scotch' (*ibid.*, p. 332), were trifling. One fresh clause specifically exempted Commissioners of the Equivalent from being excluded from the house of commons as 'new officers'. It was not, of course, necessary in 1708 to repeat the repeal of the Privy Council and Place clauses of the Act of Settlement embodied in the 1706 act.

added new categories to the civil offices already (from 1694) declared incompatible with the holding of a seat in the house of commons, and at the same time removed from the House the two types of pensioner most vulnerable to Court pressure. Moreover clause 24 of the 1708 act did appear to provide fairly effectively against one of the worst fears of the country gentlemen, the rapid escalation of 'influence' through the expansion of the Civil Service and the multiplication of new offices.

In reality, though, the gains were less impressive than they seemed, and the fervour with which the Place bills of 1710–12 were promoted in the Commons leaves no room for doubt that this was soon realized. For one thing, not everyone appointed to a 'new office' was automatically disqualified in practice, as the cases of Martyn and Murray in 1714 showed. Also, if the country interest cherished any hope that large numbers of placemen, forced to seek re-election under clause 25 of the second Regency act, would be rejected by their constituents, they were soon disillusioned. The Court had suffered an occasional shock in the second half of Anne's reign, notably when the newly-appointed master of the household, Sir William Pole, was thrown out at a by-election in Devon in 1712.[1] But an unopposed return had proved much the likeliest contingency in the circumstances.[2] Most borough electors were only too well aware of the advantages of being represented by a member who had some pull with the ministry to spare much thought for the health of the body politic. Again, the aggravated problem of the invasion of the Commons by officers of the armed forces remained completely unsolved, although the end of the Spanish Succession war gradually brought its own measure of relief here in the natural course of events. Finally, what was perhaps the biggest loop-hole of all for future exploitation, the power of the Court to 'oblige' M.P.s by conferring places, preferments and commissions not on them but on their relatives, friends, neighbours and clients, remained wide open in 1716; indeed, the leading Country Whigs and Tories of the early eighteenth century seem to have been curiously unconcerned with this aspect of the problem of 'influence'—an aspect which only Economical Reform could remedy in the end.

The Place campaigns of 1702–16, therefore, applied a brake to the 'influence of the Crown' but did little more. To the historian, however, their interest lies not only in their net result but in the paradoxical features of their story. For instance, during Anne's reign, when country zeal was still

[1] For other instances see A. B. Beaven, 'List of opposed elections on taking office', *Eng. Hist. Rev.*, xxvi (1911), 140.

[2] The anxiety of prospective placemen, as general elections approached, to have their appointments made between the dissolution of one parliament and the choice of the next was more often due to a natural wish to be spared the trouble and expense of a second election, even of an uncontested one, than to the fear of defeat in such a contingency. See, e.g., Hist. MSS. Comm., *Portland MSS.*, iv. 575, 591, 602: Thomas Conyers, Lady Oglethorpe and Charles Caesar to Harley, 25 Aug., 6 Sept., 28 Sept. 1710; Brit. Mus., Loan 29/138: Sir Simon Harcourt to the same, 27 Sept. 1710 (cf. *Portland MSS.*, iv. 608).

high, the political system was in fact providing two checks of its own against the domination of the house of commons by the court, both more effective in practice than any legislation which found its way on to the statute book. One was triennial elections, which meant frequent changes in the composition of the House,[1] while the other was the pull of party principles and party loyalties, which quite often proved stronger than the disciplines imposed by office. It is ironical that the attacks on 'influence' should have lost their impetus after 1716, at precisely the time when the first check disappeared and the second was already diminishing in force. The Septennial act of 1716 created a far stabler political world than had existed for two decades, an atmosphere in which 'influence' could breed and flourish, while the decline of party rivalry, once the tories lost their credibility as competitors for power, put a new premium on the value of place to the Crown and its leading ministers as a counter in the political game.

But there is a still greater irony about the attack on 'the influence of the Crown' between 1702 and 1716. At no stage did it seriously concern itself with the problem of the management of the house of lords by the Court. Yet here office-holders and pensioners together represented a far higher proportion of the active membership of the House than did their counterparts in the Commons.[2] Furthermore, it was the most formidable weapon which the Crown possessed in the house of lords, the power to make new creations, which in the end frustrated the efforts of the country members to secure that measure of 'freedom' in the Commons which they craved. For the tiny margins by which the Place bills of 1712 and 1714 both failed in the Upper House would certainly have been eliminated but for the reinforcement of the Court party in the last two and a half years of Anne's reign by Oxford's 'dozen'—the unprecedented block creation of twelve new peers over the Christmas recess of 1711–12. Thus by this most dubious of constitutional expedients the smooth working of the eighteenth-century constitution, which owed so much to the lubricant of 'influence' in preserving good relations between executive and legislature, was indirectly ensured.

[1] Counting the last parliament elected in William's reign which continued in session for a while after Anne came to the throne, and the first 'Parliament of Great Britain' of 1707–8, Anne actually met 7 different parliaments in 12 years, though that of 1707–8 was only technically different as far as the English and Welsh members were concerned.

[2] In Feb. 1714, for instance, some 50 peers occupied places of profit and a further 18 held unpaid offices of trust (mainly lieutenancies and seats at the privy council table) at a time when the total membership of the house of lords was 179. Moreover, the average daily attendance of peers during the 1714 session (the highest, incidentally, since 1689) was only 87, and since office-holders were naturally among the most regular attenders, the basic strength of the Court's position was at all times formidable.

3

THE FALL OF HARLEY IN 1708 RECONSIDERED

(WITH W.A. SPECK)

In February 1708, after a short but intense trial of strength at Court and inside the Godolphin ministry, the senior secretary of state, Robert Harley, was forced out of office and carried three of his closest followers with him. The causes and circumstances of this crisis have always intrigued and baffled students of the reign of Queen Anne. What has made the problem so intractable is the unusual scarcity of authoritative, first-hand evidence bearing upon it. Even at the time a dearth of unimpeachable information led to all manner of speculation. Most contemporaries in fact were utterly in the dark about the significance of the whole episode: as late as 1711 one of them wrote: 'The Spring of his Disgrace at Court . . . has so many intricate Pipes which lead up to it, that we must at present lodge it amongst the Mysteries of State'.[1] Modern scholars, lacking the clear testimony of the active participants in the crisis, have been equally puzzled. Since the 1870s a succession of historians from Stanhope down to Walcott have offered at least half a dozen different explanations of Harley's fall. But the emphasis as to which factor, or even which combination of two or three factors, was really decisive has continually shifted; so that the picture still remains exceedingly confused, and Professor Walcott was recently driven to the desponding conclusion 'that the true story of Harley's fall had never been written and could perhaps never be written'.[2]

No modern authority has been content to attribute the secretary's resignation to the discovery of scandalous negligence in his office, brought to light in December 1707 with the arrest of one of his clerks, William Greg, on a charge of treason. Nor has another theory once favoured by the Whig historians of the nineteenth century stood the test of time: namely, that the failure of the duke of Marlborough and Lord Godolphin, ever since August 1707, to persuade the queen to nominate whig candidates to the vacant sees of Exeter and Chester had convinced them of Harley's malevolent intentions towards them.[3] In fact neither the Greg theory nor the bishoprics theory have been serious runners in this century, and they no longer warrant

1. P. H., *An Impartial View of the Two Late Parliaments.* (1711), p. 117.
2. Robert Walcott, *English Politics in the Early Eighteenth Century* (Oxford, 1956), p. 153.
3. For a full discussion of the affair of the bishoprics, and of Harley's part in it, see G.V. Bennett, 'Robert Harley, the Godolphin Ministry and the Bishoprics Crisis of 1707', *E[nglish] H[istorical] R[eview]*, 82 (1967).

detailed consideration as major factors. Another traditional theory, more persistent than these two, interpreted the crisis of February 1708 in terms of Harley's backstairs intrigues with the queen, which it was believed were aimed at increasing the tory element in the ministry, and ultimately at establishing his own supremacy. This interpretation has never been disproved, but Professor Morgan has been alone among twentieth-century historians in wholeheartedly accepting it.[1]

Instead, the causes of Harley's downfall have been sought mainly in his parliamentary activities. Some contemporary observers believed or suspected that there was a link between the secretary's resignation and the chaotic situation in parliament preceding that event.[2] Subsequently historians have attempted to establish a similar connection. Sir Keith Feiling, for instance, dated the decision of Marlborough and Godolphin to drop Harley from 'the last week in the year', stressing the parliamentary situation in December 1707 as the crucial factor. Under heavy fire from both parties over the affair of the Scottish Privy Council and the conduct of the war in Spain,

1. W. T. Morgan, *English Political Parties and Leaders in the Reign of Queen Anne, 1702–1710* (New Haven, 1920), pp. 312–15. We shall later hope to show that Morgan did in fact reach the right answer, but for the wrong reasons. He was generally content to accept rumours from sources potentially hostile to Harley at their face value, and without trying to verify them.

2. Lord Somers was 'persuaded the carrying of the Bill for taking away the Scottish Privy Council was no little ingredient towards making the changes which have since happened' (Brit. Mus. Add. MSS. 34515, fos. 207–8: Somers to the earl of Portland, 14 Feb. 1708. The original is in Nottingham University Library, MSS. PWA 1188). What Somers apparently had in mind was that the success of this measure, carried through the Commons in January and the Lords in early February against strong government opposition by a powerful combination of tories and dissident whigs, compelled a reconstruction of the ministry to accommodate the second of these hostile factions. But in this connection it is of some interest that Alexander Cunningham, another contemporary observer, who was subsequently British envoy to Venice, throws a very different light on the passage of the Privy Council bill. His story is that shortly before his fall Harley had turned his coat in the house of commons on this very measure. Having originally supported Godolphin in his attempt to ensure the continuance of a separate Edinburgh Council the secretary 'suddenly changed his sentiments', according to Cunningham, and so materially helped the opposition to force through the bill. (A. Cunningham, *The History of Great Britain from the Revolution in 1688 to the Accession of George the First* [London, 1787], ii.138–9).

Were it possible to attach any real weight to Cunningham's evidence on this point it would obviously have a very important bearing on our problem. Unfortunately its value seems relatively slight. Although apparently in touch at this time with a number of Scottish M.P.s and peers in London, Cunningham is frequently an unreliable authority, writing many years after the event and with a bewildering disregard for chronology. It is striking that no other contemporary, except the vindictive Lady Marlborough, impugns Harley's attitude to the Privy Council bill, although well-informed sources like Addison, Burnet, and above all James Vernon, who was a government member in the Commons at the time, all deal with the affair. Cunningham himself, it may be noted, does not relate the supposed incident in any direct way to Harley's fall, which he subsequently sees (*ibid.* ii. 141–3) mainly as a result of petticoat-politics at Court. And since the issue of the Privy Council was before the House for most of December, and subsequently up to 23 Jan., it is impossible even to date the alleged *volte-face* with anything approaching accuracy. In the absence of confirming evidence, then, it has seemed safer to leave Cunningham's story out of account in trying to elucidate the problem of Harley's fall.

the two chief ministers were forced to decide in favour of an unqualified alliance with the whigs; and this, so Feiling's argument runs,
made the continued presence in the ministry of Harley, the apostle
of non-party government, impossible.[1] More widely supported at
one time was the idea that the secretary's resignation was demanded
after he and Henry St. John had deliberately mismanaged a vital
debate on the battle of Almanza, which took place in the house of
commons on 29 January 1708.[2] This theory was strongly favoured up
to 1951, when Godfrey Davies argued in a skilful article[3] that the
Almanza debate was not the sensational affair historians had made of
it. Dr. Davies effectively disposed of the charge of treachery against
Harley and his friends and concluded that the debate was 'the
occasion rather than the cause' of the secretary's departure from the
ministry, although he was non-committal about what the cause
actually was. Even more recently, Professor Walcott has added a new
refinement to the 'parliamentary' explanations of Harley's fall, still
considering the Almanza debate decisive, but in a different sense. He
thinks it likely that Godolphin saw it as an example not of perfidy
but of 'the worst kind of carelessness on the part of two responsible
ministers', and that it convinced both him and Marlborough that
Harley had lost his *raison d'être* as a parliamentary manager.

It has seemed to us that the first step towards a reappraisal of this
whole problem, in the light of new evidence as well as old, is to clear
from the path the impediments of these various 'parliamentary'
theories. It was the apparent coincidence between the date of the
Almanza debate and the date of the first overt intimation of
Godolphin's displeasure with Harley[4] which originally suggested to
some scholars that the two events were connected. Yet it is hard to
see how this connection was ever confidently maintained in view of
two facts deducible from sources long in print. For one thing, although
the open breach between Godolphin and Harley, on the latter's own
evidence, took place on the night of 29 January, the big debate on the
war in Spain in the house of commons went on until three o'clock on
the morning of the 30th; so that the treasurer presumably cannot
have been aware of its outcome when he sent his fateful message to
Harley via Sir Simon Harcourt – the message severing their long
alliance.[5] Equally significant is a phrase in Marlborough's letter of
resignation to the queen, printed by William Coxe, a phrase which

1. Sir Keith Feiling, *A History of the Tory Party 1640–1714* (Oxford, 1924), pp. 398–9.
2. Originating with Carl von Noorden, *Europaische Geschichte im Achtzehnten Jahr-hundert* (Leipsig, 1883), iii. 219–20, this theory was adopted by Sir Winston Churchill, *Marlborough: His Life and Times* (1933–8), iii. 351–2, and with reservations by G. M. Trevelyan, *England under Queen Anne*, ii (1932), 327.
3. G. Davies, 'The Fall of Harley in 1708', *E.H.R.*, lxvi (1951), 246–54..
4. For the latter see Hist. MSS. Com., *Bath MSS*. i. 189: Harley to Godolphin, 30 Jan. 1708.
5. *Ibid.* i. 189; *Vernon Correspondence* (ed. G. P. R. James, 1841), iii. 328: James Vernon o Shrewsbury, 29 Jan. 1708.

has been for some reason overlooked. In this letter, which Bishop Burnet states quite plainly was written some time in the week preceding the Cabinet meeting on 8 February,[1] Marlborough referred to the 'unwearied pains' he had taken *'for these ten days'* to convince the queen of Harley's duplicity. The implication is that these efforts at conversion can hardly have begun later than 28 January; that is, the day before the Almanza debate.

These chronological arguments against the Almanza theories can now be strikingly reinforced by one of a series of unpublished letters between Harley and Marlborough, preserved in the Portland Loan to the British Museum.[2] The first letter in this series was written by the secretary on 28 January, and in it he informed the duke that he had just seen the queen, who 'had the goodness to let me know that I had been represented to your Grace to have said something which had given your Grace dissatisfaction'. The date of this letter proves conclusively that this 'dissatisfaction' cannot have arisen out of the proceedings in the house of commons on the 29th. At the same time it casts doubt on the suggestion of Sir Keith Feiling that Marlborough and Godolphin had determined before the end of December to get rid of Harley. Feiling's thesis is that events in January, especially the Greg affair, were merely used by the two managers as pretexts for parting with a politically embarrassing colleague. But this leaves two important questions unanswered. In the first place, why should the ministers have postponed the break until the very end of January? After all, the evidence of Greg's treachery came to light as early as 31 December. Secondly, why, when they did serve notice on Harley, should they have done so in terms which imply anything but a put-up job, and which certainly suggest that his offence went far beyond the realms of mere parliamentary strategy and management?

The second question is the more important, and any attempt to relate the immediate cause of Harley's fall either purely or largely to the parliamentary situation falls at this hurdle, once it is accepted that there was nothing perfidious about the behaviour of the secretary and his friends during the Spanish enquiry on 29 January. It is hard to see how one can ignore the language employed by the 'duumvirs', both to and about Harley, during this crisis. At times it is vivid, to say the least. Two phrases in particular from their letters stand out: Godolphin's outburst to the secretary, 'God forgive you!', and Marlborough's words 'the false and treacherous proceedings of Mr

---

1. G. Burnet, *A History of My Own Times* (1833), v. 353 (hereafter cited as Burnet). Burnet apparently derived some of his information about the crisis from his wife, via her friend the duchess of Marlborough, and it is generally reliable.

2. Brit. Mus. Loan 29/12/5 and 6; 29/130/3. There are eight letters in this series. (i) 28 Jan. H[arley] to M[arlborough] *draft*. (ii) 29 Jan. 'Thursday'. M to H. (iii) 29 Jan. 'Thursday night'. M to H. (iv) 1 Feb. H to M. *draft*. (v) 6 Feb. H to M. *draft*. (vi) 7 Feb. M to H. (vii) 18 Feb. H to M. *draft*. (viii) 8 Mar. H to M. *draft*. We are grateful to His Grace the duke of Portland for permission to make use of this collection.

Secretary Harley to lord treasurer and myself'.[1] Somewhere behind these melodramatic lines must lie the key to the whole mystery. In Godolphin's case, especially, not merely the isolated phrase but the whole letter of which it is a part – an immediate reply on 30 January to Harley's endeavour to justify himself – gives every impression of having come from the heart rather than from the head. There is nothing cold and calculating about it. It is a passionate outburst, all the more remarkable coming from a politician of conciliatory temper and notorious timidity. Harley had committed some specific and apparently recent offence, and Godolphin clearly considered the crime so heinous, and above all so blatant – 'I cannot help seeing and hearing', he told him, 'nor believing my senses' – that it did not admit of any excuse, or even of any further discussion. But what was it?

From the exchange of letters between the four main protagonists, Harley, Marlborough, Godolphin and the queen, 28 January – 7 February, it seems clear that the nature of Harley's offence was twofold. He had 'said something' which had incurred the displeasure of Marlborough and Godolphin. And he had also done something 'false and treacherous' which had roused their wrath. What precisely Harley had said we shall almost certainly never know. But we can be reasonably sure of the identity of the person to whom he said it. It was from the queen, during an interview he had with her on 28 January, that Harley first learned that some remarks of his had offended the duke. Knowing what we do of the importance of Harley's private audiences with the queen in the autumn and winter of 1707–8, and of the apprehensions which they had long aroused in his two colleagues, it would be a fair assumption, even without confirming evidence, that the offending words had first been addressed to Anne, possibly at the secretary's previous meeting with her which had taken place either on 22 or 23 January.[2] The grounds for thinking so are reinforced by one of Harley's own accounts of the 1708 crisis, given two and a half years later in the celebrated pamphlet 'Faults on Both Sides'.[3] Here it was frankly stated that just before his fall Harley 'had faithfully discover'd to the Queen some mismanagement of the ministers that would be of ill consequence if not redress'd in time'. Whatever these revelations were – and of their precise nature Harley gives us no hint – the evidence supports the hypothesis that Harley had said something privately to the queen, something highly derogatory to the 'duumvirs', and especially perhaps to Godolphin,

---

1. Hist. MSS. Com. *Bath MSS*. i. 190: Godolphin to Harley, 30 Jan. 1708; Marlborough to the queen, N.D., printed W. Coxe, *Memoirs of Marlborough* (Bohn edn., 1848), ii. 191 (hereafter cited as Coxe).

2. Hist. MSS. Com. *Bath MSS*. i. 189: the queen to Harley, 21 Jan. 1708.

3. This piece has been attributed both to Daniel Defoe and to another Harleyite propagandist, Clement. But in any case it is generally agreed that it was written at Harley's dictation.

which had then come to the ears of his colleagues. The leak may well have occurred through the channel of Prince George and the Prince's admiralty councillor, George Churchill, Marlborough's brother.

It is perhaps anybody's guess what was the 'mismanagement' of which Harley complained to Anne. There were several ministerial activities which were being severely criticized in the current session of parliament. One, however, eventually proved the most damaging of all. This was the frightful discrepancy between the number of men voted for service in Spain for the year 1707 and the much smaller number of troops which was actually present in the Peninsula at the time of the Almanza disaster. On 29 January the opposition was to point out in the Commons that of the 29,395 men for whom a supply was voted only a mere 8,660 had been in Spain in the previous April. This revelation had the ministry reeling; and, as we have seen, the government's discomfort has been attributed by some historians to the mismanagement of the debate, either carelessly or deliberately, by Harley and St. John. But the likeliest explanation of the admittedly poor showing which Harley and his friends put up in the debate on the 29th is that they had been genuinely shocked themselves by the discrepancy, which had been first revealed on 16 January. On that day James Brydges, the Paymaster, had given the Commons a statement of the number of forces which should have been in Spain, only four days after St. John had reported the numbers actually present at Almanza. Harley's own subsequent account of the debate[1] implies that he had been appalled at the difference between these two figures and resented having to defend the maladministration which lay behind it, calling it a 'fatal miscarriage', and 'a matter wherein the nation had been notoriously abused'.[2] Months later, when he was out of office, Harley wrote to his friend Harcourt, from whom he had nothing to hide: '. . . how easy and light I find myself that I have nothing to answer for but my own faults, and that nothing of the miscarriages of others, or their misfortunes, will call for any apology from us, but like the day of doom they must be judged by their own works'.[3]

There is therefore a distinct possibility – and that is the most one can say – that the mismanagement of the ministers which the secretary of state revealed to Anne was connected with their handling of Spanish affairs. Indeed it seems the most reasonable explanation of what it was he had *said* which turned Marlborough and Godolphin against him.

1. *Faults on Both Sides* (London, 1710), p. 30. (Printed in *Somers Tracts* [1814], xii. 693).
2. In his article 'The Supply of Infantry for the war in the Peninsula 1703–1707', *Bull. Inst. Hist. Res.* xxviii (1955), 56–57, I. F. Burton argued that 'all the missing men can be accounted for . . . without any suggestion of misappropriation of money'. Even so, the immediate reaction to the revelation of the discrepancy, from responsible politicians as well as from bigoted partisans, was that there had been scandalous mismanagement, an impression which the ministry failed to remove.
3. Hist. MSS. Com. *Bath MSS.* i. 192: Harley to Sir Simon Harcourt, 16 Oct. 1708.

There can be more certainty about the deeds which brought about their hostility. These, we can say with confidence, were connected in some way with the schemes for reshaping the ministry to his own specifications which were laid to his charge at the time by whig observers. Burnet, Swift, Addison and Montagu all tell stories which, though they differ on points of detail, have some essentials in common; all agree that Harley before his fall was at the centre of a conspiracy aimed at removing many leading Cabinet ministers; three of the four versions make it clear that the tories were to be the beneficiaries of the intended changes; while two of the four plainly suggest that Harley was aiming to head the new administration himself. That there was some scheme in the air in January and February 1708 has always been suspected, and few historians who have examined the problem of Harley's fall have been prepared to discount entirely the possibility that the two were connected. On the other hand, few have cared to commit themselves to details, and some have rightly baulked at accepting whig evidence alone on so crucial a point.

It is admittedly not easy to decide, even from whig sources, just how far these plans of Harley's were meant to go, and what exactly they involved. Swift told Archbishop King on 12 February that 'the men are named to whom the several employments were to be given'.[1] Sir James Montagu, the solicitor general, informed Lord Manchester quite categorically 'we are here in very whimsical circumstances. Mr. Secretary Harley, Mr. Comptroller, Mr St. John and Mr Attorney Harcourt are turned out, for setting up a faction against my Lord Duke of Marlborough, and Lord Treasurer, and their friends'. But having said so much, Montagu then became coy as to details: 'what was aimed at in particular, I am not well able to tell, and it will not be fit to write what we talk here.'[2]

Fortunately Joseph Addison was less reticent and sent the earl of Manchester some particulars. On 13 February he wrote: 'It is said Mr. Harley and his friends had laid schemes to undermine most of our great officers of state and plant their own party in the room of 'em. If we may believe common fame he himself was to have bin a peer and Ld Treasurer, tho others say the Ld R(ocheste)r was designed for that post. Mr. Harcourt was to have bin Ld Chancellour, Mr. St. John Secretary of State, the Duke of Buckingham Ld Privy Seal and so on.' Two weeks later he was able to make corrections and fill in more details:

It seems my Lord Rochester and Mr Bromley were taken no care of in the intended promotions, and tis supposed were not in the secret. The Treasury they say was to have been in Commission and Mr Harley at the

1. *The Correspondence of Jonathan Swift* (ed. Elrington Ball, 1910), i. 76 (hereafter cited as *Swift Corr.*).
2. *Court and Society from Elizabeth to Anne* (ed. from the Kimbolton MSS., 1864), ii. 282: Montagu to Manchester, 17 Feb. 1708 (hereafter cited as *Court and Society*).

head of it in order to have it broken in a short time and himself to have been Ld High Treasurer of Great Britain. Mr St. John and the Earl Pawlett were, as it is said, to have been Secretarys of State and Harcourt Ld Chancellour. Sr T. Hanmore too was to have come in for his share but I have forgot his post.

This revised list of Addison's, unlike the first which was based merely on 'common fame', he could give some credit to 'as having from good hands' – no doubt from his departmental chief, the earl of Sunderland, and other Junto contacts.[1]

Yet it must be said that the assurance with which Addison retailed his account of Harley's ministerial stratagems seems far from justified when set against the contemporary testimony of the secretary himself. The letters Harley wrote to Marlborough and Godolphin, both during the crisis and after, are profuse in their protestations of innocence – at least of any designs against the 'duumvirs' personally. His denials noticeably do not extend to his proposals for bringing more tories into the government: this aspect of his recent conduct his letters do not touch on at all (which is what we should expect, since for some time past he had made no secret of his hopes of concessions to the tory party, and it would have been futile for him to disclaim them). All the same, these letters, in conjunction with certain other Harley-inspired material,[2] make it just possible to argue that he was guiltless of conspiring against the duke and the treasurer, and that, in seeking his dismissal, they were countenancing the most malicious whig rumours and even the wildest coffee-house gossip against the word of a close colleague.[3]

The direct conflict of evidence between whig sources and Harleian sources on so vital a point of interpretation would have made our whole problem exceedingly difficult to resolve, but for the discovery of fresh material among Harley's private memoranda and unpublished correspondence, and also among the papers of the 3rd earl of Shaftesbury in the Public Record Office. This new evidence makes it possible not only to test the genuineness of the secretary's pleas of innocence but also to make a detailed reconstruction of the

---

1. *The Letters of Joseph Addison* (ed. W. Graham, 1941), pp. 91, 95 (hereafter cited as *Addison Letters*).

2. E.g. the 'Memoirs' of Auditor Harley, in Hist. MSS. Com. *Portland MSS.* v.6 41–69. It is also of interest that two years later, in 1710, when he was on the threshold of power once again, and Marlborough and Godolphin were very much on the defensive, Robert Harley was still sticking to the same story. Arthur Mainwaring told the duchess of Marlborough in a letter probably written on 12 May 1710 of a recent talk which Godolphin had had with the duke of Shrewsbury, then Harley's closest ally: 'And I took notice of one thing which [Godolphin] said, that [the duke] had told him [Harley] protested he could not yet tell what fault he had ever committed against [the Lord Treasurer] or [the duke of Marlborough]'; which, Mainwaring added, 'was pretty impudent'. Blenheim MSS. E29 (the names are given in a numerical code).

3. Such is the defence of Harley's conduct made by A. J. D. M. McInnes in an unpublished analysis of the crisis. See 'Robert Harley, Secretary of State' (University College of Wales, Aberystwyth, M.A. thesis, 1961), pp. 135–9.

situation at Court during the eventful days of late January and early February 1708. The remainder of this paper is based on these materials, and all the available evidence is re-examined in the light they shed upon it.

It would seem that the roots of the 1708 crisis must be traced back as far as the general election of 1705, which left the placemen holding the balance in the new house of commons between a more or less equal number of whigs and tories, and so gave rise to a fundamental difference of opinion between Lord Godolphin and Robert Harley over parliamentary management. This is usually represented as a clash between Harley's 'moderation' and ideal of non-party government and the treasurer's willingness to work with party men even to the point of surrendering to the Junto. Yet during the weeks immediately preceding the secretary of state's resignation the truth was somewhere near the opposite of this. Throughout December 1707 it was Godolphin who was the apostle of non-party government, trying 'to make a party of Whigs and Tories' to support the court against the manoeuvres of the party leaders on both sides.[1] Significantly, even after the fall of Harley the first promotions went not to the Junto and their satellites but, as Professor Walcott pointed out, to the 'Lord Treasurer's Whigs'.[2] Harley's political principles, too, were opposed to party rule. But by this he did not mean rule without party. He was astute enough as a politician and parliamentary manager to realize that no ministry could keep control of parliament indefinitely without taking many of the leaders of one or other of the parties into its confidence. No ministry could get anything like a majority merely by relying on men of moderate or indeterminate opinions, or by pooling the personal adherents of the ministers themselves. There were far too many 'independents' for operating a system of management through patronage alone; and in the business of attracting the support of these independent backbenchers the 'moderates', almost by definition, stood little chance against the appeals of the party leaders. Therefore a ministry composed entirely of 'moderates' could hardly hope to achieve stability in parliament.

Harley's case was that in order to obtain parliamentary stability it was necessary for the ministers to bring into partnership party men who had the talent for leadership. He himself was probably indifferent as to which party the court chose to encourage, provided – and this was an all-important proviso – that the leaders of the chosen party should not be able to *dictate policy* to the Crown. They were to be treated strictly as junior partners in the business of running the country. This explains why in 1706–8 he eventually came to prefer the tories to the whigs when seeking the direction in which to bestow the Court's favours. The whigs were much better organized than the

1. See letters from Sir John Cropley to the earl of Shaftesbury for Dec. 1707 in P[ublic] R[ecord] O[ffice] 30/24/20: 136, 138, 140, 141.   2. Walcott, *op. cit.* p. 149.

tories under one group of acknowledged leaders – the Junto. Consequently there was a very great risk that leaning towards the whigs would eventually entail admitting the Junto into policy-making posts as the price for their continued support.[1] The leadership of the tories by contrast was not in the hands of a similar group. The earls of Nottingham and Rochester were greatly respected figures in the tory ranks, but they did not always see eye to eye, nor were they undisputed leaders of a party. Equally important, in the session of 1707-8 Sir Edward Seymour, the veteran champion of the tories in the house of commons, lay on his death-bed at Maiden Bradley, and his position in the party was being taken over by younger men who had never been tried in office: men like William Bromley and Sir Thomas Hanmer. Such considerations led Harley to the conclusion that by relying mainly on the tories the ministers would not be yielding power to a faction, whereas reliance on the whigs would ultimately involve a surrender to the dreaded Junto.

Such was the trend of his persistent arguments with Godolphin on the subject of handling parliament between 1705 and 1708.[2] Events in those years added substance to his views as more and more concessions were yielded to the whigs only to cause the Junto lords to become more insistent than ever in their demands for high office. By December 1707 they were calling for Lord Orford to be put in charge of the admiralty, a demand doubly obnoxious to the queen because her husband, Prince George, was at the time head of naval administration.[3] Godolphin's attempts to stave off their advance, without at the same time conciliating the tories, brought about a formidable coalition of both against the ministry in the fall of 1707. Shortly after parliament reassembled on 7 January 1708, the hopelessness of attempting to beat down this opposition without conceding the force of Harley's arguments and siding with one or other of the parties became more and more apparent. During the Christmas recess Greg's treasonable correspondence had been detected, and it seemed that the opposition leaders could hardly fail to exploit the incident – perhaps to the point of impeaching Harley – embarked as they were on a crusade against incompetence in high places, which meanwhile was being sustained by attacks on the admiralty and on the direction of the war in Spain. This was the

1. It seems that he did not reach this conclusion immediately. As late as the autumn of 1706 he was still prepared to admit that a stable Court party might be maintained on the basis of a whig preponderance, provided adequate safeguards were applied. See Brit. Mus. Loan 29/10/19, draft in Harley's hand; Hist. MSS. Com. *Bath MSS.* i. 110–11: Harley to Godolphin, 15 Oct. 1706.

2. See especially the correspondence between them in Hist. MSS. Com. *Bath MSS.*, vol. i, and *Portland MSS.*, vol. iv; also the Harley-Marlborough-Godolphin correspondence in Coxe, vol. ii, *passim. Cf.* Harley's memorandum dated 25 Sept. 1706 in Brit. Mus. Loan 29/9/38.

3. P.R.O. 30/24/20/140 and 141 i: Sir John Cropley to Lord Shaftesbury, N.D. and 30 Dec. 1707.

parliamentary situation when on 13 January Harley wrote to the lord steward to acquaint him 'that I am commanded to send to all the Gentlemen who have formerly met yr Grace at the chanc^{lr} of the Excheqrs house to be there tomorrow being Wednesday at eight a clock at night'. The following day he wrote also to Godolphin to give 'notice of summons at eight this night at Mr Boyle'.[1] The convening of this conference and its significance in the story of Harley's fall has not hitherto been noticed.

Private meetings of this kind were summoned frequently in the reign of Queen Anne to discuss tactics to be pursued by the ministry in parliament. But there is reason to think that the calling of this particular conference for 14 January 1708, was a decisive turning point in the events which led to Harley's resignation less than a month later. Years afterwards Swift, referring to those events, told the following story which he claimed to have had from Harley and St. John: 'that the Duke of Marlborough and the Earl of Godolphin had concerted with them and their friends upon a moderating scheme, wherein some of both parties should be employed, but with a more favourable aspect toward the church: that a meeting was appointed for completing this work'.[2] A memorandum in Harley's hand endorsed 'preliminaries Jan. 13 170$\frac{7}{8}$ and Jan. 14' proves beyond all reasonable doubt that this was just such a meeting as that referred to by Swift. As this document is of considerable interest it is reproduced here[3]:

> To agree to join in nothing wch is ill, and wrong
> 1. That we may not break friendship tho either or any of us should happen upon particular points to differ from each other.
> 2. To desire they will consider now or any other time of proper Points that we may be helpful and assistant in . . .
> 3. To find out proper heads in wch we may join and begin to found a confidence wch it is reasonable to hope will increase by Degrees.
>> 1. Receivers.
>> 2. Bill of Justices.
>> 3. As to Spain etc.
> 4. to speak with the Whiggs etc. to prevent them from taking Alarm, and to shew them that nothing is designed but public good.
> examine leased farms
> of the Revenue

The meaning of these 'preliminaries' is not crystal clear, but they obviously refer to the forging of a political alliance, and clause 4

1. Brit. Mus. Loan 29/264, pp. 202–3; 29/64/1. It is very interesting to find that in this letter to Godolphin of 14 Jan. 1708 Harley anticipated the early surrender of his seals of office – probably fearing the outcome of a parliamentary attack over the Greg affair.
2. Swift, *Memoirs relating to [the] change . . . in the Queen's Ministry in the Year 1710.* (*The Prose Works of Jonathan Swift*, vol. viii, ed. Davis and Ehrenpreis, p. 113).
3. Brit. Mus. Loan 29/9/51.

shows that this was not to be with the whigs, so that it must have been designed to bring in the tories. It can be said, then, that in the middle of January 1708 Robert Harley was working actively towards a rapprochement with the tories; and moreover that these plans had been put on a semi-official footing. They were being discussed by some at least of his ministerial colleagues, and those consulted included Court whigs like Boyle, the chancellor of the exchequer, and Devonshire, the lord steward. In this connection a point of obvious relevance is that the Junto attack on the admiralty in December 1707 had alienated some of their more moderate associates – Newcastle, Cowper, Somerset and Devonshire – who had showed themselves prepared to support the ministry against further attacks from the whig leaders.[1] As for Boyle, he had long been anti-Junto. The presence of Boyle and Devonshire at the meeting on the 14th is a strong indication that Harley was hopeful of getting this group of 'rebels' to carry their support as far as sanctioning a marked readjustment in the party equilibrium of the ministry. So much was open and above board towards the end of the second week in January.

But some time during the third week in January Harley's schemes went underground. We hear no more of business meetings of ministers to discuss them, but we do very soon afterwards hear rumours of secret approaches to tories by Harley and his friends. On the day before the secretary's fall Vernon informed Shrewsbury of a rumour 'publicly spoken of, that messages have been carried as from the Queen to several leading men among the Tory party, to engage them to stand by her Majesty against the Whigs, whose management she was dissatisfied with, and no less with the influence they had upon her ministers'.[2] No correspondence between Harley and the tory chiefs has survived to give substance to this rumour, but this does not clear him of suspicion since all the political leaders were in London attending a very lively session of parliament at the height of the crisis, and were therefore available for private meetings – a safer and more practical method of carrying on an intrigue than by correspondence. In the absence of such first-hand information one of the multitude of begging letters which Harley received later in the reign when he was earl of Oxford and lord treasurer takes on an unusual significance. On 10 November 1713, Thomas Brereton informed Oxford that 'at the instance of Sir Thomas Hanmer, Sir Henry Bunbury and Mr Shakerly I came to Town, they telling my father *they believed they had interest enough* to recommend me into your Lordship's office, your Lordship being then Secretary of State. I had not been ten days in Town, but your Lordship quitted that office –'.[3] The three

---

1. P.R.O. 30/24/20/141 i and 235 : Cropley to Shaftesbury, 30 Dec. 1707 and N.D.
2. *Vernon Correspondence*, iii. 345.
3. Brit. Mus. Loan 29/127/7. The italics are ours.

men named in this letter were not associates of Harley in 1708; they were prominent party men of an extreme tory stamp, all of them having supported the motion to 'tack' the occasional conformity bill to the land tax bill in 1704. One of them indeed – Hanmer – was leading the tory attack on the ministry in the house of commons during the very period referred to by Brereton. Therefore Harley was at least giving those tories reason to believe that the Court was prepared to countenance them, even if he was not actually intriguing with them. Moreover, we know from a different source that on 17 January he had started bargaining with a less prominent tory, William Clayton, the member for Liverpool.[1]

It is interesting that Bishop Burnet, who also mentions 'messages to the tories', asserts that when Anne was charged by Marlborough and Godolphin with authorizing Harley and his friends to carry such messages she denied it. The charge is more convincing than the denial, for the queen was not averse to lying her way out of a tight corner, nor to putting on a convincing act when it suited her.[2] Further information on her personal role in Harley's schemes is given by a Hanoverian agent in London, who claimed that Anne had commanded Harley 'to act with his friends and to set in motion the wheels of their party i.e. the Tories and malcontent Whigs who seemed to have formed a considerable party in the House of Commons'.[3] All in all the conclusion seems inescapable that during the last fortnight in January, and with the backing of the queen, the secretary was negotiating secretly with tory politicians in London with an eye to a radical reconstruction of the Godolphin administration.

However, we are still confronted with the much more taxing problem of what place Godolphin and Marlborough themselves occupied in Harley's schemes. Harley, as we have shown, always denied that he at any time contemplated the removal of either. In 'Faults on Both Sides' he attributed the rumours of such an intention that so freely circulated early in February solely to the malice of his whig enemies: 'the party [i.e. the Junto Whigs] gave out that he had been working underhand to throw out the very ministers themselves, whereas the utmost of his aim could be to reform or ballance [the ministry]; for to think of displacing and disgracing them at that time of day, was fit for no man in his wits'.[4]

In Godolphin's case, however, these protestations of Harley's have always had a hollow ring. Harley, after all, was an interested party; his

1. See p. 74 below.
2. See, *e.g.* Hist. MSS. Com. 8th Rep., pt. i (*Blenheim MSS.*), p. 38: Somers to Marlborough, 19 Jan. and 2 June 1710.
3. Letters from de Beyries in London 13/24 and 17/28 Feb. 1708 reproduced from the originals in the Hanover State Archive by B. W. Hill in 'The career of Robert Harley, Earl of Oxford, from 1702 to 1714' (Cambridge, Ph.D., 1961), pp. 142–3 here translated.
4. *Faults on Both Sides*, p. 31 (*Somers Tracts*, xii. 693).

uncorroborated evidence must obviously be treated with the utmost reserve. Admittedly the whigs, too, had an interest – in maligning Harley. But although it is a fact that most of the charges that he planned to displace Godolphin seem to have stemmed, like those of Addison and Swift, from the whig side, this is not true of all of them. It is of some note, for instance, that Roger Coke,[1] who claimed to have had his information not from the whigs but from 'a considerable Tory, but about four days before the discovery was publickly made' [of Harley's plot] had no doubt that 'The Project was to remove the Lord Treasurer out of his office' or that 'the Earl of Sunderland was to be out of his Secretary's place such a day, he being the person they resolved to begin with'. Unless Harley was playing an unusually deep game, even for him, such a project can hardly have been firmly decided on between the queen and himself by mid-January, when he was still corresponding amicably enough with the treasurer[2] and when he was, as we have just seen, discussing the new pro-tory scheme with him in an open and above-board manner. And yet we know that no later than the 24th[3] Harley had brought the most damaging accusations against Godolphin before Anne, hardly the action of a loyal colleague, and from then on there is scarcely a single piece of evidence from any source, contemporary or subsequent, to suggest that the queen herself made the slightest push to conciliate her treasurer or try to keep him in office, in itself a most significant fact.

So it would seem that some time in the third week of January, at the very time when Harley's negotiations with the tories went underground, there was a marked change in his attitude towards Godolphin. The reasons are not difficult to deduce. Quite apart from the basic conflict in the political thinking of the two men Godolphin must have realized that Harley's plans for a change in the party-emphasis of the ministry would involve for him a loss of personal prestige and status, even if he retained the treasurer's staff. At the conference of ministers held at Boyle's house on the 14th he may, perhaps, have made his distaste for the new scheme perfectly plain and convinced Harley that he could not expect the earl's co-operation. And if, a few days afterwards, the last shreds of Harley's respect for the lord treasurer were destroyed by the startling revelations of the Spanish papers just laid on the table of the house of commons, as seems possible, there can no longer have been a permanent place for Godolphin in the secretary's plans.

Admittedly Harley's letters to Marlborough on 28 January, 1 February and 6 February all beseech the duke to heal the breach between Godolphin and himself.[4] But these protestations, couched in

---

1. *A Detection of the Court and State of England* (1719), iii. 323.
2. Brit. Mus. Loan 29/64/1: Harley to Godolphin (draft), 14 Jan. 1708.
3. See p. 161 above and Brit. Mus. Loan 29/12/5.
4. Brit. Mus. Loan 29/12/5; 29/12/6.

the inevitable Harleian generalities, inspire little confidence. They may well signify nothing more than that the breach had come a little too soon for the secretary's liking; that it had caught him unawares before his own plans were fully matured, and in particular before his approaches to the tories had begun to bear fruit. According to Sir John Cropley, the M.P. for Shaftesbury, who had his ear very close to the ground at this time, it was not until the first week of February that Harley 'at last secured a good reception with the tories'.[1] It would not be surprising, then, if the premature springing of the mine at the end of January had found Harley at a disadvantage and made him anxious to postpone the final trial of strength with the treasurer for a little while. But it is barely credible that Harley still hoped for a permanent reconciliation with his chief.

Marlborough's case, however, was very different. It is significant that Harley, in his letters to Marlborough, assumed right up to 6 February that there was no great dispute between him and the duke, and that at bottom his quarrel was only with the lord treasurer.[2] Most, though not quite all, of the whig observers assumed that Marlborough was to have been preserved as head of the army. And, as we shall see subsequently,[3] the queen's attitude to the duke in the final days of the crisis, from 6 to 9 February, an attitude so strikingly different from her treatment of Godolphin, proves that these assumptions were right. Here, at least, Harley's protestations of innocence ring true. For 'to think of displacing and disgracing' the captain-general, the country's main hope of a swift and decisive victory in the land war, and a figure whose political support was regarded by Harley as an essential factor in winning the confidence of the independent tory gentlemen in the new scheme, this was indeed 'fit for no man in his wits'. And no one could accuse Robert Harley of being lacking in political judgment. The intriguing feature of the situation is not just that Harley and the queen aimed to separate Marlborough at this juncture from his old friend Godolphin, but also that they were reported to have had good hopes, at one time, of success. 'They did not question it seems', wrote Addison in his second and better-substantiated account on 27 February, 'but my Lord Marlborough woud have acted with them'. Even more startling is the evidence of another whig, in this case a Treasurer's Whig, fairly close to both Marlborough and Godolphin, and one who claimed moreover to have played a personal role of some importance in these transactions. This is the account of Lord Coningsby, the vice-treasurer of Ireland and M.P. for Leominister.[4]

Coningsby's version of the crisis is that as soon as Harley 'became

1. P.R.O. 30/24/145: Cropley to Shaftesbury, Thursday [5 Feb. 1708].
2. Brit. Mus. Loan 29/12/6: draft, Harley to Marlborough, 6 Feb. 1708.
3. See pp. 78-9 below.
4. 'Earl Coningsbies History of Parties; presented to King George the First', printed in *Archaeologia*, xxxviii (1860), 7-8.

strong enough to form a scheme of government in which the first proposition was, to remove my Lord Godolphin', Marlborough found himself faced with a very real dilemma. Because of his 'inclination to the Tories, and more particularly to St. John, Harcourt and Mansell (and at this instant, even to Harley himself) on account of their inveteracy to the Junto Lords', and still more because of his fear of Junto domination, which seemed to him the certain outcome of Godolphin's parliamentary strategy, the duke's first reaction was to sacrifice his friend: 'if he had not underhand promoted and advised the Queen to make this change at this time, [he] had most certainly determined to be passive in it, and submit to it'. He only changed his mind after he had been convinced by Coningsby himself that the treasurer's whigs in the house of commons would never support a remodelled ministry under Harley. Even then, Marlborough planned only 'to cut Harley singly', hoping to retain Harley's closest friends in the ministry as a bulwark against the Junto and a means of keeping up his own interest with the queen, whom he knew to be backing Harley's scheme.

The natural tendency, of course, is to distrust Coningsby. He did not write until 1716; he was malicious and he was egotistical. Historians have discreetly buried his story. Yet it has never seemed inherently improbable. The Marlborough-Godolphin correspondence printed by Coxe leaves no room for doubt that the former was always the more reluctant of the two to commit himself to the whigs, and that he continued to show the same reluctance for some months even after Harley's fall. It is also certain that he had a high opinion of some of the secretary's closest associates, especially of St. John and Harcourt. Marlborough must have known, furthermore, that the treasurer's credit with the queen by the beginning of 1708 was weaker than his own (it was Godolphin who had had most of the dirty work to do in the past two years in bullying Anne into making concessions to the whigs); and some of his private transactions during 1707, especially with the duke of Shrewsbury, suggest that his attachment to Godolphin was not so unqualified that for the sake of it he was prepared to close all other political doors.[1]

All the same we should probably, on balance, have to discount Coningsby's account were it not for the discovery among the Shaftesbury Papers of a striking piece of corroborative evidence. It occurs in an invaluable postscript which Sir John Cropley added to a long letter to Lord Shaftesbury on 19 February:

Since I writ in the Speakers Chamber Stanhop has dined with me. I never saw him eat so heartily. . . . He confirms the great shake at home . . . and I learn one secret I did not know, that it was ames ace as they say

1. See especially *The Private Diary of Earl Cowper* (ed. E. C. Hawtrey, 1833), p. 43; Hist. MSS. Com. *Buccleuch MSS*. ii. 719: Shrewsbury to Buckingham, 8 Dec. 1707; Brit. Mus. Add. MSS. 34518, fo. 127: Shrewsbury to Marlborough, 27 Dec. 1707; Coxe, ii. 156–7: Marlborough to Sunderland, 8/19 Sept. 1707.

whether my Lord Treasurer's old friend had not sacrificed him and given him up. Stanhop came full with resentment agst that person. But for the sake of the public puts up all.[1]

The source of the evidence is almost unimpeachable. General James Stanhope, recently back in England from service in Spain, was at this time, like Coningsby, a close follower of Godolphin. But he was a much more balanced and sober witness than 'Gaffney's Hangman', and it is clear from Cropley's letters that Stanhope was conversing with the treasurer fairly regularly at the time of the crisis. At the very least his information reflected Godolphin's own strong suspicions about the duke; most probably it was, in essentials, correct.

The one serious problem of interpretation that remains is to decide what restrained Marlborough in January 1708 from committing his fortunes to Harley and the tories. One explanation, Coningsby's, has already been noticed. But this is unlikely to be the whole truth. Roger Coke surely comes nearer to the mark when he writes: 'The Duke of Marlborough was the person that now stemmed the tide, positively, but in very dutiful terms refusing to command the army any longer if the Lord Godolphin was put out, seeing he could not rely on any other for the necessary supplies, to carry on the war with success against the common enemy'.[2] The war, for Marlborough, was indeed the vital consideration. It is often overlooked that on 3 February the ministry's whole conduct of the war in Spain was strongly censured. Harley and his friends, as we shall see,[3] failed to protect the government from this vote. One observer, commenting later on his fall, actually attributed it to this failure, concluding that 'the grand fault is that they did not prevent the House of Commons coming to the resolution they did relating to Spain'.[4] Indeed, many suspected that so far from preventing the hostile address on 3 February, Harley had secretly encouraged it.[5] Marlborough undoubtedly shared this view,[6] and in the end was deterred from falling in with Harley's project, despite all its undoubted attractions, by the conviction that to achieve his ends the secretary was employing 'false and treacherous' means.

Once the cause of the 1708 crisis has been diagnosed, and the motives and aims of the leading protagonists established, it becomes

1. P.R.O. 30/24/21/150; Cropley to Shaftesbury, N.D. [19 Feb. 1708].
2. *loc. cit.* iii. 323–4.   3. Below p. 77.
4. *The Norris Papers* (ed. Thomas Heywood for the Chetham Society) [1846], p. 167: Thomas Johnson to Richard Norris, London, 12 Feb. 1708.   5. Burnet, v. 348.
6. *Private Correspondence of the Duchess of Marlborough* (hereafter cited as *Priv. Corr.*) [1832], ii. 12: Dr. Francis Hare to the duchess of Marlborough, Amen Corner, Friday night [Dec. 1710]. Hare took it for granted that Harley deliberately 'brought about the Almanza business in the Commons' to sabotage the Court's relations with the Junto. As chaplain-general to the army in Flanders, and an intimate of the Churchills, he must have heard so from the duke.

possible to reconstruct the sequence of events with a fair degree of certainty. Here the new evidence is again of great value, for it illuminates many of the darker areas of a canvas which extends from mid-January, when Harley was still co-operating with Marlborough and Godolphin, to mid-February, when the triumvirate of 1704–8 finally broke up and 'Mr Secretary' left the government and went into open opposition.

Towards the middle of January mounting parliamentary pressure from both High Church and Junto flanks had at last persuaded the duke and the lord treasurer to listen more attentively to Harley's project for an accommodation with the tories. And so the secretary was asked to convene a meeting of ministers at the chancellor of the exchequer's house in order to discuss it. The discussion can have been no more than exploratory; for a second conference was soon afterwards arranged for eight o'clock on the evening of 14 January, and before it met Harley drew up a list of 'preliminaries' – heads to serve as the basis of an agreement with the tories. The reaction of Marlborough and Godolphin on learning the details of Harley's schemes can only be deduced from subsequent events; but it seems more than likely that, while the lord treasurer's immediate reaction was unfavourable, the duke was less critical and even gave Harley enough encouragement to persuade him to go ahead secretly with his plans, despite Godolphin's coldness.

Whatever was transacted at this second conference, Harley's open approach to the reconcilation of the ministry with the tories was from then on at an end. Three days after the meeting he was observed engaging in some rather furtive business in the house of commons. On 17 January he approached William Clayton, tory member for Liverpool, and, saying that he must speak with him, took him behind the Speaker's chair. There he offered Clayton the nomination to a post of collector of the customs which was about to be made vacant.[1] This cloak-and-dagger bid for the support of an obscure backbench tory can hardly have been an isolated act, and must have been linked with secret approaches to other tories, including more prominent members than Clayton.

That the queen was privy to these approaches, and that she gave her blessing to them, is virtually certain. Some time in the following week, either on 22 or 23 January, she held one of her periodic conferences with Harley; and it was either at this meeting or within a day or two of it that the secretary revealed to her some 'mismanagements' of the two chief ministers of which he had just become aware. We have suggested the possibility that these mismanagements were connected with the gross neglect of the Spanish theatre of war, which had led to the forces in English pay being woefully under strength at the battle of Almanza in 1707.[2] At all events, the charges Harley made

1. *The Norris Papers*, pp. 161–2.   2. See pp. 61-2 above.

must have been serious, for when the news of his revelation eventually leaked out to Godolphin the effect was conclusively to confirm all the treasurer's suspicions about his slippery colleague.

These suspicions, however, had already been very much alive for several days. On Saturday, 24 January, that is shortly after Harley's meeting with the queen, Marlborough had dropped some timely words of warning in the secretary's ear relating to the lord treasurer: and though we cannot be sure of their exact import, it seems highly probable that the duke informed his colleague that Godolphin was growing suspicious of his shady dealings with the tories.[1] Four days later, at another private interview with Anne, Harley learned that Marlborough, too, was now displeased with him, and had already begun to indicate his displeasure to the queen.[2] Some derogatory remarks of Harley's – presumably made at his earlier audience the previous Thursday or Friday – had come to the duke's ear and offended him. Anxious as he was to retain the services of the captain-general in his 'shadow cabinet', Harley naturally professed complete innocence and begged a meeting with the duke in order to clear himself. Marlborough's reply, written on 29 January, was surprisingly amicable; he promised to call in at the secretary's office on the afternoon of the 30th, half-an-hour before the business meeting of the Lords of the Committee at the Cockpit.[3]

These arrangements were rudely disturbed, however, by a dramatic development on the very night that Marlborough wrote his mild reply. It was then that Godolphin despatched attorney-general Harcourt to Harley to convey what was tantamount to a declaration of war from him. Harcourt was unable or unwilling to pass on any details of the treasurer's reasons, and Harley had no time to reply immediately, for he and his friends spent most of the night of the 29th in the house of commons, unhappily defending the government in the heated debate on the battle of Almanza.[4] Next morning, however, he received another note from Marlborough wherein the duke asked Harley to call on him at his home about noon, pleading that his foot was too uneasy to enable him to keep their appointment

1. What the duke said can only be inferred from the reply Harley made a few days later, when he had had time to chew over Marlborough's words: 'I do most solemnly assure you', he wrote, 'that I have the utmost regard and affection for his Lsp. and his great merit and I am ready to give any demonstration of it yr Grace shall judge proper if there is any where the least doubt'. It bears all the marks of a typical Harleian reaction to a charge of infidelity. See Brit. Mus. Loan 29/12/5: Harley to Marlborough (draft), 28 Jan. 1708.

2. Coxe, ii. 191: Marlborough to the queen. N.D. [6 Feb. 1708].

3. Brit. Mus. Loan 29/12/5: Marlborough to Harley, 29 Jan. 1708; Brit. Mus. Loan 29/10/2 (Harley's Cabinet memoranda); Hist. MSS. Com. *Bath MSS*. i. 189: Queen Anne to Harley, 27 Jan. 1708.

4. N. Luttrell, *A Brief Historical Relation of State Affairs* (Oxford, 1857), vi. 262, 31 January 1708 notes that Harley, St. John and Brydges spoke for the ministry on the 29th. *Cf. Vernon Correspondence*, iii. 329–30; *Court and Society*, ii. 272: J. Addison to Manchester, 3 Feb. 1708.

at the Cockpit that afternoon.[1] Anxious to discover what had provoked the sudden change in the lord treasurer's attitude from mere
distrust to violent hostility, the secretary paid the suggested visit to
Marlborough's house and there learned 'the particulars' of his
alleged crime. Once enlightened, he lost no time in writing to
Godolphin and protesting against 'misrepresentations or mis-
constructions, or the application of things said generally to a particular purpose which was never thought of; for I do solemnly protest
[he added] I never entertained the least thought derogating from
your Lordship or prejudicial to your interest'. He ended by asking
Godolphin to let his actions attest to his innocency. But the lord
treasurer was not taken in by all this. It must have seemed to him
that Harley protested much too much. He had by now seen with his
own eyes and heard with his own ears enough to convince him that
the secretary's activities were far from innocent, indeed that they
were highly prejudicial to his personal interest. As far as Godolphin
was concerned, that was the end of the matter: 'I am very far from
having deserved it from you. God forgive you!'[2]

While Godolphin was for firmly shutting the door in Harley's
face, therefore, Marlborough, although protesting to the queen at
the secretary's conduct,[3] was still willing to keep it open. Nothing
reveals more clearly the different attitudes which the two ministers
took to their colleague's activities than the contrasting tones of their
letters at this time. Marlborough's notes of 29 January were accom-
modating, if not friendly, while Godolphin's outburst of the 30th
was a point blank refusal to consider the matter any further. Once
he had received that inflexible communication, Harley must have
realized that there was no time to lose if he was to save himself and
his schemes from disaster.

His sense of urgency was further stimulated by two other considerations.

In the first place, his negotiations with the tories had so far made
disappointing progress. It is true that about the end of January Sir
Thomas Hanmer, Sir Henry Bunbury and Peter Shakerley felt
sufficiently in his confidence to be recommending posts for their
friends.[4] Nevertheless most high tories were still reluctant to fall in
with his schemes. Quite apart from the inbred suspicion of 'Robin the
Trickster' which most of them shared, there was an understandable
anxiety to know whether or not Marlborough and Godolphin were
prepared to underwrite a new Court-tory alliance, especially since
Harley's own reputation had suffered as a result of the Greg affair.
The tories had no desire to come into an unworkable scheme, and

1. Brit. Mus. Loan 29/12/5 iii: Marlborough to Harley, 'Thursday night', endorsed by
Harley, 'D:M: Jan. 29: 1707/8. RX Friday Jan. 30'.
2. Hist. Com. MSS. *Bath MSS*. i. 189–90: Harley to Godolphin; and reply, 30 Jan.
1708.   3. See pp. 59-60 above.   4. See pp. 68-9 above.

they felt that any administration which excluded the captain-general would certainly prove so, while even the treasurer's absence might be fatal.

Secondly, Harley knew that the lords of the Junto were exerting tremendous pressure on the 'duumvirs' to force his removal from the government. Their minions in the Commons had rescued the ministry from a humiliating defeat in the Almanza debate on 29 January by moving for an adjournment of the inquiry until 3 February.[1] To Harley it must have seemed that a final agreement between Godolphin and the whig lords was imminent. The Junto motion for an adjournment had made it clear that their assistance was only designed to give the ministry the shortest of respites, and was accompanied by a scarcely-veiled threat to 'go to the bottom of it to know whether the public money had been misapplied' unless their terms were met. Harley himself was in no doubt that those terms included his own dismissal.[2]

When, therefore, the Almanza inquiry was resumed on 3 February, Harley's behaviour was governed by these two overriding considerations: it was essential to give the tories a firm pledge of his sincerity, and at the same time 'to bring the ministry off from the new engagements they were gone into'.[3] Consequently, though St. John as secretary-at-war went through the motions of departmental duty by presenting a fresh account to the House of the state of the forces in Spain,[4] Harley, it would appear, did not speak at all, while the attitude of his friends was observed to have been 'very cold and passive'.[5]

This conduct achieved his first objective, for commenting on the Commons' proceedings two days later, Sir John Cropley observed 'Harley has at last secured a good reception with the tories. . . .'[6] But his second intention was foiled. Assuming that the Junto whigs would again come to the rescue of the Court as they had done four

1. *Vernon Correspondence*, iii. 330: Vernon to Shrewsbury, 29 Jan. 1708.

2. *ibid.* In later years Harley was to point to the whig hold over the ministers as a factor largely instrumental in his fall, while Sir John Cropley, for one, had no doubt at the time that the Junto were 'tearing them to pieces for not parting with Harley'. *Faults on Both Sides (Somers' Tracts*, xii. 693); P.R.O. 30/24/21/146: Cropley to Shaftesbury, 'Feb. 7 1707/8'. Harley may have over-stressed the direct responsibility of the Junto lords for his fall (Somers and Halifax later professed themselves in the dark as to what ultimately caused his resignation. See their letters of 14 and 19 Feb. 1708 to the earl of Portland in the duke of Portland's loan of manuscripts to Nottingham University Library. PWA 118 and 945), but he was right to assume that, once in the saddle, they would have had no mercy on him.

3. *Priv. Corr.* ii. 12: Dr. Hare to the duchess of Marlborough [Dec. 1710].

4. *Commons' Journals*, xv. 524–5. These new figures produced a minor amendment which mitigated the discrepancy to some extent by adding commissioned and non-commissioned officers, and their servants, to the total number of forces present at Almanza.

5. Burnet, v. 348. Clement, in *Faults on Both Sides (Somers' Tracts*, xii. 693), noted that 'the address went without any more than a little faint shewish opposition'.

6. P.R.O. 30/24/21/145: Cropley to Shaftesbury, 'Wills Feb. 4 1707/8'.

days earlier.[1] Harley apparently hoped that a defeat for the ministry, if only a narrow one, would serve to demonstrate to Marlborough the futility of a Court-Junto alliance and at the same time reinforce the logic of his own political arguments ever since 1706, by emphasizing the power of the united tory interest in the Commons. As Marlborough's chaplain later remarked, however, 'he miscarried in his attempt',[2] for the Junto whigs, to Harley's astonishment and discomfiture, changed their tactics on 3 February. 'The Junto wanted at this time so fair an opportunity to bite the ministers, and force them into a complyance with what they had long been bargaining for, and therefore directed their creatures by all means to let the Address pass as smart as the Tories would have it.'[3] Hence the 'terrible vote of 21,000 absent soldiers' passed without a division,[4] and Harley had not only failed to outmanoeuvre the Junto, but had only succeeded in virtually convincing Marlborough of his own perfidy.

Of this last fact, however, Harley remained ignorant for four more days.[5] Checkmated in parliament, he now saw only one course open to him: to persuade the queen herself to intervene and force the duke to a decision.

When Mr Harley, Harcourt the Attorney General, and St John, the Secretary for War gave the Queen to understand that they did not have enough authority to set their party in motion over such an important matter, when people more readily believed than they and who enjoyed the confidence of Her Majesty would not put themselves out in order to make her intentions known, she decided to write to the Duke of Marlborough in a letter which was given into the charge of Mr St. John. . . .[6]

In this letter the queen informed Marlborough that she was resolved, if need be, to part with the lord treasurer.[7] The issue had now been well and truly forced.

It was on Friday, 6 February that Anne despatched St. John to the duke, at the same time giving the secretary-at-war *carte blanche* to broadcast her intention 'about the town'. Godolphin had no intention of serving under Harley in any circumstances, and made up his mind there and then to quit. Marlborough, torn between two men and two policies, finally decided to stick by 'his old friend'. That same Friday night he wrote to the queen and told her that neither he nor

1. That Harley did make this assumption is plainly suggested in *Faults on Both Sides* (*Somers' Tracts*, xii. 693) and it was justified by the fact that the Junto's only representative in the Cabinet, his mortal enemy lord Sunderland, was technically responsible for the sphere of operations in the peninsula as secretary of state for the south.

2. *Priv. Corr.* ii. 12.   3. *Faults on Both Sides* (*Somers' Tracts*, xii. 693).

4. P.R.O. 30/24/21/148: Cropley to Shaftesbury, 19 Feb. 1708; *Commons' Journals*, xv. 525. The Address asked the queen for an explanation for the discrepancy between the numbers voted and the forces actually present at the battle of Almanza.

5. This is reflected in his still buoyant mood on 5 Feb. *Swift Corr.* i. 75.

6. Letter from de Beyries in London, 17/28 Feb. 1708, quoted in B. W. Hill, *loc. cit.* p. 143, here translated.   7. *Swift Corr.* i. 74-76.

the treasurer could serve her while Harley enjoyed her confidence.[1]
Something which St. John had said when delivering Anne's letter
had apparently clinched the matter, for next day the general wrote to
Harley in words which plainly revealed that their special relationship
was at an end. 'I have been very exactly informed of all the transactions
for some days past; and particularly what was said under the
sanction of a message yesterday morning.'[2]

However, it was one thing for Marlborough and Godolphin to
declare war on the secretary of state, and quite another thing for them
to achieve victory. The next few days bore astonishing witness to
the tenacity and courage of Queen Anne, in defence of her prerogative of choosing and dismissing ministers at will. The two men
from whom she had once said she 'must never part' had given her
three days to consider their ultimatum. She told them that she would
give her final answer on Sunday, 8 February, at Kensington, where a
meeting of the Cabinet was to be held. On that day Godolphin and
the duke and duchess of Marlborough met Anne in a private apart-
ment, adjoining the Cabinet-room where the lords of the council
were already assembled. What took place there was related to Sir
John Cropley by James Stanhope a few days later[3]:

first 'Ld Trea(surer) told the Q(ueen) he came to resign the staff, that
serving her longer with one so perfidious as Mr H(arley) was impossible.
She replied, in respect of his long service she would give him till tomorrow to consider. Then he should do as he pleased, with all she could
find enough glad of that staff.

Then came Lady Duchess with great duty and submission, that she had
served her ever with affec(tion) and tenderness: her utmost had been her
duty and she had been faithful in it. The reply is said to be: "You shall
consider of this till tomorrow, then if you desire it, I shall then advise you
to go to yr little house in St Albans and there stay till *Blenheim house* is ready
for yr Grace."[4]

Then entered the duke prepared with his utmost address. He told her he
had ever served her with obedience and fidelity, that (he) had used that
sword he must now resign her to her honour and advantage; that he must
lament he came in competition with so vile a creature as H(arley); that his
fidelity and duty should continue so long as his breath; that it was his duty
to be speedy in resigning his commands that she might put the sword into
some other hand immediately, and it was also his duty to tell her he feared
the Dutch would immediately on that news make a peace very ruinous for
England. "And then, my Lord", says (she), "will you resign me your

1. P.R.O. 30/24/21/146: Cropley to Shaftesbury, 'Feb. 7, 1707/8'. It is practically
certain that the undated letter of resignation drafted by Marlborough and printed in
Coxe, ii. 191 was that of 6 Feb. 1708 referred to here by Cropley.

2. Brit. Mus. Loan 29/12/5: Marlborough to Harley, 7 Feb. 1708.

3. P.R.O. 30/24/21/150: Cropley to Shaftesbury, N.D. [19 Feb. 1708].

4. Sarah's own version of this interview was very different. 'She [Anne] declared, that
she could not bear the thought of my leaving her and that it must never be.' *An Account
of the Conduct of the Dowager Duchess of Marlborough* (1742), p. 213.

sword. Let me tell you", says (she), "your service I have regarded to the utmost of my power, and if you do, my lord, resign your sword, let me tell you, you run it through my head." She went to the council, begging him to follow; he refusing, so the scene ended.' [1]

When Anne went into the Cabinet-room she found her husband, the lord chancellor, the lord president, the lord steward, the duke of Somerset, and the two secretaries already transacting business. After the Cabinet had called in the prince's council and Sir Charles Hedges to discuss admiralty business, Harley then delivered Spanheim's memorial 'about the 100^m estm for the Emperor'.[2] 'Upon which the duke of Somerset rose, and said, if her Majesty suffered that fellow (pointing to Harley) to treat affairs of the war without the advice of the General, he could not serve her; and so left the Council. The Earl of Pembroke, though in milder words, spoke to the same purpose: so did most of the lords.'[3] The memorial was accordingly shelved until the next full Cabinet meeting, and meanwhile it was agreed that it should be considered by the lords of the committee the following Thursday, with Marlborough present. But the Sunday meeting did not break up in disorder at this point, as is usually said. It went on to discuss the exchange of prisoners and terminated with the reading of a memorial from the Portuguese envoy, and of some Irish papers by the earl of Sunderland.[4] The last word, it seems, was with the earl of Pembroke, who moved the closure with a reference to the stormy scene they had just witnessed and a plea 'that all fair means possible might be used to compose these dissentions, before they should come to the ears of the people'.[5] All the same, Somerset's flamboyant action was the decisive event of the meeting. It was a sure sign that the group of ministerial whigs was now abandoning the secretary, and soon after, we are told, the 'Duke of Newcastle, Harley's friend, at last pressed the Q(ueen) to part with him. The Duke of Devon(shire) and Lord Chancellor declared they would also resign.'[6]

Harley himself must have known in his heart on this Sunday evening that the game was up. The whig magnates of the centre had made it clear that they would not serve without Marlborough, and Harley was too clear-sighted not to recognize that, with the war in its present state, Marlborough was still a *sine qua non* of any ministry. Even so, Anne would not admit defeat. Next morning, on 9 February, she was still fighting, canvassing whatever tory support she could against the Churchills, who had left town.[7] But an event which

1. Burnet bears out Stanhope's story in all essentials. Burnet, v. 353–4.
2. Brit. Mus. Loan 29/9/52: 'minutes Kensington Feb. 8 1707/8'.
3. *Swift Corr.* i. 74–76: Swift to Archbishop King, 12 Feb. 1708.
4. Brit. Mus. Loan 29/9/52: Harley's Cabinet minutes, endorsed 'Last Time'.
5. A. Cunningham, *The History of Great Britain*, ii. 142.
6. P.R.O. 30/24/21/146: Cropley to Shaftesbury, 'Feb. 7 1707/8'.
7. Burnet, v. 354: Dartmouth's note.

occurred later in the day finally broke her resolve. This was the reaction in parliament to the news that she had broken with the captain-general and the lord treasurer, and 'would abide and trust to Mr Harley's scheme for all, for her Crown and her people's safety'.[1] 'The Commons', Burnet noted, 'let the bill of supply lie on the table, though it was ordered for that day'.[2] The reaction of the Lords was still more disturbing: 'after a warm Report that the Queen was not to be prevailed on by the D. of Marlb. and Ld Treas[rs] united Requests to part with Sec. Harley, Ld Wharton made a motion to enquire into the matter of Greg's condemnation. Whereupon the House (by Balloting) chose the following seven lords as a select committee to examine the man etc. viz. D. of Somerset, D. of Bolton, D. of Devonshire, E. of Wharton, Ld Viscount Townshend, Ld Somers and Ld Halifax'.[3]

The meaning of this move by the Junto was transparent: Swift was assured that there were 'endeavours to bring in Harley as a party in that business, and to carry it as far as an impeachment', while Cropley thought it was intended to go even further, with a bill of attainder not out of the question. Harley's Achilles' heel was but too plainly visible, and Anne simply could not allow her favourite to be exposed to so violent a parliamentary attack. 'So in the heat after the Lord(s) had begun the Q(ueen) sent for the Duke and told him she would comply'.[4]

On the following day, the 10th, Robert Harley had his last interview with Anne as secretary. Something of the poignancy of the occasion comes through the scribbled memorandum of the meeting which is preserved among his papers: 'concurr for your sake . . . ready to serve you . . . leave for Controler, Attorney, Mr St. Johns . . . stay a day or two . . . The Prince'.[5] These jottings, like so much of the evidence for this crisis, contain only suggestive clues to the words actually spoken by the leading actors in a drama which had been unfolding for nearly a month, had reached a climax, and was now entering the final scenes. On 11 February Harley resigned his seals, and was accompanied out of office by his friend Thomas Mansell the comptroller of the household. Next day Sir Simon Harcourt and Henry St. John also laid down their commissions, though much to Marlborough's distress, and in the case of St. John against the advice of some of his friends. James Brydges, the paymaster-general, and vice-chamberlain Thomas Coke were expected to do likewise, while

1. P.R.O. 30/24/21/146: Cropley to Shaftesbury, 'Feb. 7 1707/8'.
2. Burnet, v. 355.
3. Bishop Nicolson's diary, 9 Feb. 1708 [Tullie House, Carlisle].
4. *Swift Corr.* i. 74–76: Swift to Archbishop King, 12 Feb. 1708; P.R.O. 30/24/21/146 and 148: Cropley to Shaftesbury, 'Feb. 7 1707/8' and 19 Feb. 1708. It should be remarked that Harley's resignation did not, as the queen obviously hoped, put a prompt end to the Junto attack, though it drew its sting and contributed to its ultimate failure.
5. Brit. Mus. Loan 29/9/52.

Henry Paget, an admiralty councillor, was yet another junior minister and M.P. associated with Harley whose resignation was thought 'uncertain'.[1] In the end all three thought better of it.

All the same, the resignations that did take place were a remarkable example of group loyalty in the political context of the day.

The reasons they give are because Mr Harley was turned out, which they looked upon as a full declaration of the ministry's intention to join entirely with the Whigs, which they though was inconsistent with the declarations they [the duumvirs] had made to them, and the assurances which by their authority and commission, as also by the Queen's commands, they had given the Tories that no such thing should be done.[2]

The Harleyites, reported Sir John Cropley, 'swear a time will come to deliver the poor Q(ueen), as they style her, out of her bondage'.[3]

On this defiant note Harley's audacious bid to check the drift towards the Junto by forging a partnership with the tories, even at the price of parting with Godolphin, came to an end. His scheme, as Addison so shrewdly observed soon after his fall, 'came to light before its time'.[4] It was this piece of ill-luck, plus the sheer impossibility of constructing an administration at this juncture without the duke of Marlborough, which proved his undoing. Even so it was reckoned 'the greatest piece of Court skill that has been acted these many years'.[5]

1. 'Earl Coningsbies History of Parties: presented to King George the First', printed in *Archaeologia*, xxxviii (1860), 7–8; *Swift Corr.* i. 74–76: Swift to Archbishop King, 12 Feb. 1708; P.R.O. 30/24/21/146: Cropley to Shaftesbury, 'Feb. 7 1707/8'.

2. *Huntington Library Quarterly*, xv. (1951–2), 39–40: James Brydges to William Cadogan, 12 Feb. 1708.

3. P.R.O. 30/24/21/146: Cropley to Shaftesbury [11 Feb. 1708].

4. *Addison Letters*, p. 95: Addison to Lord Manchester, 27 Feb. 1708.

5. *Swift Corr.* i. 74–76: Swift to Archbishop King, 12 Feb. 1708.

POSTSCRIPT

In his article 'Godolphin and Harley: A Study of their Partnership in Politics', *Huntington Library Quarterly* 30 (1967), Henry L. Snyder constructed a different hypothesis from that advanced here to explain the reasons for Harley's fall. Although we prepared prepared a paper at the time challenging his arguments at many points, the journal refused us a right of reply.

4

THE HAMILTON AFFAIR OF 1711-12:

A CRISIS IN ANGLO-SCOTTISH RELATIONS

IN two and a half centuries of tolerably healthy life the Union of Scotland and England has acquired every appearance of permanence and and a distinct air of ' inevitability '. The hazards which attended its birth and infancy may seem, in contrast, remote and even a little unreal. Yet the fact remains that the partnership concluded in 1707 was essentially experimental, and that more than once during its first, uncertain, years preceding the '15 rebellion the experiment came perilously close to failure. This was palpably so during the Malt Tax storm in 1713, when the Union survived a hostile division in the house of lords by a mere four votes;[1] and it is scarcely less true of the crisis which arose some eighteen months earlier over the question of the duke of Hamilton's patent. But the Hamilton affair has, for some reason, been so sketchily treated by even the best secondary authorities that its full significance is not generally appreciated.[2] In particular, the conspicuous part it played in the party politics of the day has virtually escaped notice, although it was this which, more than anything, accounted for the excitement the affair aroused and for the serious blow it dealt to the stability of the Union.

[1] This crucial division on 1 June 1713 followed a long debate on a motion of the earl of Findlater for leave to bring in Repeal, though it was not a vote on the motion itself. See G. M. Trevelyan, *England under Queen Anne*, iii. 242 n. The political manoeuvres leading up to the debate of 1 June are described in detail by the Jacobite M.P., George Lockhart of Carnwath in [*The*] *Lockhart Papers* (2 vols., London, 1817), i. 418-34. The fullest printed account of the debate itself is in *The Parliamentary History of England*, vi. 1216-20, drawing largely on the contemporary histories of Boyer and Oldmixon. (POSTSCRIPT: In 1982 Clyve Jones and I published a full account and analysis of the ｜wider 1713 parliamentary crisis. See paper 5, pp. 109-38 below.)

[2] For instance, two such standard works of reference as Sir George Clark's *The Later Stuarts* (Oxford History of England, 2nd edn., 1955) and Sir Lindsay Keir's *The Constitutional History of Modern Britain* (5th edn., 1953) surprisingly make no mention whatever of the Hamilton affair, while on the Scottish side the often admirable work of W. L. Mathieson, *Scotland and the Union . . . 1695 to 1747* (Glasgow, 1905), dismisses it in half a page. Where the case is discussed at all it is cited usually as a demonstration of the mutual antipathy which still existed between the former peers of Scotland and England, sometimes as a question of constitutional interest, very occasionally, *e.g.* in A. S. Turberville, *The House of Lords in the 18th Century* (1927), pp. 150-5, as both. Michael Foot, *The Pen and the Sword* (1957), pp. 332-3, 337-8, is almost alone in conveying some idea of its importance in the party war and in giving a brief account of the debate of 20 Dec. 1711 in the Lords.

Among the sixteen representative peers elected by the Scottish nobility on 10 November 1710 to sit in the third parliament of Great Britain was James Douglas, fourth duke of Hamilton. Earlier that year Hamilton had abandoned his alliance with the Godolphin ministry in London—an uneasy and incongruous alliance for one who was the champion of the Scottish Jacobites—and had hitched his wagon to the rising star of Robert Harley. When Harley began to construct a new ministry in August the duke had given him the support of his powerful northern interest, and at the subsequent general election, as well as in the election of Scots peers, had worked actively on his behalf.[1] In return he had come to regard as his due some special mark of the queen's favour.[2] He had watched fellow-countrymen like Queensberry, Montrose and, recently, Argyll prosper since the Union and expected for himself a reward commensurate with his royal lineage and extensive estates, for he recognized no superior north of the Border.

To begin with his pretensions did not meet with much encouragement. Harley found it inconsistent with his own essentially moderate objectives to give high office to men with patent Jacobite connections; so that for a while Hamilton had to rest content with such meagre crumbs as the lord lieutenancy of Lancashire and a seat in the privy council. But it was not political rewards alone he hankered after. For some time past he had set his heart on adding a British dukedom to his Scottish title. On the face of it, it seemed a perfectly reasonable ambition to cherish, since the only two Scotsmen of similar stature, Argyll and Queensberry, had already received comparable honours[3] and sat in the house of lords on the strength of them. Yet even here Hamilton met with initial disappointment. His first approaches in the summer of 1710 led to nothing, and it was only when he renewed his request to the queen in the following spring that he found the climate more favourable.[4] His own credit at Court was by this time good; Anne herself saw no objection to granting such a peerage; while Harley (now earl of Oxford and lord treasurer)[5] was probably relieved to find this seemingly innocuous way of satisfying the duke's ambition.

However, the proposal to confer a British title on Hamilton soon ran into unexpected difficulties. It was opposed in the Cabinet by secretary Dartmouth, who challenged its constitutional

[1] H[istorical] M[anuscripts] C[omission], *Portland MSS*. x. 342: Sir James Erskine to [earl of Mar?], 19 Sept. 1710; *ibid*. pp. 349–50: Mar to Harley, 7, 9 Nov. 1710.

[2] *Ibid*. pp. 330–1, 333: Mar to Harley, 20, 21, 25 Aug. 1710.

[3] In Argyll's case, the *English* earldom of Greenwich (1705); in Queensberry's the *British* dukedom of Dover (1708). The peerage of England, like that of Scotland, was ' frozen ' at the Union and all fresh creations thereafter were in the new peerage of Great Britain.

[4] H.M.C. *Portland MSS*. x. 333; *ibid*. v. 5.

[5] He was raised to the peerage on 23 May 1711, at roughly the same time as Hamilton applied for his British title.

validity in the light of the terms of the Act of Union; [1] and according to Lockhart of Carnwath the news ' was no sooner publick than the greatest part of the English Peers (Whigs and Tories) exclaimd against it '—not on rational grounds, he implies, but as a sort of conditioned reflex induced by anti-Scottish prejudice.[2]   Lockhart's diagnosis of the cause of this reaction was superficial,[3] ana his picture of Tory hostility was certainly exaggerated.   But the existence of *some* opposition on the Tory side was indisputable;   and this, from Hamilton's point of view, seemed the most ominous feature of the situation.   His British peerage, even if granted, could still be challenged in the house of lords, and with an evenly-balanced Upper House it needed relatively few tory dissidents to cause the ministry embarrassment.   The serious alarm with which the Scots viewed the reaction of the English peers is demonstrated by the warning which Lord Mar gave to Oxford as early as 10 June. Hamilton was by no means alone in his aspiration for a British title,[4] and Mar left the treasurer in no doubt whatever how he and his colleagues regarded the duke's case: as a precedent of such importance to their entire order that the whole future of Anglo-Scottish relations might depend on its outcome.   ' . . . should that hardship of the peerage be putt upon us, so contrair to all sense, reason and fair dealing, . . . how is it possible', asked Mar, ' that flesh and blood can bear it? and what Scotsman will not be wearie of the Union, and do all he can to get quitt?'[5]   Faced with the certainty of Scottish hostility if the peerage were *not* granted and the threat of English hostility if it were, the treasurer preferred to risk the latter.   But he allowed more than three months to elapse after the queen had consented to the grant before issuing Hamilton's patent, by which time most of the potential trouble-makers had dispersed to their country houses for the parliamentary recess and

[1] Mainly, it seems, on the ground that if Hamilton took his seat in the Lords in virtue of a British title it would contravene article xxii of the Treaty of Union—the article which fixed the representation of the Scottish peers in the united parliament. ' now they are like to interpret the 22. art. of Union as perversely as they did interpret soundly the act agt. intruding ', wrote Lord Balmerino to Harry Maule of Kellie on 9 June (S[cottish] R[ecord] O[ffice], Dalhousie MS. 14/352).

[2] See *A Letter from a Scots Gentleman residing in England to his Freind at Edinburgh* (London, 12 June 1711), reprinted in *Lockhart Papers*, i. 529-48.

[3] See p. 94 below.

[4] *E.g.* Mar himself pressed the treasurer for such a title at the same time as Hamilton on the strength of a former promise from the queen, and there were other Scottish peers who, even as early as May 1711, were ' talked of ' as likely candidates: H.M.C. *Portland MSS.* x. 355, 409; S.R.O., Dalhousie MS. 14/352: Balmerino to Maule, 19 May.

[5] H.M.C. *Mar and Kellie MSS.* p. 490: Mar to Oxford, 10 June 1711. *Cf.* a letter from Sir David Dalrymple to Oxford, written five days earlier: ' It is yet but the Skeatch of an Union (pardon the Expression). Real advantages are necessary to make an incorporating Union . . . if slavery or discontent prevail upon us here, the Gangrene must needs spread hastyly all over . . .' Brit[ish] Mus[eum]. Portland Loan (Harley MSS.), 133. I am much indebted to the duke of Portland for permission to use these papers.

he could hope for a more amenable House by the next session.[1] Not until 10 September 1711, then, did the patent creating Hamilton Baron Dutton and duke of Brandon in the peerage of Great Britain finally pass the Great Seal.

For a few weeks thereafter it seemed that Oxford's caution would pay dividends. Despite all Dartmouth's qualms and Mar's solemn warnings the patent had a quiet reception. Indeed it is just possible that little more would have been heard of the matter [2] but for the sudden change in the political situation in the late autumn of 1711. The signing of preliminaries of peace with France on 27 September so angered Britain's allies that the whigs were encouraged to plan a all-out attack on the ministry, to be launched as soon as parliament reassembled. Although the government's majority was impregnable in the house of commons its control of the house of lords was precarious, disturbingly dependent on a dozen or more Court whigs—' Trimmers ' who normally supported the administration, whatever its complexion, but were now under tremendous opposition pressure to vote against a Tory peace. It was this crisis which gave to the duke of Hamilton's patent a new and wholly unlooked-for significance in the eyes of both the English parties. To the tories, anxiously calculating each single vote in the Upper House, the sixteen Scottish votes became a potentially decisive factor, and for two to three weeks before parliament met on 7 December Oxford was urging his Scottish supporters to be at Westminster without fail by the first day of the new session. To the whigs too the conduct of the representative peers was a matter of the utmost concern. It was not that they had any serious hopes of their support, for they were well aware that the relative poverty of the Scots coupled with their lack of interest in English affairs normally bound them firmly to the government which had nominated them. What really perturbed the whigs was the prospect of having *more* than sixteen dependent Scots ranged against them in a finely-balanced House. For they suspected that Hamilton's new honour was not to be an isolated award, but the first of a series of such creations designed· to enlarge the Scottish representation in

---

[1] *Cf. A Letter from a Scots Gentleman* . . . in *Lockhart Papers*, i. 545. Although the delay was mainly tactical there were other factors. A caveat was entered against the patent by a group of opposition peers and there was also some difficulty in persuading Lord Dartmouth to sign the necessary warrant. According to Peter Wentworth the warrant was actually in Dartmouth's hands as early as the first week in June. See A. Boyer, *Quadriennium Annae Postremum* (2nd edn., 1718), ii. 449; Dartmouth's note to G. Burnet, *A History of my own Time* (2nd edn., Oxford, 1833), vi. 89 (hereafter referred to as Burnet); *[The] Wentworth Papers*, (ed. J. J. Cartwright, 1883), p. 204.

[2] Kinnoull's memo. to Oxford, 19 Sept. 1711: ' . . . To send down my Ld. Mar to take care of the election of a new Peer ' (Brit. Mus. Portland Loan [Harley MSS.] 146) suggests that at this stage the introduction into the Lords of the new duke of Brandon was taken for granted. Even at the beginning of November the earl of Seafield was busy furthering his own campaign to fill the expected vacancy: H.M.C. *Portland MSS.* x. 201.

the Lords.[1] Though their fears may have been unnecessary they were quite genuine,[2] and together with the parlous situation of Oxford's ministry—its very existence hanging at this point on the votes of the Upper House—they explain the fervour with which the Junto lords in December 1711 contested the duke of Hamilton's patent.

They had made their intention evident enough from early November. By the middle of that month the duke had begun to feel most uneasy about his prospects; and Oxford seems to have shared his pessimism, for he seriously thought of sending Hamilton on a diplomatic mission to Vienna and so evading the issue of the patent until the ministry had weathered its other storms.[3] As for the rest of the Scottish peers, they now experienced afresh all the anxiety they had felt earlier in the summer and resumed their warnings to the government.[4] Alarm was not confined to one party in Scotland, or even to those whose immediate prospects were affected. Baillie of Jerviswood, for instance, though an opposition member, was by no means at one with his English allies at Westminster in their hostility to the patent: ' If he [Hamilton] lose it ', he wrote to Lord Polwarth on 13 November, ' the Union must break. What will be the consequences God knows, and therefore I cannot understand the meaning of the Whigs; for one would think that this will force Scotland to espouse the Pretender's right '.[5] It is not altogether surprising in the circumstances that when the second session of parliament opened on 7 December the new duke of Brandon did not take his seat in accordance with his recent title. Not until the ministers could guarantee his position would he expose himself to the indignity of a possible challenge; and so on this day of all days, when it was threatened with the repudiation of its whole peace policy, the government was deprived not only of Hamilton's own vote but also of those of several of his colleagues whose proxies the duke carried with him.[6] In the event only five Scottish peers out of sixteen attended, and though the ministry had

---

[1] *I.e.* creations leaving vacancies which would, in turn, be automatically filled by government nominees. Brit. Mus. Add. MS. 17677 EEE, fo. 395.

[2] At the beginning of December, when the queen was canvassing Lord Cowper's support both for the peace preliminaries and for the Hamilton grant, she made a point of denying any intention of making fresh Scottish creations: ' . . . In speaking on this subject was pleas'd to say to me, " That the House of Lords was already full enough. I'll warrant you, I shall take care not to make them more in hast ", etc.' *The Private Diary of Earl Cowper* (Roxburgh Club, 1833), p. 53. Cowper, formerly Godolphin's lord chancellor, was a moderate whig.

[3] H.M.C. *Portland MSS.* v. 107: Hamilton to Oxford, 9, 13 Nov. 1711; Brit. Mus. Lansdowne MS. 1236, fo. 262: The Queen to Oxford, 16 Nov. 1711.

[4] H.M.C. *Portland MSS.* x. 230: [Seafield] to Oxford, 1711 [probably November].

[5] H.M.C. *Polwarth MSS.* i. 2.

[6] *Wentworth Papers*, p. 224: Peter Wentworth to earl of Strafford, 14 Dec. 1711. ' As many proxies as could be got ready ' were despatched by Lord Kinnoull by ' the flying packet ' from Edinburgh on 3 Dec.: H.M.C. *Portland MSS.* v. 121.

the support of all five it was defeated in two vital divisions on the question of 'No Peace without Spain' by majorities of one and eight.[1]

The poor response of the Scots to the treasurer's recent appeals was a significant reflection of growing tension in the relations of the two countries. Oxford may have preferred to explain it away as an accident caused by flooded roads in the north;[2] but, as with the continued truculence of the Scottish peers throughout the next three months, it had its roots in personal frustrations and disappointments which had been building up for the best part of a year. In the first place, few of 'the sixteen' felt that the ministry had done anything like enough to reward their own services, with either offices or gratuities. The refusal to appoint a Scottish secretary of state after the death of Queensberry was a prime source of discontent, especially with Mar and Islay, the two leading aspirants to the post. It is true that the establishment of a new trade commission for Scotland in November 1711 had stayed some of the criticism, but though it gave employment ultimately to five of the sixteen only Eglinton and Balmerino were genuinely gratified by their new offices (Annandale, in fact, regarded his appointment as beneath his notice and at first declined it). Another grievance, not unconnected with the first, was the government's failure to purge public employments in Scotland of the members or allies of the hated 'Squadrone', in particular its reluctance to dismiss Montrose and Glasgow.[3] Indeed, since the end of the previous session Oxford had been receiving a steady stream of solicitations, exhortations and complaints of every kind from beyond the Border, and a plan for holding weekly meetings with Lord Mar to iron out Anglo-Scottish problems had produced little appreciable improvement.[4] On top of all this had now come the peerage dispute, which threatened to close, perhaps indefinitely, one of the most attractive avenues opened up to the Scottish peerage by the Treaty of Union. The cumulative effect was to subject the Union to its most serious period of stress since the attempted invasion of 1708 at the very time when the Oxford ministry most needed a quiescent Scotland, represented in the house of lords by a pliant contingent of peers.

Only a direct challenge to Hamilton's patent in parliament was needed to precipitate a genuine crisis out of these discontents, and this was not long delayed. Flushed with their triumph of 7 December, the whigs saw in the duke's affair an ideal opportunity to cause the government yet more acute embarrassment: not least because, by treating it as a *constitutional* rather than a political issue, they could

---

[1] H.M.C. *Polwarth MSS.* i. 3: George Baillie to Lord Polwarth, 8 Dec. 1711.
[2] *Letters and Correspondence of . . . Viscount Bolingbroke* (ed. G. Parke, 4 vols, 1798), ii. 49.
[3] Brit. Mus. Portland Loan (Harley MSS.) 146: Kinnoull to [Dupplin], 27 Oct. 1711.
[4] H.M.C. *Portland MSS.* x. 409.

hope for the sympathy and even support of a number of otherwise loyal tories. Despite ministerial protests that any discussion of the patent would infringe the prerogative, the Lords rejected, by a majority of three, a government motion for an adjournment on the 12th and ordered a full debate on Thursday, 20 December.[1] ' I designe to get into the house to hear the debate ', wrote Peter Wentworth on the 14th, ' for there's a great deal to be said of both sides, and if ever any cause was debated without party this will be so'.[2] And when the Lords assembled six days later the crowded benches and galleries plainly testified to the uncommon interest which the case had aroused. There were 114 peers present—only two fewer than on the momentous opening day of the session—and four recent arrivals from the north had brought the Scottish representation up to nine,[3] even though Hamilton himself still held aloof. The Court had left no doubt that it intended to fight the case with the utmost energy, even persuading the queen to attend *incognito* in the hope that her presence would influence wavering peers on a question affecting her own prerogative. In fact, with the house of lords so clearly holding the balance of political power in the existing crisis,[4] here were all the ingredients of a great parliamentary occasion.

Since legal issues were involved the debate was preceded by the hearing of counsel on Hamilton's behalf. The duke had instructed two of the most eminent lawyers of the day, Sir Thomas Powys and Serjeant Pratt, and Powys's opening speech was a masterly piece of legal exposition that did full justice to the occasion.[5] He began by asserting that the queen's prerogative with regard to the conferring of honours and dignities was clear and unchallengeable and that *all* the subjects of the new United Kingdom of Great Britain were equally entitled to receive such honours at the queen's hands. No one would question the right of the commons of Scotland to such a privilege. How then was it possible to make a single exception in the case of the Scottish peers? To debar them from receiving honours was to make a quite invidious distinction in one particular

---

[1] [*House of*] L[*ords*] J[*ournals*], xix. 342; Boyer, ii. 689–90.

[2] *Wentworth Papers*, p. 225.

[3] *Viz.* earls of Mar, Home, Loudon, Rosebery, Orkney and Islay; Viscount Kilsyth; Lords Balmerino and Blantyre. Six were still in Scotland: H.M.C. *Polwarth MSS.* i. 3; *L.J.* xix. 345.

[4] *Cf.* Earl Poulet's remark to Strafford in a letter written on the same day as the Hamilton debate: ' . . . the House of Lords prevailes over the Queens management with us and the strongest House of Commons that ever meet.' Brit. Mus. Add. MS. 22222, fo. 188.

[5] Speaker Onslow, who heard the debate as a young man, later remarked that Powys's speech ' was deemed a great performance ' (note to Burnet, vi. 86). Peter Wentworth, however, dissented from this view. To his mind ' they both [*i.e.* Powys and Pratt] seem'd as if they lay under difficulty, that they had no lawyers to answere, but was to suppose what objections were to be made ' (to Strafford, 21 Dec. 1711. *Wentworth Papers*. pp. 226–7).

case: indeed to reduce the Scots nobility to criminal status. Furthermore, Powys argued, to challenge Hamilton's patent was to claim that the royal prerogative of creating peers was restricted. Yet it was an accepted maxim of the constitution that the Crown could lose no prerogative that it had not already given up by the express words of an act of parliament. The Act of Union of 1707 contained no such specific limitation. It merely stated that the peers of Scotland were *by virtue of this treaty* to be represented in parliament by sixteen of their number, and the very use of these words, he suggested, seemed to intimate that other Scottish lords might sit by virtue of other rights, namely creation or succession. By the time Sir Thomas had concluded his case there was little left of a purely legal and constitutional nature for his second-string, Pratt, to say. The latter was content mainly to expatiate further on the prerogative and to insist that if the patent itself were acknowledged to be legal it entitled his Grace of Hamilton not merely to call himself duke of Brandon but to take his seat in the House in that capacity.[1]

Though the debate which followed lasted until eight o'clock, a very lengthy sitting by the standards of the day, the queen is said to have stayed in the House from start to finish.[2] To begin with their lordships clearly felt inhibited by Anne's presence—the departure of the two lawyers was followed by a long, embarrassed silence —but once the tory peer Lord Guernsey[3] had broken the ice, opposing Hamilton's right to sit as duke of Brandon, the leading partisans were soon warmly engaged. Throughout the debate the argument centred on two essential questions: one a question of legal interpretation (in this case, interpretation of the 22nd article of the Union, dealing with Scottish representation in the united parliament), the other a question of precedent (created by the elevation of the duke of Queensberry to a British peerage in May 1708 and the fact that he had sat and voted unchallenged, as duke of Dover, in two successive parliaments up to his death in July 1711). Opposition spokesmen naturally preferred to avoid the second question as far as possible. About Queensberry Lord Sunderland, for the Junto, could only argue that while the matter had been passed over

---

[1] Burnet, vi. 87; H.M.C. *House of Lords MSS*. N.S. ix. 173.

[2] *Wentworth Papers*, p. 226; Boyer, ii. 691. The Dutch agent, L'Hermitage, gave a different version: ' La reine alla a la chambre un peu devant 2 heures et S.M. y resta jusqu'a pres de 5 heures pour entendre les debats ': Brit. Mus. Add. MS. 17677 FFF, fo. 11. Altogether the proceedings lasted eight hours, having begun at noon: *L.J.* xix. 345.

[3] Formerly Heneage Finch, the celebrated lawyer. He was a man who normally commanded the respect and attention of the House, and the sophistry to which he appears to have resorted on this occasion illustrates the flimsiness of the opposition case: S.R.O. Dalhousie MS. 14/352: Balmerino to Maule, 24 Jan. 1712, reporting the debate of 20 Dec. Guernsey was the brother of Lord Nottingham who had deserted the tories earlier in the month over the issue of ' No Peace without Spain '.

in silence this did not necessarily validate his claim; nor was Hamilton's case thereby prejudged.[1] With the first question, however, the whigs felt on safer ground. They took up Powys's maxim that the prerogative could only be limited by act of parliament, and Halifax bent his considerable oratorical gifts to seek to show that such a limitation was imposed by the Act of 1707. He urged that the Act of Union had made *all* peers of Scotland peers of Great Britain in every respect except two: namely, voting in the house of lords (a power vested only in their sixteen representatives) and sitting in judgment on their peers.[2] Opponents of the patent had long since claimed that to increase Scottish representation beyond sixteen by any means would be to give the Scots a greater share of the legislative power than was designed at the time of the Union,[3] and Halifax reiterated this argument.[4] In short, the Opposition did not dispute the queen's right to bestow what titles she pleased upon the Scots; but although conceding that she was free to create Hamilton duke of Brandon they argued that she could not give him the right to sit and vote in that capacity.[5]

From the government benches it was urged, especially by Lord Abingdon, that Hamilton's case was in every way identical with Queensberry's and that by its failure to take any action in 1708 the House had already prejudged the matter. The only right of Queensberry's which had been challenged, insisted Abingdon, was his right of voting in elections of ' the sixteen ', and the very fact that this right was denied him by the House in January 1709 was itself clear proof that his status as a peer of Great Britain was accepted.[6] The most impassioned speeches from the Tory side, as was to be expected, came from the Scots themselves, with Islay, Loudoun, Balmerino and Mar their chief spokesmen. Their answer to the argument that the number of Scottish peers in parliament, as Scotsmen, must be confined to sixteen precisely in order to maintain the ' legislative balance ' was simple and categorical: since the proportion of Scots to English in both Houses had been carefully assessed in 1707 on the basis of comparative revenue, the ' freezing ' of the former could not in justice be accompanied by the

---

[1] Burnet, vi. 88; *Wentworth Papers*, p. 227. The fact that the Books of the House, recording Queensberry's introduction in 1708, referred to his ' claiming ' his place was used by Sunderland as evidence that the case was never decided.

[2] Halifax based this argument on the 23rd article of Union.

[3] *Lockhart Papers*, i. 342; Boyer, ii. 689.

[4] As reported in *Wentworth Papers*, p. 229: Peter Wentworth to Strafford, 21 Dec. 1711. See also Burnet, vi. 88.

[5] This was a distinction on which tory dissidents, notably Guernsey, laid particular stress as being perfectly consistent (so they claimed) with solicitude for the prerogative: *Wentworth Papers*, p. 227.

[6] *Ibid.* p. 227. See also Hume Brown, *op. cit.* iii. 142. Dr. W. Ferguson has pointed out to me that it was Hamilton himself who first pressed for Queensberry's disfranchisement after the 1708 election. See Wm. Robertson, *Proceedings relating to the Peerage of Scotland from . . . 1707 to . . . 1788* (Edinburgh, 1790).

elevation of any Englishman to the new peerage.[1] Like Powys,
the Scots made great play in the debate with the words *by virtue of
this treaty* in the 22nd article of the Union, and those who had helped
to negotiate the treaty reinforced his interpretation by insisting
(unanswered by the opposition) that these words were put in for
the very purpose of leaving the door open for peers other than the
sixteen to sit by creation or succession.[2] Well before the end of
the debate neither the House nor the ministers could have been in
any doubt of the genuinely bitter feelings the whole affair had
aroused in Scotland, and the bishop of Salisbury noted that the
speeches of the Scottish peers were interspersed with 'intimations
of the dismal effects that might follow, if it should go in the
negative'.[3]

As he listened to these prognostications Oxford could no longer
evade the unpalatable truth that something more than the existence
of his own ministry was in danger. Now that the Hamilton case
had become inextricably involved with the other elements in the
general political crisis Mar's former prophecy that the Union itself
might founder over this sorry affair seemed dangerously near to
realization. In his own speech the treasurer had tried desperately
to outmanoeuvre the whigs by proposing that the House should
seek the opinion of the judges, as the question was primarily one of
law; but though supported by two other Cabinet ministers, Poulet

---

[1] *Cf. Lockhart Papers*, i. 343; S.R.O. Dalhousie MS. 14/352, Balmerino's report of
the debate.   On the ratio of representatives to wealth and population see *The Treaty
of Union of Scotland and England* (ed. G. Pryde, 1950), pp. 43–44.

[2] This, without doubt, was the most unanswerable part of Hamilton's whole case
and the one which cast most discredit on the whigs, especially those Junto lords who had
themselves been active in the Union negotiations.   It also explains the singular bitterness with which the Scots reacted to the attack on the patent.   ' . . . it is too certain ',
writes Lockhart, ' that severall of the Scots Peers were cajoled and amused [in 1706]
with the hopes nay assurances (as is well known to severall English lords) of being
created hereditary Peers . . .': *Lockhart Papers*, i. 343.   Again, in the memorial which
was presented by twenty Scottish peers to Anne on 1 Jan. 1712 [see p. 269 below] this
particular grievance is emphasized more than any other: ' the Commissioners for
Scotland . . . did condescend to this Declaration, That they did not insist for greater
Numbers (by virtue of this Treaty) of Representatives in the House of Peers, than
Sixteen.   Having been assured at that Time, by several of the Commissioners for
England, that Your Majesty's Prerogative could never be thereby construed to be
restrained from granting new Patents of Honour to the Peers of Scotland, with all the
Priviledges depending thereupon; the Commissioners for Scotland thought it more
reasonable, that the Peers of that Kingdom should, by their Zeal for Your Majesty's
Service, endeavour to merit Your future Favour, as the Sole Fountain of Honour,
than to interrupt the Progress of the Union . . . with any further Demands upon Your
Majesty's Prerogative by Vertue of the Treaty.   Upon the Faith of these Assurances,
and the sacred inviolable Force of Publick Treaties, the Commissioners concluded the
Treaty, and the Parliament of Scotland did ratify the Union.'   *A Representation of the
Scotch Peers 1711/12 on Duke Hamilton's Case* (London (?), 1712): the printed version
of the Memorial, in pamphlet form.

[3] Burnet, vi. 88.   The chief prophet of doom was Islay who, in the course of what
Wentworth found ' a very moving speech ', said that ' he trembled to think of the
consequence . . . for he was sure 'twould be deem'd a breach of the Union ': *Wentworth
Papers*, p. 229.

and Harcourt, his proposal was opposed by Sunderland and Wharton on the specious ground that the matter was one of privilege rather than law, and was rejected on a vote by a majority of fourteen.[1] The flat refusal of the Junto lords to consult the judges on a matter so wholly within their province as the interpretation of the words of an act of parliament showed quite clearly that, for all their avowed solicitude for the constitution, they regarded the Hamilton affair primarily as a matter of political advantage. Nor were they interested in reaching any compromise on the main question. When an independent tory peer, Lord Pembroke, suggested towards the end of the debate that Hamilton's patent should be admitted only for the duration of his own life the idea was soon brushed aside. But despite the ruthlessness with which the whig leaders pressed their point and assailed the prerogative—a ruthlessness which disturbed some of their closest supporters and allies [2]—they were still strong enough to carry the final division by 57 votes to 52 on the resolution ' that no Patent of Honour granted to any Peer of Great Britain who was a Peer of Scotland at the time of the Union can entitle such Peer to sit and vote in Parliament or to sit upon the Trial of Peers '.[3] And not even Anne's presence was sufficient, in the event, to deter a number of non-ministerial tories or even two members of the government itself (Dartmouth and Berkeley of Stratton) from voting with the Opposition.[4]

Why did the house of lords reach this historic decision? Party motives, we can be sure, governed the hard core of uncompromising whigs; but this was not so with the Court whigs and tory rebels whose votes were the decisive factor. Were their judgments really swayed by the kind of legalistic or constitutional argument which had dominated the debate, or were there less obvious undercurrents at work? These are questions to which it is hard to give

[1] *Wentworth Papers*, p. 229; Brit. Mus. Add. MS. 17677 FFF, fo. 11: L'Hermitage to the States-General, 21 Dec. [O.S.], 1711. The voting was 63 to 49: H.M.C. *House of Lords MSS.* N.S. ix. 174. A Protest subsequently entered in the Journals of the House in the name of the Scots and ten other peers stressed the illogicality of this decision. To allow the hearing of counsel but refuse to hear the judges on the self-same question seemed singularly wrong-headed, especially as the judges had been specifically ordered to attend on the 20th and the opposition had acquiesced in this order: *L.J.* xix. 345,347.

[2] According to L'Hermitage ' un fort grand nombre ' of whig peers either absented themselves or executed a tactical withdrawal before the final division, and while he exaggerated the scale of the abstentions their existence is worth noting: Brit. Mus. Add. MS. 17677 FFF, fo. 11. Marlborough and Godolphin were among those sufficiently embarrassed to leave the Chamber before the second vote : *Wentworth Papers*, p. 229. Speaker Onslow later wrote: ' I was then a very young man, in all the warmth of party on the Whig side, yet I was much scandalised, I remember, at this behaviour of those I wished best to [*i.e.* the Junto] . . .' (note to Burnet, vi. 87).

[3] H.M.C. *House of Lords MSS.* N.S. ix. 174.

[4] See Dartmouth's note to Burnet, vi. 89. Other tories voting against Hamilton included Nottingham, Guernsey and Scarsdale: H.M.C. *House of Lords MSS.* N.S. ix. 174. There is a full division-list in Brit. Lib. Loan 29/163/10.

a clear-cut answer. To any peer approaching the debate with an open mind the case which the lawyers, the government and the Scots together put forward on the duke's behalf must have seemed convincing. But it is unlikely that very many of the 'marginal' voters in the House came prepared to assess the matter purely judicially. Lockhart, as we have seen, presupposed the existence of a widespread, almost instinctive, anti-Scottish prejudice in the light of which he normally interpreted most English behaviour. The Hamilton affair, to him, was certainly no exception, and his verdict has too readily found support among both Scottish and English historians.[1] In reality the motives of the tory and moderate whig lords who voted against the patent on 20 December were at once more complex and more subtle. Some doubtless shared Dartmouth's genuine constitutional scruples and so were predisposed in favour of the arguments advanced by the Junto. But the attitude of the majority was more probably determined by two considerations of a different nature. One was the jealous concern many English peers felt for their own order and their apprehensions lest it should be swamped by a flood of Scottish creations:[2] this was prejudice, no doubt, but not of the crude variety which Lockhart depicts. The other, and more powerful, factor was the general aversion which both whig and tory peers had developed for the whole system of choosing sixteen Scottish representatives to sit in the Upper House. The most recent example of this system in action, the proceedings at Edinburgh in 1710, had conclusively confirmed that the so-called 'election' was a ludicrous formality, with success a virtual certainty for anyone on the official ministerial list of recommended peers; and the effect, as at least one Scotsman admitted, had been to make the English nobility as a whole 'weary of our elections'. Some weeks after the debate of 20 December the earl of Mar wrote pessimistically to his brother that 'as long as they [the elections] last they have such an apprehension of the acquisition of strength the Crown gets by us, and as it were in opposition to both their parties, that they will ever treat us as enimies, Whige and Torie being alike affraid of the power of the Crown'.[3] This 'apprehension', unuttered though it was (for obvious reasons) in the debate itself, may well provide the most important key to the alarm and *furor* created in the Lords by the grant of Hamilton's patent, a grant which focussed new attention on the iniquities of the elective system by the threat of frequent 'by-elections' which it seemed to carry.

[1] *E.g.* James Mackinnon, *The Union of England and Scotland* (1896), p. 423; Turberville, *op. cit.* p. 151.

[2] H.M.C. *House of Lords MSS.* N.S. ix., intro., p. xxii; *Lockhart Papers*, i. 341; Brit. Mus. Add. MS. 17677 FFF, fo. 11.

[3] H.M.C. *Mar and Kellie MSS.*, pp. 492, 495: Mar to Sir James Erskine, 27 Dec. 1711, 17 Jan. 1712.

The full consequences of the events of 20 December were not immediately apparent. It is true that the Scots, both at Westminster and north of the Border, reacted with considerable anger to the Lords' decision. Quite clearly they regarded it as a national rebuff, not merely as a personal one, and as early as the 21st 'some hot head fellows' were already proposing, according to Wentworth, ' that neither Commoners nor Lords of that Nation ought to come into the house any more '.[1] But these extreme counsels did not at once prevail. Burnet tells how a meeting of the Scottish representative peers in London [2] resulted instead in a decision to make a formal representation to the queen, complaining of the Lords' vote as ' a breach of the union, and a mark of disgrace put on the whole peers of Scotland '. This memorial, drafted jointly by Mar, Islay and Hamilton, was submitted for the approval of the Scottish commoners at a further meeting on Sunday the 30th, before being signed by the peers on the 31st and presented to Anne on New Year's Day. The version subsequently printed [3] makes it plain that this was something more than a statement of grievances preceding a request for redress. It was intended to serve as a further reminder to the Court that failure to provide redress might well lead to the dissolution of the Union. True, the threat was decently veiled by fulsome professions of loyalty to the queen; but that it was meant to be implicit there can be no doubt.[4] What is not so certain is how this threat was interpreted by the signatories themselves. There were those who honestly saw in a formal dissolution of the Union the only honourable satisfaction for their grievances and who believed, like Rosebery, ' that the Whigs, Tories and Scots all desyre it . . . and that nothing stops it but the Court ';[5] but there seem to have been just as many who regarded it as a useful instrument of political bargaining, the likeliest way of bringing pressure on the ministry, rather than as a practicable expedient. ' As to dissolveing the Union in a Parliamentary way, I despair of it ', wrote the earl of Mar on 27 December, ' or if it were possible in doing of it, they would fix the succession, and in that case Scotland wou'd lose any aw it could have over England ';[6] and developing this theme in a later report to his brother in Edinburgh he explained that ' Tho' both

---

[1] *Wentworth Papers*, p. 229: Peter Wentworth to Strafford, 21 Dec. 1711. See also H.M.C. *Mar and Kellie MSS.* p. 491.

[2] Probably on 28 Dec. See H.M.C. *Mar and Kellie MSS.* p. 492.

[3] See note 2, p. 266.

[4] The crux of the matter was contained in this paragraph from the *Representation*: ' We beg leave to assure Your Majesty, That whatever may be Our Fate, we shall always be ready *either in a united or separate State* [my italics] to sacrifice every Thing that is dear to us, for the Defence of the Prerogative of the Crown, and for the Honour of Your Majesty and Your Successors.' See also Burnet, vi. 90–91; H.M.C. *Polwarth MSS.* i. 5: Geo. Baillie to Lord Marchmont, 1 Jan. 1712; *Wentworth Papers*, p. 236.

[5] H.M.C. *Mar and Kellie MSS.* p. 492: earl of Mar to Sir James Erskine, 27 Dec. 1711; S.R.O. Dalhousie MS. 14/352; Balmerino to Maule, 15 Jan. 1712.

[6] H.M.C. *Mar and Kellie MSS.* p. 492.

parties be wearie of the Union, they will upon no tearmes that I can yett see quitt with the Union in a legall way. . . . With you [in Scotland] I have no doubt but the dissolveing of the Union is thought to be possible and pritty easie in a Parliamentary way; but that I cannot conceave, and I fear it will be found so, and I wish our countrymen could be made to understand this.' [1]

That Mar and his sympathizers succeeded for a while in impressing caution on their colleagues is proved not only by the generally restrained tone of the memorial but by the attitude of the peers to a more extravagant representation made by Hamilton personally. The duke was satisfied neither with the memorial nor with the queens' encouraging reply, and in a personal audience with Anne he demanded 'in the name of the whole nation' that she should dismiss her secretary of state, Lord Dartmouth, from the government for voting against the patent, 'for they could never believe her majesty was ine arnest, whilst a man that had her seals in his pocket voted against them, and received no mark of her displeasure'. We have Dartmouth's own account of what took place at this interview:

> The queen said, she had done all she could to persuade me to comply: but I understood it to be against law, and she believed I acted sincerely, with affection to her service, and zeal for my country; therefore had deceived nobody; . . . [she] did not think it for her own service to comply with them in that particular: for she believed it would give great offence to the English lords, and do the Scotch more harm than good. Then duke Hamilton proposed, that an act of parliament might be brought in to confirm his and the duke of Queensbury's patents; to which the queen gave him no answer. [2]

If Dartmouth's story is accurate the duke was inviting a snub, and the fact that it was duly administered does not seem to have caused his colleagues much distress. They thought his action ill-advised and did not hesitate to say so. Indeed, the duke of Atholl called on Dartmouth the day after Hamilton's audience to disassociate both himself and the rest of the Scottish peers from what had been said and to ask him to convey their views to the queen. [3]

But while they were not prepared as yet to commit themselves publicly to extreme demands, in their private talks with ministers the peers made little secret of their growing exasperation. The treasurer, at least, was aware by the end of December that even if the Union itself managed to survive the immediate shock dealt it by the Hamilton affair the whole Scottish contingent was likely to prove most unreliable for weeks, possibly months, to come. Its leaders

---

[1] H.M.C. *Mar and Kellie MSS.* pp. 494-5: Mar to Erskine, 17 Jan. 1712.

[2] Dartmouth's note to Burnet, vi. 89. For several days after the vote of 20 Dec. there was a strong belief at Court that Dartmouth would be dismissed. See *Wentworth Papers*, p. 233: Peter Wentworth to Strafford, 28 Dec. 1711.

[3] Burnet, vi. 89 n.

had already taken care to warn the ministry unofficially that unless prompt satisfaction was forthcoming from the government side they would ' all join with the other partie ', and Oxford believed this to be a threat more capable of swift realization than the more spectacular official warnings about the fate of the Union.[1]   In fact this situation may well have had more to do than is generally realized with the remarkable and highly controversial step which he took at the close of the Christmas recess, when twelve new peers were created *en bloc* to ensure the safety of his government and the passage of the peace preliminaries through parliament.   Certainly, when Dartmouth subsequently asked him the reason for such a desperate measure Oxford's reply was that ' the Scotch lords were grown so extravagant in their demands, that it was high time to let them see they were not so much wanted as they imagined; for they were now come to expect a reward for every vote they gave'.[2]

When the house of lords reassembled on 2 January 1712 the first division, on a Court motion for adjournment, demonstrated to all but the most obtuse political observers that the treasurer's gamble had succeeded, at least in its immediate objective.   Barring unforeseen developments the government could now expect to survive the current crisis; and this meant automatically that the problem of appeasing the duke of Hamilton in particular, and the Scots in general, lost something of its pressing urgency in ministerial eyes.   ' Lord Treasurer's dozen ' had made ' the sixteen ' less indispensable.   Nevertheless the problem had still to be resolved and it continued to exercise both the Cabinet and the queen a great deal during the first weeks of the new year.   The crux of the problem was now this: since the events of 20 December it had been pretty clear that nothing short of an act of parliament reversing the decision of the Lords and restoring the *status quo* of 1707 would appease Scottish opinion at large; [3] yet the ministry, for all its recent accession of strength, could not guarantee the success of any such bill.   Some Scottish peers, Mar for instance, might privately have accepted the justice of alternative schemes of compensation, but with feeling running so high and ' the bent of the country . . . so much for the dissolution of the Union ' they could scarcely afford publicly to accept any compromise.[4]   On the other hand, as

---

[1] H.M.C. *Mar and Kellie MSS.* p. 493.   Whether the Scottish leaders could have persuaded their more rabid tory colleagues, Eglinton and Balmerino for instance, to pursue such a policy is by no means certain.   Eglinton avowed two weeks later that ' if we please he shall absent but if he be present by God he will never let the Whigs gain a vote of the tories if he cane help it ': S.R.O. Dalhousie MS. 14/352: Balmerino to Maule, 15 Jan. 1712.

[2] Dartmouth's note to Burnet, vi. 95.

[3] This was what the duke had insisted on in his audience with Anne, and though his colleagues had not supported him then many of them believed in the necessity of such a measure.

[4] H.M.C. *Mar and Kellie MSS.* pp. 492, 495.

long as the peerage question continued to cut across normal party divisions [1] any expedient (like the proposed bill) which preserved the existing system of electing Scottish peers was sure to arouse sufficient tory opposition to jeopardize its success.

Such was the government's dilemma; and however sincere it was in its desire to accommodate the Scottish aristocracy [2] it could not be optimistic about its chances of reaching an acceptable settlement. Still, there was one circumstance in its favour. In the continued absence of any firm offer of terms from the whig opposition the Scots stood to gain little, at this juncture, by an immediate and open breach with the Court; they could hardly refuse to negotiate. In fact on Sunday, 13 January, their leaders [3] accepted a ministerial invitation to a joint meeting at the Cockpit in Whitehall with a group of Cabinet ministers. Its purpose was strictly limited—to discuss the preliminary steps to be taken after the adjournment [4]— but within this context it was successful. It was agreed that the representative peers should continue for the time being to support the ministry, pending an address to the queen to ' lay proposals ' before the House, and that if the address were carried these proposals were to be discussed beforehand with the Scots. [5]

The ministry's first objective, that of persuading the house of lords formally to reopen the peerage question, was successfully attained. In the course of her message to the House on 17 January Anne once again made her own views patently clear: she referred to the extreme concern felt in Scotland at the fact that the royal prerogative had been ' strictly barred ' against the Scottish peers alone, reminded the lords that this was ' a matter which sensibly affects her ' and requested ' their advice and concurrence in finding out the best method of settling this affair to the satisfaction of the whole Kingdom '. [6] After Oxford, in the brief debate that followed, had reiterated the absolute necessity of doing something ' to satisfie so great a part of the Nation ' the House agreed to a suggestion of Godolphin's that it should go into committee on this question the following day. [7] No doubt the fresh rumours that had

---

[1] In a letter to his brother, dated 17 Jan, Mar wrote: ' . . . As to this affair of ours, there is nothing so like a Whige as a Torie and nothing so like a Torie as a Whig—a cat out of a hole and a cate in a hole ' : H.M.C. *Mar and Kellie MSS.* p. 495.

[2] Even Balmerino, reluctant as he was to concede the existence of any good will on the part of the English, was forced to admit that ' certainly the queen is most heartie in our affair, so is the Treasurer, Shrewsbury, Paulett & Lord Keeper & some others ': S.R.O. Dalhousie MS. 14/352: to Maule, 15 Jan. 1712.

[3] They included Mar and Islay, but not Hamilton.

[4] Following the sitting on 2 Jan. parliament had been adjourned for a fortnight.

[5] H.M.C. *Portland MSS.* v. 138; *Mar and Kellie MSS.* p. 494. At the same time the Scots ' endeavoured to show the impractibility [*sic*] of any [expedient] succeeding ': *ibid.* 495.

[6] L.J. xix. 358; H.M.C. *Polwarth MSS.* i. 6: George Baillie to earl of Marchmont, 19 Jan. 1712.

[7] *Wentworth Papers*, pp. 253-4: Peter Wentworth to Strafford, 18 Jan. 1712.

begun to circulate of an intended parliamentary boycott by the Scots [1] helped to make the Lords more responsive to the promptings of the Court. In any event, a Committee of the Whole House, meeting on 18 January under Lord Ferrers's chairmanship, began an exhaustive discussion which was subsequently prolonged over three further sittings—on 21 and 25 January and on 4 February.[2]

Ironically the speed with which the Lords acted appears to have caught the ministry unprepared. Its own proposals were not ready by the 18th and government spokesmen on that day were forced to confine themselves mainly to generalities and the expression of pious hopes.[3] Nothing concrete was forthcoming from the government benches until the 21st and the suggestion made then was one that had already been privately canvassed for some weeks.[4] The House was invited to consider ' whether it would not be to make the Union more complete if a number of the Lords of the North part of Great Britain sat here by inheritance and not by election ', provided the rest of the Scottish peers consented to the change.[5] Discussion of this proposal occupied the rest of the sitting on the 21st and was then adjourned to the 25th without a vote being taken, but even on the first day it was clear that, as it stood, the plan would not command general support, so much so that Oxford had already begun to devise new expedients by the 24th.[6] For one thing, there was the practical difficulty of deciding how many Scottish peers should be given hereditary seats if the representative principle were abandoned. If opposition to the idea in Scotland was to be overcome the number would have to be high, and thirty-two seems to have been the minimum asked for by the Scots. To Lord Wharton, on the other hand, ' a number of hereditary peers meant only 16, not half a peer more '; and this was probably the view of most Junto whigs and not a few tories.[7] There was also the more basic problem of whether the representative

---

[1] Rumours that were not entirely without foundation. The idea had been seriously discussed by ' the sixteen ' at a private meeting on 15 Jan. but only Annandale was in favour of giving immediate effect to it: S.R.O. Dalhousie MS. 14/352: Balmerino to Maule, 15 Jan.

[2] H.M.C. *House of Lords MSS.* N.S. ix. 174–5.

[3] *Ibid.* 174. The treasurer, who had probably expected the House to rest content at first with an address to the queen to lay proposals before it, does not seem to have begun to formulate his own ideas until the following day. His draft notes, endorsed ' Scotland ' and dated 19 January 1711/12, are in Brit. Mus. Portland Loan (Harley MSS.) 29/218.

[4] Mar had told his brother on 27 Dec. of a proposal ' to offer us a considerable number of our families to be chose and made by the Queen peers, with all the priviledges of sitting, etc., as they are here to the number of perhaps thertie or some more; that the incapacity should be taken off the rest of us; that our titles and precedencies should continue, and that we should be capable of being elected in the House of Commons ': H.M.C. *Mar and Kellie MSS.* p. 492.

[5] H.M.C. *House of Lords MSS.* N.S. ix. 174; Burnet, vi. 99.

[6] Brit. Mus. Portland Loan (Harley MSS.) 29/218.

[7] S.R.O. Dalhousie MS. 14/352 : Balmerino to Maule, 24 Jan. 1712.

principle *could* legally be abandoned without dissolving the Union. The debate[1] mainly hinged, in fact, on which of the articles of the Union were ' fundamental ', and therefore unalterable by parliament, and which were not; and more especially on whether the article providing for an elective representation of Scottish peers should be considered ' fundamental '. At length, after a great deal of wrangling, the committee did manage to agree on the 25th that this article *was* alterable by parliament without any violation of the Union, provided it was done ' at the request of the Peers of Great Britain who were Peers of Scotland before the Union '.   But the very use of the phrase ' at the request of ' in the resolution represented a defeat for the Court.   The ministers had favoured a different formula, one which stipulated only the ' consent ' of the Scottish peers, not their ' request ', but the opposition objected that this word implied a retention of some legislative power by the Scots and sustained their objection in a division by 60 votes to 52; [2] so that the government was forced to accept an alternative which it well knew to be impracticable—for there was little or no chance of a full muster of the Scottish peers in Edinburgh agreeing to make the proposal which the resolution envisaged.[3]

Oxford had not quite shot his bolt, however.   Between the third meeting of the committee on 25 January and its next appointed meeting on 4 February he made a new offer privately to the Scots.   As Mar reported it, this was

> that the Queen should be enabled by an Act of Parliament to call the peers of Scotland togither to lay this matter before them, in order to their laying before her Majestie what they wou'd propose in this affair, and then betwixt and [*sic*] that meeting the Queen's servants wou'd concert with the Scots here a reasonable scheme to be laid before them. . . .[4]

The plan was open to two technical objections: that the peers of Scotland had no power to act alone, that is without the other two estates, least of all in effecting any modification of the treaty of

[1] The debates in the committee are nowhere well reported.   Visitors were being fairly regularly excluded from the House at the time: see *Wentworth Papers*, p. 260.

[2] *Ibid.* p. 260; H.M.C. *Mar and Kellie MSS.* p. 496; *House of Lords MSS.* N.S. ix. 174.

[3] See H.M.C. *Mar and Kellie MSS.* p. 496: Mar to Sir James Erskine, 14 Feb. 1712. The Scots were being required, in effect, to propose the abolition of the existing system of election before being assured of any satisfactory substitute.

[4] *Ibid. Cf.* Oxford's memorandum of 24 Jan. in H.M.C. *Portland MSS.* x. 167; also the rather different scheme envisaged in his note of 19 Jan.: ' An Act to enable her matie to convene all the Peers of Great Britain who were Peers of Scotland at the time of the Union or the successors to their honors to meet & elect out of such Peers a limited number to be commissioned by her matie to treat with the like number of her Peers of Great Brittain in the like manner commissioned to consider of proper methods of rendring the Union more compleat with respect to the Peers of Scotland sitting in the Parliamt. of Great Britt.   And that the Proceedings of the sd. Comrs. to be laid before her matie & the Parlmt. of Great Brittain in their next Session ': Brit. Mus. Portland Loan 29/218.

1706; and that a meeting of all three estates could be construed as an *ipso facto* dissolution of the Union.[1] But neither was really responsible for the chilly reception given to the treasurer's offer when it was put before a meeting of Scottish peers and M.P.s at Westminster. The main complaint was that it was merely a delaying tactic on Oxford's part and, for this reason alone, should be emphatically rejected. If it were proposed in the House, the ministers were told, the Scots would vote against it. In consequence, when the committee met on 4 February there was no move at all from the government side for a fresh approach to the problem. The Scots, for their part, remained frankly unco-operative. Lord Mar announced bluntly to the committee that ' they had nothing to propose ', while Islay ' declared for himself and his country Lords that he wished rather than hoped anything can come from it '.[2]

Thus the government's attempt to solve the problem in parliament ended disappointingly, if not surprisingly, in total deadlock. As the Dutch agent in London remarked, no party had shown any genuine willingness to compromise;[3] and in the last fortnight, at least, only the ministry had demonstrated any real enthusiasm for a settlement or any conviction that a solution was possible. More serious, it seemed that the only result of reopening the matter in parliament had been still further to aggravate the grievances already present, for the Scottish peers now proceeded to carry out their long-rumoured threat of boycotting the house of lords. They had already shown their hand on 31 January when they staged a ' walk-out ' just before an important vote was due on a Bill to repeal the Naturalization Act,[4] and the decision to carry out the full-scale boycott was taken at the same meeting as rejected Oxford's final proposal—that is, before the Committee of the Whole House held its final session. A cautious minority appear to have had private doubts of the wisdom of such a step (the failure of the token walk-out on the 31st to embarrass the ministry in any way had been only too apparent),[5] but they were swept along by their more militant colleagues who saw it as the best way left of bringing pressure both on the Court and on the tory peers as a whole. ' We did not resolve to abandon the House entirely ', explained Mar subsequently, ' but to neglect attending it, or when any of us should be

[1] S.R.O. Dalhousie MS. 14/352: Balmerino to Maule, 15 and 26 Jan. 1712.

[2] H.M.C. *Mar and Kellie MSS.* p. 496; *House of Lords MSS.* N.S. ix. 175.

[3] Brit. Mus. Add. MS. 17677 FFF, fo. 38: L'Hermitage to the States-General, 29 Jan./9 Feb. 1712.

[4] Even before this two of the sixteen, Annandale and Balmerino, had been making their own private protest by deliberating absenting themselves for several days: S.R.O. Dalhousie MS. 14/352: Balmerino to Maule, 24 and 26 Jan. 1712. See also Balmerino's letter to Oxford, 29 Jan. 1712, in H.M.C. *Portland MSS.* v. 141.

[5] A tory victory by 18 votes in the division on the repeal of the Naturalization Act had suggested that, on party issues anyway, Scottish support was certainly not indispensable: *Wentworth Papers*, p. 261.

there on a summons or by accident, we should not act til it was by the consent of the major parte of the sixteen present here '.[1]   To the English tories, however, it was plain desertion; and to everyone the action seemed all the graver in view of fresh storms in Anglo-Scottish relations that were rapidly blowing up from the house of commons.   Here the high tories, much to Oxford's embarrassment, were giving enthusiastic backing to a measure which had long been dear to the hearts of episcopalian members like George Lockhart and Sir Alexander Erskine: a Bill for according greater toleration to the episcopal church in Scotland.   The alarm which presbyterians felt at the progress of the Toleration Bill was intensified by the prospect that it would be followed by a still more offensive measure, the restoration of rights of patronage in Scotland.[2]   All in all, the outlook for the Union could not have seemed much bleaker than at the beginning of February 1712.

Then, quite suddenly and to the apparent astonishment of all observers, came a relaxation of tension.   After only two days' absence from the House, on 7 and 8 February, the Scottish peers returned; and Burnet tells us that from then on they continued to take part in parliamentary business, without further protest, for the remainder of the session.   As we shall see, Burnet rather exaggerates the suddenness with which the crisis was resolved.   But it is fairly plain that from the time the Scots resumed their seats on 9 February the atmosphere began to improve, so that by the end of the month only the habitual Jeremiahs were prophesying the imminent demise of the Union.   The causes of this transformation were naturally the subject of a good deal of speculation.   The ministers vaguely explained that ' an expedient would be found that would be to the satisfaction of the peers of Scotland ', but when no such expedient was forthcoming the politicians were left to draw their own conclusions.   The whigs clearly assumed, with the bishop of Salisbury, that such satisfaction as had been given the Scottish peers must have taken an essentially ' private and personal ' form.   Indeed, Burnet's dark hints about the inroads made into the civil list at this time by Oxford probably reflect a supposition that was fairly

[1] H.M.C. *Mar and Kellie MSS.* p. 496.   The original intention was for the Scottish commoners to join the peers in their stand, but this idea was eventually dropped: S.R.O. Dalhousie MS. 14/352: Balmerino to Maule, 24 Jan. 1712.   John Anderson, in his *Historical and Genealogical Memoirs of the House of Hamilton* (Edinburgh, 1825), gives a brief and thoroughly unsatisfactory account of the Patent dispute in which he states that the boycott began after the adverse vote of 20 December and *ended* after the vote of the Committee on 25 January—a sorry confusion of the facts.   Anderson believed, quite mistakenly, that the second vote went far towards appeasing the Scottish peers.

[2] See *Lockhart Papers*, i. 339-40, 378-9.   The resentment aroused by the encroachment of a ' Prelatic Parliament ' on Scottish religious preserves can only be fully understood in the light of earlier presbyterian reactions to the Greenshields case (1709-11). See Trevelyan, *op. cit.* iii. 236-8.

general among both parties. The venality of the Scottish aristocracy was, after all, already a by-word among politicians; the assumption that the treasurer could only have extricated his government from the Hamilton crisis by scattering its *largesse* even more generously than before was, in the circumstances, perfectly logical.

Whether the assumption was correct is not so certain. It is a point on which Oxford's own voluminous papers do not fully enlighten us, but there is strong evidence to the contrary. In particular, it is possible to say with some confidence that the collapse of the boycott was not primarily brought about by material inducements. The best the peers appear to have got from the ministry at this juncture was vague promises of what would be done for them as soon as the signing of peace made parliament less dangerous,[1] and months later their expectations were as far from being fulfilled as in February.[2] Nor, as far as is known, was Hamilton himself bought off. At the time it was confidently predicted that he would be made master of the horse, a coveted Court appointment left vacant in mid-January by the dismissal of the duke of Somerset, but expectation was disappointed ; similarly ungratified were the supposed ambitions of the duchess of Hamilton to be groom of the stole, for all the coffee-house gossip that she ' hath made her stays of late with loops for the gold key '.[3] But in any case it is possible to find a perfectly adequate motive behind the Scots' decision to resume their attendance in the Lords without searching for examples of bribery and corruption. The truth is that the experiment of the boycott, brief though it was, had not been a happy one. Hamilton had suffered more than anyone, since as a direct result of his colleagues' absence he was defeated in an important vote on 8 February during the hearing of his law-suit over the Gerrard estate.[4] But the main trouble was that the boycott coincided with the arrival in the Upper House of the Toleration Bill (officially the Episcopal Communion [Scotland] Bill), which passed the Commons on 7 February by 152 votes to 17, was given its first reading in the Lords

---

[1] H.M.C. *Portland MSS*. x. 266, 272: Mar to Oxford, 21 May, 4 June 1712.

[2] ' People will be so soured with delays ', wrote Mar in May 1712, ' . . . that most of that country will not attend next sessions ' (*ibid.* x. 267). The light thrown by the Harley papers on certain individual cases suggests that in the lifetime of this parliament (*i.e.* up to the summer of 1713) the Scots were fed mainly on promises and but little on hard cash. *E.g.* Eglinton in the early part of 1712 was given every reason to expect a payment of £500, euphemistically described as a sum ' due to me before the Union ' ; but he was still waiting ruefully for the money in Aug. 1713: *ibid.* x. 196, 203, 300. Northesk, another who was promised the Queen's ' allowance ' during the 1712 session, had no satisfaction until the end of 1713 and even then had to be content with reappointment to the Scottish trade commission: *ibid.* x. 204-5.

[3] *Wentworth Papers*, p. 258: Lord Berkeley of Stratton to Strafford, 25 Jan. 1712.

[4] H.M.C. *House of Lords MSS*. N.S. ix. 189; *Mar and Kellie MSS*. p. 497; *Wentworth Papers*, p. 248. Hamilton's opponent in this law-suit was Lord Mohun, with whom he fought his celebrated fatal duel in Nov. 1712.

on the 8th and was due for its second reading three days later.¹
So angry were the tories at losing Scottish support for their other
business that a number of them decided to withhold their support
from this Bill unless the Scots returned; some even resolved to
vote with the whigs against it.

> This [Mar tells us] made severall of us think again, and tho' some
> of us would not have been for bringing in the bill at this time had
> they been consulted, yet since it was past one House we thought it
> being lost in the House of Lords would be of worse effects; . . .
> if the bill should chance to miscairie by our not attending we should
> get little thanks from our constituents at home.²

Accordingly a meeting of the representative peers was called at
Hamilton's house, either on the evening of the 8th or on the morning
of the 9th, to discuss the new turn of events. Of the twelve who
attended five were opposed to returning to the house of lords,
including Islay and Hamilton (the latter being openly antagonistic
to the Bill itself); the other seven, including Mar and Home,
favoured a return on the grounds that since the Bill ' only or prin-
cipally concerned Scotland and not [*sic*] a bussiness of the parties
here, it was not breaking our resolution to go to the House on this
occation, espetially since our resolution was not to abandon the
House but only to neglect attending it . . . '. Hamilton was reported ' exceeding angrie ' at the majority decision and tried to
reverse it at a new meeting the following day, but without success.³

On 9 February, therefore, ten Scottish peers took their seats;⁴
and while the proceedings on the Episcopal Communion Bill continued (*i.e.* on the 11th, 13th, and 15th) there were never fewer than
this number in the House, all of them firmly supporting the measure.
Again on the 23rd and 26th, after the amended Bill had been sent
up again by the Commons for final consideration, the Scots were
duly represented.⁵ What many contemporary observers do not tell
us,⁶ though the fact is plain enough in the *Lords' Journals*, is that the
boycott continued to operate on every parliamentary day between
the 9th and 26th on which the House was not directly concerned
with the Toleration Bill.⁷ It was only when the Scots appeared in
strength on 27 February—the day after the Lords had completed
their work on the Bill—that they formally abandoned their policy

---

¹ *House of Commons' Journals*, xvii. 73; L.J. xix. 373, 375.

² H.M.C. *Mar and Kellie MSS.* p. 497.

³ *Ibid.* The names of the peers attending these meetings are given in cipher but
some can be identified from a similar cipher in H.M.C. *Portland MSS.* x. 342.

⁴ The queen came to the House on this day, a Saturday, to give her assent to a
number of bills and the Scots tried to pass off their reappearance by announcing ' they
went purely out of respect to the Queen ': *Wentworth Papers*, p. 248.

⁵ L.J. xix. 374–9, 383–5; Brit. Mus. Add. MS. 17677 FFF, fo. 56.

⁶ This is true not only of Burnet but of L'Hermitage and Peter Wentworth.

⁷ L.J. xix. 377 380–2.

of harassing the tories into revoking the decisions of 20 December and 25 January. But though the final capitulation was delayed, and was even now qualified by the continued resistance of two of the rebels,[1] it was none the less inevitable. The inconsistency of their recent conduct had further reduced the effectiveness of a stand which even at the start had been of questionable value. ' Our Scots Peers ' secession from the House of Lords makes much noise ', as a minister of the Kirk had written, ' but they doe not hold by it. They somtimes come and somtimes goe, and they render themselves base in the eyes of the English.' [2]

With the end of the boycott the whole peerage question receded for some time into the background. From March 1712 until the malt tax precipitated a new crisis in the following year Anglo-Scottish relations subsided into a relative, if still uneasy, calm. Hamilton himself made his peace with the ministry in the summer of 1712, although he characteristically maintained his personal protest against the Lords' proceedings by still refusing to enter the House.[3] In November a fatal duel with Lord Mohun ended his own interest in the case; but his death did not remove the lingering resentment of his countrymen. A fresh petition to the queen from the peers of Scotland in January 1713, though it failed to stimulate the government to fresh action, demonstrated how much the events of twelve months earlier still rankled.[4] It was no surprise, therefore, that the vote of 20 December 1711 provided a major grievance of ' the sixteen ' when they joined with the whigs in the great attack on the Union on 1 June 1713; [5] nor that it remained a firm barrier

---

[1] ' The Scots Peers are all boughted [enclosed in the fold] again, except the Duke of Hamiltoun and another [the marquess of Annandale] ', notes Wodrow in March 1712: Rev. R. Wodrow, *Analecta* (Maitland Club, 1842), ii. 30.

[2] *Ibid.* ii. 8 (20 Feb. 1712). One must recognize, however, that the dilemma created by the Toleration Bill was a genuine one. There is little specific evidence to support Mackinnon's charge that the stand of the Scottish peers collapsed mainly because of ' the self-seeking spirit of the Earls of Mar and Kinnoull, who, consulting their private interests rather than the honour of their order and their country, broke away from their colleagues in the course of the quarrel ': *The Union of England and Scotland*, p. 423.

[3] It is clear from the *Lords' Journals* that neither he nor the truculent Annandale took any part in the remainder of the session. Sir Herbert Maxwell, *A History of the House of Douglas* (2 vols, 1902), ii. 213, was wrong in thinking that the duke returned to the House along with his colleagues, *i.e.* at the end of February. Hamilton's reconciliation to the ministry came with his appointment as ambassador in Paris in Aug. 1712, and he was later confirmed in favour by the grant of the lucrative office of master general of the ordnance in September and the award of the Garter in October.

[4] This petition is printed in H.M.C. *Portland MSS.* x. 167–8. See also a petition of the Scottish peers [1712] concerning the creation of a hereditary parliamentary peerage: *ibid.* 474.

[5] Brit. Mus. Add. MS. 17677 GGG, fo. 202: L'Hermitage to the States-General, London, 9 June [N.S.] 1713. *Cf.* also [earl of Mar] to Oxford, 12 June 1713: ' If you do not now contrive some relief as to the Malt Tax in Scotland and some redress for that of the peerage, it will not be in the power of man to prevent addresses from all in Scotland against the Union by the meeting of the next Parliament ': H.M.C. *Portland MSS.* x. 296.

against reconciliation in the remaining troubled months of the reign, when the bulk of the Scottish contingent in both Houses was in semi-opposition.

Nothing could prevail, however, against the stubborn determination of the Lords to preclude any possibility of a Scottish ' invasion ' of their House. The apprehensions which lay at the root of this determination, as we have seen, defy any superficial analysis; but whether they sprang from plain anti-Scottish prejudice, or from a jealous solicitude among peers of English birth for the privileges of their own order, or from a purely political objection to strengthening the hand of the ministry of the day, they had this much in common: they persisted long after the purely party motives affecting the decision of December 1711 had lost all validity. They were still strong enough by 1720, for instance, to defeat an attempt by the second duke of Queensberry to claim the seat which his father had filled, as duke of Dover, up to the time of his death in July 1711.[1] In fact, a further sixty years and more were to elapse before the issues raised by Hamilton's patent were formally and conclusively settled. In the interim not only the dukes of Hamilton but every Scottish peer with a British title [2] remained technically subject to the disqualification imposed in 1711, in addition to the disfranchisement effected by the Queensberry decision of 17 January 1709.[3] Moreover the very combination of these two disabilities aggravated the injury done in the former case, as well as creating an injury out of the latter. The 1709 decision had remained a just one ' only so long as what was implicit in it remained true, namely, that such Scottish peers were allowed to sit as members in their own right '.[4] But, as Vicary Gibbs has pointed out, ' First to tell a man that because he is Duke of Brandon, he cannot vote as Duke of Hamilton . . . and to follow that up 2 years later by telling him that because he is Duke of Hamilton, he cannot sit and vote as Duke of Brandon . . . seems the height of injustice '.[5]

Yet despite the obvious unfairness of these two votes and the illogicalities which they involved [6] the resentment they caused in Scotland gradually died down, and by the seventeen-twenties, at any rate, it would be stretching the evidence to claim that they still imposed a violent strain on Anglo-Scottish relations. The fact

---

[1] W. S. Holdsworth, *History of English Law*, xi. 7.   G. E. C., *Complete Peerage* (ed. Vicary Gibbs), iv. 447 n.

[2] Though not, ironically, those with a pre-Union English title, like Argyll.

[3] That is, the decision to deny a vote in the election of ' the sixteen ' to peers awarded a peerage of England before the Union, or of Great Britain after it.   See p. 91 above.

[4] *Treaty of Union*, ed. Pryde, p. 53.

[5] G.E.C., *Complete Peerage*, iv. 447 n.

[6] See also Sir James Fergusson, *The Sixteen Peers of Scotland* (Oxford, 1960), p. 39. Not the least inane feature of the whole situation was the fact that English peers with Scottish titles were entitled to both the privileges denied to Scottish peers with British titles.

that for the greater part of the eighteenth century this double incapacity never affected more than a tiny proportion of the whole body of Scottish peers obviously played its part in assuaging the feelings of Scotsmen as a whole. But it was Walpole's government which, together with the house of Lords, provided the most effective balm. Acting on a precedent which, curiously enough, had been established by Oxford himself in December 1711, the whig ministry secured British earldoms in 1722 for the *eldest sons* of both Montrose and Roxburghe. Ten years before, at the very height of the Hamilton crisis, the heir of the earl of Kinnoull had been summoned to the house of lords as one of Oxford's ' dozen ' and had taken his seat unchallenged in his British dignity of Lord Hay. When in 1719 he succeeded to the earldom on his father's death the Lords decided that this did not invalidate his right to sit in virtue of his British title.[1] Presumably George I's ministers assumed in 1722 that these precedents would still hold good, though the fact that they chose to elevate two minors who could not take their seats for some years suggests a conscious effort to avoid any appearance of political sharp-practice. In any event, once Earls Graham and Ker had been accepted as members of the Upper House—as they were in 1727 and 1730, still during the lifetime of their fathers—they could hardly be ejected if and when they succeeded to their Scottish dukedoms of Montrose and Roxburghe.[2] By a simple yet ingenious device a way was thus found of evading, in certain individual cases, the consequences of the Hamilton vote. Had it ever been abused the dying embers of the Hamilton affair would probably have been stirred up afresh; but in fact it was an expedient employed very sparingly indeed.[3]

Not until 1782, however, did it finally become unnecessary. It was then that the eighth duke of Hamilton resurrected the seventy-year-old claim to a seat in the house of lords as duke of Brandon. This time the judges were consulted, and their opinion was unanimous that the royal prerogative was not curtailed by the Act of Union and that the duke was fully entitled to *all* the privileges of a

[1] Turberville, *op. cit.* p. 152.

[2] The 1st Earl Graham did not, as it happened, outlive his father; but his brother William succeeded to the British earldom in 1731 and then, without prejudice to his hereditary seat, to the Scottish dukedom in 1742. The 1st Earl Ker eventually succeeded his father as 2nd duke of Roxburghe in Feb. 1741.

[3] In 1766 Argyll's eldest son was created Lord Sundridge; but as the vote of Dec. 1711 had never affected the dukes of Argyll this was not a comparable case. In 1776 the heirs of the earls of Marchmont and Bute also received British peerages with the titles of Lord Hume of Berwick and Lord Cardiff (G.E.C., *Complete Peerage*, iv. 448 n.), but the former died during his father's lifetime (the earldom of Marchmont became extinct in 1794) and by the time Lord Cardiff succeeded to the earldom of Bute in 1794 this particular road to a hereditary seat at Westminster was no longer necessary. Professor Mark Thomson's statement that ' frequent advantage was taken of this way of giving the Scottish nobility hereditary seats in the House of Lords ', *A Constitutional History of England, 1642-1801* (1938), p. 185, is, I think, a little misleading.

peer of Great Britain.   When it decided to endorse this verdict on 6 June 1782 [1] the House not only remedied a personal and national injustice; it supplied an ending long overdue to a chapter of much importance in the early history of the Union.

[1] *L.J.* xxxvi. 517.

5

TRADE, THE SCOTS AND THE
PARLIAMENTARY CRISIS OF 1713

(WITH CLYVE JONES)

The parliamentary session of 1713, which ran from 9 April to 16 July, saw the first major setback for the Harley ministry in the House of Commons since its leader had taken office in August 1710. At the same time it witnessed a serious crisis in the House of Lords, which took the ministry to the brink of defeat. Once again a Tory administration was threatened with loss of control over the upper House, a fate it had only escaped in December 1711, following defeats over 'No Peace without Spain' and the case of the Duke of Hamilton's British peerage,[1] by persuading the Queen to make a block creation of 12 peers. And once again it was to be questions raised by the peace negotiations with France and by the grievances of Scotland's parliamentary representatives that placed the government of Robert Harley, Earl of Oxford, in peril.

From the 1711–12 session of Anne's fourth Parliament the ministry had finally emerged in triumph and its Whig opponents, both commoners and peers, in retreat and disarray. But the opening of the 1713 session had been many months delayed pending the conclusion of the final peace at Utrecht, and during the intervening winter Tory nerves became stretched and Whig morale recovered. Eventually, on the last day of March the British plenipotentairies, Lord Strafford and Bishop Robinson of Bristol, were able to put their signatures on the Treaties of Peace and Commerce with France. Three days later the treaties arrived in London, and on 7 April the Queen in Council ratified them. The making of peace was undoubtedly part of the Crown's prerogative, and thus the final terms of the peace treaty did not need formal parliamentary approval. Nevertheless, Parliament did have a part still to play, for the commercial treaty with France needed legislation to give it effect. The two crucial articles, the eighth and ninth, could not come into force until existing anti-French protectionist acts were repealed and the new articles were ratified in what would, in practice, be a money bill. Other than obstructing this bill, the only possible shot left in the Whigs' locker after their long battle against Oxford's peace was to try to persuade both Houses to withhold their blessing from the settlement as a whole in their votes over the address in

For discussions of the two crises of December 1711 see C. Jones, 'The Division that Never Was: New Evidence on the Aborted Vote of 8 December 1711 on "No Peace without Spain"', *Parl. Hist.*, 2 (1983), pp. 191-202; and G.S. Holmes, 'The Hamilton Affair of 1711–12: A Crisis in Anglo-Scottish Relations', *E.H.R.*, 77 (1962); above, 83-108. We should like to thank the following for allowing us to use and quote from their papers: the Duke of Atholl, the Marquess of Bute, the Marquess of Downshire, Lord Binning and Sir John Clerk of Penicuik.

reply to the Queen's Speech.

To judge by Oxford's calm and methodical preparations for the opening of Parliament, he was confident there would be no direct attack on the peace. His continuing contacts with one of the lords of the Whig Junto, Halifax, gave him a sure understanding of their now resigned attitude to the dynastic and territorial settlement. His apprehensions, if any, were focused on the signs that the Whigs might be planning to switch public attention, as soon as they judged the time ripe, to the sensitive issue of the Protestant Succession. The Queen's assurance in her speech from the throne on 9 April that a 'perfect friendship' subsisted between the courts of Hanover and St James's was plainly written in by the Treasurer with an eye to forestalling any early move by the opposition; and it appears to have been sufficient, for the time being at least, to calm the fears of the many Tories with Hanoverian sympathies.[2] With Hanover and the Whigs unable to decide for many weeks on a course of joint action, the Whigs had to wait until almost the very end of the session for their first suitable opportunity to make direct use of the Succession issue.

Balked on this front, they sought for other weapons with which to embarrass and wound the ministry; and six weeks went by before these weapons came to hand. Two issues then arose to which the government's armour suddenly appeared unexpectedly vulnerable: the cause of Scotland over the malt tax and the flaring-up of opposition to the Bill of Commerce. By exploiting them, like the seasoned parliamentary campaigners they were, the Whigs were able by June 1713 to recapture the political initiative they had lost since February 1712.

The earliest faint sign that the government might be heading for trouble was detectable in the Commons' Committee of Ways and Means on 22 April, though at the time the setback seemed relatively mild and the ministry may even have been prepared for it. The government wanted to bring the land tax down to three shillings in the pound, a one-shilling reduction on the standard wartime rate. But it was forced to yield to the pressure of the country gentlemen on the back benches, who had expected a halving of the tax and would settle for nothing more than two shillings in the pound. With a general election only a few months away, the Tory country gentlemen saw no better way of recommending themselves to their constituents than a substantial reduction of direct taxation after 11 years of unremitting burden.[3] The instinct of self-preservation proved stronger than any ties of obligation to the ministry. The Court party in the Commons, making the best of a bad job, promised to co-operate with the back-benchers in securing a two-shilling rate, while the latter undertook in return to see that the resulting shortfall of £500,000 in revenue was made up in some other way. And even at this early stage at least one Scottish Member, George Baillie, the Squadrone M.P. for Berwickshire began to voice fears that one result of this bargain would be an increase in the malt

[2] J. Macpherson, *Original Papers; Containing the Secret History of Great Britain, from the Restoration to the Accession of the House of Hanover*, (2 vols., 1775), II, 488–9.
[3] Berkshire R.O., Trumbull MSS., Alphab. LI, Thomas Bateman to Sir William Trumbull, 17 Apr.

tax and its imposition on Scotland.[4]

The ministry, however, was to experience a less tractable spirit from the Commons over the field of trade regulations with France. The Treaty of Commerce provided for two major changes in Britain's commercial relations with her neighbours. It accorded to France the most-favoured-nation treatment which, since 1703, had been virtually (if not officially) enjoyed by Portugal, our ally under the Methuen Treaties. It also stipulated that the tariff on French goods was to return to the low level at which it had stood in 1664, before the protectionist policies of Colbert had inaugurated an era of bitter commercial rivalry between the two kingdoms.[5] The ministry, realizing that the legislation needed to repeal the anti-French trade laws might delay the passing of the Commerce Bill until the end of June, introduced a preliminary and interim measure, which it believed would be less controversial. The bill was designed to effect a two-month suspension of the additional, prohibitive, duties levied on French wine since 1696. Its attempted introduction on 2 May proved less encouraging than had been expected. After the Whigs, with James Stanhope as their chief spokesman, had skilfully played on anti-French sentiments, the government received a majority of only 29 on the motion to put the question and one of 40 on the question for its introduction.[6] The narrowness of the margin was somewhat disturbing, especially when it was clear that the Whigs had gained the support of some independent Tories.

The ministry now ran into opposition from the Portuguese envoy in London who delivered a memorial threatening an embargo on the import of British woollens into his country if Portuguese wines lost the preferential position in the British market which they had enjoyed since 1704.[7] The leading Whigs in the Commons made full play with the damage such an embargo would inflict on the British economy. In consequence the ministry carried the second reading of the Wines Bill on 6 May by a mere 25 votes. However, the next division on the same day on the commitment of the bill was carried by a majority of 102 after many Tory M.P.s had flocked into the House. The circumstances of the second vote strongly suggest a good deal of 'whipping'; but the scale of the success was mainly due to a concession by the ministry, in promising to reveal the terms of the Commerce Treaty before the committee stage of

---

[4] *Ibid.*, Add. MS. 136/3, Ralph Bridges to Trumbull, 21 Apr.; Mellerstain Letters, (Lord Binning, Mellerstain, Berwickshire), V (unfol.), [George Baillie to his wife], 23 Apr. As early as 8 April there had been a joint meeting of Scottish M.P.s and peers to discuss 'matters of the Utmost consequence': Huntington Library, LO 9116 (Loudoun MSS)., George Lockhart to Loudoun, 7 Apr.

[5] *C.J.*, XVII, 333–4. For a valuable analysis of the economic background and implications of the eighth and ninth articles of the treaty, of the economic grounds of the opposition to the bill giving effect to them and of the consequences of its defeat, see D.C. Coleman, 'Politics and Economics in the Age of Anne: The Case of the Anglo-French Trade Treaty of 1713', in *Trade, Government and Economy in Pre-Industrial England*, eds. D.C. Coleman and A.H. John (1976), pp. 187–211.

[6] *C.J.*, XVI, 310, 315.

[7] B.L., Add. MS. 17677 GGG, f. 164, L'Hermitage despatch, 8/19 May (hereafter cited as L'Hermitage).

the Wines Bill was reached on 12 May.[8] It was doubtless seen at the time as a tactical ploy; but the Court managers were to have good cause to regret it. On 9 May the Commerce Treaty was laid before the House and Members soon saw that by the side of its more controversial articles, the Wines Bill seemed a very minor matter. The committee stage was, against the wishes of the Court, put off for a further week. On the 14th the storm broke over the Commerce Treaty and the Wines Bill was never heard of again.

The Portuguese memorial submitted earlier in the month against the Wines Bill had alarmed the textile interest in many parts of the country. Petitions began to pour into the Commons.[9] As the Commerce Bill could be expected to affect the same interests and many more besides, Whig tactics were naturally dictated by the hope of delaying its early stages as long as possible to enable maximum opposition to the bill to build up.[10] The chances of defeating the bill in the Commons seemed negligible in the light of the vast Tory majority;[11] but the more effective the rearguard action which the Whigs managed to fight in St Stephen's Chapel, the brighter, it seemed, would be the party's prospects when the measure reached the Lords. Since it was a money bill the peers would not be constitutionally entitled to amend it. But they could reject it.

On 14 May the ministry sought the Commons' approval to bring in the Bill of Ratification, and the debate, largely owing to the delaying tactics of the Whigs, lasted until 10 p.m. Although the Court put up a spirited defence of the terms of the Commerce Treaty and mustered an impressive team of businessmen to put its case, the Whigs appeared at the time to have had the better of the economic arguments.[12] On the other hand, Sir Thomas Hanmer, one of the knights of the shire for Suffolk, gave every impression of speaking for the solid body of the Tory landed interest in urging the introduction of the bill: and it is of particular note, in view of his remarkable change of opinion the following month, that at this stage Hanmer was seemingly unafflicted by doubts of any kind. When at length the question was called for, something like 40 M.P.s had already left the House since the start of the debate, ten hours before; but the Court still achieved a heavy majority, recording 252 votes against 130. The next day the Hanoverian resident, Kreienberg, was to purvey an astonishing report to his government that the minority was made up of 60 Whigs (all those of that party then left in the House, according to his information) and 70 Tories. But this is simply not credible and finds no support in any other account. On the other hand, it is clear that the Whigs managed to capture

[8]   For the proceedings on 6 May, see W. Pittis, *The History of the Third Session of the Last Parliament* (1713), pp. 92–3; Berks. R.O., Trumbull Add. MS. 136/3, R. Bridges to Trumbull, 8 May; *C.J.*, XVII, 315; L'Hermitage, 8/19 May.
[9]   *C.J.*, XVII, 355–8.
[10] L'Hermitage (f. 177), 15/26 May.
[11] For a view of the optimism of the ministry see *The Wentworth Papers*, ed. J.J. Cartwright (1883), p. 333.
[12] Coleman, 'Politics and Economics in the Age of Anne', casts doubt on the validity of some of their arguments. A good contemporary account of them is in Niedersächsisches Staatsarchiv, Hannover, Cal. Br. 24 England, 113a, ff. 76, 106, Kreienberg despatch, 15/26 May 1713 (hereafter cited as Kreienberg).

some Tory votes; and that among perhaps a dozen to 20 defectors were at least two Tory businessmen — Robert Heysham, a West India merchant, and the scrivener, Sir George Newland — who had supported the opposition from the floor of the House as well as with their votes.[13] Significantly, there were also some welcome Scottish reinforcements to the minority.[14] None the less, as both the Dutch agent, L'Hermitage, and Kreienberg reported on the following day, there was a general consensus of opinion that the bill would pass the Commons with little difficulty; and L'Hermitage felt that even in the Lords, where opposition was expected to be more effective, the Whigs could have small chance of ultimate success.[15]

However, the leading Whig, General Stanhope, in his speech on the 14th had touched upon the argument which was in the event to prove decisive for the future of the bill. He made a strong plea that the Commerce Bill should be divorced from the peace settlement, which must be accepted as a *fait accompli*. The bill should not be considered a party measure, and should be judged on its own merits in regard to its effect on the economy of the nation.[16] By this, of course, he had hoped to detach Tory Members from its support. Here again, time was a fundamental ingredient in Whig strategy: not only time to enable them to organize representations against the bill, but time to give the Tories a chance to shed their original attitudes to the treaty, based as they were largely on party bias and a general enthusiasm for the peace settlement as a whole. By a strange irony, the ministry itself, though its supporters were urging all possible speed,[17] allowed a delay of more than a fortnight to go by before the Bill was introduced on 30 May. This may have been due to difficulties in drafting the proposed Bill of Ratification. But whatever the reason the delay enabled the Whigs to orchestrate a propaganda campaign against the bill which soon produced results.[18] Meanwhile the House of Lords had begun to show a lively interest. On 18 May Lord Somers had moved for a host of papers relating to Anglo-French trade since 1696 to be laid before the House by the Board of Trade. He had carried his point without opposition, many leading ministers being absent from the House at the time. This was to be the origin of a long-drawn-out Lords inquiry into the background of the recent Commerce Treaty; and when it eventually got under way on 28 May the government made a confident and effective start. Oxford defended the treaty in 'a noble and cunning

---

[13] *Ibid.* For the proceedings on 14 May, see also *Wentworth Papers*, pp. 334–6; L'Hermitage (ff. 176–7), 15/26 May; A. Boyer, *The History of the Life and Reign of Queen Anne* (1722), pp. 632–3; *C.J.*, XVII, 353; Mellerstain Letters, V, [Baillie to his wife], 14 May, postscript 16 May.

[14] See H.M.C., *Polwarth MSS.*, I, 10, for George Baillie's reasons for opposing the bill at this stage (especially the threat to the Scottish fishing trade).

[15] L'Hermitage, 15/26 May; Kreienberg, 15/26 May.

[16] See brief accounts of Stanhope's speech in Boyer, *Anne*, p. 633, and *Wentworth Papers*, p. 335.

[17] Kreienberg, 15/26 May.

[18] The first petition presented directly against the treaty (as opposed to the earlier Wine Bill) came before the Commons on 25 May. It was followed on the 26th, 27th and 30th by seven more (*C.J.*, XVII, 377–9, 385–6).

speech in answer to Wharton, Coupar [Cowper] and Halifax', promising in due course to lay his opinion before them. According to Lord Balmerino, 'Halifax was forced to say, "Nobly spoke"'.[19]

All the same, on the eve of the Commerce Bill's introduction into the Commons, some ministers were beginning to betray traces of anxiety about the future.[20] It was disturbing to contemplate the possibility that the issue might ultimately be decided not by party prejudice, which would have reacted in their favour, but by national prejudice, which was more likely to work against them. As one of them put it, 'it hath been soe long a receiv'd opinion that a trade with France is prejudicial to this kingdom that it is noe easie task to beat them out of it'.[21] Old bogies died hard.[22] The first reading in the Commons on 30 May passed off without serious alarms, despite two divisions unsuccessfully forced by the Whigs. The only portent, it seemed, was that 'in both questions all the Scots were on the losing side'.[23] Before the second reading on 4 June, however, the steady stream of petitions against the trade treaty had suddenly become a flood; no fewer than eight were laid before the House on the very day of the bill's next stage.[24] The debate on that day proved to be another marathon of nine hours,[25] and the division which took place on the motion for commitment provided clear evidence that the Whigs were gaining ground, if only slightly. The Court secured 202 votes, the opposition 135;[26] so that although there were 45 fewer Members voting, compared with the first big clash on 14 May, the opposition vote actually rose by five while the government's vote dropped by 50. There was still no suggestion that the bill could ultimately be defeated in the lower House — so far most Tories who felt uneasy about the prospect of a freer commerce with France were still tending to absent themselves rather than join forces with the Whigs.[27] But the attitude of the Scots was further confirmed, with the greater part of their Tory Members again deserting the Court,[28] and their alienation now began to look distinctly ominous. For should there be a corresponding move by the 16 representative peers when the Commerce Bill came to the Lords, the position of strength

[19]   L'Hermitage (f. 182), 19/30 May; *L.J.*, XIX, 549; Scottish R.O., GD45/14/352/18 (Dalhousie MSS.), [Lord Balmerino to Henry Maule], 28 May.

[20]   *Letters and Correspondence . . . of . . . Lord Visc. Bolingbroke*, ed. G. Parke (4 vols., 1798), IV, 138.

[21]   *Wentworth Papers*, p. 331.

[22]   How hard, and why, in this case, is explained in Coleman, 'Politics and Economics in the Age of Anne', 196–205.

[23]   *C.J.*, XVII, 386; Mellerstain Letters, V, [Baillie to his wife], 30 May.

[24]   *C.J.*, XVII, 391–3. On 3 June the Whigs had scored an unexpected success in the Commons over the demolition of Dunkirk: *ibid.*, 390; L'Hermitage,(f. 209), 5/16 June; Berks. R.O., Trumbull MSS., Alphab. LI, T. Bateman to Trumbull, 3 June.

[25]   L'Hermitage (f. 210), 5/16 June; Mellerstain Letters, V, [Baillie to his wife], 4 June.

[26]   *C.J.*, XVII, 402.

[27]   This is confirmed by L'Hermitage (f. 210) who noted on 5 June that a number of Tory M.P.s were staying away from the House in order to avoid making an unpleasant choice between the political interests of the Court and the economic interests of their own constituencies.

[28]   *Ibid.* A recently discovered division list showing how the Scottish M.P.s voted on 4 June is printed below in the Appendix.

which the government had enjoyed there since January 1712 would be completely undermined.

It is doubtful whether any member of the Oxford ministry would have been prepared at the beginning of June to rule out this possibility, for it was the government's misfortune that at this particular juncture its problems had been suddenly complicated by a sharp deterioration in Anglo-Scottish relations. The Union had suffered recurrent stresses since the first year of its life, most of them over issues with parliamentary consequences.[29] But the most serious shock yet to the fabric of 1707 occurred in late May and early June 1713. The Treaty of Union had guaranteed that taxation in Great Britain would be imposed on a basis of general equity. In addition article 14, as amended by the Scottish Parliament, had granted Scotland explicit exemption from payment of the malt tax for the duration of the war. When, therefore, the Commons on 22 May passed a Malt Tax Bill which imposed a levy of 6d. per bushel on English and Scottish malt alike, there were instant and bitter complaints from the Scots that both provisions had been ignored. The second, admittedly, had been no more than a technical infringement: fighting was over, even though the signatures had yet to be appended to the treaties between Britain and Spain. But the first had undoubtedly been disregarded. There could be nothing 'equitable' about an act which taxed all British malt at the same rate, regardless of the fact that Scottish barley was much inferior to English in quality and commanded much lower prices. Why, then, did the Oxford ministry risk arousing Scottish hostility, especially at a time when it was engaged in shepherding a major piece of legislation through Parliament?

The fact is that the controversial clause of the Malt Bill, in the form in which it eventually passed the Commons, was not the work of the ministry at all. It was essentially a back-bench measure, forced on an unwilling Court by 'the countrey gentlemen of England'. Without doubt there was sympathy in the Cabinet with the Scottish plea for a reduction of the tax, and at the time the bill was introduced official hints were dropped that some redress would be made in committee.[30] Moreover, in spite of Lockhart's charge of insincerity,[31] the ministers do seem to have done their best to ensure that justice was done. It is true that when Lockhart himself, at the committee stage on 18 May, proposed that Scotland should be granted total exemption he got no official support; but a subsequent suggestion from the Scottish Members that a duty of 3d. a bushel instead of 6d. should be levied north of the border did receive ministerial backing, and was carried by the casting vote of the chairman,

---

[29] For example, over the abolition of the Scottish Privy Council (1708); the Treasons Act (1709); the depriving the Duke of Queensberry of his right to vote in the election of Scottish representative peers (see C. Jones, 'Godolphin, the Whig Junto and the Scots: A New Lords Division List from 1709', *Scottish Historical Review*, LVIII [1979], 158–74); the Greenshields case and the Hamilton peerage case of 1711, and the Scottish Toleration and Patronage Acts of 1712.

[30] *Bolingbroke Corresp.*, IV, 138; H.M.C., *Polwarth MSS.*, I, 9; Mellerstain Letters, V, [Baillie to his wife], 12 May. A series of detailed arguments against the Scottish malt tax submitted to Oxford can be found in B.L., Loan 29/218.

[31] *The Lockhart Papers*, ed. A. Aufrere (2 vols., 1817), I, 416.

John Conyers.[32] The very next day, however, the Commons refused to accept the amendment and ordered it to be recommitted. According to one source, the opposition came from 'the Whiggs & Octr. Clubb', who overrode a combination of 'the Scots and the Court' by 125 to 100.[33] But perhaps the deciding factor was the attitude of independent Country Tories representing some of the northern, western and Welsh counties, who felt aggrieved that the Scots should receive preferential treatment while their own economically-poor constituencies had to shoulder the full burden.[34] In the second committee, on the 20th, the Court once again struggled hard to carry the reduction: but this time, though there was again only one vote in it when the committee divided on the clause, the decision went against them and the Scots.[35] On 21 May,

> upon reporting the bill [wrote Baillie] to the Commons, the 6d was agreed to 139 to 104 and upon a motion for leaving out the clause relating to Scot[land] it passed in the negative 147 to 115 so that there is nothing left to us now but to try to get the time of commencement of the duty allowed from June to December [1713].

The next day in the Commons the bill passed 'and the attempt that was made to alter the Commencement of the duty had the same fate with the rest'. Baillie's advice to his fellow Scotsmen was to 'make all the Malt they can before the middle of June'.[36]

From then on events moved quickly to a climax. On 12 May there had been a preliminary meeting, called together by Lord Balmerino on the insistence of the Scottish M.P.s, at which Balmerino had hoped for a unanimous resolution to bring in a bill for the dissolution of the Union. He pinned his faith on Ilay (still in Scotland), who would 'be more alerte on this head than many of our Lords because he is discontented'. The meeting, however, 'ended in the general opinion that it would be impossible to get free of this Malt tax . . . that ane endevour to throw the whole bill out would be in vain But our commons thought they would get some abatement'.[37] These hopes having by 22 May clearly proved illusory,

[32]   Mellerstain Letters, V, [Baillie to his wife], 19 May. Conyers was the chairman of Ways and Means.

[33]   Berks. R.O., Trumbull Add. MS. 136/3, R. Bridges to Trumbull, 1 June; *C.J.*, XVII, 359. According to George Baillie, 'the Whigs have dealt basely by us for they either left the house or went against us' (Mellerstain letters, V, [to his wife], 19 May).

[34]   Pittis, *Third Session*, p. 113; H.M.C., *Polwarth MSS.*, I, 9. For some of their names see tellers for the opposition in *C.J.*, XVII, 359–73, *passim*.

[35]   By 132 to 131. What most of the justly aggrieved Scots overlooked, however, was that no fewer than 12 of their own number were out of town on the day in question, and a thirteenth, William Livingston (Aberdeen Burghs) was absent from the House though in London; so that to some extent the Scots contributed to their own misfortunes. See H.M.C., *Polwarth MSS.*, I, 10, Baillie to Polwarth, 21 May.

[36]   Mellerstain Letters, V, [Baillie to his wife], 21 and 23 May.

[37]   Scottish R.O., GD45/14/352/16, [Balmerino to Maule], 12 May. It was reported that Ilay, who had gone to Scotland 'upon some concert, to feel the pulses of some upon this [the dissolution]', had 'at a public entertainment, drunk a new kind of health, even to the speedy and legal dissolution of the Union!': *The Correspondence of the Rev. Robert Wodrow*, ed. T. M'Crie (3 vols., Edinburgh, 1842–3), I, 461, [Wodrow] to J[ames] H[art], 8 June and Hart to Wodrow, 30 May.

on the following day a meeting of the Scottish commoners[38] was 'warmly pressed' by George Lockhart and Sir Alexander Erskine to move for a bill to dissolve the Union. Lockhart did not hold out extravagant hopes of success at the first attempt, but in view of the party divisions in England he thought it 'not improbable that some considerable party might take us by the hand and carry our business through'. That the meeting approved this startling proposal almost unanimously is indicative of the extent to which normal political differences among Scottish M.P.s had become submerged by a national sense of grievance. The Squadrone Members and the Whigs among them were placated by a promise to include guarantees of the Protestant Succession in the proposed bill, while ministerialists like Pringle, William Cochrane and Sir Hugh Paterson stifled whatever misgivings they might have felt. Robert Pringle, for one, was under no illusions as to the practicality of dissolving the Union. He was later to remark that 'theres never one knowing man in England has any such thoughts as to be free of us, whatever may be pretended at this time'; for it was clear that the Union was 'the strongest Bullwark for the Protestant Succession'. Nevertheless the meeting concluded with the Members agreeing to seek the co-operation of the representative peers.[39]

On 26 May the joint meeting of M.P.s and peers took place at the Blue Posts tavern in the Haymarket. According to George Baillie, there was no debate for there was general agreement on the course to be taken.[40] The only counter-arguments were put forward by Baillie himself, in order to gain time (he had not been at the meeting on the 23rd). He urged that the poor prospects of success at the present juncture 'would tye down the Union the harder upon Scotland and consequently defeat all hopes of success upon other occasion'; that this would increase divisions in Scotland and make it impossible for them to unite against future measures; that it was too great a step to be taken without the advice of their constituents. He suggested a constitutional obstacle too; in his view the Union could not be dissolved without the consent of the Parliaments of both kingdoms. Baillie stood alone, and the meeting came to a unanimous resolution to bring in a bill of dissolution. The Duke of Argyll, Lord Mar, George Lockhart and John Cockburn were deputed to inform the Queen. Balmerino, like others, was realistic enough to recognize no hope of success this session, but with an election in the offing, he saw the attempt at breaking the Union as a step towards endeavouring 'to have nather Lord nor Commoner chosen next parl[iamen]t who is not of this mind

---

38   We are fortunate that George Baillie, whose letters are so illuminating for this session of Parliament, also compiled a memorandum on the malt tax crisis which details the political moves of the Scots and the Whigs against the ministry from 23 May to 2 June. Though written in the third person — Baillie being referred to as Jerviswood — it is in Baillie's own hand (Mellerstain Miscellaneous Papers, 1st Series, Box 4, Item 384, 'Memorandum about the Union').

39   H.M.C., *Polwarth MSS.*, I, 12; *Lockhart Papers*, I, 422; Scottish R.O., GD18/3150/3 (Clerk of Penicuik MSS.), Pringle to John Clerk, 6 June.

40   There was a meeting of the Scottish peers arranged by Lord Mar at Ilay's lodgings an hour before the joint meeting where they were 'all very unanimous and zealous to agree to the Commons proposal' (GD45/14/352/17, [Balmerino to Maule], 26 May; Huntington Library, LO 8868, Mar to Loudoun, 25 May).

and who will have it in their hand to force the ministrie . . . to let us go'.[41]

In the meantime, the Treasurer, whose intelligence system was as usual working well — Bolingbroke had a meeting with several Scottish Members on the evening of 25 May — had got wind of what was afoot. Indeed he had already tried to deter the leading conspirators, without success.[42] Similar efforts by William Bromley and Hanmer were equally unavailing, and so were those of Anne herself when the Scottish deputation had their audience on 26 May, and were told by the Queen that their intentions were 'rash'. All they achieved was to convince the Scots that their chances of gaining any significant support from the Tories were slight, and therefore to persuade them to make their first attempt, at the earliest opportunity, in the House of Lords, where Whig assistance — could they secure it — was more likely to prove effective.[43] This decision was taken at a meeting on 27 May, at which Argyll and Ilay, supported by General Ross, suggested that the Scots should oppose all English parties in everything if they would not support the dissolution of the Union.[44] Baillie demurred, claiming the freedom to vote as he saw fit, particularly concerning the Treaty of Commerce which he believed would 'prove the ruin of the trade of Scot[land]'. His stand apparently gave Lord Mar and others the excuse 'to declare they would not oppose the Court in the Treaty of Commerce', a step which (Baillie claimed) 'otherwise they durst not have ventured upon, for they say if it be reasonable that Jerv[iswood] be at liberty on the one hand it is as reasonable we be at liberty on the other, supposing we think it a good Treaty of Commerce'. The general opinion of the meeting appeared to blame Baillie for thus causing a split in the otherwise united ranks of the Scots. He, however, had been playing a tactical game, and he was not displeased with the result. He had ensured that by furnishing certain lords 'with a handle not to oppose the Court' they could not join with the Whigs whole-heartedly and thus be 'more favourably stated with them than the Squadrone'. This, he calculated,

41   Mellerstain 'Memorandum'; Mellerstain Letters, V, [Baillie to his wife], 28 May, in which the M.P. confessed his despair: 'I mean whither the Union is broke or continued, both must bring ruin on Scot[land]'. Balmerino reported that 'Jerviswood was full of shifts to put it off . . . but finding not one man of his mind (some I believe there were but durst not own it) he did agree' (Scottish R.O., GD45/14/352/17, [to Maule], 26 May).

42   *Lockhart Papers*, I, 424–6; GD45/14/352/17. Bolingbroke also dined with Eglinton and Rosebery on the evening of 27 May (GD45/14/352/18, [Balmerino to Maule], 28 May). John Crookshanks, comptroller-general of the Scottish customs living in London, had told Oxford on 26 May that the Scottish M.P.s were influenced by some of the peers 'for accomplishing their private views more then the publick good, and when they are satisfyed, the Clamour for the Country ceases' (B.L., Loan 29/218).

43   *Lockhart Papers*, I, 426–9, 432–3; L'Hermitage (f. 196), 29 May/9 June; GD45/14/348/ 3, Sir Alexander Erskine to [Maule], [2 June] misdated 2 May; Kreienberg (f. 114), 29 May (for Anne's reaction).

44   Lockhart reported that the two brothers on 27 May did 'roar and exclaim bloodily against the Union, and seem very positive that the Whig Lords would join to dissolve if our peers would help in the meantime to slap the ministry'. He went on to hint, as did another observer, that there was personal pique behind their position: National Library of Scotland, MS. Acc. 7228/1 (Newhailes Papers), [Lockhart to ? Sir David Dalrymple], 28 May [1713]; Atholl MSS. (Duke of Atholl, Blair Castle, Blair Atholl, Perthshire), 45/11/29, John Douglas to Atholl, 13 June 1713.

would give him and his Squadrone friends 'the means to ruin their credit at the next Election by laying the blame upon them for the failing of the dissolution and at the same time might keep their ground with the Whigs'.[45]

Despite these differences, the Scots inevitably had to make approaches to the Whigs, and in order to strengthen their bid they began openly to co-operate with the opposition in the Commons, where in one division on 28 May a combination of the two inflicted a minor defeat on the Court.[46] On the same day the Earl of Findlater moved in the House of Lords for a day to consider the state of the nation. He was seconded by Lord Eglinton, and Monday, 1 June was agreed upon. Lord Treasurer Oxford, normally the most phlegmatic of men, commented acidly to Balmerino that the Scots were like a man with the toothache who was prepared to have his own head cut off in order to cure it.[47]

Everything depended now on how the Whigs would react to these developments. Their leaders were in a particularly awkward posi.ion. They could scarcely fail to appreciate the possibilities of exploiting the new parliamentary situation which had arisen; and while it was unfortunate that during the proceedings on the Malt Bill their followers had been noticeably unsympathetic to the Scottish cause,[48] a sudden change of face when the measure came before the Lords would involve no betrayal of party principle. But the future of the Union was a different matter. For the Junto lords to identify themselves now with a deliberate attempt to break it up, when seven years before they had done their utmost to bring it into being, would be both cynical and discreditable. Nevertheless, it has been the generally accepted verdict of historians that the Junto succumbed to the temptation put before them, and that they supported the demand for a bill dissolving the Union in the hope of binding the Scottish contingent to the opposition for the remainder of the session.[49] But this view is based on a misunderstanding of the events of the last few days of May, and more particularly of the crucial debate of 1 June

---

[45]   Mellerstain 'Memorandum'; Mellerstain Letters, V, [Baillie to his wife], 28 May. Lockhart described Mar, Findlater and Loudoun as being against opposing the Court for 'they believed the Whigs would be as much against us as the Court' (N.L.S., MS. Acc. 7228/1).

[46]   Scottish support enabled the Whigs to uphold the right of the Quakers to vote in parliamentary elections without taking the statutory oaths (C.J., XVII, 385; B.L., Loan 29/45J, newsletter, 2/13 June; cf. Bolingbroke Corresp., IV, 140; GD45/14/352/18, Balmerino reported that the votes were carried 'only by 19 or there about which shows how we can cast the balance'; N.L.S., MS. Acc. 7228/1, Lockhart wrote that after the defeat the confounded Court 'fell a flattering us').

[47]   Mellerstain 'Memorandum'. There had been a meeting of Scottish peers on the evening of the 27th to co-ordinate their moves in the Lords the following day (GD45/14/352/18). Lockhart reported that at this meeting Kilsyth and Linlithgow were against opposing the Court (N.L.S., MS. Acc. 7228/1).

[48]   Berks. R.O., Neville MSS., D/EN. F23/2, [Charles Aldworth to the Duke of Northumberland, 20 May 1713]; H.M.C. Polwarth MSS., I, 10–11.

[49]   See K. Feiling, A History of the Tory Party (Oxford, 1924), p.449; W.L. Mathieson, Scotland and the Union 1695–1747 (Glasgow, 1905), pp. 293–4; G.M. Trevelyan, England under Queen Anne (3 vols., 1930–34), III, 241; E.L. Ellis, 'The Whig Junto' (Oxford D.Phil. thesis, 1961), pp. 770–1; and, more recently, B.W. Hill, The Growth of Parliamentary Parties 1689–1742 (1976), p. 139.

in the House of Lords, and does rather less than justice to the integrity and sense of responsibility of the Whig leaders.

As late as 29 May, L'Hermitage still believed that the majority of Whigs, like most Tories and all the Court dependants, would positively oppose any dissolution of the Union.[50] And three letters written by Lord Halifax to Oxford, from the 26th to 28th, suggest (if they are not to be taken as deliberate pieces of deception) that his first impulse and that of several of his fellow leaders was to support the Treasurer in opposing 'the wild proceedings with which we are threatened'.[51] But concerned as they were with their failure to gain ground in the House of Lords this session, few of the leading figures in the party felt, at the eleventh hour, that they could afford wholly to ignore what seemed an ideal opportunity of winning over 'the sixteen'. The problem was, how far could they reasonably go in responding to the overtures of the Scots? Wharton, characteristically, seems to have been prepared to go farther than most; Somers to have exercised the most restraint. Ill-health had by this time drastically restricted Somers's parliamentary activities; but he still kept something of his moral hold on the party, and at a crucial Whig policy-meeting held at the Duke of Somerset's house at the end of May it was his sage counsel which prevailed, and not the more extreme course advocated by Wharton. In fact the latter's normal equanimity and good humour was so disturbed by the cautious tone of the meeting that he dissociated himself from the whole proceedings and retired to his seat in Buckinghamshire.[52]

Yet it was natural, after all, that the majority of his fellow leaders, finding themselves in this extremely delicate position, should want, and try to get, the best of both worlds: to secure the Whigs the immediate advantage of Scottish support, without doing any permanent damage to the Union, or endangering the Hanoverian Succession, which had been their main concern in championing the Union in the first place. And the only hope of achieving this, at least temporarily, was to keep the question of dissolution in play for as long as possible, encouraging the Scots with general professions of sympathy without ever firmly committing themselves to a decisive step. There seems small reason to doubt that these were the tactics finally decided on by the Whig lords, and that Burnet was justified, therefore, in claiming that 'they did not intend to give up the Union, yet thought it reasonable to give a hearing to the motion'.[53] The refusal of the Whigs to give the Scots any firm promises before the great Lords debate of 1 June is, in itself, significant enough; and it may have been this which confirmed Baillie in his own conviction that 'the Whigs were not for breaking the Union'.[54] But conclusive evidence in favour of the Whigs is to be found in their attitude during the debate itself.

The Scottish peers met at the Earl of Mar's lodgings at 10 o'clock in the morning of 1 June to discuss the wording of the motion that was to be put

50   L'Hermitage (f. 197), 29 May/9 June.
51   H.M.C., *Portland MSS.*, V, 292-3.
52   Berks. R.O., Trumbull MSS., 136/3, R. Bridges to Trumbull, 9 June.
53   G. Burnet, *A History of My Own Time* (6 vols., Oxford, 1833), VI, 161.
54   *Lockhart Papers*, I, 45; Mellerstain 'Memorandum'; see also Atholl MSS., 45/11/25, John Flemyng to [Atholl], 8 June 1713.

to the Lords, and it was agreed that Lord Findlater should seek leave 'for bringing in a bill for dissolving the Union and securing the protestant Succession as it is presently by law established'.[55] In the House, Findlater 'very copiously moved for leave to bring in the bill',[56] rehearsing the grievances that the Scots had suffered since the Union — the dissolution of the Scottish Privy Council, the Treasons Act, the barring of Scottish peers with British titles from sitting in the Lords, 'but above all our many taxes, especially the Malt tax bill, and the ruin of our trade and manufactorys'.[57] After all this fighting talk, however, the speech ended remarkably lamely.[58] It seems that at the meeting earlier that morning, Findlater had shown himself 'very unwilling or rather affraid to make the motion for disolving and therefore [in the House] ended his speech without it'. This piece of equivocal 'nonsense' had received the approval of a majority of the Scots peers at Mar's lodgings, but in the Lords 'some of the English muttering that he had concluded nothing, particularly Anglesey said so to himself, then he [Findlater] rose up and read it'.[59] The motion having been seconded by Eglinton, there followed a lengthy and — as the Hanoverian resident thought — a gloomy silence, 'la cour, je veux dire les ministres, regardant les Whighs et ceux-cy regardant les ministres'.[60] The Junto and their allies were content to go on sitting tight and leave the field to the Scots on the one hand — for whom Eglinton, Ilay, Argyll, Loudoun and Balmerino were briefed to support the motion — and the ministry on the other. The Court side at length opened their case with Lords North and Grey and Peterborough, with the latter in skittish mood.[61] Then Lord Trevor and the Lord Treasurer (the latter putting his finger on the very constitutional point that Baillie had anticipated)[62]

attaqued us, they insisted that our grivances might be just and therefore we

[55] Scottish R.O., GD45/14/352/19, [Balmerino to Maule], 2 June. Baillie and Lord Tullibardine confirm that the motion included both the ending of the Union and the settlement of the 'Succession as it is now' (Mellerstain Letters, V, [to his wife], 2 June; Atholl MSS., 45/11/17, Marquess of Tullibardine to Atholl, 2 June). Findlater was probably chosen, despite his closeness to the Court, because as the former Lord Chancellor of Scotland he had signed the engrossed Act of Union in 1707.

[56] Mellerstain Letters, V, 2 June.

[57] GD45/14/352/19. This list of grievances is very similar to one drawn up by the Duke of Atholl in April 1712. See Bute (Loudoun) MSS. (Marquess of Bute, Mount Stuart House, Bute), bundle A261.

[58] It was reported that when Findlater concluded his speech 'It was hard to know whither, He was for dissolving yea or nott, which made all the Court to Smile, and he was likeing after all to desert our other peers, and goe in to the Courtt until Illa pelted him back again' (Atholl MSS., 45/11/24, John Douglas to [Atholl], Edinburgh, 8 June 1713, reporting accounts of the debate from London).

[59] GD45/14/352/19, postscript, 2 June. There is some evidence that not only was Findlater pressurized into making the motion against his better judgment, but that he would have regarded the dissolution as 'a great loss to Scotland': Scottish R.O., GD 248/561/48/37, 42 (Seafield MSS.), J.L[orimer] to his uncle [William Lorimer, Findlater's chamberlain], London, 13 May, John Philp to William Lorimer, Edinburgh, 8 June 1713; Atholl MSS., 45/11/19, John Flemyng to [Atholl], Edinburgh, 3 June 1713, reporting a letter from Findlater.

[60] Kreienberg (ff. 120–1), 2/13 June 1713.

[61] Cobbett, *Parl. Hist.*, VI, 1217.

[62] *Ibid.*, 1218.

might desire redress but why a dissolution? We maintained that no other remedy could sett things right.[63]After two or 3 hours debeat (No English man helping us all the while) at lenth Nottingham made a long and excellent discourse.[64]

Nottingham's speech, in fact, was a curious mixture. The rebel High Tory, who had left the Court party over the question of the peace preliminaries in December 1711, began by expatiating on the natural advantages which Union ought to have brought, had each party properly carried out its share of the contract. He went on to disagree with Oxford and assert the constitutional right of the Parliament of Great Britain to dissolve the contract if it so wished, but then concluded with a motion for adjourning the debate to some future date. It was important, he claimed, to give the Lords more time to produce an effective alternative guarantee of the Protestant Succession. No one, he reminded the House, had opposed the Act of Union more strongly than he in 1707; but the second article, settling the Succession in Scotland, he had never objected to at the time, and he declined to lend his hand now to dissolving or weakening the Union without guarantees for the House of Hanover, at least as secure as those in the act. Nottingham's carefully judged contribution set the tone for the Whigs who followed him in the debate; and not surprisingly, Balmerino believed that he 'had concerted it with the Whiggs'.[65] The Whig lords and their supporters who spoke — Sunderland, Halifax, Townshend, Scarbrough, Bishop Burnet of Salisbury, Cowper, Pembroke, Guernsey — all in turn supported the adjournment and all, with the exception of Sunderland, whose speech marked him out (in Balmerino's words) as 'clear for us', hedged on the main question of whether they were in favour of breaking the Union or not.[66]

What is quite plain is that Nottingham's ploy had not been discussed beforehand with the Scots peers. The first reaction of the latter, as expressed by Mar and Findlater,[67] was to reject any suggestion of delay. It was only after Halifax's speech had made it fairly clear that they had no hope of support except on these terms that the Scots appear to have given

---

[63]   For a more detailed report of these exchanges, see GD45/14/352/26, [Balmerino to Maule], 23 June.

[64]   GD45/14/352/19. The whole debate lasted 'near five hours' (Atholl MSS., 45/11/17).

[65]   GD45/14/352/19; Kreienberg, 2/13 June.

[66]   L'Hermitage, (ff. 203–4), 2/13 June; Loan 29/45J, newsletter, 2/13 June. Pittis, *Third Session*, pp. 113–21, states that Sunderland was for dissolving the Union. This is supported by Balmerino (GD45/14/352/19), who described Sunderland as 'the only honest hot whig which I know'; by Baillie (Mellerstain 'Memorandum'), who noted that the Whigs spoke 'without opening their minds as to the dissolution except the latter [Sunderland] who declared of it'; by Sir Alexander Erskine (GD45/14/348/3), who recorded that 'my Lord Sunderland was the only on[e of the Whigs] I saw seemd inclynd frankly to the dissolution'; and by James Gray (Atholl MSS., 45/11/20), who wrote that 'non of the Whigs appeared for the dissolution of the Union except Sunderland'. Only L'Hermitage states that Sunderland qualified his support of dissolution (f. 204).

[67]   L'Hermitage, f. 204; GD45/14/352/19. Cobbett, *Parl. Hist.*, VI, 1219 gives Mar and Loudoun.

way.[68] Only this interpretation of the Whig attitude and of the final Scottish capitulation enables us to make sense of the division on 1 June, which was not a vote for or against the Union, but in effect a vote on delaying the discussion to a later date. The technical question voted on was the previous question, called for by the Court peers, of whether to vote on Findlater's motion for leave to bring in a bill. The Whigs opposed the question in order to delay consideration; the Scottish peers, apart from Oxford's son-in-law Lord Dupplin, who was not one of 'the sixteen', unenthusiastically followed suit;[69] but Oxford and his colleagues, encouraged by the patent lack of understanding between the Whigs and the Scots, 'proposed to go on to the motion instantly'.[70]

The ministry, not unnaturally, was determined to try to remove all uncertainty and prevent the future of the Union being imperilled again this session at least; and the Treasurer must have calculated that, with at least nine Whigs absent from the House (some of them with proxies), the time for a show-down was there and then.[71] It seems, however, that he was more confident of success than the subsequent division warranted, for in the event the Junto's gambit only failed by a very narrow margin. At the first count, among the peers present, the two sides were exactly equal with 54 votes each, but when proxies were called for the Court motion for putting the question was carried by four votes. One of these was the proxy of the Duke of Richmond which had been procured by Lord Poulet and was cast — not very scrupulously in view of Richmond's Whiggery — for the Court.[72] This, plus the fact that two Low Church bishops with proxies in their pockets, Ely and St Asaph, left the chamber before the division at 6 p.m., proved just enough to save the day for the government: 'had they [the bishops] staid', wrote Edmund Gibson, the chaplain to the Archbishop of Canterbury, to his friend Bishop Nicolson, 'it had come to what our friends desired, namely the appointment of a day to hear the

---

[68] 'Halifax told Mar that they would not joyn us on that [Findlater's motion]', and if the Scots insisted 'they would put a question they were sure to lose, upon which Mar stood up and said, that no man was more sincere and hearty than he for the disolution and that he thought the question as he had moved very proper, yet since he found it was misconstructed he retracted and was for a delay' (GD45/14/352/19). See also Pittis, *Third Session*, pp. 119–20.

[69] Kreienberg, 2/13 June.

[70] *More Culloden Papers*, ed. D. Warrand (5 vols., Inverness, 1923–30), II, 34. That the Whigs did not vote against the Union on 1 June, but for an adjournment of the issue, was first spotted by Trevelyan (*England under Queen Anne*, III, 242, n.) using Forbes's letter. Sir Alexander Erskine, an eyewitness, confirms Forbes's second-hand account: 'the Whigs desynd to have tym to considder of what proposals cold be made to them for their satisfaction [concerning the Succession] so all our peopell went in to that to hav had the delay but they lost itt by four votes and proxes' (GD45/14/348/3, to [Maule], [2 June] misdated 2 May).

[71] L'Hermitage (ff. 204–5), 2/13 June.

[72] Berks. R.O., Trumbull MSS., Alphab. LI, T. Bateman to Trumbull, 1 June; Atholl MSS., 45/11/24, John Douglas to Atholl, 8 June. There was also a rumour that Atholl's proxy had been left with the Lord Treasurer and thus used against dissolution, but Atholl countered by explaining that Mar held his proxy (*ibid.*, items 24–6, 29, 30, Breadalbane to Atholl, 9, 13 June, Douglas to Atholl, 8, 13 June, John Flemyng to [Atholl], 8 June; *More Culloden Papers*, p. 35). Unfortunately no official proxy records have survived for the 1713 session.

proposition on the part of Scotland with regard to the succession, that they might have taken an estimate from thence, whether they are in earnest for it . . .'[73] As it was, the government was able to go on to clinch its victory by defeating Findlater's original motion without a vote. The Scots declined to divide the House on it, well aware that if they did they would be deserted by the Whigs, many of whom had deliberately left the House before the main question was put so that they would not be forced to declare for or against the dissolution.[74] Balmerino claimed that the Whigs had deserted them because they could not 'get a Secret Capitulation with us upon a nice point . . . it is presently to bring over H[anover]'. The events of the following spring suggest that what the Junto may have had in mind was a parliamentary initiative to invite the Electoral Prince to England.[75]

The Oxford ministry had weathered its first major hazard of the 1713 session; but the storm created by the malt tax was very far from having blown itself out. The Malt Tax Bill itself had still to pass the Lords, where it was clear that, money bill or no, the opposition would fight it all the way in combination with 'the sixteen'.[76] Bolingbroke, and perhaps others in the Cabinet also, would have liked the ministry to follow up its victory on 1 June with an immediate counter-attack. It had caused some remark that Oxford's chief rival in the Cabinet had taken no part in the debate itself: indeed Kreienberg noted that he had still to make his maiden speech in the Lords since his promotion to the peerage the previous summer.[77] Now, however, the Secretary began to talk of a bill making it a treasonable offence to attempt the dissolution of the Union 'by any overt act'.[78] But this was not the Treasurer's way. His first concern was to pilot

[73] Bodl., MS. Add. A. 269, f. 23, 6 June. The story of the two bishops leaving, each with a proxy, is confirmed by Baillie (Mellerstain 'Memorandum'), Balmerino (GD45/14/352/19), Sir Alexander Erskine (GD45/14/348/3), and John Douglas (Atholl MSS., 45/11/22).

[74] H.M.C., *House of Lords MSS.*, new ser., X, 112; L'Hermitage, f.205; Trumbull Add. MS. 136/3, R. Bridges to Trumbull, 1 June; Mellerstain 'Memorandum'. Tullibardine reported that those who were for bringing in the bill 'after they had gone without the barr, gave it up without telling, for they found it would then be lost by a greater majority then the former vote', while another stated that only Somerset and Sunderland, of the Whigs, joined the Scots in this vote (Atholl MSS., 45/11/17, 25, Tullibardine and Flemyng to Atholl, 2, 8 June; cf. *ibid.*, item 22, Douglas to Atholl, 6 June, where the number of Whigs is put at 'but three or four').

[75] GD45/14/352/19. Sir Alexander Erskine thought that the Whigs would not join in the dissolution until something was done for the security of 'the Protestant Succession in the hous of hannover, whi[ch] indeed I beliv they would have proposd to bring him over' (GD45/14/348/3). See also Atholl MSS., 45/11/24, Douglas to [Atholl], 8 June, for Ilay's strong condemnation of the Whigs' tactics over this point.

[76] 'All this was a concerted piece of management not without Jerv[iswood]', wrote Baillie about the Whigs' tactics over voting on 1 June, 'in order to bring over the Scots peers to joyn with them against the Court in the Trade Bill and other matters . . . [but] Jerv[iswood] believed this will have little weight with many of the Scots for tho some are satisfied that the Whigs acted a right part even for carying throw the dissolution . . . yet there are others who say the Whigs have tricked them. But this they could not know there having nothing appeared like it in the management' (Mellerstain 'Memorandum').

[77] Kreienberg (f. 122), 2 June.
[78] *Bolingbroke Corresp.*, IV, 140.

the malt tax safely through — the government simply could not afford the loss of another lucrative source of revenue after its enforced concession over the land tax — and then, if possible, to reach some sort of private compromise with the Scottish peers; for he was reasonably sure that many of the latter would remain susceptible to Court pressure provided they were not further antagonized. This analysis was given some weight on 2 June by a meeting of Scottish lords and M.P.s which decided not to move for the dissolution of the Union in the Commons, but to wait for a more proper occasion.[79]

The passage of the malt tax, however, proved hazardous in the extreme. Sunderland, representing the Junto, visited Balmerino on 4 June with the message that his friends:

> would all to a man joyn us [the Scots] if I would move to delay Committing of the bill till Munday 8 [June] and that then they would take into Consideration the state of the nation in relation to the 14th and other articles of union which relate to this tax — But he said [that] on munday when I opened the debeat I must oppose the bill not only with regard to Scotland but to England and not offer to amend it but to throw it out — I said I would agree to any motion that might retard the ruin of my Country But that amending it would throw it out, for the commons will not pass a Money bill that we amend — he said that was thrue but the other way was better — I said I should talk to my Scots friends of it – I apprehend that the Court will oppose this and get it committed in spite of all we can do.[80]

The joint opposition of the Whigs and Scots did divide the House of Lords on the bill, and each time the margin was uncomfortably narrow, but each time, as Balmerino predicted, the ministry scraped home. On 5 June, in a very full House assembled for the second reading, the ministry had a majority of only two.[81] Balmerino himself opened the debate as planned, vigorously seconded by Ilay, and the struggle lasted three hours. Besides trying to get the second reading put off until the eighth, Balmerino, who was sitting amongst the Tories, had a message from the Whigs 'to insist against the bill itself'. He and Ilay were strongly supported by Argyll, Mar and Findlater; but the best speech for the opposition came from Nottingham. Balmerino concluded that they had had the better of the debate, and the Court were so wearied that though the House consented to a commitment it was agreed not to proceed until the eighth. Though the Scots and Whigs were deserted by some Tories who had declared they were against the tax, the narrow defeat was squarely laid at the door of the

---

[79] GD45/14/352/19; GD45/14/348/3. According to Baillie, only General Charles Ross and Alexander Murray were for going on (Mellerstain 'Memorandum'). Murray himself, along with Lockhart, was in favour of both peers and Commoners unanimously opposing the Court in everything. For Murray's detailed reasoning in support of this action see GD45/14/364, Murray to [Maule], 2 June.

[80] GD45/14/352/20, [Balmerino to Maule], 4 June.

[81] All sources agree on the size of the majority but there is disagreement on the figures themselves. Cobbett, *Parl. Hist.*, VI, 1219 has 85–83; L'Hermitage (f. 211, 5/16 June) has 76–74 (the same as the official figures recorded in the Manuscript Minutes of the House of Lords); while Thomas Bateman (Trumbull MSS., Alphab. LI, 5 June) gives 77–75.

Scottish peers themselves. The absence of Lord Wharton (with a proxy), Lord Derby and the Duke of Grafton was more than balanced by 'the poor old Bishop [of] London, D[uke of] Leeds and others [who] were wanting on the Court side'. It was the Duke of Argyll who told Balmerino that the Scots 'had lost it by Lord Duplin's being with the Court[82] for his vote would have made us equall, and we being for the negative (not a 2d reading) we had carried it'.[83] To cap it all the 'poor E[arl] of Home (meaning no ill) had got his bottle over night and came not to the house till after our vote, and that he was sent for'.[84] Balmerino and Argyll, however, were not in possession of the full facts on the vote of 5 June. The anxiety which Oxford felt about his prospects in the House that day may be gauged from one extraordinary measure he resorted to in order to make sure of his majority. On the very morning of the second reading he bought the support of the independent Whig Earl of Warrington with a promise that the arrears of £6,500 on the pension granted to Warrington's father by William III, outstanding since 1694, would be paid. 'I believe your Lordship would gladly that morning have given double that sum and paid it down', claimed Warrington later, 'to have been sure of Carrying that Bill at that time.'[85]

There was another long debate on 8 June, in which the Scots and the Whigs, led by Nottingham, Sunderland, Cowper, Balmerino, Findlater, Ilay, Mar and Argyll, were answered by Oxford, Bolingbroke, Leeds, Peterborough and North and Grey. Oxford agreed with the Scots that the levying of the duty would be very hard on them 'but that it was like the exaction of it would not be strict'. Others also 'on the Court side insisted to insinuate that it would not be exacted'. This led to a heated discussion on the Queen's dispensing power which involved Oxford and Sunderland

[82]   Though a Scot, the Viscount of Dupplin (heir to the Earl of Kinnoull, one of 'the sixteen') sat by right of his British peerage as Baron Hay of Pedwardine (one of Oxford's dozen peers of 1711/12). He was also married to Oxford's youngest daughter, and was one of his father-in-law's chief lieutenants in the Lords. See C. Jones, ' "The Scheme Lords, the Neccessitous Lords, and the Scots Lords": The Earl of Oxford's Management and 'the Party of the Crown' in the House of Lords, 1711 to 1714', *Party and Management in Parliament 1660–1784*, ed. C. Jones (forthcoming). Baillie confirms that the vote of Dupplin was crucial to the division (Mellerstain Letters, V, [to his wife], 6 June), while Forbes (*More Culloden Papers*, p. 35) states that Wharton had two proxies.

[83]   By the rules of the House in a tied vote the negatives carry the question.

[84]   GD45/14/352/22, [Balmerino to Maule], 6 June. Baillie again confirms that Lord Home's absence helped to defeat the opposition (Mellerstain Letters, V, 6 June; see also *More Culloden Papers*, p. 35). Home, one of the poorest Scottish peers, had recently been given the post of General to the Scottish Mint worth £300 a year, so his hangover may have been diplomatic. He was to be given a royal bounty of £150 in December 1713: G. Holmes, *British Politics in the Age of Anne* (1967), p. 394; *Calendar of Treasury Books*, XXVI, 85, 519; XXVII, 464.

[85]   B.L., Loan 29/127/1, Warrington to Oxford, 10, 24 Apr. 1714. Warrington had by that time received only £1,000 of his arrears (paid December 1713) and it was in an attempt to extract the remainder that he reminded the Treasurer of 'that matter of soe great consequence barely carryed by that vote soe askt by your Lordship'. For a discussion of this incident in the context of Warrington's finances see J.V. Beckett and C. Jones, 'Financial Improvidence and Political Independence in the Early 18th Century: George Booth, 2nd Earl of Warrington', *Bulletin of the John Rylands University Library*, LXV, No 1 (1982).

swapping insults.[86] Lord North then flew off at such a tangent on the laws of Scotland that Argyll refused to let Balmerino answer him. At 5 o'clock in the afternoon, 'after many good and many ridiculouse speeches . . . it was put to the votes [and] we were 56, they 64 — we did not call for proxies knowing them to be equal — 19 to 19'.[87] Again the Court had scraped through, and this despite the fact that the opposition was this time strengthened by the reappearance of Wharton, whose 'zeal to do mischief', we are told, 'got the better of him and brought him up . . . to be against the bill'.[88] The larger majority for the Court on the eighth was largely due, according to Kreienberg and Balmerino, to the actions of three moderate Whigs, the Duke of Kent, and Lord Herbert, 'who had all along been with us, [but who] deserted to the enemy, els we had only lost it by two'; also to the unavoidable absence of Lord Guernsey (Nottingham's brother) and the Whig Bishop Fleetwood of St Asaph.[89] A protest against the vote was entered into the Journal two days later. Composed by Balmerino, it was vetted by Nottingham, Sunderland and Halifax, and signed on the 12th by 19 peers.[90] Baillie summing up the whole course of the Malt Bill concluded that

> There has all along been something odd in this affair. It carried in the Committee of the house of Commons by the absence of a Scots member and a second reading in the house of Lords by a Scots man. If either of these had not happened we had bee[n] free of it. The thing itself does not trouble me so much as the consequences that are likely to follow upon it.[91]

It is certainly the case that more than the malt tax alone was at stake in the Lords division on 5 June 1713. The question before the House at the end of a long afternoon's debating was whether the Malt Bill should be given its second reading forthwith, or whether this stage of the measure should be deferred for several days. Both the Whigs and the Scots were in favour of delay; and both for the Whigs and for the government such a delay was of the utmost tactical importance. For the Whigs, as Oxford must have been well aware, had their eyes now not just on the defeat of the Malt Bill but on what, to them if not to the Scots, was much more important — namely, the defeat of the Commerce Bill, and until the latter reached the House of Lords — as both parties still assumed it would — it seemed essential to the Junto to keep some material hold over their Scottish allies.

---

[86]   Cobbett, *Parl. Hist.*, VI, 1219–20 puts this exchange into the 1 June debate, but Balmerino (GD45/14/352/22, 9 June) clearly places it in the 8 June debate on dispensing power.

[87]   GD45/14/352/24,[Balmerino to Maule], 9 June. The number of proxies available had only increased by one over the vote on 5 June (Court 19, opposition 18), despite Balmerino reporting on the 6th that 'there are expresses on all hands to the country for proxies' (GD45/14/352/22).

[88]   Berks. R.O., Trumbull Add. MS. 136/1, R. Bridges, 9 June.

[89]   GD45/14/352/24; Kreienberg (f. 135), 9/20 June.

[90]   *L.J.*, XIX, 567; GD45/14/352/24, 23, [Balmerino to Maule], 9, 11 June. Of the 19 who signed, 14 were Scottish representative peers (including Kinnoull); the others were the Duke of Argyll (who was not a representative peer, but sat by right of his English Earldom of Greenwich), the Duke of Somerset, the Earls of Sunderland and Scarbrough, and Viscount Lonsdale. The two missing representative peers were Atholl, who was in Scotland (Mar held his proxy, see n. 72 above) and Annandale.

[91]   Mellerstain Letters, V, [to his wife], 8 June.

Hence their anxiety 'to have their turn served first, and the Scots to trust them, rather than they trust the Scots', as they would have to do once the fate of the malt tax had been decided.[92] Hence also Oxford's endeavours first to prevent the retarding of the money bill, and subsequently, as soon as it was safely through on the eighth, to bring back the straying Scots to the fold.

To get the whole political scene in clear focus, as it unfolded in the second week of June, we must remember that right through the period of crisis over the Union and the malt tax the House of Lords' inquiry into Anglo-French commercial relations, begun on 28 May, had been steadily proceeding. On the second, fourth and ninth of June, in fact, the Lords had given the greater part of their time to it. Already it was becoming clear to the Treasurer that a body of Tory opinion in the House was hardening against the new trade treaty. A list which he drew up on 13 June of the Commerce Bill's potential supporters and opponents in the Lords[93] shows that as early as this Oxford expected as many as 13 or 14 Tory peers to divide with the opposition when the bill arrived. If he lost the Scottish vote as well, the upper House would be almost certain to repudiate the treaty. Once again therefore, as in the aftermath of the Hamilton peerage case in February 1712,[94] it seemed that the Scots contingent held the key to the immediate political situation. An astounding turn of events in the House of Commons, however, was about to render these calculations irrelevant.

It was against a background of mounting public excitement and increasing strident criticism of the ministry's economic policy that the Commons began[95] on 9 June the first of five exhausting days of committee work on the Commerce Bill. It was this stage which undoubtedly determined the bill's fate. From the start the atmosphere of the House was tense and over-charged. There was a struggle over the chairmanship, which took the Court by surprise but which was eventually resolved in favour of Oxford's friend, Sir Robert Davers.[96] Next day, 10 June, spokesmen for the Levant and Peninsula trade and for the Italian merchants were allowed to present evidence, and Members on both sides became extremely heated after Nathaniel Torriano, who was speaking on behalf of merchants trading with Spain and Italy, had interspersed his economic data with some barbed political reflections on the government's competence.[97] Upbraided by Robert Benson, for the ministry, Torriano[98]

[92]   Berks. R.O., Trumbull MSS., Alphab. LI, T. Bateman, 5 June.
[93]   B.L., Loan 29/10/3, printed in Holmes, *British Politics*, pp. 422–3.
[94]   See Holmes, 'Hamilton Affair', 257–82.
[95]   A shower of petitions descended on the Commons between 4 and 9 June (see B.L., Add. MS. 31138, f. 188), while pamphlets critical of the trade treaty circulated freely. Robert Pringle complained that the treaty 'in place of makeing of advantageous to the nation, it is made an handle of parties . . . [and] that everie bodie speaks as they effect even merchants contradicting one another' (GD18/3150/3, [to John Clerk], 6 June).
[96]   *C.J.*, XVII, 411.
[97]   L'Hermitage (f. 220), 12/23 June; A. Baldwin, *The History and Defence of the Last Parliament* (1713), p. 241.
[98]   According to Kreienberg (f. 136, 12/23 June) the offender was not Torriano but the princely Portugal merchant, James Milner. For Milner, see H.E.S. Fisher, *The Portugal Trade* (1971), p. 104.

was defended by the Whig Sir Peter King, who pleaded eloquently for freedom of speech for those giving evidence. Many Tories joined Lechmere, Stanhope and Smith in supporting King's appeal. The Court, disturbed by the warmth generated, and not least by a surprise intervention by Charles Aldworth, a High Tory Member for Windsor, dropped its motion to have Torriano censured: a small enough concession in itself; but one that for the opposition was to mark the turn of the tide.[99]

In the remaining committees on the bill the spirit of uneasiness which had begun to settle on the Tories became more and more noticeable. Besides the prospect of an approaching general election, which made many Tories less likely to disregard the views of their constituents — more than 50 sat for seats which had petitioned either against the Commerce Bill or the earlier Wine Bill — there were a growing number who were doubtful of the economic wisdom of the ministry's policy. In addition, and more disturbing still from the Court's point of view, the granting of most-favoured-nation treatment to France in the recent treaty had given fresh alarm and brought fresh reinforcements to that small but determined group of Tories which had for more than 18 months suspected the whole drift of the government's peace policy. The anti-French and anti-Jacobite spirit of the 'peace rebels' of December 1711[100] and of the March Club of 1712 was again abroad, and in its latest form it was proving dangerously infectious. What made the Commerce Bill opposition more formidable than its predecessors was that by the middle of June it had attracted the support of two or three men of real influence within the party, men who had sufficient pull to draw together in temporary association the diverse elements of the bill's opposition.

The most important convert in the House of Commons was Sir Thomas Hanmer. He had begun by favouring the Treaty of Commerce but during the committee stage of the bill there was a marked change in his attitude and he began to campaign strongly against it. His speech on 18 June indicated that the reasons for this change were chiefly economic. The county of Suffolk, which he represented, had some stake in the woollen industry, and like many other Tory gentlemen, Hanmer must have been affected by pressures in his locality as well as by the arguments he heard in the Commons. But at the same time, from his subsequent record as the champion of the Hanoverian Tories in the next Parliament, one can assume that already he had political as well as economic reservations about the ministry's policy.[101]

---

[99] L'Hermitage (f. 220); Pittis, *Third Session*, p. 122; Boyer, *Anne*, p. 637; Berks. R.O., Trumbull MSS., Alphab. LI, R. Bridges, 15 June; (for Aldworth's intervention) Kreienberg (f. 136), 12/23 June.

[100] See G.S. Holmes, 'The Commons' Division on "No Peace without Spain", 7 December 1711', *B.I.H.R.*, XXXII (1960), 223–33.

[101] Hanmer's public motives as expressed in his speech may have hidden a more private one of his impatience with Oxford for not pursuing a thorough enough Tory policy. It is worth remembering that Hanmer's fellow knight of the shire, Davers, had played a key role on behalf of the bill, and thus was presumably immune to any pressure from the woollen interest. In any case this pressure was not as great on Suffolk M.P.s as it appears to have been on those from the neighbouring county of Norfolk, where the manufacturing centre of Norwich and its hinterland had a very considerable influence on county elections. On these points we should like to acknowledge the help of David Hayton of the History of Parliament.

Even Hanmer's defection, however, did not appear to threaten the ministry with defeat in the Commons; although general feeling in London by 16 June was that the majority there would be small, and just a few were by now allowing themselves to think the unthinkable — that the lower House might actually throw the bill out ('il semble', Kreienberg hastily added in his report to Hanover, 'que ceux qui raisonnent ainsi, vont trop vite').[102] What continued to cause Oxford most concern was the bill's prospect in the Lords. Here the events of the past two or three weeks had alarmingly eroded much of the ground which the Court had so painfully regained since the spring of 1712. In his assessment of support and opposition, the Treasurer's first calculations produced a total of 77 votes for each side.[103] Second thoughts suggested a maximum of 79 votes for the opposition and 84 for the government, but the latter figure was based on the supposition that all but three of the disaffected Scottish peers[104] would eventually come to heel — and this, in the circumstances, was no better than a gamble. The 14 Tory peers whose allegiance Oxford considered doubtful or discounted included most of the Nottingham contingent,[105] plus Pembroke (now almost a Whig by adoption), and a prominent rebel of more recent vintage, Bishop Dawes of Chester; but there were also two significant new names bracketed with the Whigs, the Earls of Anglesey and Abingdon, the former being the more important politically. The defection of these two peers was just as damaging to the ministry as that of Hanmer; for each held office, each was an active politician, and together they enjoyed quite important connexions and influence in the Commons as well as the Lords.[106] Moreover, while Abingdon's opposition seems to have been mostly factious, possibly grounded on disappointment that he and his family had not been especially favoured,[107] it was believed that Anglesey was acting largely from anti-French and anti-Jacobite feelings, reinforced probably by self-interest.[108]

The rebellious state of the Lords, and in particular the disaffection of the Scots and the hostility of Abingdon and Anglesey, who both denounced the Commerce Treaty openly in the House on 17 June,[109] confronted the

[102] H.M.C., *Portland MSS.*, VII, 144; L'Hermitage (ff. 225–6); Kreienberg (f. 140), 16/27 June.

[103] See above, n.93.

[104] Argyll, Ilay and Balmerino.

[105] Nottingham, Guernsey, Weymouth, Berkshire (whose proxy seems to have been held by Weymouth), Carteret and Hatton (whose name appears on both lists). Thanet is the one notable absentee in this group.

[106] See Holmes, *British Politics*, pp. 281–2 and n. 283 for details of Anglesey's and Abingdon's connexions in the Commons. Two of Anglesey's followers in the Lords, Mountjoy (the former M.P. Lord Windsor) and Conway, are also noted as possible opposition recruits in Oxford's list. They had for some time past maintained a 'strict connection' with the Duke of Argyll (Macpherson, *Original Papers*, II, 495) whose breach with Oxford was now virtually complete.

[107] See H.M.C., *Portland MSS.*, VII, 143 for a comment on the formation of the Abingdon 'party' since Christmas 1712.

[108] See Macpherson, *Original Papers*, II, 495–6; Holmes, *British Politics*, pp. 278–9; D. Hayton, 'The Crisis in Ireland and the Disintegration of Queen Anne's Last Ministry', *Irish Historical Studies*, XXII (1980–1).

[109] Boyer, *Anne*, p. 638.

ministry on the eve of the report stage of the Commons with a most awkward decision. Should they drop the bill or carry on in the hope of a still-expected victory in the Commons which might rally some of the waverers in the Lords? Powerful pressure from loyal Tories persuaded the ministry to go ahead.[110]

On 18 June, after Davers had reported the amendments made in committee, the motion was made by the ministry that the bill be engrossed. The resulting debate lasted eight hours with no fewer than 35 speeches. A list of speakers in the debate which has survived[111] shows that of the 18 speeches made against the bill, seven came from English Whigs, one from a Scots Whig merchant,[112] one from a Scottish Court Whig,[113] one from a Squadrone Member,[114] the rest from disaffected Tories. The turning point in the debate came when Hanmer unexpectedly appealed to the 'country' instincts and to the self-interest of the Tory gentlemen.[115] The opposition cause was further helped by the fact that the supporting speeches from the Tory side came from a very fair cross-section of the party: three Hanoverian Tories in the March Club tradition, and two merchants,[116] one October Club stalwart, and one professional politician and placeman.[117] When the heads were finally counted at 11 p.m. the motion for engrossment was rejected by 194 to 185. The Oxford ministry had suffered its first major defeat in the Commons since November 1710.

The existence of a printed division list which is exceptionally precise, and the recent discovery of George Baillie's listing of the votes of the Scottish M.P.s,[118] makes it possible to analyze the various factors contributing to the government's defeat. Such an analysis reveals the extraordinary scale of the Tory rebellion against the Court. The printed list shows 76 Tories voting against the bill (there were also two Tory tellers) along with 104 English Whigs and 14 Scots opposition Members;[119] and yet in the final reckoning it was Tory abstentions, rather than hostile Tory votes which cost the government the day. The narrow margin of nine votes could easily have been made up if the Court could have polled even a fraction of the absentee Tories. But there can be little question that many of the absences were politic and deliberate. Out of the key group of 51

---

110   *Bolingbroke Corresp.*, IV, 165–6; Boyer, *Anne*, p. 638; J. Oldmixon, *History of England during the Reigns of King William . . . Queen Anne, King George I* (1735), p. 520; GD45/14/352/26, [Balmerino to Maule], 26 June.

111   See Pittis, *Third Session*, p. 128.

112   Thomas Smith, M.P. Glasgow Burghs. The English Whigs were Sir Peter King, James Stanhope, Nathaniel Gould, William Pulteney, Richard Hampden, John Smith and Edward Wortley Montagu.

113   Sir David Dalrymple, Lord Advocate since 1709.

114   George Baillie.

115   For the speech and its effect see Pittis, *Third Session*, p. 127, and Berks. R.O., Trumbull MSS., Alphab. LI, T. Bateman, 19 June.

116   Sir Arthur Kaye, Gilfrid Lawson and Charles Cholmondeley; Robert Heysham and Paul Docminique.

117   Francis Annesley (cousin of Anglesey) and John Aislabie respectively.

118   For details see Appendix.

119   The Baillie list for 18 June gives 16 Scots voting against the bill (for details see Appendix). If Baillie is more accurate than the contemporary printed list, then two fewer English M.P.s must have voted against the bill than indicated on the printed list.

Tories who sat for constituencies which had petitioned against a freer trade with France, only 17 actually voted with the Whigs. Significantly, however, no fewer than 15 of the remainder did not attend the House. Both in this closely interested group and among Tory M.P.s as a whole a surprising number of previously highly active politicians — men who normally never missed a key division — were on this occasion absent; among them office-holders like Sir William Drake, Francis Scobell and Sir Simeon Stewart, and leading October men like the two Strangways, Sir William Barker and Sir Gilbert Dolben.[120]

Taking into account both the Tories who voted against the bill and the absentees, the importance of the attitude of the two High Church peers, Anglesey and Abingdon, becomes evident. At a conservative reckoning, their joint following in the Commons in the summer of 1713 was about 15 Members.[121] Of these only four failed to vote against the bill, and only one — Henry Bertie (Beaumaris) — actually supported the Court. Thus the friends and connexions of the two earls more than account for the small opposition majority. The impact of Hanmer's *volte-face* is much more difficult to assess from the lists, since like that of Speaker Bromley, Hanmer's influence in the Commons was based much more on his political authority than on a personal connexion. Many of the group of High Church Tories with whom Hanmer had been most closely associated in the past had also been associated with Nottingham, and for several of them the vote against the Commerce Bill was not their first revolt against the Court.[122] Such as it is, the evidence does appear to suggest that Hanmer's immediate influence on the Court's defeat, which later became part of political legend, may have been exaggerated.

There is some evidence to suggest that Oxford played a fairly passive role in whipping up support for the bill at the report stage.[123] He subsequently told Swift that 'he did not care whether Parliament passed the Commerce, or no, and that the next should have the honour of it'.[124]

---

[120] Dolben, a judge in Ireland, had landed at Dublin on 18 June, the day of the crucial Commons' vote, to take up his duties. He may have been unable to postpone his visit, for he appears to have favoured the bill, chairing the committee on the French Commerce Treaty and on 2 June urging Sir Justinian Isham to appear in the House on the sixth 'on the account of the trade, which has many enemies, their number being increased by the total apostacy of the Scots': Northamptonshire R.O., I.C. 2791, 4735 (Isham MSS.), Dolben to Isham, 2 June, Elizabeth Baggs to Isham, Dublin, 23 June. Thomas Strangways sr did not stand in the 1713 general election and died in December 1713. Stewart, Scobell and Drake all seem to have been much less active parliament-arians in the 1712 and 1713 sessions (in the case of the two former after appointment to office). Barker, for whose absence no satisfactory explanation can be found, was to be returned, almost certainly through Hanmer's influence, at Thetford in 1713, though he did not subsequently take a Hanoverian Tory line in the 1714 Parliament and appears instead to have followed Bolingbroke. We are grateful to David Hayton for this information.

[121] See above, n. 106.

[122] This was certainly true of John Ward, Peter Shakerley, Sir Roger Mostyn, Heneage Finch and William Hedges. On the other hand Sir George Warburton, Ralph Freman, Edward Duncombe and the Earl of Barrymore were, like Hanmer himself, 'first offenders'.

[123] *Wentworth Papers*, p. 338.

[124] *The Correspondence of Jonathan Swift*, ed. H. Williams (5 vols., Oxford, 1963–5), I, 375.

Yet it is noteworthy that the Treasurer spoke in favour of the treaty in the Lords on 17 June; also that it was his brother Edward, seconded by Vice-Chamberlain Coke, who opened the Court's case in the Commons on the 18th, expatiating at some length on the advantages of the bargain with France.[125] The testimony of at least one experienced Court Member, Josiah Burchett (Secretary to the Admiralty, M.P. for Sandwich) acquits the ministry quite firmly of any obvious slackness in managing the proceedings;[126] and on the whole the division list supports this view. Admittedly the names of five Tory office-holders can be found among the ranks of the bill's opponents;[127] but this is a surprisingly small number considering the warmth of feeling which the trade treaty had generated, and in any case four of these five had been unreliable for some time past. Had the head of the ministry himself been evidently negligent or even indecisive in his attitude one would have expected this to be reflected far more clearly in the votes of Court Members.

What do the two George Baillie lists for the votes on the Commerce Bill on 4 and 18 June tell us about the behaviour of the Scottish M.P.s? With the exception of the six who abstained on the fourth, only three voted differently on the two occasions: Sir James Campbell, who had opposed the bill on the fourth, was absent on the 18th, while Sir David Dalrymple and Sir Patrick Johnston, absent on the fourth, opposed the bill on the 18th. The significant switch in voting was performed by the six abstainers of the fourth who supported the Court on the later vote. The explanation may well lie in the fact that five of the six were Jacobites (Erskine, Hamilton, Houston, Lockhart and Paterson), and the Pretender had sent instructions (dated 29 May/8 June, which would have arrived in England shortly after the 4 June vote) to support the Court in Parliament.[128] Baillie's only general comment on the voting was that 'all merchants of our countrey members of the house both whig and tory voted against it'.[129]

The Parliament still had a month to run, but the closing weeks of its third session were something of an anti-climax for the Whigs after their triumph of 18 June.[130] The Lord Treasurer, in contrast to Bolingbroke, was as phlegmatic as ever. Lord Somers viewed the future with cautious reserve. He realized that the defeat of the Commerce Treaty might turn

---

[125] L'Hermitage (f. 229), 19/30 June; Kreienberg (f. 145), 23 June/4 July.
[126] B.L., Add. MS. 31138, f. 199, Burchett to Strafford, 19 June.
[127] *Viz.* John Aislabie, Heneage Finch, Sir Roger Mostyn, John Ward and Dixey Windsor.
[128] Macpherson, *Original Papers*, II, 416. We should like to thank Daniel Szechi for this information.
[129] Mellerstain Letters, VI (unfol.), [to his wife], 4 July. In contrast, three days later, Lockhart reported from Scotland 'that most of all our trading people are extremly exasparated att the Loss of the Bill of Commerce' (B.L., Loan 29/15/3, [to Oxford], 7 July).
[130] As active a parliamentarian as Lord North and Grey had left London by 26 June on his way to Newmarket thinking that 'the business of Parl[iament] seems pretty well over', Recalled by Oxford for a probable struggle over the Civil List, he was again on his travels by 3 July, believing that 'the right will prevail without my weak succor' and leaving his proxy (B.L., Loan 29/308, North and Grey to Oxford, 26 June, 3 July; Bodl., MS. North b.2, f.17, Oxford to North and Grey, 29 June).

out to be the Whigs' one and only success, due to a combination of factors which were unlikely to coincide again; 'our power', he warned his colleagues, 'does not answer our inclinations'.[131] His prognostication appeared to be proved right by the events of the next fortnight: the Commons voted a 'palliative address' thanking the Queen for the benefits of the peace treaties while the Whigs failed to prevent the voting of £500,000 to pay off the debts on the Civil List, which the Court alleged had been incurred before 1710.[132]

The greatest disappointment to the Junto was, perhaps, the unwillingness of the Scots peers in the House of Lords to extend their temporary co-operation at the time of the malt tax crisis into a permanent political alliance. Here again Oxford's calm appraisal of the situation earlier in the month, and his confidence that, properly handled, 'the sixteen' could be coaxed back into their former state of dependence on the Court, proved sounder than the more extravagant reaction of Bolingbroke.[133] As early as 11 June the Treasurer had prudently arranged a meeting with the disgruntled peers.[134] On the 25th he received a deputation of Scottish peers and M.P.s at St James's Palace, and suggested possible expedients to enable Scotland to escape part at least of the burden imposed on her by the controversial malt duties.[135] Findlater, the spokesman for the deputation, returned a guarded reply, but after a second meeting the following day the antipathy of the peers, at least, towards the Court noticeably relaxed. By early July Ralph Bridges was able to report the government's recovery of strength in the upper House: 'for last week the Wh—g grandees made an overture to the Scotch, that they would heartily joyn with them and by the first opportunity break the Union, provided they would come into their measures. But the Sc[otch] Lords refused it, and only the D[uke] of Argyle and 3 more of his Party will oppose the Court any more this Session.'[136]

The Whigs, having thereby lost the initiative in the Lords to the Court, had only one way left to them by which to maintain the momentum gained by the defeat of the Commerce Bill. This was to bring the question of the Succession at last before Parliament. For tactical reasons they chose to concentrate on a demand for the removal of the Pretender from his

131   Surrey R.O., Somers MSS., 0/2/50, [Mrs Cocks] to her brother, [end of June 1713].
132   For the proceedings on the Civil List see Burnet, *History*, VI, 173–4; Boyer, *Anne*, pp. 639–40; *C.J.*, XVII, 441–7; *Wentworth Papers*, pp. 338–9; H.M.C., *Portland MSS.*, V, 467; L'Hermitage (f. 250), 30 June/11 July.
133   See H.M.C., *Portland MSS.*, V, 300.
134   Scottish R.O., GD220/5/309/1 (Montrose MSS.), Oxford to [Montrose], 11 June.
135   L'Hermitage (f. 244), 26 June/7 July. The meeting had again been arranged by Oxford: GD45/14/352/26, [Balmerino to Maule], 23 June. For one of Oxford's suggestions — farming the malt tax — see GD45/14/352/25, [Balmerino] to Maule, 16 June. From Scotland, Lockhart later reported to Oxford 'in Generall that what your Lordship proposed for easing this countries of the Malt tax is very acceptable' (B.L., Loan 29/150/3, 7 July).
136   Berks. R.O., Trumbull MSS., Alphab. LV, to Trumbull, n.d., but from internal evidence probably written a few days before 8 July. Cf. Atholl's letter to Oxford, 1 July, in H.M.C., *Portland MSS.*, V, 302; *Lockhart Papers*, I, 416–17 for Lockhart's lament on the lack of 'spirit' and 'courage' shown by the Scots peers in face of Oxford's blandishments.

refuge in Lorraine, and after careful planning the 'Lorraine motions' were introduced into the Lords on 30 June and into the Commons on 1 July. The Lords' motion, introduced by Wharton, had been organized with some skill and caught the ministry off balance. It proposed an address to the Queen, begging her to use her influence with the Duke of Lorraine and with other friendly rulers to ensure that the Pretender would be offered no asylum in their territories. Oxford was wise enough to avoid being drawn into a vote, and the Whigs were sufficiently elated by their success in the debate to accept an amendment offered by Lord Paget, which thanked the Queen for the (entirely fictitious) efforts she had already made to secure the Pretender's removal.[137] In the light of all that was to happen in 1714, in the first session of the next Parliament, the bloodless success of the Lorraine motions may seem very significant. In fact, however, beyond a short-term tactical victory, they achieved very little at the time for the Whigs. The Tories, though evidently disturbed by the question of the Pretender, had contrived to evade a pitched battle and had denied the Whigs the material evidence of their uneasy consciences that would have come from dividing either House. With the dissolution of Parliament following a fortnight later, the Whigs had no immediate opportunity, at Westminster at least, to pursue the scent further.

Although the Oxford ministry, after treading dangerously for over a month and suffering one very painful fall, at length survived the parliamentary crisis of 1713, the session had held important lessons alike for the members of the government, for its supporters, for its Tory critics and for its Whig enemies. It had placed further strain on the fabric of ministerial unity, with the result that by the time Parliament rose Bolingbroke was confirmed in his decision to challenge Oxford's leadership more openly than before.[138] It had shown once again how very far from monolithic the early eighteenth-century Tory party was: and yet had not offered the Whigs any realistic hope that without numerous gains in the coming elections they would be able seriously to undermine the government in the House of Commons. The loss of the Commerce Bill had certainly been a humiliation for the administration and its loyal backers; but the issues involved had been so very special that no one believed that desertions on this scale would occur again. According to the shrewd compiler of the detailed division list for 18 June 1713 in *A Letter to a Member of the House of Commons*,[139] possibly Defoe, only 36 out of the 76 trade rebels were 'very Whimsicals indeed'. Of the rest, he commented that they were 'I hope . . . very far from lost sheep, which were hardly ever known to straggle from us but this once, and I hope never will again'.[140] Among those he listed were Sir Thomas Hanmer and several other prominent back-benchers, like Ralph Freman (Hertfordshire) and Lord Downe (Yorkshire), and there was no indication as yet that men of

---

[137] For the debate L'Hermitage (ff. 249–50), 30 June/11 July; *Wentworth Papers*, pp. 340, 342; Boyer, *Anne*, p. 640; B.L., Lansdowne MS. 1024, f. 420, White Kennett's journal.

[138] See G. Holmes, 'Harley, St. John and the Death of the Tory Party', below, chapter 6, pp. 148-9.

[139] See Appendix.

[140] *A Letter to a Member*, p. 25.

such calibre were likely to become committed opponents of the ministry in the last critical session of Anne's reign. As for the Junto, the session had underlined once again how far their hopes of salvation were bound up with the balance of power in the House of Lords, and how tantalizingly short they still were of tipping that balance decisively in their favour. On the other hand, the hostility to the ministry revealed in recent weeks by the Earls of Abingdon and Anglesey was the most promising shift in the situation there since December 1711. What the Junto needed next was a sustained campaign less opportunistic than the struggle over the malt tax and the Union had been, and certainly less dependent on the uncertain favour of the Scots.

One thing the 1713 session had shown very clearly was the strength and the weakness of the Scots in the British Parliament. In both Houses the representatives of North Britain formed an important bloc, with the 16 representative peers clearly the more important in view of the shakier Court majority in the upper House. Sufficiently aroused, and acting together, they had the capacity to inflict embarrassment on the government in the Commons and defeat in the Lords. The causes which agitated the Scots were nearly always domestic, and between the Union in 1707 and 1713 several such causes had arisen, the cumulative effect of which was the outburst of anti-Union feeling in May and June of 1713. The weakness of the Scots lay in their inherent inability to work together for long as a group. Divided by party, religion, clan, dynastic loyalty and economic interests they were rarely able to overcome these differences. The summer of 1713 was the closest they came to succeeding. Even here the Scottish M.P.s remained partly at odds with each other, but in the Lords 'the sixteen' did achieve a temporary cohesion. The fissiparousness of the Scots was, of course, invaluable to the ministry in restricting the political damage that might be caused by Scottish discontent. And as far as the representative peers were concerned, the government held a trump card whenever there was a general election in the offing. Influencing the elections of the Scottish M.P.s was difficult for the ministry, and at the general election in the autumn of 1713 the Whigs were to triumph in Scotland as a result both of the malt tax issue and growing fear of the Jacobites. The management of the peers' election was a different matter. The relatively small electorate was open to various forms of pressure, and from 1710 onwards the government's 'list' for 'the sixteen' was invariably returned. Lord Ilay was to find to his cost that his opposition to the ministry over the malt tax in 1713 led to his being dropped from the list at the autumn election and to his consequent non-election.[141] One lesson the Oxford ministry (and subsequent ministries) did learn from the troubles of 1713 was the need for more assiduous management of the Scots. It cannot have been a coincidence that the post of Secretary of State for Scotland, which had lapsed on the death of Queensberry in July 1711, was revived for Lord Mar in September 1713.[142]

[141]   Ilay's brother, Argyll, was, of course, unaffected by the election — his English peerage gave him a 'safe seat'. For the election see P.W.J. Riley, *The English Ministers and Scotland 1707–27* (1964), pp. 249–50.

[142]   See *ibid.*, pp. 246–7 for the appointment of Mar upon the breakdown of Oxford's system of personal management of Scottish business.

APPENDIX: *The voting of Scottish M.P.s on the French Commerce Treaty Bill, 4 and 18 June 1713*

The two division lists reproduced below, showing how the 45 Scottish M.P.s voted on the French Commerce Treaty Bill at the second reading on 4 June, and at the engrossment stage on 18 June, at which the bill was rejected, are from the papers of George Baillie (Mellerstain Papers, Series 1, Bundle 343). The two lists are in Baillie's hand and there is no reason to doubt that they were drawn up by him at, or shortly after, the two divisions. The list for 4 June (which is the only list known for this Commons division)[143] is set out in the form of four sections: those 'for committing the bill' (10), those 'against commitment' (15), those who 'went out' (6), and those who were 'absent' (14). The second list for 18 June is set out in three sections: 'Against engrossing the Bill' (16), 'For engrossing' (16), and those 'Absent' (13). There is a complete division list for the division on 18 June, 'An Exact List of those who voted for and against Engrossing', appended to *A Letter from a Member of the House of Commons Relating to the Bill of Commerce, with a True Copy of the Bill,* printed by J. Baker in 1713. It gives 187 names for the bill; 196 against it, of which 120 are marked 'W' for Whig and 36 'Wh' for 'whimisical', to distinguish them from the Tories (unmarked) who voted against the Court. Two other variants of this list were printed in 1713,[144] but the one printed in 'A Letter from a Member' is probably the more accurate as the figures for the vote correspond exactly with those given in the *Commons' Journals*, plus two tellers each side.[145] In fact, this list has been described as 'the most reliable division list to be published during Anne's reign'.[146] There are three differences between this printed list and Baillie's recording of the vote of 18 June. The M.P. for Dumfries Burghs is given as John Hutton, who in fact died in December 1712, and was replaced at a by-election by Sir William Johnstone (correctly given by Baillie). The printed list gives Alexander Reid as absent, whereas Baillie records him as 'pro', and Baillie records the Hon. John Stewart as 'con' while the printed list gives him as absent. Thus the printed list has two fewer Scottish M.P.s voting than Baillie's list.

---

[143] See *A Register of Parliamentary Lists 1660–1761.* eds. D. Hayton and C. Jones (University of Leicester History Department Occasional Publication No. 1, 1979), p. 106.

[144] For details see R.R. Walcott, 'Division-Lists of the House of Commons, 1689–175', *B.I.H.R.*, XIV (1936–7), 35–6.

[145] The Commons figures are 194 to 185 (*C.J.*, XVII, 430).

[146] W.A. Speck, 'The House of Commons, 1701–14: A Study in Political Organisation' (Oxford, D. Phil., 1965), p. 80. In the list printed in 'A Letter from a Member', 8 M.P.s are wrongly labelled: 3 'Whimsicals' are in fact Whigs, and 5 'Whigs' are either Whimsical Tories or even Tories who in this issue voted for the first time against the Court (*ibid.*).

The Lists

'pro' = voted with the Court; 'con' = voted against the Court; 'a' = absent from the House; 'went out' = at the House but left before the vote.

Names	4 June 1713	18 June 1713
Abercromby, Alexander	pro	pro
Baillie, George	con	con
Campbell, Sir James	con	a
Campbell, Hon. John	a	a
Carnegie, John	pro	pro
Cochrane, Hon. William	a	a
Cockburn, John	con	con
Cumming, Sir Alexander	pro	pro
Cunningham, Henry	con	con
Dalrymple, Sir David	a	con
Douglas, Sir Alexander	a	a
Douglas, Hon. George	a	a
Dunbar, Sir James	a	a
Eliott, Sir Gilbert	con	con
Erskine, Sir Alexander (Lord Lyon)	went out	pro
Gordon, Sir William	a	a
Grant, Alexander	con	con
Hamilton, George	pro	pro
Hamilton, Sir James	went out	pro
Houston, John	went out	pro
Johnston, Sir Patrick	a	con
Johnstone, Sir William	a	a
Livingstone, William	pro	pro
Lockhart, George	went out	pro
Mackenzie, Alexander	a	a
Mackenzie, George	a	a
Mackenzie, Sir Kenneth	a	a
Malcolm, Sir John	a	a
Montgomerie, John	con	con
Munro, Robert	con	con
Murray, Alexander	con	con
Murray, Lord James	pro	pro
Murray, Hon. James	pro	pro
Oliphant, Charles	went out	pro
Oswald, James	con	con
Paterson, Sir Hugh	went out	pro
Pollock, Sir Robert	con	con
Pringle, John	pro	pro
Ramsay, Sir Alexander	a	a
Reid, Alexander	pro	pro
Ross, Hon. Charles	pro	pro
Smith, Thomas	con	con
Stewart, Hon. John	con	con
Stewart, John	con	con
Yeaman, George	con	con

6

HARLEY, ST. JOHN AND THE DEATH OF
THE TORY PARTY

IN September 1714, a month after the death of the Queen whom he had served for four years as Secretary of State, the fallen Lord Bolingbroke mourned the passing of a political era: 'the grief of my soul is this, I see plainly that the Tory party is gone'. Gloomily he foresaw a future in which tens of thousands of his countrymen would continue to profess themselves Tories, but would no longer be credible competitors for power in the new Britain of George I.[1] Behind this lamentation lies one of the strangest riddles in British political history. Why did a party which commanded a natural majority of the political nation, which had enjoyed since 1710 a position of unprecedented strength in the House of Commons, and whose members had engrossed by 1714 almost every important civil office in the kingdom, thereupon disappear from the political map, as a potent force, for three-quarters of a century?

This is the problem on which this essay will focus. A possible solution, and one with much substance in it, is that the two most able Tory politicians of the day, Bolingbroke himself (the former Henry St John) and Robert Harley, earl of Oxford, engaged in a mutually destructive quarrel which divided the party, paralysed its leadership and delivered it into the hands of its enemies. A number of myths have grown up around this great political duel which can too easily befog the political scene of Anne's later years; and these we must try to dispel. But further questions will still require to be answered. Why, for instance, were there no other helmsmen ready and able to take the wheel when the captain and the first mate were swept from the bridge in that fateful summer of 1714? Is it feasible to explain the party's astonishing collapse solely in terms of leadership? Was it not the whole body, and not just the head, of Toryism that was mortally afflicted at the time of Anne's death? And, finally, can the assumption that underlies these questions – that the Tory party was indeed doomed in August 1714 – be itself sustained in the teeth of evidence which scholars have recently marshalled against it?[2]

1. James Macpherson, *Original Papers containing the Secret History of Great Britain* (1775), ii, 631: to Bishop Atterbury [1 or 2 Sept].
2. e.g. J. H. Plumb, *The Growth of Political Stability in England 1675–1725* (1967), pp. 159–60; *The Divided Society*, ed. G. Holmes and W. A. Speck (1967), pp. 1–2, 33–7. For the traditional view see K. Feiling, *History of the Tory Party* (1924), p. 479.

I

To assess the contribution of Harley and St John to the Tory *débâcle* involves some understanding of the origins of their struggle, of the main stages in its development, and above all of its underlying causes. But the first necessity is to look back before the quarrel itself to the famous political friendship which preceded it. It is only when the nature of that close but strange relationship is understood that the reasons for its breakdown and for the bitter antagonism this engendered can be appreciated.

In the first place it was never an equal relationship. Harley was by fifteen years the senior, with over a decade more of parliamentary experience behind him. In the period of their closest association, during the first half of Queen Anne's reign, St John was merely the most talented member of a political group which looked to Robert Harley (Speaker in three successive Parliaments from 1701 to 1705 and Secretary of State from 1704 to 1708) for leadership and patronage. 'Robin' was the 'Master'; Harry the 'faithful' pupil. Later, when Harley formed a new administration in 1710 and St John received his first taste of Cabinet office, the latter's position remained – whether he liked it or not – that of a subordinate. Their Tory friends recognised this by the nicknames they gave the two men then, 'the colonel' and 'the captain' respectively. It is often imagined that right from the start the Queen's last ministry suffered from divided command – that it was 'the ministry of Harley and St John';[3] but this was not the case. The administration of 1710–14 was already half-way through its life when a noted confidant of its leading members wrote: 'the court is so luckily constituted at present, that every man thinks the chief trust cannot be anywhere else so well placed; neither do I know above one man that would take it, and it is a great deal too early for him to have such thoughts'.[4]

Apart from being an unequal relationship, Harley's friendship with St John had also represented, to an extraordinary degree, the attraction of opposites. Indeed, perhaps the oddest feature of their story is not that later in Anne's reign their paths so sharply diverged, but that they should ever have come together in the first place. They might never have done so but for the factious obstructionism and religious fanaticism

3. This legend owes its popularity to that most widely read survey of the seventeenth century, G. M. Trevelyan's *England under the Stuarts*. See Pelican ed. (1960), pp. 484–5.

4. *The Works of Jonathan Swift*, ed. T. Roscoe (1888), ii, 483: Swift to Archbishop King, 30 Sept 1712.

shown by the champions of traditional High Toryism in the first two years of Anne's reign, which all but forced a disillusioned young St John into the welcoming arms of the Speaker, then casting around for Tories of every shape and size to rally them to the support of the Godolphin administration. But although their political alliance was accompanied by warm comradeship, there was never an integration of like minds and outlooks, let alone a harmony of temperaments. St John was by nature frank, impulsive, volatile; Harley secretive, oblique and phlegmatic. Their political talents were sharply contrasted, with St John the more brilliant debater and more indefatigable administrator and Harley the subtler negotiator and more skilful parliamentary manager. Their concepts of public life and its obligations were likewise very different. Harley was not only personally incorruptible, but meticulous in his attitude to public money; whereas St John, as he showed over the Quebec contracts (1711) and the commercial negotiations with Spain (1713–14), believed that nests were meant to be feathered.

Still more remarkably at variance were their basic political attitudes. To Harley the existence of party, as it had evolved by the end of King William's reign – with the deepest division that of Whig against Tory rather than of Country against Court – was a necessary evil. That is why a political spoils-system, in which party allegiance was the sole governing factor, was always unacceptable to him, particularly when it threatened the professional fields of administration. Although, in reaction against the Junto, he had severed nearly all his former Whig connexions by 1702, he consistently resisted the efforts of his friends to press him into a wholehearted commitment to Toryism, and more especially to foist on him after 1707 the mantle of party leader. Sharing as he did most of the opinions of a 'moderate Tory', such detachment became increasingly difficult to sustain as the head of a largely Tory administration between 1710 and 1714. Yet, however others saw him, he always conceived of himself as the Queen's 'manager', carrying on her business in the Sunderland–Marlborough–Godolphin tradition. St John, on the other hand, wore the habit of 'moderation' like a hair shirt. By nature and inclination he was deeply partisan, an extremist who showed his true colours in his fledgling years as an M.P. when he was a sponsor of the first two Occasional Conformity bills. His championship of right-wing policies and of unqualified single-party government later in Anne's reign was no more than a reversion to type.

The origins of the conflict between Harley and St John have long been a subject of speculation and confusion. The truth is, there was no sudden break, but rather a progressive deterioration of relations over

2. Queen Anne in Parliament, c.1710. This is the first known painting of the interior of the House of Lords.

Peter Tillemans. *House of Lords Record Office*

3. Robert Harley, earl of Oxford, as Lord High Treasurer, c.1714

Speaker of the Commons 1701-5 and Secretary of State from 1704 until his fall in 1708, he became (1710-14) the first and last Tory prime minister of the eighteenth century. The subtlest politician of his day, Harley was 'secretive, oblique and phlegmatic' but 'personally incorruptible'.

Sir Godfrey Kneller. *National Portrait Gallery*

more than six years: first a period of friction rather than direct conflict; then a period when conflict still remained to some extent below the surface, a source of embarrassment to Harley rather than a serious threat; and lastly a period when it was open and avowed, a real menace to Harley's supremacy and a dangerous source of weakness to the Tory party. The key dates emerge as 1708, 1711 and 1713.

In all three phases there were common denominators. There was disagreement over the extent to which Harley was committed, both by past promises and present professions, to the cause of Toryism. The element of personal animus was also constant throughout, limited to St John alone in the first phase, but becoming mutual in the last two. But the conventional view that theirs was essentially a clash of temperament and personality, underlain more by motives of jealousy and ambition than by a fundamental collision of principles[5] is wholly at odds with the evidence. In each phase there were major issues in dispute, and the way these issues were resolved or left unresolved was to prove of critical importance to the Tories. In the first period the argument was mainly over tactics – an argument over how the reign of Godolphin and the Whigs could best be terminated and their recovery prevented. But subsequently matters of policy and ideology became paramount, above all the issue of peace in the second period and the issue of the succession in the third.

The idea that Henry St John remained a loyal Harleyite for at least a decade must also be discounted. In fact, firm links were not forged until his third winter in the House of Commons (1703-4) and within five years these links had begun to show the first signs of stress. They were still apparently indissoluble in February 1708, when the young Secretary-at-War generously followed Harley out of office after the failure of his chief's first bid to overthrow Godolphin. Had Harley's February *coup* succeeded it was generally believed that St John would have replaced Lord Sunderland as Secretary of State for the South. This is a fact worth bearing in mind when considering St John's reaction to Harley's next attempt at a ministerial revolution, in 1710. The turning-point in their special relationship, however, had already come long before then. We can trace it back as far as the General Election of May 1708, an event which thus assumes an ominous significance for the future of the Tory cause. At this Election St John lost his seat at Wootton Bassett. All efforts to accommodate him elsewhere failed, and

5. See, for example, M. Ashley, *England in the Seventeenth Century* (1952), pp. 246-8; G. N. Clark, *The Later Stuarts*, 2nd ed. (Oxford, 1955), pp. 239, 245-6.

he was left with a strong grudge against his fellow Tories for not exerting themselves more strongly on his behalf. Some of this resentment rubbed off on Harley, although both he and his lieutenants seem to have done all they reasonably could do to assist 'the Thracian' in his plight.[6]

The next two years of enforced political inactivity, much of them passed on his country estate in Berkshire, changed the course of Henry St John's life. For one thing, they gave him prolonged insight, at first hand, into the grievances of the ordinary Tory gentleman, the private 'country esquire'. Between 1708 and 1710 the exile cf Bucklebury found himself increasingly in sympathy with the attitudes of such men: with their war weariness; with their opposition to costly land operations in the Low Countries; above all with their hatred of Whiggery in all its manifestations, especially the Whiggery of the 'war profiteers' in the City. The other effect of St John's exclusion from the House of Commons was that for almost eighteen months down to the spring of 1710 it cut him off from the political mainstream, and to some extent from the Harleyite main body. While he was exhorting the 'Master' by letter to put himself 'at the head of the gentlemen of England', Harley himself was carefully preparing the ground for his second attempt to undermine the Godolphin ministry; and the agents of destruction which he planned to use (the Queen, the royal favourite Abigail Masham, and a group of discontented Whigs, the most notable of whom was the duke of Shrewsbury) were very different from the methods being advocated by his disciple. Together with the imperative need for secrecy in the work, they precluded close co-operation with St John in this vital phase.

The strain caused by these tactical disagreements was suddenly increased in March 1710, when St John discovered to his astonishment how Harley and Shrewsbury were planning to dispose of the spoils once the Godolphin ministry was overthrown, and realised that he himself had no place in their shadow Cabinet. As in 1708, Sunderland was earmarked as one of the first victims of the plot. But now there was no mention of St John among the bevy of candidates whose names were canvassed for the secretaryship before the choice fell in June on the uncontroversial Lord Dartmouth. Not until September, when Harley finally gave up his efforts to persuade an old comrade-in-arms of the 1690s, Henry Boyle, to stay on as the other Secretary of State, was the way opened for St John's promotion.[7] How can one account for this

6. Levens MSS: St John to James Grahme, 18 July 1708; see also G. Holmes, *British Politics in the Age of Anne* (1967), pp. 319, 506 n 123.
7. HMC *Portland MSS* ii, 218.

obvious reluctance to give him Cabinet office ? One factor undoubtedly was the attitude of the Queen, who at this time disapproved of his political principles as well as of his unsavoury private life and his freethinking.[8] But it seems equally apparent that Harley himself, aware of St John's drift to extremism in the past two years, foresaw that it would be increasingly difficult in future to curb the younger man's natural bent. Both he and Shrewsbury realised the need for moderate policies at home while the new ministry was carrying out its first major task – that of putting peace negotiations on a firm footing, while fighting one more vigorous campaign abroad. They may even have feared that the negotiations themselves might be jeopardised with so positive a personality as St John in an office which gave him a large measure of control over the country's foreign relations.

It would have been asking too much of St John not to resent the obvious intention to exclude him from high office. His acknowledged gifts, and his self-sacrifice in 1708, entitled him to anticipate a more alluring prospect from the ministerial revolution of 1710 than an invitation to return to his old job at the War Office. His eventual appointment as Secretary of State for the North on 20 September was not in itself enough to remove the scars left by the events of the previous few months; and it should not be overlooked that two of the basic factors which were to sustain and embitter the quarrel which developed between Harley and St John in the years from 1711 to 1714, a personal grudge and a sharp divergence of political attitudes, were both present from the very start of the new ministry's life.

Friction, then, had been present since 1708. But the first real breach, disturbing to Harley's equanimity and to some extent disruptive of party unity, did not occur until 1711. It was in the spring of that year, while Harley still lay on his sick-bed following an attempt on his life by a French adventurer, that St John, jealous perhaps of the wave of sympathy for the victim, foolishly tried to detract from his colleague's near-martyrdom by claiming that Guiscard's knife had been intended for him. To Harley's anxious relatives such reckless and blatant seeking after the limelight was hard to forget and forgive; and we know that the invalid himself was deeply offended. But for him St John's indiscretion was adding insult to injury, for twice already the prime minister had been given good grounds for regretting his reluctant decision to admit his old friend into the Cabinet. Trouble had erupted in the Cabinet itself as early as January 1711, when St John, powerfully swayed by

8. Herts RO Panshanger MSS: Hamilton's diary, 21 Sept 1710, 14 Dec 1711.

traditional Tory arguments in favour of a maritime strategy, first brought forward his proposal for an expedition to capture Quebec. Anxious not to subject the government's precarious financial position to unnecessary strain, and suspicious perhaps that the Secretary's motives were not entirely disinterested, Harley had cold-shouldered the scheme; but he had been unable to prevent the Cabinet finally approving it in the early days of his illness. Meanwhile, however, he had acquired a new and much stronger grievance against his ambitious colleague. Early in February the House of Commons had witnessed the first concerted effort against the ministry by a formidable pressure-group of Tory backbenchers, the October Club; and Harley had good cause to suspect that St John was in some measure privy to its secrets and even involved behind the scenes in its activities.

It was common knowledge that 'the captain' sympathised with both the main aims of the Octobrists: the punishment of every Whig against whom a charge of financial malpractice in office could feasibly be brought and a total purge of that party's adherents, as he himself later put it, from all 'the employments of the kingdom, down to the meanest'.[9] It can scarcely be a coincidence that the Club's opening salvoes, including an unmistakable threat to hold up the voting of supply, were fired on 5 February 1711; and that over three years later Harley recalled to the Queen's memory, with unerring precision, that it was at 'the beginning of February 1710 [1711], there began to be a separation in the House of Commons, and Mr Secretary St Johns began listing a party, and set up for governing the House'.[10] How long St John continued to play so dangerously with fire in this way we cannot be certain. He was sobered to some extent in late February or early March by the remonstrances of a group of fellow ministers dining at his house; but during Harley's two-months' absence from the Commons after the Guiscard incident, the Secretary was seemingly tempted to at least one more major indiscretion. The humiliating fiasco over the leather duty at the end of March, when the government was defeated on a vital revenue measure by the votes of the Octobrists, and was able to recover only by the discreditable expedient of proposing the same tax the following day, disguised under a new name, was largely St John's fault. And the contemporary evidence to support a charge of connivance as well as negligence certainly cannot be lightly discounted.[11]

9. Bolingbroke, *A Letter to Sir William Windham* (1753), pp. 21–2.

10. BM Loan 29/204: paper dated 6 June 1714.

11. See, for example, Arthur Onslow's note to Burnet, *A History of my own Time* (1833), vi, 31; Edward Harley's 'Memoirs of the Harley Family', in HMC *Portland MSS* v, 655.

If by his extraordinary tactics between January and March 1711 St John had hoped to discredit Harley's administration, force his resignation and then step into his shoes, he must have been bitterly disappointed by the outcome. When Harley returned to active politics at the end of April, after his convalescence, his own star was much higher than it had been two months earlier and his ministry more firmly established, while the Secretary's stock had plummeted. In the late spring of 1711, in fact, St John's dismissal from office was confidently forecast. By great good fortune he survived. He did so mainly because Harley could at this time afford to be generous to his would-be rival. His own primacy was now unquestioned, and was soon to be confirmed when a grateful Queen made him earl of Oxford and Lord High Treasurer. Also, St John's acute mental grasp and formidable capacity for work could not lightly be dispensed with after 2 May 1711, when Lord Rochester's sudden and unexpected death deprived the government of its most experienced member; and this only a few days after the Cabinet, St John included, had been admitted to the secret that peace negotiations with France were afoot. But it is the fact of St John's survival rather than the reasons for it which is important. For this was the first of two crucial occasions during the life of Anne's last ministry when Harley allowed his erring and dangerous colleague to escape the penalty of his political sins and recover all the ground that he had lost. The second, as we shall shortly see, occurred in the autumn of 1713. Each episode appears in retrospect to have been a nail driven inexorably into the coffin of the Tory party.

The latter occasion took place shortly after the Harley–St John struggle had entered its third and most serious phase. For most of the preceding two and a half years, since April 1711, the dominant theme in the two men's relations with each other had been the making of peace. Over the same period, likewise, the government's peace policy had become the governing factor in setting the Tory party as a whole on a perilous and injurious course: 'the very work which ought to have been the basis of our strength', as the 'man of mercury' himself came to acknowledge,[12] 'was in part demolished before our eyes, and we were stoned with the ruins of it'. How St John was for long kept in ignorance of the 'Jersey stage' of the negotiations in 1710–11; how Oxford tenaciously preserved his own diplomatic control from April 1711 until the consummation in April 1713; and how St John constantly chafed and fretted at his inability to put his own stamp indelibly on the

12. *Letter to Windham*, p. 50; 'man of mercury' was yet another of St John's nicknames.

proceedings – this modern research has established.   But there are three aspects of the Tory peace-making which, because of their bearing on our own problem, merit special emphasis.

The first is that for Oxford important principles were at stake in the foreign as well as the domestic policies of his administration. From the first his Cabinet had been generally agreed on the need for peace, as well as on the fact that British interests had been sacrificed by the Whigs to those of the allies. Yet over the timing of negotiations, the methods by which peace should be sought, and the objectives it should secure, there were important ministerial differences, above all between the first minister and the Secretary for the North; and these reflected still wider differences within the Tory party at large.[13] Harley did not exclude St John from the 'Jersey stage' because, as is sometimes maintained, he was jealous of the younger man's talents. He excluded him primarily because he wanted the broad principles of agreement to have been reached between Britain and France, and accepted by the allies, before St John's own views – his unashamed anti-Europeanism, his almost pathological hatred of the Dutch, and his consequent indifference to the protection of most allied interests – had had the chance to obtrude themselves. The attempt did not succeed; but the subsequent history of the negotiations, once St John was involved in them, proved that it was well justified.

The second point to be stressed about the personal conflict over the peace, seen in the context of ultimate Tory disaster, is that on the one occasion in these two years when St John broke free from Oxford's stranglehold, during his brief mission to France in August 1712, he committed indiscretions even more shattering than his parliamentary frolics of 1711 and certainly more damaging in their effects. This was a mission from which he himself expected much, as a means of breaking down remaining obstacles to peace, but from which Oxford expected little or nothing. The Treasurer sanctioned it only in the hope that it would help to salve St John's wounded pride, after the Queen had conferred the viscountcy of Bolingbroke on him instead of the earldom he had expected; and he made certain that his colleague's commission would be narrowly circumscribed. But even Oxford could hardly have foreseen that Bolingbroke would exceed his instructions quite so extravagantly or perpetrate the crowning solecism of allowing himself to be seen in public with the Pretender. The result was a stormy Cabinet meeting on 28 September 1712, at which the Treasurer succeeded in

13. See Holmes, *British Politics*, pp. 78–80.

getting Bolingbroke's actions and immediate objectives repudiated, but at the same time discovered to his chagrin that the Secretary was now able to command more support from other leading ministers, and even – on some points – from the Queen, than he had imagined possible. The importance of this Cabinet as a stage in the breakdown of ministerial cohesion should not be overlooked.

At the same time it must be seen in perspective. For although the ministry's peace policy added a fresh source of friction to those already present in the relations between Oxford and St John, it was also the main factor in postponing for so long a complete and final rupture. Cabinet disputes over the peace there certainly were. But the over-riding necessity of completing the great work to which all its members were committed led them, on each occasion, to stifle resentments and patch up differences which in other circumstances would have led to resignations or dismissals. Very significantly it was only after the final treaties with France had been signed in April 1713, and very soon after-wards at that, that Oxford noted the formation of the first genuine 'confederation' or 'combination' against him.[14]

This confederacy was born out of the troubles of the session of April–July 1713 (the last session of the old Parliament). Both inside and outside the ministry there were prominent Tories who by 1713 had lost faith in Oxford's leadership, or believed that now peace had come at last he had outlived his usefulness to the party. At their head, needless to say, was Bolingbroke. He and his closest allies, Lord Chancellor Harcourt and Francis Atterbury, the new bishop of Rochester, unjustly laid the onus of all the government's parliamentary difficulties – over the malt tax, the Union with Scotland and above all the commerce treaty with France – on the Lord Treasurer's shoulders, and protested that nothing positive had been done to advance the interest of the Tory party or the Anglican Church. By the end of the session, though still far from certain of the Queen's good will,[15] Bolingbroke had come to the conclusion that now was the time to make his bid for glory. 'If your brother will not set himself at the head of the Church party', he informed Edward Harley, 'somebody must'.[16]

Thus the Oxford–Bolingbroke conflict became for the first time a direct struggle for power. It was fought out in the corridors of Kensington and Whitehall during the last week in July and the first week in

---

14. 'Set on foot against the next Parliament'. BM Loan 29/204: paper dated 15 June 1714; cf. HMC *Portland MSS* v, 466.
15. *The Lockhart Papers*, ed. A. Aufrere (1817), i, 412–13.
16. HMC *Portland MSS* v, 660.

August, and it ended in rout for Oxford's opponents. They were forced to submit not just to his continued premiership, but to a remodelling of ministerial offices which directly curtailed their own departmental authority and placed 'Treasurer's men' at almost every strategic point available. When Oxford journeyed into Cambridgeshire at the end of August to preside over his son's marriage to Lady Harriet Holles, one of the most coveted matrimonial prizes in England, it seemed that he was setting the seal of social triumph on a great political achievement.

No-one, least of all Oxford himself, could have expected the tide of fortune at this juncture to turn so quickly against him. It did so for three reasons. The first was four weeks' almost continuous absence from Windsor by the Treasurer, which gave Bolingbroke an unexpected opportunity to rally his broken forces and to win over the influential favourite, Lady Masham. The second was Oxford's request in mid-September for the dukedom of Newcastle for his son, Edward, which caused the first real breach in the unique relationship which Oxford had enjoyed with Queen Anne since 1706. The third was Masham's betrayal of this request to Bolingbroke, who did not scruple to propagate the slander that Oxford was prepared to sacrifice all other interests, public and party, to those of his family advancement. The truth is that Oxford had been forced into this unhappy predicament mainly by the vindictiveness and self-consequence of Lady Harriet's mother.

More serious, however, than these immediate causes was the prolonged bout of apathy, verging on despair, which assailed the Treasurer from late September until well into December. This was the product partly of the damage inflicted on his relationship with the Queen (the extent of which was magnified greatly by his own paranoia), partly to a great personal tragedy he suffered in November – just when he was beginning to haul himself out of the trough – with the death of his favourite daughter. For the Tory party this phase of the Oxford–Bolingbroke struggle was to prove perhaps the most important of all. For although by December 1713 Bolingbroke had almost succeeded in convincing the Queen that his *policies* were the right ones for the government to pursue, he had still to convince her that they were best entrusted to his own hands. Anne could as yet see no obvious alternative to Oxford without turning again to the Whigs. One can only conclude that had the prime minister looked to his defences late in 1713, instead of giving way to defeatism, he would very probably have regained fairly quickly much of the ground he had lost in September; and in that case it is more than possible that he would still have been firmly in the saddle when Anne died the following August (the fact that he clung on to an infinitely weaker position till almost the end of July surely justifies this assumption). The Tory party would then not have had to face the most critical year of its existence in 1714 with a ministry which had no authoritative leadership, no clear objectives, and indeed no sense of direction.

It is this final phase of the battle for command over the Tory ministry, from January to August 1714, which has attracted most attention; and partly for this reason, partly because there is less that is new to be said about it, we may be excused for devoting the minimum of space to it here. The lack of direction in the government was nowhere more obvious, and nowhere more fatal, than in its succession policy. By the terms of the Act of Settlement of 1701, the second in line to the throne if Anne died without direct heirs was the Elector George Lewis of Hanover. Only his aged mother, the Princess Sophia,[17] stood between him and the legal Protestant succession. Ever since the winter of 1711–12 this fact had confronted the Oxford ministry with a most uncomfortable dilemma. For the Elector was a convinced supporter of the claims of the Habsburg Charles VI to the throne of Spain; he was also a soldier with a warm admiration for the duke of Marlborough. The news, that winter, of Britain's determination to abandon Spain to the Bourbons, followed by the dismissal of Marlborough from his command, had done serious damage to good relations between the ministry and the Hanoverian court. To the Elector these steps argued a favourable disposition towards the cause of the exiled Stuarts, and few Tories doubted by December 1713 that his succession would mean for them at least a temporary loss of royal favour. Had this seemed a distant prospect it would have been less disturbing. But at Christmas the Queen fell desperately ill, so ill that for two or three days her life was in genuine danger, and from every Tory, inside and outside the government, an agonising reappraisal of the succession question was called for.

Bolingbroke's priorities from now on were: first, to try to persuade the Pretender to acknowledge a purely nominal conversion to Protestantism, and second, in case this approach failed (and it had done so comprehensively by early March), to seek to ensure that Tory command of all the institutions of Church and State, and above all of the armed forces, was so unchallengeable that whoever succeeded Anne would be forced to make his terms with the party and with its leaders. Bold as he was, even Bolingbroke was not hardy enough to stake everything on the Pretender's cause. But by assiduously cultivating the Jacobite leaders in

17. Sophia died in May 1714.

Parliament, by holding out the prospect of a repeal of the Act of Settle-ment and by showing himself totally unconciliatory in his attitude to Hanover, he left few politicians or observers in any doubt where his real sympathies lay. Oxford, galvanised at last into action by the Queen's illness, was convinced in the last six months of his ministry's life of the Secretary's Jacobite inclinations. He himself had never been anything but a Hanoverian at heart. And although for a month or two at the beginning of 1714 he was put so much out of patience by Hanoverian intrigues with the Whigs that he allowed himself to be associated with the appeal to the Pretender on the religious issue, his attitude towards the succession very soon became dominated by two overriding concerns.

The first was to take advantage of what parliamentary opportunities occurred (for example, over the Whig proposal to offer a reward for the Pretender's capture in June) to demonstrate his sincerity to Hanover and to the 'Hanover wing' of the Tory party. His main concern, however, was the purely negative one of clinging on to office as long as possible, in the conviction that this was the best service he could render the Hanoverian cause. Only twice did he veer from this course: for a few days in March, when, under renewed attack from Bolingbroke and his followers, he seriously contemplated throwing in his hand; and in the last fortnight in June and the first week of July, when he saw his last chance of destroying Bolingbroke by a vigorous counter-attack over the conduct of the Spanish commerce negotiations. But in the main his aim was to act, as one scholar has strikingly put it, as the 'drag anchor' on Bolingbroke's ambitions.[18] So well did he succeed in the end in fulfilling this self-appointed role – staving off the inevitable for four months at least after he had totally lost the Queen's confidence, and after his defeat had been widely predicted, and leaving his rival a mere four days' grace before Anne's death overwhelmed him – that he is entitled to no small share of the credit for frustrating the Pretender's hopes. Unfortunately for the Tories, of course, the very success of this long-drawn-out delaying action, accompanied as it was by open warfare both in Cabinet and Parliament between Oxford and Bolingbroke factions, further increased the possibility that the party itself would not long survive the fall of the Lord Treasurer on 27 July 1714. Though heavily outnumbered in the House of Commons, the Whigs had achieved complete unity and cohesion in 1714 over the succession question; and from the morning of 30 July, when Queen Anne, brought

18. B. W. Hill, 'The Career of Robert Harley, earl of Oxford, from 1702 to 1714' (Cambridge Ph.D. thesis, 1961), fo. 332.

by the distress and anxiety of the past few months to the end of her tiny stock of physical resources, fell into the coma that was to mark the start of her last illness, 'Mercurialis', the victor of the moment, saw all the hopes and schemes of the past twelve months rendered irrelevant. The initiative was wrested from his hands, first by the Privy Council,[19] and secondly, after the Queen's death, by the Council of Regency for which the Whigs had made such careful provision in the Act of 1706. Once George Lewis had been peacefully proclaimed King at St James's Palace gate, and it became apparent that the Jacobites were not prepared for any swift countermove, the remorseless logic of party conflict and of two and a half years of bad relations between the Oxford ministry and Hanover could only mean the end of Tory government, at least in the immediate future.

II

But did it also mean, or need it have meant, the end of the Tory party? Certain it is that there were major obstacles in the way of the party's revival and recovery. And none was more formidable than the poverty of its leadership.

The essence of the Tories' plight in 1714 was not that they were entirely lacking in young men with the potential of leadership: men such as Sir William Windham, the Chancellor of the Exchequer, who in the 1720s and 1730s was to become an able enough spokesman of those Tory backbenchers by then reconciled to the Hanoverian dynasty. But what the Tories needed in the aftermath of Queen Anne's death was assets that were more solid and more immediately realisable; and the sorry truth was that there was no-one who could *at once* (and this was the key point) fill the vacuum left by the fall of Oxford in July 1714 and of Bolingbroke in August. The Whigs were utterly determined to hound both these men out of public life at the earliest opportunity, using the recent peace negotiations as their excuse. In any case Oxford's constitution had already been badly undermined by illness and bouts of heavy drinking, and two years in the Tower awaiting trial from 1715 to 1717 completed the ruin of his health. As for Bolingbroke, he was still young and, for all his dissolute life, immensely vigorous (it is sometimes forgotten that he lived until 1751). But even if he had not sealed his own political fate by fleeing to France in anticipation of arrest in 1715, he would still have been out of the reckoning for several years.

19. See *The Divided Society*, ed. Holmes and Speck, pp. 176–7.

The absence of any outstanding personality capable of rallying the demoralised forces of Toryism after August 1714 and, equally important, of holding them together in face of the fresh shocks they suffered over the next two years, can partly be explained on natural grounds. The most important seam of Tory leadership since 1688 – that old generation of High Church Tories whose primacy had been established by the political battles of the 1670s – had been virtually worked out. Sir Edward Seymour had died in 1708, the earl of Rochester in 1711, and the duke of Leeds (the former Danby) in 1712. The only prominent survivor of this vintage, Lord Nottingham, might have given the lead the party so desperately needed in the early months of George I's reign but for one crippling disqualification. In November 1711, prompted in part by pique, in part by principle, he had renounced his support for the Oxford ministry, made a pact with his old adversaries the Whigs, and gone into permanent opposition. Many Tories never forgave him; and even those strong pro-Hanoverians who co-operated with him in Parliament in 1714 were disillusioned when he agreed to accept a Cabinet office along with the Whigs in George I's first ministry.

Of the younger generation only three men, apart from Bolingbroke had established any real claim before 1714 to inherit the mantle of Nottingham, Rochester and Seymour. These were Sir Thomas Hanmer, one of the wealthiest commoners in England and Speaker at the time of the Queen's death; the earl of Anglesey, who had been Vice-Treasurer of Ireland under Lord Oxford; and the Northern Secretary of State from 1713 to 1714, William Bromley of Baginton. The first two had emerged since the summer of 1713 as the undisputed leaders of the Hanoverian Tories. But as fomenters of open rebellion against the ministry they had made themselves highly controversial figures, and in some Tory quarters unacceptable. Moreover Hanmer, despite a good intellect and an impressive oratorical style, remained a backbencher at heart, far more at home as a critic than as a pillar of government. The man incomparably best fitted to lead the Tory party through the wilderness in 1714 was Bromley. He had a quarter of a century of parliamentary experience behind him. Ever regarded as a staunch Churchman, he nonetheless had friends and admirers in every section of the party. In the previous four years he had filled the Speaker's Chair as well as the Secretaryship with credit. Though far more a party man than Harley, he had backed the Treasurer against the wilder excesses of Bolingbroke from 1711 almost to the end, but had refused to join in intrigues with the Whigs. Hanover believed him loyal, and he was offered a Household appointment by George I soon after his accession.

Yet, with all these advantages, Bromley incomprehensibly missed the opportunity which awaited him in 1714. He continued to sit in the House of Commons until his death in 1732, but the last eighteen years were a slow downward drift into relative obscurity. Even in the Parliament of 1715–22 he became of less account on the attenuated benches of the Tory opposition than lesser figures like Windham, Shippen and Hynde Cotton. It may have been a failure of character, of ambition, or simply of faith. Whatever it was, it cost the Tory party dear; it could be argued that it cost it its best, if not its only, chance of surviving the disaster of 1714 and competing again for power.

The problem of leadership was not, of course, a new one for the Tories. It was all too familiar. The party hierarchy had never approached the cohesion which the Whigs derived from the dominance first of Shaftesbury and later of the Junto. Neither could it consistently secure united action from the lower ranks. The Country Tory backbencher and the backwoods Tory peer earned a just reputation both in William's reign and in Anne's for their independence of mind and for being unamenable to discipline. Not surprisingly, the capacity of the parliamentary Tories for fragmentation in certain circumstances was remarkable; and it was never more in evidence than in the session of 1714. The contrast with the Whigs was extraordinary. Both in 1702, when William III died, and in 1710, when the Godolphin ministry fell, the Whigs faced great difficulties and possible disintegration. That they lived to fight another day was due in no small measure on each occasion to the command which the five lords of the Junto could exercise over the party in times of adversity. In 1715–16, when three of these lords died and a fourth retired from active political life, the Whigs had a new generation of leaders ready to assume control: a generation represented by Walpole, Townshend and Stanhope and, of the younger vintage, by Pulteney and Carteret.

At the same time too much emphasis can be placed on these essentially personal factors. The Whigs survived the shocks of 1702 and 1710 not only because of talented and coherent leadership but also because in both crises the rank and file of the party were, and remained, united on essentials. Those who would maintain that the Tory party was a doomed party from the moment Queen Anne died must rest their case, at least in part, on the demonstrable lack of any comparable unity in its ranks, at least since the summer of 1713.

For a party which traditionally stood for 'Church and Crown', the Glorious Revolution, involving as it did a spectacular disavowal of the

High Anglican political creed, had necessarily been a damaging experience. Yet it was one from which, to most appearances, the Tories had recovered with startling rapidity. Their great strength in the constituencies, the early favour shown them by King William,[20] and the fact that their ideological base, though undermined in 1688, had by no means been destroyed, had all played their part in this recovery. A comparison between their situation and fortunes in 1688–9 and in 1714–15 is both valid and instructive. On each occasion Tories were faced with the same basic choice – Church versus King (though in the latter case it was not the King in possession but the titular James III, 'the Gentleman over the Water', whose right was in question). On each occasion the vast majority came in the end to the same decision: they chose to reject the Stuart king in order to preserve the Anglican Church. Having made that decision once at the expense of their traditional belief in hereditary right, and what is more confirmed it thirteen years later by accepting the parliamentary exclusion of the legitimate Stuart line, the choice should logically have been much easier to make on the next occasion. In fact it proved far more difficult, and was delayed so long that the Tories were overtaken by events and, in marked contrast with 1688–9, lost control of them.

What was at the root of this dilemma? Lack of firm leadership, though of the greatest importance as we have seen, cannot have been the whole answer. Nor had the Tories experienced any diminution of their Anglican zeal in the past quarter of a century. And yet the Pretender's refusal to compromise on the religious issue in March 1714, so far from resolving their paralysis of will, only served to intensify it. Without doubt, their consciences were still sorely troubled about the Revolution and about the Act of Settlement of 1701 that had been its logical sequel. The old creed may have been denied in 1688–9; it may have seemed for some years thereafter to lose much of its relevance; but it had not been forgotten. When, for the first time since the Revolution, an oath abjuring allegiance to the Pretender was imposed on all officials and members of Parliament in 1702, it took Lord Nottingham (stout Anglican though he was, and later a doughty fighter for the Protestant succession) three months to change his first opinion, that 'the safest side *in conscience* is to refuse it'.[21] The refusal of the 'Church party' four years later to support the practical measures proposed in the Regency bill, to ensure the peaceful establishment of a Protestant

20. G.Holmes, ed., *Britain after the Glorious Revolution* (1969), pp. 120-5, 160-1.

21. Lloyd-Baker MSS, box 4, bundle Q55: Nottingham to Archbishop Sharp, 10 Jan 1702. My italics.

successor when Queen Anne died, was another straw in the wind; and during the impeachment and trial in 1710 of Dr Henry Sacheverell for preaching a violently anti-Revolution sermon in St Paul's Cathedral, the arguments voiced by Tory after Tory proved beyond doubt that the principle of hereditary right still commanded wide support, and that even the notion of passive obedience was far from being extinct.

Such is the ideological background against which we must view the Tories' reaction to the growing breach between the Oxford ministry and the Elector of Hanover after the winter of 1711–12. Despite this estrangement, the Protestant succession still claimed its quota of genuine supporters inside the party. A handful of committed pro-Hanoverians nailed their colours to the mast as early as December 1711; more followed suit in 1712 and 1713; and by 16 April 1714 almost a quarter of the 340 Tories packed into the Commons' chamber in St Stephen's Chapel (more than had ever attended since the Revolution) were prepared to vote against the government motion that the succession was in no danger. More significant, however, was the attitude of the remainder, who either frankly repudiated or simply shirked an open commitment to Hanover. At least half the party was still torn in the spring of 1714 between the legal and religious arguments in favour of Hanover and the emotional and ideological factors, not to mention considerations of party interest, which pulled them in the opposite direction.

How this great mass of 'floaters' would have reacted in the 1714 session, had Bolingbroke been in a position to introduce – as the Jacobite members begged him to – a bill to repeal the Act of Settlement, we can only speculate. The stirring demonstration of Tory support for Edward Harley, after his unequivocal speech on 24 June in favour of a reward of £100,000 for the Pretender's capture, suggests that since April more waverers had moved towards Hanover than away from it.[22] What really mattered, however, as far as the party's future was concerned, was that so many of its adherents sat irresolutely on the fence for so long that neither Bolingbroke's hand nor Oxford's could be sufficiently strengthened by parliamentary backing to put an early end to the disastrous war of attrition at Court, a war in which there could only be one eventual victor – the Whigs.

Since the succession paralysis of 1714 was, in a sense, a delayed result of the violent shock which the Tory creed had suffered in 1688–9, it

22. Staatsarchiv Hannover, CBA 24 England, 113a, folios 298–9: Kreien-berg's report, 25 June; Add. MS 22201, fo. 101: [Boyer] to Stafford, 25 June.

could be maintained that the party died 'from natural causes'. But taking a wider range of evidence into account, the coroner-historian would be more justified in deciding that it took its own life. It cannot be too strongly emphasised that except on the succession the Tories were not a fatally divided party in 1714. On religious policy, though some were prepared to go further than others to attack the toleration, there were no fundamental disagreements among Tory laymen, while the return of a Whig administration from August 1714 onwards lent renewed force to the old rallying cry of 'the Church in danger'. On social policy, there was still widespread acceptance of the need to shore up the landed interest against its supposed rivals in the City and in the professions, although with the end of the war the conflict of interests[23] inevitably lost something of its edge, and it would lose more as the years went by. Had Bolingbroke had his way and negotiated a new alliance with France and Spain, a serious split might conceivably have developed over foreign policy, but most Tories would have agreed in 1714 on the need for a large measure of disengagement from Europe. The death of Anne and the subsequent loss of the power it had enjoyed for the past four years did not overnight destroy the whole *raison d'être* of the 'Church party'. It still had something to live and fight for; and no less because for the great majority of Tories the succession problem virtually solved itself with the peaceful proclamation of George I. And yet, after August 1714, as for months before it, the party behaved as though the death-wish had taken possession of its spirit. Firm but judicious measures might still have resuscitated an ailing patient. Instead almost everything that was done served to hasten the end.

It is true that the final decline after August 1714 was at least partly attributable to the destructive power of the Whigs. The resignation of Shrewsbury, Oxford's successor as Lord Treasurer, within a few months of his appointment meant that for the first time since 1694 there was no 'manager' at the helm to restrain the vindictiveness of a triumphant set of party leaders or control the vast patronage of the Crown. For this reason the loss of power which the Tories suffered between August and December, first at the centre, then in the localities, was more than just a swing of the party pendulum, like those which had gone against the Whigs in 1702 and more recently in 1710. No party since the Revolution had been so dangerously exposed to the fury of its opponents as was the Tory party by the end of 1714. But at the same time no party could

23. See W.A. Speck, 'Conflict in Society', in *Britain after the Glorious Revolution*, pp. 135-54.

have done more to increase its own vulnerability. The most extraordinary feature of British politics in the two years following Anne's death was the well-nigh incredible folly of the Tories in squandering their last reserves of strength. By spurning the limited yet important favours which George I was prepared to bestow on them,[24] by bungling their election campaign in the winter of 1714–15 and so failing to capitalise on a natural majority in the constituencies,[25] by withholding their support but not their sympathy from the rebels of the '15, they virtually offered themselves up as a sacrifice to their enemies.

The 1715 Election, on which the party had pinned its hopes, was not in itself a holocaust. With over 200 seats in the new House of Commons the Tories were better placed, numerically, than their opponents had been after the previous contest in 1713. But whereas the Whigs in 1713 still had their leaders, their discipline and their faith to hold them together, the Tories by 1715 lacked all three. They were also too discredited both at Court and in the country, especially after the disastrous decision of Bolingbroke to bolt to France in March 1715 and enlist in the Pretender's service, to escape the stigma of Jacobitism and treason when the '15 Rebellion broke out in Scotland later in the year. Even though few English Tories actively supported it, the rebellion gave the Whig ministers a perfect excuse by 1716 to carry through a purge of office-holders 'down to the meanest', such as Bolingbroke had dreamed of in 1710 but had never been strong enough to accomplish. It also enabled them to pass the Septennial Act, which on the grounds of public safety extended the maximum life of the existing Parliament from three years to seven. It was thus made impossible for the Tories to profit, with the strength remaining to them in the constituencies, from the great Whig schism of 1717 or from the South Sea Bubble scandals of 1720. From these final blows in 1716 there could be for the old Tory party no hope of recovery.

To sum up. The first Tory party did not die in 1714 but in 1716; nor even then did it die a natural death. The inquest of history, while con-

---

24. Add. MS 47027, pp. 342–8. Of particular importance was the rejection by Bromley, Hanmer and the latter's friend and ally Ralph Freeman of the King's invitations to join the Nottinghamites in the ministry (Oct 1714). Unlike Nottingham, these three leaders had no past sins to purge, and their acceptance would have ensured, as nothing else could, that the Tories did not fight the General Election of 1715 as a truculent opposition faction.

25. A spectacular example of their indiscreet electoral propaganda was Francis Atterbury's 'English Advice to the Freeholders of England' (1714). See *Somers Tracts* (1815), xiii.

ceding that the party's constitution had been weakened by the shocks of 1688–9 and 1701, must look elsewhere than the Revolution and the Act of Settlement for the real agents of destruction. It must find that the party was gravely wounded between 1711 and 1714 by the two men best able, in their very different ways, to give it a new lease of life; but must add the *caveat* that the protracted duel in which these injuries were inflicted was, in part at least, the reflection of broader differences of opinion among Tories at large, over basic questions of home and foreign policy. It must accept the evidence that in the months of crisis at the beginning of George I's reign the party was recklessly neglected or abused by its own physicians, and reach the verdict that at the last, despairing of the future and implacably harried by its foes, it committed suicide.

POSTSCRIPT

This essay was written in 1968. Even then it was never its intention to argue a case for the 'destruction' of the Tories as a *party*, in 1716 or at any other time in the early 18th century (cf. J.C.D. Clark, 'A General Theory of Party, Opposition and Government, 1688-1832', *Historical Journal,* 23, 1980, p. 296n.); but rather to explain their disappearance 'as a potent force', as 'credible competitors for power', under the first two Georges (p. 139 above). On reflection, it would have been more prudent to avoid the over-dramatic metaphor of 'death' both in the title and in the conclusion. That the Tories *had* ceased by the 1720s to have realistic hopes of ever again dominating the King's ministry, as long as either George I or his successor lived, would hardly be denied even today by any serious student of 18th-century politics. Since 1968, however, our knowledge of the development of party between 1714 and 1760 has been so much advanced that the extraordinary resilience and organizational coherence of the Tory party, even after it had been consigned to permanent opposition for three to four decades, is now accepted. Especially important have been two works. *The History of Parliament: House of Commons 1715-1754* (ed. R. Sedgwick, 1970), vol. I, revealed that at the 1722 General Election the Tories put more candidates into the field than ever before (albeit with depressing results); while Linda Colley's definitive *In Defiance of Oligarchy: The Tory Party, 1714-60* (Cambridge, 1982) demonstrated that, even when down in strength to less than a quarter of the Commons, and reduced to a remnant in the Lords, Tories remained alert to the possibility of exploiting Whig divisions. Thereby they hoped to re-acquire some share of power at the centre and to regain a fair measure of the Crown's favour locally.

None of the work of the past seventeen years (which has included a full-scale biography of Bolingbroke by H.T. Dickinson [1970]) has changed my conviction that the passing of the Septennial Act in 1716 dealt the decisive blow to the two-party system as it had operated under Queen Anne. But I would now argue that it was not until after the crushing Tory defeat at the 1722 Election and the revelation of the Atterbury Plot in the same year that the system conclusively crumbled, to be replaced over the next few years by the political system of the age of Walpole and the Pelhams.

4. Sir Robert Walpole, K.G., as First Lord of the Treasury.
Jean Baptiste van Loo. *National Portrait Gallery*

Robert Walpole, born 26 August 1671, third but first surviving son of Robert Walpole, MP, of Houghton, Norfolk, and Mary, daughter of Sir Jeffrey Burwell. Educated at Eton and King's College, Cambridge. Married (1) 1700 Catherine, daughter of John Shorter, Baltic merchant, three sons (Robert, later Lord Walpole, Edward and Horace) and two daughters. (2) 1737 Maria, daughter of Thomas Skerrett, two illegitimate daughters. Whig MP for Castle Rising 1701-2, King's Lynn 1702-Jan. 1712 (expelled from the House for alleged corruption), Feb.-Mar. 1712 (election void) and 1713-42. Member of Prince George's Admiralty Council 1705-8; Secretary-at-War 1708-10 (Acting Secretary Jan.-Sept. 1710); Treasurer of the Navy 1710-11 (dismissed); Paymaster of the Forces 1714-15; Chancellor of the Exchequer and First Lord of the Treasury 1715-17 (resigned); Paymaster of the Forces 1720-1; Chancellor of the Exchequer and First Lord of the Treasury 1721-42 (resigned). KB 1725; KG 1726; created Earl of Orford 1742. Died 1745.

7

SIR ROBERT WALPOLE

Sir Robert Walpole[1] is traditionally considered the first British prime minister; and traditions, however capriciously and illogically their seeds are planted, are notoriously difficult to uproot. In this case tradition will serve as usefully as anything else to mark one of the major watersheds in Britain's political and constitutional development. For how does one define a 'prime minister' in an age when no such office was legally recognised and the term itself, more often than not, was used pejoratively? The criteria are so variable that we would do well to recognise that a cast-iron definition of the indefinable is impossible.

There were many respects in which even Walpole cannot be compared with a modern prime minister. He was not carried to power on the tide of a party electoral victory: that was not how the political system worked in the eighteenth century. What is more, for twenty years Walpole led a government which was never certain, in the twentieth-century sense, of commanding a majority in the House of Commons. He was never asked by either of the two kings he served, George I and George II, 'to form a ministry'; and in the early years of his supremacy he had to share office with some very uncomfortable bedfellows. There were many of his party, the Whigs, to whom he became anathema, who rejected his primacy and who opposed him venomously.

On the other hand he was by no means the first English politician to be labelled 'prime minister' by his contemporaries. A macabre opposition pamphlet of 1733, entitled *A Short History of Prime Ministers in Great Britain*, found abundance of historical material for its cautionary tales. More reputably, there were several seventeenth-century precedents, especially Danby in the 1670s; and two far stronger ones in the early eighteenth century, Lord Godolphin and Robert Harley, Earl of Oxford, who presided over the Treasury in succession from 1702 to 1714. It was after the Revolution of 1688, when Parliament finally came to stay, with automatic yearly sessions of four to six months' duration, that the Treasury took on a new political dimension. Since 'govern-

[1] The name is often spelt 'Walpool' in contemporary correspondence, which suggests that this is how it was pronounced.

ment business' and 'financial business' were largely synonymous, and the Treasury was the most obvious channel of official patronage, it was always easier after the Revolution for the effective head of the Treasury to undertake with more success than any other minister the maintenance of a regular working partnership between the executive and the legislature. And the long wars against Louis XIV's France made this new task crucial.

Under William III royal control remained too firm to allow a 'prime minister' to emerge. But under the invalid and far less able Anne both Godolphin and Harley wielded a good deal of the power, and enjoyed much of the status, that Walpole made his own as First Lord of the Treasury from 1721[2] to 1742. They also experienced – as Walpole did – some of the limitations attendant on any minister's authority at a time when the royal prerogative still carried meaning and when possessing the sovereign's full confidence was an essential ingredient in political mastery. There were, however, important differences. Walpole, for instance, was every inch a party man, serving the national interest as he saw it but wearing his Whiggery as proudly as he wore his Garter ribbon and star. Godolphin and Harley, under whom the young Walpole had served, were birds of a different feather. Though forced to work within the existing two-party framework, each was fundamentally anti-party, concerned as the Queen's 'Manager' or 'Undertaker' with harnessing the power of the dominant party to the working needs of government, while keeping at bay as far as possible its most violent partisans.

This led to two further differences of significance between their primacy and Walpole's. The Cabinets over which they effectively presided, under the Queen, were generally less homogeneous than those of the later era and invariably more difficult for the chief minister to dominate (though the solidarity even of Walpole's Cabinets can be exaggerated); while the discipline which Walpole at his peak was able to impose on *all* office-holders was far more rigorous than anything Godolphin or Harley could achieve. In this respect, perhaps more than any other, Sir Robert's long ministry saw the emergence of a prime ministerial authority without precedent and, as it seemed to many contemporaries, unconstitutional.

[2] Space does not permit discussion of the controversial question of how far Walpole was, in effect, prime minister in his first year at the Treasury, and whether he could have triumphed over his chief rival, Sunderland, had not the latter been prematurely removed from contention by death in April 1722.

Finally, although Godolphin was a competent parliamentarian and Harley a skilful one, their position rested more on the trust of the monarch than on the approbation of Parliament. Walpole's rested equally on both; and his personal dominance over Parliament was certainly more complete. A basic factor here was his realisation that in order to be in the best position to control Parliament the King's leading minister must sit, and continue to sit, in the Commons. It cannot be overstressed how much Walpole was an innovator in this respect; how far he defied convention when in 1723 he accepted a peerage for his son, Robert, instead of for himself; and how important in the long term his innovation was – even if not all his successors followed his pattern. And for Walpole mere presence in the Commons, and periodic participation in key debates, was not enough. Until 1733 he was the only Commoner in the Cabinet; and both before and after that he acted as the day-to-day leader of the House, piloting it through its business with the aid of a handful of loyal subalterns and, from 1727 onwards, of his invaluable 'Governor', Speaker Onslow. Considering also the 'incredible . . . variety and quantity of business he dispatched',[3] one can fairly say that in terms of sheer burden of work he could comfortably stand comparison with any modern peacetime prime minister.

Rarely, if ever, have two decades of British history seemed to historians so overshadowed by the figure of one man – other than a king or queen – as the 1720s and 1730s seem to be by Walpole. This is altogether natural. To contemporaries the presence of 'the great man' (George II's *gros homme*) was just as engulfing. Not since Burghley had there been such an epic period of continuous high office. And in length there has been no equal since 1742. It has a mesmeric quality which can easily tempt the unwary into assuming that all these twenty-one years, save the last two or three, saw Walpole's power at much the same pitch of unquestioned supremacy. This was not so. A graph of his authority in the ministry and at Court, for instance, would start relatively low; would begin to rise quite steeply in April 1722, when the Earl of Sunderland died, and sharply again after the defeat of a younger rival, Lord Carteret, in 1724; but would only reach the highest plateau in 1730, when Townshend resigned. And from 1737, the year Walpole's position was damaged by the Prince of Wales's quarrel with his parents and by the death of Queen Caroline, the year too that loyal Cabinet colleagues

[3] John, Lord Hervey, *Some Materials Towards Memoirs of the Reign of King George II*, ed. Romney Sedgwick (London, 1931), i, 17.

such as Newcastle and Hardwicke first began to kick over the traces, the line would fall progressively. Even in Parliament, throughout his career from 1721 to the election of 1741 there were peaks and troughs. The Excise crisis is well known. But there were other near-disasters. Only through the abstention of forty Tories did Walpole escape defeat over the emotive issue of the Prince's allowance in February 1737. Twelve months later an Opposition motion to reduce the Army only failed by fifteen votes in a crowded House of 518. The Walpole 'machine' was no automaton.

In certain respects Walpole left his stamp on eighteenth-century England less by what he did than by how he did it. His methods, for good or ill, provided the blueprint for the next two generations of Whigs. This is not to say the positive achievements of his regime were negligible. In some fields they were very far from that. But (in spite of his massive personal authority) it is not easy in every case to assess just how far Walpole himself was responsible for them.

This is true even of the most conspicuous legacy of the 1720s and 1730s, the legacy of political stability. For close on a century prior to the Revolution of 1688 the Constitution had been in a state of acute imbalance. The natural governing class of the country, the aristocracy and landed gentry, had been for much of this time divided in interest and loyalty. Religion and politics had been mutually embroiled. After 1689 the more serious constitutional problems were slowly resolved, but the division of both the political and the religious nations into two contesting parties, ideologically at odds, persisted. Relatively little of the social order remained untouched by the violence of Whig–Tory conflict, and in particular great bitterness was engendered between the landed interest of the country, the overtaxed, economically struggling 'mere gentry', and the rising power of High Finance, which as Henry St John wrote in 1709 was 'a new interest . . . a sort of property which was not known twenty years ago'.[4] An uncertain or insecure succession to the throne and two unpopular foreign rulers stimulated Jacobite intrigue; and although the 1715 rebellion did much to discredit the Tory party and open the way to an unchallengeable Whig supremacy, fear of conspiracy persisted. Also the Whigs in their hour of victory fell prey to fratricidal struggles; and in 1720 – the year Walpole returned to office for the third time as Paymaster-General – the whole political

4 Bodleian Library MS Eng. Misc. e.180, f. 4: to Lord Orrery, 9 July 1709 (copy).

world was convulsed by a major scandal, the South Sea Bubble. By 1721 nine Englishmen in every ten must have seriously doubted whether even under their 'Revolution Constitution' a strong, stable government, commanding widespread support in the country and based on a tranquil social order, would ever be attainable.

The next twenty years were to prove that it was attainable. And clearly it would be absurd to minimise Walpole's personal contribution to a political edifice whose strength and durability long outlived him.[5] The pursuit of tranquillity and stability, social as well as political, had been an overriding concern of his administration. He saw them both as ends eminently desirable in themselves and as prerequisites for the preservation of security; and this – the security of the Hanoverian dynasty and the security of the new United Kingdom of Great Britain from Jacobite activity and foreign threats – was with Walpole a persistent, almost obsessive, preoccupation. By the late 1730s Walpole could point to twenty-five years without major war, to substantial though not universal economic prosperity, low taxation, the repair of the social fabric by the reconciliation of the landed and moneyed interests, and a marked lowering of the political temperature – all part of the climate that made stability possible and all traceable, to a greater or lesser degree, to his specific policies.

And yet the achievement of political calm under the first two Hanoverians was far from being a one-man miracle. Even in the turbulent atmosphere of Anne's reign important lessons had been learnt, especially about the manipulation of patronage and the techniques of imposing effective executive control on the legislature. Between 1714 and 1721, too, there were strong favourable currents running which Walpole was later able to channel, and without which the most outstanding political talent must have been powerless. One such current was steadily bearing away much of the ideological debris of Stuart England, in particular its more violent religious emotions: one has only to compare the electoral issues and propaganda of, say, 1710 with those of 1722 to appreciate this. Another current was carrying along the electorate itself, so volatile and unmanageable since the late 1670s, towards certain captivation. The crucial event here was the Septennial Act of 1716.

By establishing the convention that Parliaments should last for their

[5] See J. H. Plumb, *The Growth of Political Stability in England 1675–1725* (London, 1967), especially the masterly final chapter.

statutory maximum of seven years, except when interrupted (as in 1727) by the death of a monarch, this Act exposed Walpole to only three general elections in nineteen years after 1722. Had he been forced to fight ten elections in just over twenty years, as his predecessors had under the Triennial Act between 1695 and 1715, it is hard to imagine that either he or the stable political system he created could have survived as long as they did. While it is true that large sums of money had been staked on the roulette wheel of electoral fortunes during the fierce Whig–Tory conflict of 1690–1715, the obviously enhanced value of parliamentary seats after the passing of the Septennial Act encouraged still heavier investment in the constituencies, by the great landed magnates and also by the Treasury. As these investments became more secure, so contests became fewer. In the process the contribution to Walpole's remarkably successful electoral organisation of the 'government boroughs', which could return thirty to forty members, of the big local overlords, such as Edgecumbe and Newcastle, and of such large-scale borough owners as Bubb Dodington, was made possible.[6]

Walpole reaped a further harvest from the Septennial Act. The patronage of the Crown appreciated in value no less than the parliamentary seat. When the recipient of an office early in the lifetime of a Parliament could look forward – provided he behaved with reasonable discretion – to at least a six- or seven-year tenancy, the Government's purchasing power could hardly fail to benefit. The contribution of Walpole's patronage system both to political stability and to the solidity of his own regime is now a historical commonplace. The truth is, however, that the total fund of patronage was not as great as it had been under Anne (there had of necessity been some contraction of the inflated wartime administration, and Walpole was apt to complain that there was 'not enough grass for the beasts to feed on'); but the scope of the patronage directly at Walpole's disposal as First Lord, together with the patronage of other departments which he voraciously engrossed, was certainly wider than any previous minister had enjoyed. The key to his position at the heart of the web is a factor often overlooked. The position was one which the great party chieftains of 1689–1714 would have dearly prized; but it was always denied them by the prejudices of the the Crown and the interposition of the Crown's 'Managers'. It was only when the post-Revolution generation of

[6] cf. the situation from 1701 to 1715 in W. A. Speck, *Tory and Whig: The Struggle in the Constituencies* (London, 1970).

Managers finally died out in 1714, with the fall of Oxford and the resignation of Shrewsbury, England's last Lord High Treasurer, that for the first time since the Revolution a political party found itself in direct control of the administration. And for almost seven years before Walpole became prime minister his party used this control to eliminate its opponents from all positions of influence, great and small. The way was thus prepared for him not merely to concentrate this power, uniquely, in one pair of hands, but to turn it in time as ruthlessly against rival or dissident Whigs as against Tories.

In one other respect Walpole found himself rowing with a powerful tide after 1721. He belonged to a generation which from youth to mature manhood had experienced the two most ambitious and costly wars that Englishmen had ever known. The Utrecht peace settlement of 1713 was born of mutual exhaustion. Although war had yielded Britain rich dividends, it had bled the gentry white by its financial demands, had seriously burdened other sections of the community, had added new ferocity to party conflict and had imposed heavy strains on society. Even the Whigs who had supported the struggle against France and the Bourbons most eagerly had been satiated by 1713; and Walpole himself shared in this universal reaction and repugnance scarcely less than the most xenophobic Tory squire. Peace alone did something to repair the damage to the body politic in the eight years after Utrecht. But the Fifteen rebellion, and the South Sea crisis five years later, followed inside two more years by the uncovering of the Atterbury plot, all seemed to emphasise how sick the patient still was; and they made it the more receptive thereafter to the tranquillising medicine that Walpole prescribed.

Most directly the post-war reaction ensured a strong body of support at almost all times until the late thirties for the foreign policy of the Walpole administration. This had a constant aim – to secure the dynasty and the Protestant succession and to maintain the European balance of power by diplomatic negotiation and combination – but varying emphases, resulting in the main from Walpole's own profound ignorance of Europe in 1721. He had no linguistic ability and at 44 had never set foot on continental soil. To earn and keep the confidence of a German monarch, as well as to make a respectable showing in the House of Commons, he had perforce to improve his grasp of European issues and take a stronger interest in them. But as long as his brother-in-law Lord Townshend, Secretary of State for the North, conducted foreign policy in broad accord with the prime minister's priorities, the First Lord interfered as little as possible. After the eruption of a major European crisis in 1725–6, however, Townshend began to develop in Walpole's eyes a rather alarming capacity for brinkmanship, not to mention a disturbing disregard both for the traditional Whig friendship with the Habsburg Emperor[7] and for the financial implications of an over-ambitious policy. This is why from 1728 onwards Britain's foreign policy began increasingly to bear the Prime Minister's own more conciliatory, conservative and pacific stamp. And from 1730, when Townshend resigned in disgust, until 1738, Walpole dominated the country's European relations, through two compliant Secretaries of State,[8] just as thoroughly as he dominated every other field.

In the early years of his activity he claimed two important diplomatic *coups*, the Treaty of Seville with Spain (1729) and the second Treaty of Vienna with the Emperor Charles VI (1731), which seemed at first blush to have settled the outstanding problems of these two powers not merely with Britain but with each other. Of both treaties Walpole was inordinately proud, and they gave him a quite misplaced confidence in his own talent and far-sightedness as a diplomat, a confidence he unwisely backed to the hilt in the Polish Succession crisis of 1733–5. In this crisis he used his now titanic authority to overbear the judgement of George II, Queen Caroline and most of his colleagues in order to preserve Britain's neutrality.

Walpole always remained unrepentant about this crucial decision. But in the light of subsequent events his foreign policy after 1733 is hard to defend with conviction. By 1735 Britain was more isolated than she had been for almost twenty years. Her *entente* with her old enemy, France,[9] which had been the cornerstone of both Townshend's and Walpole's diplomacy, was in ruins, though Walpole perversely refused to recognise the fact. Charles VI was alienated; and Spain, which had commercial and colonial differences with Britain, was encouraged to pursue them in the assurance that Walpole would never resort to force. Nor would he have done so even in 1739, when he reluctantly embarked on the so-called 'War of Jenkins's Ear', if his parliamentary support, his hold over the King and above all his authority over his long-docile fellow ministers had not threatened to crumble as a result of his attitude. 'It is your war,' he acidly told the Duke of Newcastle, 'and I wish you joy of it.'

[7] Since 1711, Charles VI.   [8] Newcastle and Harrington.   [9] Dating from 1716.

The peace Walpole had kept in the 1730s had not been peace with honour. But neither had it been peace at any price. He always maintained, and reiterated in a great speech to the Commons in 1739, that in both Britain's economic interests – 'the interests of a trading nation' – and those of her Protestant dynasty, a policy of neutrality and negotiation was profitable and right. His opponents sneered at his argument that war would provide the Jacobites with an opportunity they could never hope for in peacetime; the Jacobite bogy, they insisted, was just a convenient screen for Walpole to hide behind; but in the end the Forty-five rebellion was to prove him right. The economic argument was more controversial. So far as we can tell from statistics of somewhat questionable validity, some important branches of trade and many industries did make mildly accelerated progress during the years of 'business as usual' in the thirties; and the merchant shipping fleet, notoriously vulnerable in wartime, unquestionably expanded. On the other hand the aggressive mercantilist war against Spain which more and more of the Government's Whig opponents were demanding in the late 1730s, and even such a war undertaken as early as 1733 against France and Spain combined, might *if vigorously and efficiently conducted* (and this was both the crux of the matter and the great imponderable) have paid off more handsomely in terms of colonial gains and valuable future markets.

Walpole, for his part, could justifiably claim that his pacifism had at least been in the interests of the landed classes, that it had kept the Land Tax low and helped to cement the social harmony he had consciously sought since the start of his ministry. But to argue, as he did in his 1739 speech, that it had also preserved 'the balance of Europe' was self-delusion. On the contrary, the scales had been decisively tilted in favour of the Bourbon powers, by then in close alliance; Britain's international prestige was probably at its lowest ebb since the 1680s; and the pathetic failure of Walpole as a war minister in the years 1739–42 reflected in some measure the deflation of national morale as well as his own patent lack of stomach for the job in hand. If France had not been deterred from entering the colonial war by the death of Charles VI, Walpole's political career might have ended not merely in disappointment but in humiliating defeat.

It would be unjust, however, to assess him as a prime minister on his record in foreign policy. Walpole, after all, was First Lord of the Treasury. It was his reputation as the leading Whig financial expert which enabled him to lay claim to this office in the first place. It is primarily on his record as a finance minister, and on the success of his superintending interest over the whole field of the economy, that history must judge him.

It is significant that three of the most important and imaginative of Walpole's financial achievements predated his premiership: they were the fruits of earlier spells of office. His financial blueprint for untangling the ravelled affairs of the South Sea Company in the winter of 1720-1 helped to restore public confidence and government credit, so badly shaken by the Bubble crisis. The decisive first step in his plan to reduce the interest payable on most segments of the long-term National Debt had been taken earlier still, in 1717;[10] and in that same year one of his few genuine innovations, the 'Sinking Fund', devised as a mechanism for progressively paying off the capital of the £40 million War Debt (which then seemed a ruinous burden) had been launched by Stanhope soon after Walpole's resignation from the ministry.[11] These two measures, dating from the first and more adventurous half of a parliamentary career of forty-four years, proved the twin keys to the effectiveness of much of his financial policy as prime minister, and were primarily responsible for his remarkable success in keeping peacetime taxation so low. For by persisting with the Sinking Fund to the very end of his ministry, long after anxiety about the size of the National Debt had become a thing of the past, he was able to cream off into the ordinary revenue the Fund's handsome surplus, accruing from successive interest reductions.

Thanks to the success (as he saw it) of his foreign policy, Walpole was never faced with the necessity of raising the huge sums that had annually confronted Godolphin and Harley. With a modest annual budget varying between 2 and 3½ millions, the need for loans was limited, and when it did arise Walpole had at his disposal the techniques of loan management perfected by Montagu and Godolphin. He was the fortunate heir of the 'Financial Revolution'; though he could thank his own fostering of credit and assiduous cultivation of the City and

---

[10] His scheme to consolidate the whole Debt in the first instance at 5 per cent, despite being truncated after he left office in 1717, was of great importance. It was later taken further, with a three-stage conversion to 4 per cent in the years 1727-30.
[11] The Fund was fed mainly from the appropriated taxes 'released' by the reduction of interest payments. The best treatment of Walpole and the National Debt is in P. G. M. Dickson, *The Financial Revolution in England* (London, 1967).

financial corporations for the fact that he was able to raise a £1 million loan in 1727 at an astonishing 3 per cent. Such circumstances, it might be thought, offered a glorious opportunity for a minister of Walpole's ability and authority, particularly one with his enviable faculty for making financial complexities intelligible to the most doltish back-bencher, to effect the basic reforms in the fiscal system which his hard-pressed predecessors had not had time to conceive or carry through.

Walpole's *forte*, however, lay not in striking originality but in making the existing system work more efficiently and in rationalising it – as with his radical simplification of Customs duties in 1722[12] – where rationalisation did not reduce the amount of 'grass' available for 'the beasts'. By demanding higher standards from revenue officials and extending the authority of the Customs Commissioners to Scotland, that home-from-home for smugglers, he did what he could – though it was for the most part a losing battle – to reduce the staggering amount of duty evasion. But his celebrated Excise scheme of 1733 was the nearest Walpole came to a truly courageous fiscal reform. This scheme, which involved the relief of imported colonial tobacco, and later of imported wine, from all but nominal customs, and their subjection instead to a bonded ware-house system and an internal excise duty, was far more than an anti-smuggling device to save £500,000 a year. It was the culmination of a long-term strategy for shifting the incidence of taxation away from land and property and on to consumable commodities: ultimately, Walpole seems to have hoped, there would be no direct taxation at all except in time of emergency and war. A pilot scheme in 1724 had proved a striking minor success,[13] and by 1731 the Land Tax had been reduced to one shilling in the pound. The 1733 Excise scheme would have brought this process to its logical conclusion. The case for it on financial grounds was unanswerable. But it was abandoned in the face of an exceptional display of popular hostility, incited by opposition charges that the Government was planning a General Excise and a massive invasion of personal liberty by its inquisitorial officials.

The abortive Excise project does demonstrate, however, that Walpole's policies at the Treasury had social and political as well as financial ends. In addition to a sound and efficient revenue system, he also sought

[12] See below, pp. 174, 175.
[13] Applying the excise to tea, coffee and cocoa, it had increased revenue on these goods by about £120,000 a year.

an *acceptable* system – one that would be sufficiently fair to conciliate all the important social interests in the country, as well as weaning the squirarchy from its natural Tory allegiance.

Whether Walpole's fiscal measures were part of an overall economic strategy as well is a question on which not all modern historians are agreed.[14] Some would argue that not until the Younger Pitt, at the earliest, did Britain have a prime minister or a Treasury minister who envisaged an organic connection between the raising of money and the regulation of the national economy, or who even recognised a responsibility to pursue a coherent 'economic policy'. It has certainly been shown beyond much doubt[15] that the so-called 'system' of protective tariffs, so marked a feature of Hanoverian England until the 1780s, developed fortuitously as a result of the desperate revenue problems of the governments of the war years 1689–1712, not of a planned ministerial initiative or as a response to contemporary economic dogma. So that Walpole's highly important tariff reforms of the early 1720s, with their emphasis on the deterring of foreign manufactures and the encouragement of domestic industry, should be seen largely as an attempt to impose some order on a haphazard and irrational state of affairs, with a particular eye to satisfying those struggling native industries, such as linen, silk and paper-making, which had benefited from their adventitious tariff cocoon in the previous thirty years. In addition, one can point to measures later in the ministry's life which clearly reflect the lobbying of politically influential pressure groups, the West India interest and others, rather than the implementation of any national policy for the good of the economy at large;[16] while parliamentary historians have revealed that several notable economic measures commonly attributed to Walpole, for example the South Carolina Bill of 1730, were in fact the result of backbench initiatives of which the Prime Minister did not always approve.

These examples of pragmatism dent the traditional picture of Walpole as the watchful economic overlord with a master-plan. But they do not necessarily destroy it. Walpole's rueful reference to the Carolina Act – 'that he was always against repealing old laws, made for the

14 Argument is inhibited by the fact that much economic groundwork for a close analysis of Walpole's administration still remains to be done.
15 By Professor Ralph Davis. See 'The Rise of Protection in England', *Economic History Review*, xix (1966).
16 Of these measures the Molasses Act of 1733 is but the best-known instance.

benefit of trade, and *breaking into the Navigation Act*[17] – illustrates one element of underlying consistency. And there can be no question that his Government remained faithful to the pledge given in the Speech from the Throne of October 1721: '. . . to make the exportation of our own commodities and the importation of the commodities used in the manufacturing of them as practicable and as easy as may be; by this means, the balance of trade may be preserved in our favour, [and] our navigation greatly increased. . . .' The cosseting of the re-export trade in colonial goods (its encouragement was to have been a major bonus of the Tobacco Excise Bill of 1733), and the crucial link in Walpole's mind between a pacific policy and economic progress, confirm an impression of overall coherence.

What is less certain, because of the different interpretation that can be put on the available statistics, is how far the effects of Walpole's policies answered their intentions. Historical orthodoxy long identified his regime with prosperity and economic growth. It is now apparent that there were important limits to what Walpole's or indeed any eighteenth-century government could achieve in the face of adverse circumstances of market fluctuation, or the natural rise and fall of certain branches of trade, or the discrimination of foreign governments against British goods. Thus Walpole could not possibly have sustained the extraordinary rate of progress the woollen cloth industry had achieved in the seventeenth century; nor could he prevent the relative decline of the sugar trade in the face of increasing French competition after 1720. Yet he still presided over the most prosperous economy in Europe. He had certainly by 1738 achieved his aim of a substantially healthier balance of trade; he had seen English shipping steadily though not spectacularly increase since 1723;[18] and he could point to the slow if painful advance of most of the heavily protected industries. Perhaps, as with so much else, he could have done more had he not been so preoccupied for much of the thirties with his political position and become less and less susceptible to new ideas or bold initiatives.

It is odd that two decades as important as the years 1720–40 in the evolution of the prime minister's office and power should have been in some ways retrogressive in the development of the Constitution. There

[17] Historical Manuscripts Commission, *Egmont Diary*, i, 173. Author's italics.
[18] See Ralph Davis, *The Rise of the English Shipping Industry* (London, 1962), especially pp. 27–8.

was one highly important exception. After 1733, when for the first time his administration had to fight for its life in both Houses, Walpole established the principle that *everyone* who held office or commission under the Crown, however petty, was expected politically to dance to the tune of the First Lord of the Treasury, or risk dismissal. Admittedly this principle had been foreshadowed under some of Walpole's immediate predecessors; but minor placemen had rarely been subject to more than occasional, limited purges, and Harley had held in 1706 that as long as an office-holder supported the ministry on votes of supply he should be allowed considerable latitude on other matters.[19] So the change in the 1730s was of great moment.

But what was an advance in terms of the growth of party discipline and executive control over the legislature was a setback in the development of what has been called 'the non-political civil service'. The Managers of the post-Revolution period had done much to ensure that in certain government departments[20] a solid core of experienced 'professionals' would be permitted continuity of office, regardless of the party seesaw. Walpole did not abandon this policy entirely. But even in the case of offices from which MPs were barred (and there were thousands, especially in the revenue field), he showed more political discrimination and paid less regard to professional competence or reputation. In Cabinet government, too, the newly established conventions of the post-Revolution period – regular, minuted meetings of a Cabinet of about a dozen leading ministers at which major policy issues were debated in the royal presence – were rudely disturbed by Walpole's preference for working behind the scenes with a smaller inner group of four or five. The change made for smoother policy-making; but it created suspicion and added to the reputation of the Walpole regime for autocracy and highhandedness.

In this, as in so much else, however, Walpole was a realist and not a theorist. In all his years in office there was never a time when he hankered after perfection, or let preconceived notions or ideal considerations disturb his clear-headed sense of what was attainable, or of what in political terms was necessary, merely desirable or frankly irrelevant. Much of his (in many ways misleading) reputation for 'letting sleeping dogs lie' is simply a reflection of this realism.

[19] Historical Manuscripts Commission, *Bath MSS*, i, 110–11.
[20] Most notably the Treasury, the Navy Office, the Post Office and most of the revenue departments.

In view of the host of abuses and institutions crying out for remedy in early Hanoverian England – social injustices by our standards appalling, religious discrimination, a demoralised state Church, a scandalous penal system, an administrative structure still plagued in many parts with sinecurists and enmeshed in antiquated procedures – Walpole's record of positive legislation over two decades may seem pitifully meagre.[21] But it is significant that in the 1720s and 1730s Walpole, freely slandered for so much else, was rarely criticised for this. He was observing the conventions of his day: that the prime business of government was to *govern* rather than to legislate or reform. And he could make the confession, 'I am no saint, no Spartan, no reformer' without a qualm; for he was at one with the bulk of his contemporaries in believing that government intervention to remedy most social abuses was either irrelevant or unwise at a period when society at large seemed to have rediscovered stability.

Even the historian must concede that since the years of Walpole's premiership were also years of relatively static population and prices, of a lull in the industrial advance made during the war years, and of urbanisation (outside London) at a gentle pace, the need for active paternalism was not urgent. In so far as Walpole had a 'social policy' it might appear to have been a largely oppressive one: he certainly believed in low wages on economic grounds, promoted laws against workers' 'combinations' (nascent unions), and had no hesitation in endorsing increased severity in dealing with crimes against property (it was in 1723 that the notorious 'Waltham Black Act' passed into law). And yet occasional stirrings of a social conscience can be detected. Relief of the poor was sometimes recommended to Parliament's attention (for instance in the King's Speech of 1730); though Walpole usually thought it proper to let the legislature decide how best it should be achieved, and firmly believed that, except in emergencies, the proper initiatives in such matters should be local, private or institutional. Where the Poor Law machinery or the private philanthropy of landlords and businessmen fell short there was the contribution of the Churches – the new Charity Schools, for instance, and the many

---

[21] Almost half the 600 government-sponsored Bills introduced into the Commons between 1715 and 1754 were regular supply Bills or annual mutiny Bills; and only a very small proportion of the remainder could be considered, in any meaningful sense, 'reform legislation'. See R. Sedgwick, *History of Parliament: The House of Commons 1715–54* (London, 1970), i, 5.

Societies for Reformation of Manners which had sprung up after 1688.

Walpole's attitude towards both the Church of England and Dissent was likewise pragmatic. In his apprentice years from 1701–14 he absorbed something of the anti-clericalism of the Augustan Whigs, exposed as they were to the electoral hostility of the High Churchmen, among them 80 per cent of the parish clergy; and his Commons speeches of this period also reflect his party's sympathy with Protestant nonconformity. But the Sacheverell affair of 1710, in which he was a leading prosecutor, taught him a lesson he was never to forget;[22] so too did the vital support given by the Low Church bishops to the Whig Opposition in the House of Lords in its darkest days from 1711–14. By 1721, although the Tory Occasional Conformity and Schism Acts had been repealed, the Test and Corporation Acts of Charles II's reign still remained on the Statute Book, subjecting the dissenters to continuing civil disabilities. Stanhope's attempt to neutralise these Acts in 1719 had failed, no small thanks to Walpole, who then and ever after was adamant that full civil rights for dissenters, as re-urged in the 1730s, could not be granted without offending the bishops and risking a flare-up of the ugly High Church passions of 1710. The farthest he would go in the cause of further toleration was an Annual Indemnity Bill, first passed in 1727. And since this was not always annual, and the indemnification it gave seems to have been uncertain, it left the Whigs' dissenting allies unsatisfied.

The state Church itself had little to thank Walpole for, except the retention of the Test. Politically the Church leadership gave his regime invaluable support; for the celebrated partnership of the years 1723–36 between the Prime Minister and Bishop Gibson of London, made possible by the monastic habits and infirmities of Archbishop Wake, ensured that all but a handful of bishoprics, deaneries and Crown livings in that period were filled by sound Whigs and pro-Walpoleans. Yet in return for this political support, much of it vastly time-consuming, Walpole gave Gibson no official backing for the latter's ambitious and far-reaching reform programme, including a radical administrative re-organisation; and without such encouragement the Bishop's plans withered on the vine. Walpole and his colleagues could not, of course, be entirely blamed for the Church's palpable decline in the twenties and thirties. But their cynicism assuredly did nothing to arrest it.

[22] See Geoffrey Holmes, *The Trial of Doctor Sacheverell* (London, 1973).

Britain, therefore, had some cause to rue, as well as good cause to bless, the long supremacy of Sir Robert Walpole. As well as the criticisms that can be made of specific fields of policy, it is also undeniable that the tone of politics declined between 1721 and 1742. By contrast with some of his recent predecessors Walpole's personal example was hardly edifying. Corruption and a blatantly materialistic view of politics manifestly increased during his period of office. And yet if we judge Walpole's premiership as an exhibition of the political art, in the widest sense, it would be grudging not to bestow on it the accolade.

Although he had been trained in a very different arena, he proved superbly adaptable to a new ambience in which the electrifying issues of Queen Anne's day had been defused and in which politics had become more intimate and personal than at any time since the sixteenth century. Walpole stood head and shoulders above all his contemporaries on such a scene, partly because he was so adept at balancing the major interests within the victorious party oligarchy, and partly because he was himself such a consummate master of personal relationships.[23] Above all he was one of the greatest parliamentarians who have ever lived. Patronage and discipline combined may have held together 'the Court and Treasury party', the core of his majorities in each Parliament, 1722–7, 1727–34, 1734–41. But his true calibre was shown in his peerless handling of the Independents, the 150–200 backbenchers, mostly country gentlemen, who were tied by interest neither to the Court nor to the power politicians of the Opposition. These men could in the last resort make or break any ministry. Indeed, in the end Walpole fell essentially because his foreign policy and his ineffectual war policy disenchanted too many of the country members whom he had successfully wooed for so long. For at least seventeen years, however, he had commanded their confidence and for the most part their support; commanded it by his highly effective debating skills, trenchant and direct; by his techniques of communication, to which he devoted enormous pains; by the genuine respect he showed for the House of Commons, whose 'approbation' he once declared[24] was 'preferable to all that

---

[23] Though as a matter of sober fact, because of the unfortunate gaps in his surviving correspondence, we know a good deal less about this aspect of his primacy than we should like to do – except as regards his relations with a number of fellow ministers, like Newcastle, and of course as regards the Court, where he hardly put a foot wrong until 1737.

[24] In the House of Commons, February 1739.

power, or even Majesty itself, can bestow'; and not least by his success in cultivating the image of himself, despite his vast fortune and princely style of living,[25] as just such another homespun, earthy, hearty, fox-hunting squire as the average backbencher.

In short, what set Robert Walpole apart from any other prime minister of the eighteenth century, save the Younger Pitt, was his capacity to achieve the maximum conceivable measure of influence and dominance *within the existing political system*. He accepted, and trimmed his sails to meet, all the rough weather which challenged the ambitious politician in early Hanoverian England: the fragmentation of the ruling one-party oligarchy; the uncertain favour of kings and courtiers; above all the crucial fact that because of the power of the independent member, the prime minister and his government never controlled an absolute majority of the Commons. Playing to perfection the dual role of 'minister with the King in the House of Commons' and 'minister for the House of Commons in the closet', Walpole mastered all the inherent difficulties of the political world in which he lived; and not only that, he turned them into positive and long-term assets. No politician can do more.

BIBLIOGRAPHY

The character of both Walpole and his age have been unforgettably captured in the first two volumes of J. H. Plumb's trilogy *Sir Robert Walpole* (London, 1956, 1960). The third volume, which will take the story from 1734 to 1745 is in active preparation. Meanwhile Archdeacon W. Coxe, *Memoirs of the Life and Administration of Sir Robert Walpole*, vol. i (London, 1798) remains a valuable storehouse of information. A brief single-volume study of outstanding merit is H. T. Dickinson, *Robert Walpole and the Whig Supremacy* (Teach Yourself History series, London, 1973). Through the author's kindness I was able to read the book in typescript while preparing this essay, to my great profit.

On particular aspects of Walpole's premiership the following works can be strongly recommended: C. B. Realey, *The Early Opposition to Sir Robert Walpole, 1720-1727* (Philadelphia, 1931); P. G. M. Dickson, *The Financial Revolution in England* (London, 1967); J. B. Owen, *The Rise of the Pelhams* (London, 1957).

For more recently published work on the period 1721-42, see Introduction, above, pp. ix-xviii *passim*.

25 See J.H. Plumb, *Sir Robert Walpole: The King's Minister* (London, 1960),   pp. 81-91 and *passim*.

PART TWO

8

RELIGION AND PARTY IN LATE STUART ENGLAND

THE second English Revolution of the seventeenth century, the Revolution of 1688, ushered in during the next twenty-five years a series of changes which were to be profoundly important to the ultimate development of the country. Most conspicuously, the reigns of William III and Anne released Englishmen – though not overnight – from the threat of arbitrary government and bequeathed to the eighteenth century a limited monarchy, subject to the rule of law and inescapably dependent on the regular co-operation of Parliament. But the changes of these years went far beyond the confines of the constitution, in its traditional sense. There was also a transformation in England's relationship with the Continent; and in this, as in constitutional change, Scotland was likewise involved, even before the Union of 1707 brought into being the new state of Great Britain. Elsewhere, too, radical change or new departure was the order of the age: in the processes of executive government and the development of bureaucracy; in the mechanisms of high finance and public credit; in the economy, with the birth of Protection; in society, with convulsions in the landowning sector and a rapid acceleration in the advance of the business and professional interests.

Many historians of today, unlike their predecessors of the 'Whig' school, have seen the hand of war as the all-important instrument in most of these changes. For twenty of the twenty-five years from 1689 to 1714 England was locked with France in a struggle of unprecedented dimensions and cost. And but for this, it may be argued, the inherently conservative Revolution of 1688 would have been a far less significant landmark, across the board of national life, than it now appears to have been. Be that as it may, the aftermath of the overthrow of James II proved a great deal more revolutionary than the Revolution. We are surely justified in regarding the end of the Stuart era as one of the great periods of fermentation in English history: a period of change at least as dynamic as the 1530s, at least as dynamic as the 1650s or the 1790s.

Yet whereas in so many areas these late Stuart years see the beginning of new chapters of prime significance, there was one field, the field of religion, in which quite the reverse seems to be the case: where the historian finds himself involved much more in the end of an old chapter than in the start of a new one. By the time of the Glorious Revolution, religion had been for more than 150 years – since the first meeting of the Reformation Parliament – the most continuous thread in British political history: it is difficult to call to mind more than two or three major political events or crises between 1529 and 1688 in which religious passions or ideals or divisions were not a factor of some importance. This was as true in the Revolution of 1688 as it had been in the Exclusion crisis, as true at the outbreak of the First Civil War as it had been at the sailing of the Armada, as true of the Northern Rebellion as it was of the Pilgrimage of Grace.

If, however, we look forward from 1714, only a very few years, what a different world we seem to be in! Passion, idealism, 'enthusiasm' are now frowned on. Sermons, religious tracts, even major works of theological controversy continue to be published; they still have their academic interest and their educated readership. But no longer do they pour off the printing presses to feed an avid public, as they had done under the Stuarts. Above all, there is now a completely new relationship between religion and politics. Religious issues, far from shaking the ocean bed of politics, now scarcely ruffle its surface, except for a few sudden squalls which blow up from time to time, such as the repeal of the 'tests' or Quaker relief in the 1730s.

The fact that this happens may not in itself seem very remarkable; the whole temper and intellectual climate of early Hanoverian England made such a development in some ways perfectly natural. What is remarkable is that there are so few overt signs under William and Anne that it is going to happen. There are one or two portents, which we can now recognize. But on the whole religion and religious conflict appeared to bulk just as large in the first three decades of post-Revolution England as they had done for more than a century and a half before.

The most striking illustration of this is provided by the history of political parties in England between the 1688

Revolution and the death of Queen Anne. After a decade in which a mass of relevant evidence has come under intensive scrutiny, present-day historians are now overwhelmingly agreed that the period in question saw the two-party division of the body politic, which had originated before the Revolution, fully maintained thereafter under 'the invidious names of Whig and Tory'.[1] The longer the period lasted, the deeper and more sharply defined the schism became: in elections it was of decisive importance from first to last;[2] within society it opened up cruel wounds from the mid-1690s onwards; and in Parliament after 1701 it subsumed, without ever entirely obliterating, the older distinction of Court and Country which in William's reign had periodically threatened to reassert itself.

The purpose of this pamphlet is to consider the contribution of religion to what J. H. Plumb has called 'the rage of party' in late Stuart England. 'Two set parties of men', as Lord Chancellor Cowper reminded George I, '. . . can only be kept up by some diversity of opinion upon fundamentals, at least points of consequence.'[3] The most cursory acquaintance with the years 1689–1714 will reveal that issues that were ostensibly religious in character frequently agitated both Parliament and the constituencies. But how far did these reach down to 'fundamentals'? Furthermore, what 'points of consequence' did they precipitate; and with what effects upon the parties, upon the Church and upon the nation?

It is safe to say at the outset that none of the other major sources of conflict between the late Stuart parties went deeper back into the scarred terrain of seventeenth-century history than those from which their religious animosities were charged. Although it was not until the late 1670s that Englishmen first began to group themselves into the two great confederations soon to be called Whigs and Tories, much of the interplay of

1. Abel Boyer, *The Political State of Great Britain* for 1711, Preface. For some of the chief contributions to the historiographical debate, originally stimulated by the revisionist arguments of Robert Walcott and their elision into textbook orthodoxy, see *Bibliographical Note*, below.
2. Cf. Henry Horwitz, 'The General Election of 1690', *Journal of British Studies*, xi, 1971, pp. 77–91 and W. A. Speck, *Tory and Whig: the Struggle in the Constituencies, 1701–1715* (London, 1970).
3. 'An Impartial History of Parties', printed in John, Lord Campbell, *The Lives of the Lord Chancellors* (London, 1846–7), iv, 427.

religion and party politics, then and later, only becomes intelligible in the light of what had happened in the 1640s and 1650s. Even as late as Queen Anne's reign the reverberations of the first English Revolution could still be heard and felt at times with extraordinary clarity and force. If, to take a single example, one studies the General Election of 1710, if one looks at just a fraction of its propaganda literature or examines its campaign slogans, it is hard to believe that Marston Moor and Naseby, the execution of the Lord's Anointed, the rule of the Saints, had actually taken place fifty-five, sixty, sixty-five years before. To the Tory mobs who swirled round many hustings in 1710 chanting 'No Forty Eight', 'No Tub Preachers', 'No Presbyterian rebellion', 'Save the Queen's White Neck', it was almost as though they had happened the previous week.

When the Whig and Tory parties were born in the later years of Charles II religion had played a vital part in the process. The first Whigs were so opposed to a Catholic succeeding to the throne after Charles that they tried to alter the legitimate succession by law; and at the same time most of them ended up, even if they did not start out, by championing the claims of Protestant dissenters to a measure of toleration. As for the first Tories, although most of them had no love of Popery, they were so wedded to the political theory of Anglicanism and to those high religious concepts of monarchical right and authority that had been so busily propagated by the restored Anglican ministry since 1662, that they resisted every attempt in the years 1679–81 to tamper with the succession. And likewise they resisted every attempt to encroach on the exclusive authority claimed by the restored Church of England. Such, very broadly, remained the position at Charles II's death, at which point the Whigs were in eclipse and a bleak future seemed in prospect for their dissenting allies. It was quite impossible that the religious platforms of the two parties, especially that of the Tories, should have remained unaffected by the experience of James II's reign, by the subsequent events of the 1688 Revolution or by the character of the Revolution Settlement. Neither could they have remained untouched by the tortured state of the Established Church after the Settlement; by the loss of the Nonjurors, for example – those clergy of unbending conscience who could not bring themselves to renounce their oaths of allegiance to the now-exiled James and swear obedience to his *de facto* successor; above all by the fact that from the late 1690s the Church of England was itself, like the politicians, grievously divided into two parties, the High Church and Low Church parties, in a way which had no precedent under Charles II and James II.

The effects of some of these changes, especially of the Settlement and of the emergence of clerical parties, are considered later. But these effects made no difference to one basic and continuing fact. However the nature of the interaction of religion and politics may have changed as a result of the events of 1685–9, the extent of their involvement with each other changed remarkably little. It did diminish for a while in the course of the 1690s; but from 1697 at the latest it began to increase again, and from 1701 onwards religious and political developments were as closely embroiled with each other as they had been at any time since the Reformation.

At this stage we must be quite clear on two points. In the first place, it is not contended that religious issues, or even issues with a religious content, were the only important issues which divided the Whigs from the Tories in William's reign and Anne's. Such a contention would be nonsense. The parties were in conflict over Britain's role in Europe, over the wars against France and over the making of the final peace, over the serious social tensions of the period, and over a great many more minor and specific questions as well. And all issues apart, it would be idle to pretend that naked power-seeking and place-hunting had no part in the politics of late Stuart England; though my interpretation of the evidence is that by Anne's reign the majority of the party leaders (the Whig Junto is a case in point) sought power very much more for what they could accomplish with it than for the private rewards it would bring them.

It could not be seriously argued, therefore, that religious issues were the only ones that mattered. Neither would it be logical to assume that because they remained so important a factor in politics for a further thirty years after the Glorious Revolution, this necessarily implies that England was at this period an especially devout nation. In fact much of the evidence points the other way: to the fact that attendance at places of worship was declining, at least in King William's reign; that Christian belief was being either eroded by criticism and fashionable Deistic thought or, at lower levels of society, partly submerged in apathy; and that standards of Christian morality were a good deal lower in the 1690s than they had been, say, before the Civil Wars. To open the diary of John Evelyn, who was a devout layman, almost at random in the closing years of the 17th century is to come across passages like this [May 1690]: '. . . that all our threatning Calamitie proceeded from mens Vices, and they, for want of stable, Christian and Moral principles, an universal atheistical, or sceptical, humor overspreading the nation.' Likewise with the sermons of almost any of the major preachers of the day; leaf through the pages of an average collection and it will not be long before you come across a lament on the spiritual poverty of the times or a castigation of a backsliding people. Nor is this just normal professional sales talk. More often it comes over with real feeling, as when Charles Trimnell, shortly before he became bishop of Norwich, warned the House of Commons from the pulpit of St. Margaret's, Westminster, in 1707 that God's mercies to England in the war of the Spanish Succession had not been earned by merit; rather had they been bestowed 'notwithstanding the vice and irreligion that, like a pestilence . . . now rages among us.' Certainly there were some among the governing classes who made a positive parade of their irreligion. Sir Richard Gipps, a fiery country gentleman from Suffolk, once sallied all the way down to Totnes in Devon to contest this Tory pocket borough for the Whigs; and, it is said, 'the first thing he did in that town towards gaining an interest was to single out the parson of the parish, to prove to him that there was no God.'[4]

Not surprisingly, then, among the main leaders of both political parties in Anne's reign, one finds some barely disguised sceptics and freethinkers, such as 'Honest' Tom Wharton, the third earl of Sunderland, and Lord Bolingbroke (Henry St John), and only a handful of men, by contrast, whose religious faith stands out as deep and wholly genuine. Robert Harley is an obvious example of the latter; for him it was completely in character that in February 1708, when his whole career and possibly his life hung in the balance after the arrest of his traitorous clerk, William Greg, he calmly ignored the protective

4. *The Letter Books of John Hervey, First Earl of Bristol* (Wells, 1894), i, 172.

measures urged on him by frantic friends and told his brother:
'I know nothing that I can do, but entirely to be resigned to
and confide in the Providence of God.'⁵ The earl of Nottingham,
who with Lord Rochester was the leading High Church Tory
among the laity in the generation after the Revolution, was
another whose Christian beliefs and concern for the Church
were patently sincere; so too was William Bromley, a Speaker
and Secretary of State in Anne's reign. That such leaders were
relatively few in number is quite beside the point, however.
For as we shall see, in many of the political situations which
developed under William and Anne it was not *positive commitment* to a religious cause which counted for most. A great deal
of the religious motivation of political action in late Stuart
England was of an essentially negative brand. Yet it is a commonplace of human experience that negative feelings can be every
bit as strong as positive ones; and that not infrequently they
are stronger. History testifies endlessly to the force of the most
powerful of all negative emotions, fear. And it can hardly be
stressed too strongly that much of the fuel – not all of it, but
much of it – which kept the flames of party roaring away so
furiously under the last two Stuarts was the fuel of fear.

The first half of the seventeenth century in England
bequeathed two extremely powerful phobias to the second half
of the century. And circumstances conspired to make these
phobias stronger than ever between 1670 and 1700. One was
the fear of Popery; the other was the fear of Puritan fanaticism,
of a Second Coming of the Saints.

It is arguable that the persistent distrust of Charles I, which
was primarily responsible for pushing England over the brink
into civil war between 1640 and 1642 had been rooted, more
than anything else, in the fear that he was conspiring with
Papists. At a critical point of that war, in the autumn of 1643,
it was the spectre of an invasion of Catholic troops, raised by
the 'Cessation' the King had negotiated with the Irish rebels,
which played an important part in tipping the scales against
the royal cause. After the Restoration all the latent credulity
and prejudice of the English on the score of Catholicism was
revived and heightened by the events of the 1670s, culminating
in the extraordinary hysteria of Titus Oates's Plot, while the

5. Edward Harley's Memoirs of the Harley Family, in Hist. MSS. Comm.
Portland MSS. v, 648.

experience of James II's reign inside the next decade appeared to confirm to the hilt all the gloomiest prophesies of what a Catholic King portended.

If only the 1688 Revolution had settled the future of the monarchy and of the succession beyond doubt, many of these fears would have been put at rest, and domestic politics under William and Anne would undoubtedly have been a good deal quieter: for the old Catholic recusant families were in themselves the source of relatively little apprehension, at least in the provinces. When Defoe visited Durham in Queen Anne's reign he found that 'the town is well built but old, full of Roman Catholicks, who live peaceably and disturb nobody, and nobody them; for we being there on holiday, saw them going as publickly to mass as the Dissenters did on other days to their meeting-house.'[6] As long as the laws excluding Catholics both from office and from Parliament* and subjecting them to double taxes were enforced, few Englishmen cared, except at odd moments of crisis, that the rest of the battery of anti-recusant Acts on the statute book were tacitly ignored. But 'Popery' to them had long signified much more than an unpalatable religion. The whole notion had become inseparable from the arbitrary government, the persecuting zeal and the violent methods manifested, in their eyes, by the Catholic absolutists of the Continent – most recently and most starkly by Louis XIV.[7] And so, while late Stuart Englishmen burnt Popes in effigy and still looked for Jesuits under the most unlikely beds, it was Catholic monarchy, and all that it implied, which lay at the heart of their anti-Popery phobia.

Unfortunately the Revolution did not settle the future of their monarchy. For one thing William III himself was embarrassingly unpopular, and the hopes of the Jacobites (most of them Protestants of a Nonjuring or High Anglican persuasion) that they might be able to restore King James, in spite of his religion, were therefore kept well alive in the 1690s. Such hopes, sustained to begin with by the strong possibility of a foreign invasion, were then rekindled by the prospect that

---

* The 1st and 2nd Test Acts of 1673 and 1678.

6. *Tour through the Whole Island of Great Britain* (Everyman edn., London, 1927), ii, 249.
7. This theme is well developed in John Miller, *Popery and Politics in England 1660-1688* (Cambridge, 1973), especially ch. 4.

William might be killed in battle or assassinated,[8] and revived once more after 1697 by William's growing disillusionment with the English and his threats to throw his crown back at them and retire to Holland. Even when William survived, however, the further problem of the Protestant Succession remained. Although this was laid down by the Bill of Rights in 1689* and re-ordered by the Act of Settlement in 1701, it was precarious from the start. William and Mary had no children; Princess Anne, their designated successor, had only one surviving child in the 1690s and by the time he died in 1700 it was obvious to everyone that, after sixteen fruitless pregnancies, there was nothing more to be expected from that quarter; Anne's health was even worse than William's had been; and the Hanoverians, whom Parliament nominated in 1701 to succeed her, were both distant and notably uncharismatic. From September 1701 the Stuart Pretender – the titular James III – held court at St Germains under the protection of the greatest Catholic potentate of the day. Is there any wonder that such persistent uncertainties bred among the Whigs and Tories of 1689–1714 an agitated preoccupation with the fate of the crown and the succession? They were more than enough to guarantee that fear of Popery would remain a powerful undercurrent of politics until Queen Anne's death, indeed right down to the time of the Atterbury Plot in 1722.

The second great phobia of the late Stuart period with which we are concerned – fear of a Puritan resurgence, dread that the nation might eventually be engulfed by a new wave of sectaries and 'fanatics' – was, objectively speaking, less realistic than the first. But men are not objective about their fears; and there was just enough substance to this one in the years after 1688 to make it, at times, even more explosive politically than fear of Popery. In May 1702 a young Oxford don named Henry Sacheverell was able to launch himself on a career of notoriety

* The Bill of Rights also stipulated that all persons who 'are or shall be reconciled to ... the See or Church of Rome or shall profess the Popish Religion or shall marry a Papist shall be excluded and be forever uncapable to inherit, possess or enjoy the Crown and Government of this Realm ...'

8. A serious assassination plot – the most serious of several – was uncovered in 1696. See S. B. Baxter, *William III* (London, 1966), pp. 336–7, 343. A much fuller, more partisan and colourful, but generally scholarly account is in Lord Macaulay, *The History of England from the Accession of James II* (ed. C. H. Firth, London, 1913–15), v, 2584–2602 *et seq.*; vi, 2640–87.

by preaching a widely-publicized sermon in the University Church of St. Mary's so hysterical in its obsession with Dissent that it ended with the preacher calling on all true Anglicans not to 'strike sail to a party which is an open and avowed enemy to our communion' but 'to hang out the bloody flag and banner of defiance'.[9] Not everyone took him seriously, of course. Daniel Defoe taunted Sacheverell by dubbing him 'the bloody flag-officer'. But enough Tories and enough High Anglican clergy did take Sacheverell's message to heart (he was not alone in spreading it) to ensure that for at least ten years after 1701 fear of nonconformity was like a keg of dynamite planted in the middle of the party arena. It blew up one of Queen Anne's ministries in 1704–5, after the attempted 'Tack' of a controversial religious bill to a money bill, when it backfired on the very Tories who had lit the fuse. And it was another charge from a similar keg, this time mishandled by the Whigs, which was largely responsible for demolishing the war administration of the Whig Junto and Lord Godolphin in 1710. So crucial were these two episodes in the strife of party after the Revolution, they will repay more detailed scrutiny later.

But first we must understand how such extraordinary situations came about.

In the early 1660s the leaders of the restored Anglican regime, backed by a Cavalier Parliament still haunted by the memory of 'Forty-Nine, thought they had laid the Puritan bogy for good. They had rejected Comprehension, even for the moderate Presbyterians, and they had erected instead by a series of statutes the grim penitentiary which history has labelled 'the Clarendon Code'. Later the first Test Act of 1673, though primarily anti-Catholic in intention, had the effect of adding further civil disabilities – disqualification from office under the Crown for dissenters unwilling to comply with the Anglican 'sacramental test' – to the existing religious and municipal disabilities which nonconformists suffered. Even so, on the few occasions when the dissenters, with royal connivance, were able to break out temporarily from their statutory prison

<hr />

9. H. Sacheverell, *The Political Union: A Discourse shewing the Dependance of Government on Religion in General: and of the English Monarchy on the Church of England in Particular* (London, 1710 edn.), p. 23.

(for example after Charles II's Declaration of Indulgence in 1672) Anglican Tories showed by their instant alarm that the old fear was still firmly implanted in their minds. The Revolution of 1688 made a relaxation of the penal laws against dissenters unavoidable, at least so far as their right to freedom of worship was concerned: in order to outbid James II for the support of the dissenters, Anglican leaders had to promise them nothing less than that. But once the first flush of gratitude to Dissent had passed, suspicion and apprehension soon reasserted themselves, and they are fully reflected in the critical religious settlement of 1689.

They can be seen at work in the second, and this time final, rejection of Comprehension in November of that year. Its death blow was struck by the militants in Convocation, for whom the dean of Gloucester's ringing words, '*Nolumus leges Angliae mutari*', served as a call to the barricades;[10] but its fate had been as good as sealed the previous spring in the House of Commons, where reactions to a Comprehension bill amply bore out Lord Halifax's forecast that 'the Church of England party [the High Tories] . . . had rather turn papists than take in the Presbuterians'.[11] The same distrust and fear are evident in the blunt refusal of Parliament to bow to William III's known wishes and abolish the sacramental test for office-holders, and in the patent alarm of both clergy and laity at the King's recognition of a Presbyterian state church in Scotland.[12] Not least (though the point is often overlooked), these sentiments help to explain the grudging nature of the famous Toleration Act which passed into law in May 1689. The frosty title of the Act reveals how limited in conception it was: officially it was 'An Act for exempting their Majesties' Protestant subjects, dissenting from the Church of England, from the penalties of certain laws'. At no point, in fact, did the Act

10. William Jane, dean of Gloucester, was elected Prolocutor of the Lower House of Convocation in November, defeating the pro-Comprehension candidate, Dean Tillotson (later archbishop of Canterbury).

11. *Memoirs of Sir John Reresby*, ed. Andrew Browning (Glasgow, 1936), p. 572. There is a valuable account of the final failure of Comprehension – a crucial event in the party politics as well as the religious history of the next 30 years – by Roger Thomas, 'Comprehension and Indulgence', in *From Uniformity to Unity 1662–1962*, ed. G. F. Nuttall and O. Chadwick (London, 1962), pp. 243–53.

12. Gilbert Burnet, *The History of my own Time* (Oxford, 1833), iv, 51–3. [Hereafter cited as Burnet].

proclaim a state of 'toleration'. Indeed when the bill was passing through the Commons Sir Thomas Littleton declared explicitly at the Report Stage on 17 May that 'the Committee, though they were for Indulgence, were for no Toleration.'[13] Although many Whigs and dissenters were soon talking as though such a state now existed, Tories studiously avoided the word 'toleration' altogether, and were not slow to point out that the Act promised no more in its preamble than 'some ease to scrupulous consciences in the exercise of religion'. In full accordance with this grudging spirit, the Act did not repeal outright the statutes of the Clarendon Code; it simply suspended their penal provisions, provided the dissenters met certain conditions.

It is true that there is more in this Act than meets the eye; and that one reason for its peculiarly bleak tone is that the men who originally drafted it – including Anglican Tories such as Nottingham (its chief sponsor), Sharp and Stillingfleet who were not ill-disposed at the time to moderate Dissent – intended the measure in the first place to apply only to the more extreme sectaries, and that it only came to apply to the whole body of nonconformists after a companion Comprehension bill had collapsed.[14] Nevertheless it is clear that even at this stage most committed Anglicans regarded the Toleration Act as decidely charitable;* and it is no less transparent that as the milder Tories and High Churchmen observed the results of the Act over the next ten to twenty years, they became just as nervous about Dissent as the militants had been in 1689. Meanwhile the latter, in their turn, moved further and further towards the state of almost frenzied hostility which, as we have seen, Sacheverell embodied in 1702.

Had they any serious grounds for such extremities of alarm?

---

* The veteran Tory, Sir Thomas Clarges, made a serious attempt in the Commons to limit its application to a seven-year term in the first instance, arguing that the Act ought to be 'temporary and probational'.

13. *Cobbett's Parliamentary History of England*, v (London, 1809), 266. [Hereafter cited as *Parl. Hist.*].
14. See Henry Horwitz, *Revolution Politicks: The Career of Daniel Finch, Second Earl of Nottingham 1647–1730* (Cambridge, 1968), pp. 87–93; G. V. Bennett, 'King William III and the Episcopate', in *Essays in Modern English Church History*, ed. G. V. Bennett and J. D. Walsh (London, 1966), pp. 113–16.

Was there any justification for the belief, which nine High Tories out of ten professed by the early years of Anne, that the so-called 'Toleration' of 1689 had unintentionally opened the floodgates to a tidal wave of Dissent, which might well damage the Establishment beyond repair? The truth, predictably enough, is that fear led to a wild exaggeration of the danger to the Church, but that it had sufficient foundation in fact to make the victims of the fear impervious to rational argument; and we can better appreciate their feelings if we remember, in fairness, that there were scarcely any reliable statistics available to which men could appeal to confirm or deny subjective impressions.

The growth in the number of nonconformist congregations throughout the country offers a striking illustration of the gap between morbid contemporary assumption and sober, authenticated historical fact. We now have ways of calculating this, accurately enough for us to be certain that it did take place and that it was not negligible. Leaving aside the Quakers, it would seem that the 940 or so dissenting congregations which existed (officially at least) in 1690 had swollen to around 1200 by 1716. Most Tories clearly believed that congregations were spawning much more prolifically than this. And it is very likely that they were misled (as some historians have been) by what seemed to them the staggering number of licences that were taken out for meeting-houses under article 19 of the Toleration Act. Almost 4000 new licences were issued over the course of the twenty years from 1690 to 1710. But with statistics at our disposal that were unavailable to contemporary Tories, we can now be certain that the vast majority of these licences were granted in response to applications from already-existing congregations who wished to change their meeting place, either because they wanted to move from a temporary to a permanent home, or more frequently because it had become necessary for them to shift from one set of temporary premises to another.[15]

As with the total number of congregations, so with the size of individual congregations. Undoubtedly some of these, in perhaps a score of provincial towns, did grow to impressive proportions. We know of one chapel in Taunton with 2,000 'hearers' by 1715, one in Nottingham in 1717, with 1,400, Cross

15. See Geoffrey Holmes, *The Trial of Doctor Sacheverell* (London, 1973), pp. 36 and n.†, 37.

Street meeting-house in Manchester with 1,515, and so on.[16] But what tended in this respect to magnify and distort the growth was the fact that much of it was concentrated in a limited number of places which caught the eye. Such a place was Coventry, where the much-travelled Celia Fiennes found in 1697 'the largest Chapple and the greatest number of people I have ever seen of the Presbiterian way'.[17] London's case was clearly the most startling of all, since it was under the eye of the legislature and represented a continuing offence to such High Tory watchdogs as Sir John Pakington, M.P. for Worcestershire. There were probably 500,000 dissenters in England and Wales by 1714, out of a population more than ten times that strength; and at least 100,000 of the half million were to be found in London and its outparishes.[18] But it was also noteworthy that of the six largest provincial towns in 1714, at least four (Norwich, Bristol, Birmingham and Exeter) had a still higher proportion of dissenters among their populations than the capital, not far off a third, perhaps, in each case.

Physical growth apart, there were two respects in which, to the anxious High Church Tories, the dissenters seemed to be advancing their interests in a sinister way after 1689: exploiting the vagueness of the Toleration Act, and (as Tories claimed) perverting its intentions. One was by setting up dissenting academies. The numbers, once more, were greatly inflated. It is doubtful if there were more than thirty of these academies in being by 1714, a net increase of no more than ten since the Revolution.[19] But it is true that they now operated more publicly and that some were highly successful as places of higher education, infringing the Anglican monopoly officially enjoyed by Oxford and Cambridge. And the bitterest pill, one which few Tories could stomach, was that these establishments served as training-grounds for a whole new generation of nonconformist ministers; which meant that the *schism*, as the

16. E. D. Bebb, *Nonconformity and Social and Economic Life 1660–1800* (London, 1935), p. 38 n, citing the papers of John Evans, 1715–18 (now in Dr. Williams's Library, London, MS.34.4), lists no fewer than 17 congregations at this time with more than 1,000 hearers. See also MS. 'Evans List', pp. 58, 92, 99.

17. *The Journeys of Celia Fiennes*, ed. Christopher Morris (London, 1949), p. 113.

18. I discuss the provenance of these figures in the essay 'The Sacheverell Riots: The Crowd and the Church in Early 18th Century London', *Past and Present*, 72, 1976: see below, p. 225 n. 37.

19. Holmes. *op. cit.*, pp. 38–9.

High Churchmen called it, in the religious fabric of the nation, was certain to be perpetuated into the foreseeable future, unless Parliament took statutory action to prevent it.

Even more perturbing was the way the less scrupulous dissenting laymen had managed to find a way of evading the obstacles to civil office which the Test and Corporation Acts still legally imposed. After the Revolution, and in particular under the indulgent eye of William III and his Whig ministers in the mid 1690s, there spread very rapidly a cynical practice known as 'Occasional Conformity'. This was particularly rife in the corporations, where its origins went back to Charles II's reign. Dissenters remained officially debarred from municipal office after the 1689 settlement, as they had been since 1661. But they found that provided they were prepared to take the Sacrament in an Anglican church just once, in the twelve months before they stood for local election, and provided they got a certificate to that effect from the vicar, they could then take their seats as councillors, and even become aldermen and mayors, while cheerfully repairing week after week to their own meeting-houses until the next Common Council election was in prospect.

In a number of towns contempt for the law became flagrant. In the 'fine new-built meeting-house' at Bridgwater, Defoe found to his astonishment on a visit to this quiet western port (probably in 1705) 'that they have an advanc'd seat for the mayor and aldermen, when any of the magistrates should be of their Communion . . .' 'Of their Magistrates and Companyes', Fiennes wrote of the corporation and guilds of Coventry in 1697, 'the majority of the heads are now in sober men's [i.e. dissenters'] hands, so it's esteem'd a Fanatick town'.[20] By the same year Occasional Conformity was already being so widely practised in the corporation of London that the Lord Mayor of that year, Sir Humphrey Edwin, had the supreme nerve to travel to Mead's meeting-house in full regalia, two Sundays running, with the City sword carried before him by the official sword bearer. Even Defoe, a strong dissenter himself, felt moved to accuse Edwin and his like of 'playing Bopeep with God Almighty'. Such prostitution of conscience for the sake of

20. *Journeys, loc. cit.* For Bridgwater, see Defoe, *Tour*, i, 270. (The account purports to be written in 1725, but for the likely date of the visit, 15 August 1705, see Hist. MSS. Comm. *Portland MSS.* iv, 27); and cf. MS. 'Evans List', pp, 99, 102.

office he could find 'no colour of pretence for in all the Sacred Book.'[21]

There is no doubt that by the beginning of Anne's reign Occasional Conformity had made it possible for nonconformists to get a grip on many corporations. And this in turn enabled them to influence parliamentary elections in the Whig interest in some of the limited corporation boroughs, where the councillors alone had the right to vote in the election of members of Parliament, and in even more of the smaller freemen boroughs, where the corporation in effect controlled the electoral roll. In some places the dissenters had become so cocksure that they did not even bother to occasionally conform. There was a scandalous case in the little Wiltshire town of Wilton in 1702. Here the Whig candidates were defeated at the last General Election of William's reign, and immediately afterwards the Whig mayor of Wilton announced quite openly in the Council House that 'before another election he would make so many new burgesses, there should be no occasion for the old to attend'; and what was more, 'that he would make none burgesses that were not Dissenters from the Dam's Teat; for if they chose churchmen [he said, with disarming frankness] they would always be against them.' The mayor was as good as his word. Little more than seven months later, when Anne's first Parliament was elected, nineteen new burgesses had been added to this small 'unlimited' corporation, all of them dissenters, and scarcely one of them even technically qualified under the Corporation Act. The outcome was a foregone conclusion. Wilton sent two staunch Whigs to the first House of Commons of the new reign, right against an electoral tide which in the counties and popular boroughs was running strongly for the Tories, the self-proclaimed 'Church party'.*

* It was after this General Election that an anonymous pamphleteer wrote of the electors of England '. . . Their good opinion of men will arise in different persons from very different reasons . . . But the most popular reason, and so of greatest use in the counties, cities and great boroughs, where the right of election is in the populace, is an opinion that the persons elected will endeavour the security of the religion they profess and the properties they enjoy. And for this reason men that differ in religion and interest so often disagree about the persons they would elect.' *Occasional Thoughts concerning our Present Divisions and their Remedies* (London, 1704), quoted in W. A. Speck, *Tory and Whig* (1970), p. 97.

21. *An Enquiry into the Occasional Conformity of Dissenters, in Cases of Preferment* (London, 1698).

And although a petition soon unseated one of them, it was this case which more than anything stiffened the determination of the Tories, emboldened by the accession of a 'Church of England Queen', to rid themselves by law of 'this abominable hypocrisy' of Occasional Conformity.[22]

The resulting campaign, which lasted just over two years, from November 1702 until December 1704, provides a classic example of how religion and political interest merged to feed the rage of party in this period. At a time when Britain was fighting for her life – or at least for the survival of her Protestant religion – in the early stages of the Spanish Succession War, the Protestants in Anne's first Parliament were at each other's throats to an extent which utterly disillusioned Godolphin and Marlborough, who had inherited the chief responsibility for carrying on the struggle with France; indeed, to an extent which eventually shocked even the devoutly Anglican Queen Anne. Three bills to prohibit Occasional Conformity followed one after the other in three successive sessions, the first a vicious measure with draconian penalties,[23] the second and third not quite so malevolent but stern enough. It was natural that each should have stemmed from the House of Commons, for this particular House had the heaviest Tory majority seen so far since the 1688 Revolution. Furthermore, among the politicians it was the Commons who had most at stake materially. In spite of all the high-falutin' appeals to principle in which members encased their speeches, a fear at the back of every Tory's mind was the one bluntly expressed by Sir John Pakington in the debate on the 1703 bill, namely, that 'by the benefit of this Occasional Conformity, the dissenters will come to be the majority of this House'.

Three times the bill passed the Commons, twice with ease, the third time with significantly shrunken support. And three times (to the accompaniment of a torrent of pamphlet literature) it was destroyed by the Lords; the first bill crippled by amendments by the narrowest of margins, the second and third directly thrown out. It was in the Lords that the Whigs had their main strength, and also the support of the Low Church bishops, who were by this time a majority of the bench. And it was the hostility of the Lords which finally stung the Tory

22. *Commons' Journals*, xiv, 49. See also Geoffrey Holmes, *British Politics in the Age of Anne* (London, 1967), pp. 99–101.
23. This will be found printed in full in *Parl. Hist.* vi, 61–8.

militants in the Lower House into a wild and fortunately unsuccessful attempt to force the third 'Occasional bill' through Parliament by 'tacking' it to the main bill of supply, the Land Tax bill. In other words, in the height of their partisan zeal they were prepared to provoke a major constitutional crisis and even to bring the whole war effort to a grinding halt for lack of revenue. Small wonder the Solicitor-General, Sir Simon Harcourt, wrote on the eve of the 'Tack' in November 1704 to his mentor, Robert Harley, the Speaker of the House, a letter which began: 'Dear Sir, Universal madness reigns . . .'[24] When this Parliament was dissolved soon afterwards, the next General Election, that of 1705, was dominated by the Whig efforts to destroy the notorious Tackers (134 of them) and by the Tory platform that 'the Church was in danger' under the present regime – a 'mixed' ministry having recently succeeded the strongly High Tory ministry of 1702–4. Pakington emphasized the central point of his own campaign and that of his fellow-travellers in graphic fashion by having a banner carried before him through the streets of Worcester: it showed a steeple crumbling and falling – a sign of what the electors could expect if they returned his Whig rival, William Walsh!

Politically the 1705 Election was of the first importance. Although 90 Tackers succeeded in battling their way back into the House – 'either by the prevalency of their party [St John claimed] or the absolute dependancy of their corporations'[25] – the Whigs gained some sixty seats; and Marlborough was soon urging the Queen to 'advise with Lord Treasurer [Godolphin] what encouragement may be proper to give them'. Putting John Smith in the Speaker's Chair and Cowper, the Junto's nominee, on the Woolsack was a clear indication of the way the minds of the Managers were now working: these were to be just the first stepping-stones by which the Whigs, over the next three years, strode from fringe participation in a coalition to total ministerial dominance. The High Tories were not slow to read the signs. Even before the struggle over the Tack Francis Annesley had told the archbishop of Dublin: 'the Whigs expect

---

24. Brit. Lib. Loan 29/138: Harcourt to Harley, 'Saturday Night' (endorsed by Harley: 'Sr. S. Harcourt. Abt. the Tack').
25. Blenheim MSS. A.1–20: to duke of Marlborough, 25 May 1705. I am indebted to the present duke for permission to use his family papers.

to be established, and then God preserve the Church of England.' And within weeks of the new Parliament's meeting in the late autumn of 1705 the Tories attempted in both Houses to vote 'the Church in danger' under the present administration, Lord Rochester setting the tone in the Lords by deploring 'the miscarriage of the Bill against Occasional Communion'. When, instead, a counter-motion was carried in the Lords by 61 votes to 30, declaring that 'whoever insinuates or suggests that the Church is in danger . . . is an enemy to her Majesty, the Church and the Kingdom', Nottingham concluded that 'some of us have nothing to do but to goe home and say our prayers.'[26]

The Occasional Conformity question, together with its electoral and parliamentary repercussions, reveals how powerfully religion could interact with politics in late Stuart England. It also reminds us that not all the religious and quasi-religious issues of the day found the two parties invariably divided from each other along strictly defined lines. The Tories, in particular, had their internal divisions uncomfortably exposed by two of these issues; and in the end the most serious of those divisions proved their undoing. Even on the question of nonconformity they were not at one; for whereas the great bulk of the Tories, especially the squirearchy, made common cause with the High Church clergy from the late 1690s onwards in concentrating on the threat to the Establishment from revitalized Dissent, a small but very influential minority of the parliamentary party, the followers of Harley, accepted that the Church and indeed religion itself was in danger from the spread of heresy, scepticism and atheism, yet defended the Toleration. This was natural enough, since not a few of them came of dissenting and Whig stock themselves. It was this division which came to a head in November 1704 over the third Occasional Conformity bill and 'the Tack', and which thereby opened the way to the growing Whig ascendancy of the years 1705–10.

But if there were some Tories who thought the general fear of Dissent exaggerated,* there were far more who experienced almost as strongly as the Whigs the fear of Popery. This was what had led many of them, after all, to renounce allegiance

26. Trinity College, Dublin, T. C. D. Lyons 1080: Annesley to Archbishop King, 6 May 1704; Tullie House, Carlisle, diary of William Nicolson, bishop of Carlisle, 6 Dec. 1705.   * See p. 200 n.

to James II, and after the Revolution it was the factor chiefly responsible for their party's schizophrenic attitude to the succession. The Tory conscience under the last two Stuarts was always being to some extent torn between this fear, plus the respect for the law, which together after 1701 pulled towards Hanover, and the divine right tradition and the emotional ties which pulled towards St Germains. Only a very resilient conscience could have stood the strain for so long. But when Anne's rapidly-deteriorating health brought the succession issue to a head in 1713–14, the hard core of Jacobite Tories and Hanover Tories were at last forced into irreconcilable positions. After that it was only a matter of time before the centre battalions of the party, paralysed both by their own indecision and that of their leaders, cracked and conceded the field to the Whigs.

Even the Whigs, though unanimous in their rejection of a Popish Pretender, were not entirely united in their attitude towards religious minorities at home. The pragmatic attitude of the party as a whole to the religious settlement of 1689 was well expressed by John Smith, then Chancellor of the Exchequer, in a speech at Sacheverell's trial in 1710.

> The Toleration is certainly grounded upon the best principles, upon a principle of religion and a principle of policy. I think every body will allow, that nothing can establish peace in a kingdom so well, as the granting ease and quiet to men's consciences; if they pay due submission to the Government, they ought not to be persecuted for their religion. It is for Her Majesty's interest and honour; for how can Her Majesty be the head of the Protestant Interest abroad, if Protestants are not protected at home?

A few enlightened souls such as James Stanhope, well in advance of their time, were ideologically so committed to Toleration that they were prepared to see official freedom of worship even for Catholics, in peace time. Many more, but

---

* It must be added that their numbers, even among the Harley following, had shrunk appreciably by 1709–10, by which time the social and political influence of the dissenters, especially their identification with the new 'monied interest' and an unpopular war policy, was more obtrusive than it had been earlier in the reign.

still a radical minority, wanted full civil rights as well as religious liberty for the Protestant nonconformists. The majority of Whigs, however, were by and large prepared to defend all the ground the dissenters had gained since 1689, including municipal influence through Occasional Conformity and the right to set up schools and academies, but were still apprehensive of lowering every barrier and so allowing dissenters to compete on equal terms with Anglicans for office under the Crown.

Perhaps the surest way to grasp the attitude of the late Stuart Whigs and Tories towards 'the Toleration' is to recognize that while *ideological* commitment, either way, was a variable, *interest* generally acted as a constant. Interest had bound the Anglican Whigs to the dissenters since firm links had first been forged between them in the Exclusion crisis. And in the frenetic electoral atmosphere after the 1688 Revolution (eleven General Elections between 1689 and 1713), the fact that the dissenting vote – perhaps fifteen to twenty per cent of the whole electorate in Anne's reign[27] – was on most occasions overwhelmingly Whig was an inescapable consideration for the Junto and their friends. They were expected to look after their own. In just the same way interest bound the great bulk of the Tories to the 8,000-odd High Church divines in the country. During the 1690s the tragic division of the clergy into 'High' and 'Low' parties, with sharply conflicting remedies for their Church's mental and bodily ills,[28] steadily widened and hardened; and by 1701, when the breach became irreparable, the High Churchmen had acquired something close to a siege mentality, seeing themselves as defending the ramparts of a beleaguered Church establishment against a hostile and encroaching army of fanatics. It is astonishing how the whole imagery of battle and siege became normal verbal currency in

27. The most tentative of estimates; but because the proportion of the well-to-do and the 'middling people' (tradesmen, yeomen, farmers, etc.) to 'the meaner sort' among the dissenters was very much higher than among Anglicans they figured much more prominently in the electorate than in the population as a whole. In 1715, for example, it would seem that, disregarding Quakers, dissenters made up a third of the borough electorate and 'about one 6th of the freeholders' in Devonshire, a fifth of the county and a third of the borough voters in Essex, and about a sixth of the combined county and borough electorates in Notts. See appendices V and VII (based on the Evans census) of Bebb, *op. cit.*; Dr Williams's Lib. MS. 34. 4, p. 31 and *passim*.

28. See Holmes, *The Trial of Doctor Sacheverell*, pp. 29–35, 41–5.

the sermons and writings of High Church controversialists such as Sacheverell, Milburne, Tilly and Welton. And because they believed that ultimate deliverance could only come through a period of prolonged Tory dominance in Parliament and in government, these clerics, and the thousands more who shared their views if not their flair for publicity, were as devoted in their commitment to the Tory cause in elections as the dissenters were to the cause of the Whigs. They canvassed their flocks assiduously. They rode to the poll in black-coated squadrons, two or three hundred strong, in many county elections. Above all they put their pulpits in the most bare-faced manner at the service of Tory candidates. The parson who harangued the mayor and aldermen of Durham just before the city election of 1708 took as his text

> the –th verse of the 12th chapter of the 1st of Sam[uel], and the words, they say, by hard straining, he perverted into the management of elections on which his whole discourse run, lashing all those who oppos'd Mr. Coniers [the Tory candidate], concluding that damnation would be their future lott, if they did not repent of such an heinous sin as the very attempting to reject so true and trusty a member of the Church.[29]

Of course in such circumstances the pressure on Tory politicians to take the extreme High Church line on the peril of Dissent, even when their own fears may have been tempered to some extent by realism, was irresistible.

In short, for the party politician of the years 1689–1714 religion may or may not have been a matter of strong personal conviction, but it was almost invariably an ideal stick with which to beat his opponents. It was ideal because it carried the power, and it exploited the stigma, of association. Thus, the average Whig knew well that all Tories were not Jacobites. But he also knew, and was aware that his opponents could not deny, that all Jacobites were Tories. And therefore it became a stock-in-trade of his propaganda to exploit the fear of Popery against most Tories, and certainly most High Tories, indis-

29. James Clavering to Lady Cowper, 11 May 1708, printed in 'Some Clavering Correspondence', ed. E. Hughes, *Archeologia Aeliana*, 4th series (1956), xxxiv, 17.

criminately. To quote just one of a host of examples: the duchess of Marlborough, canvassing at St Albans in 1705 against John Gape, a 'Tacker' seeking re-election, told one voter who was inclined to favour him, 'she had no prejudice to Mr Gape, but it was the Queen's desire that no such men should be chose, for such men would unhinge the government, and the Papists' horses stood saddled day and night, whipping and spurring.'[30] On the other side, the average Tory was fully aware that not every Whig was a dissenter, and that not every Whig was ill-disposed to the Church. But he had in his hands two potent weapons: the universal knowledge that virtually every dissenter was a Whig, and the widespread feeling that every time the Whigs attained power in the state, as in the years 1694–8 and 1705–10, the dissenters benefited and the Church suffered. How could he refrain from harping on such damaging associations? Or from rattling the skeletons of the 1640s into the bargain? Thus in his speech on the Second Occasional Conformity bill Sir John Pakington did not hesitate to lump Whigs and dissenters together, by implication, as

> a party of men that are against the church and government; whose principle of hatred and malice to the family of the Stuarts descends to them by inheritance; men, sir, that offered open violence to her majesty's royal grandfather; men that have not only the impudence at this time to justify that fact, but to turn the day of his murder into ridicule, and keep a calf's-head-feast in the city.[31]

In the last part of this paper we shall examine some of the other major 'points of consequence' in the post-Revolution period, apart from Occasional Conformity, which enabled the two parties to use their sharpest religious weapons, the weapons of fear and association, in a contest for survival of growing desperation.

Leaving aside the continuous bass-line of Whig propaganda, as persistent as a bagpipe's drone, there were some half a dozen

30. *Commons' Journals*, xv, 38.
31. *Parl. Hist.* vi, 153–4.

occasions of uncommon importance when the Whig leaders strove to exploit their opponents' equivocations on the succession and the nation's fear of Popery to win a major party advantage. For example, they made two attempts, the first an unsuccessful one in 1690 and the second successful in the session of 1701–2, to enforce on all office-holders, sitting peers and M.P.s an oath abjuring allegiance to James II and later to the Old Pretender. The logic behind the call for abjuration was to expose the true 'zealots of indefeasible hereditary right', and therefore the potential traitors, by stripping away from them the garments of political convenience; for it was argued by the Whigs that many who 'equivocated in the very act of kissing the gospels'[32] when swearing a carefully tailored oath of allegiance to William III would find it much more difficult so lightly to renounce allegiance to King James. The move failed on the former occasion, because William himself discountenanced it. It succeeded on the latter occasion, for one reason because the Pretender had just been recognized by Louis XIV as James III of England. And there is little doubt that many members of the Tory party, which had always steadfastly opposed an abjuration oath, might indeed have been seriously embarrassed by it, had not the sudden death of William a few weeks later and the accession of James II's daughter, Anne, deprived the issue of its immediate relevance and soothed their consciences in acquiescing. As a leading Tory peer, Viscount Weymouth, informed his brother with evident relief, at the end of March 1702: 'though I have not absolutely resolved to take this new Oath, yet . . . I am much nearer doing it than I ever thought I should bee, and may possibly submit to doe it, the case beeing soe much altered by the death of King Wm, and the old as well as new lawes beeing on the Queens side. And if conscience will allow it, I am sure prudence will prompt to strengthen her Government, and restore the Church to the ground it has lost.'[33]

Much of the ground that had been lost, in the view of Weymouth and thousands of his kind, had been treacherously abandoned by the government in the period of Whig Junto

32. Macaulay's unforgettable phrase. *History of England*, iv, 1823.
33. Longleat MSS. Thynne Papers, xiii, fo. 287: to James Thynne, 27 March 1702. I am grateful to the marquess of Bath for giving me access to the Harley and Thynne papers at Longleat.

dominance in the middle years of William. Whether or not they were right, what is noteworthy for us is what cemented that dominance in 1696, at a time when it seemed very precarious. The turning-point was the Jacobite plot to assassinate the King. This it was which enabled the Junto to achieve a major *coup* by demanding that the members of both Houses of Parliament should subscribe to what was called 'the Association' to defend their 'rightful and lawful monarch' (as William was now pointedly described) against the Papists, who were sworn to murder him. A hundred Tories in the Commons and about twenty in the Lords refused to sign: not as many as the Whigs had hoped, but enough to send Tory fortunes into a decline between this point and the 1698 Election.

The Whigs continued to raise the Jacobite bogy whenever possible, but they achieved nothing quite as successful as the Association again until the parliamentary session of 1705–6, when they had just entered their second phase of prosperity. That winter they introduced their Regency bill, a measure designed to give teeth to the 1701 Act of Settlement and prevent a collapse of authority in what everyone realized would be a perilous interlude between the Queen's death and the arrival in England of the Hanoverian heir. Their opponents cut a sorry figure by their tactics in factiously obstructing the progress of this bill without having the courage to oppose it in principle: so much so that Bishop Burnet, that arch-Whig, wrote soon afterwards in his *History of my own Time*, 'I never knew any thing, in the management of the Tories, by which they suffered more in their reputation than by this.'[34] When the bishop wrote these words he was not to know that a more terrible shoal lay ahead for the Tories, one which was to do far more than simply damage their reputation; and that he would live to see them run on to it. Well before that, however, an attempted invasion of Scotland in 1708 had given the Whigs a fresh, heaven-sent opportunity to deploy all their anti-Catholic, anti-Jacobite propaganda against the Tories – this time at the Election which, fortunately for them, followed immediately afterwards. But the Tory failure of 1708, which brought them

34. Burnet, v, 238. There are abundant instances of Tory tactics in the Regency bill debates in 'An Anonymous Parliamentary Diary, 1705–6', ed. W. A. Speck, printed in *Camden Miscellany*, xxiii (London, Royal Historical Soc., 1969), esp. pp. 49–78.

for a while to their lowest ebb since the Revolution, was followed by an unprecedented triumph of 'the Church interest' at the polls in 1710; and this, in turn, was followed by an even bigger election victory following the Tory-negotiated Peace in 1713, a victory which left the Whigs with a mere 180 members in the Commons. This was the lowest point to which either party slumped between 1685 and the decisive Tory defeat of 1722. In fact, in terms of numbers returned, the débâcle of 1722 was no more shattering for the Tories than what the Whigs experienced in 1713.[35] The Whigs, it is true, were still strong and full of fight in the House of Lords. But they were now so starved of royal favour as well as of popular support that without the Succession crisis of 1713–14 it is hard to see how they could have escaped ultimate disaster: in short, the fate which in the event, and so wholly against the tide, overtook their enemies.

It has to be emphasized, however, that what happened to the Tories in those traumatic months at the end of Anne's reign occurred not just because of the effects of the Queen's near-fatal illness at Christmas 1713 on those internal divisions we observed earlier.[36] It also occurred because the Whigs, from the summer of 1713 onwards, consistently brought a series of issues before Parliament which dramatized the threat to the Protestant Succession and the growing Jacobite proclivities of their opponents. Even at the fag-end of the old Parliament the Junto forced the ministry to accept Wharton's motion in the Lords for an address calling for the Pretender's removal from Lorraine. In the new Parliament, which met in March 1714, they caused consternation by demanding during a finance debate that the Hanoverian troops, who were subsidized by the British tax-payer, should have their arrears paid in full – including those incurred after the Queen's forces had withdrawn from the front in May 1712. And when many Tories jibbed at this in a private meeting of backbenchers, 'the Whigs [one Jacobite member wrote] made a terrible outcry upon it, affirming that now the

35. The Whigs by June 1714 were reduced to 171 members, after election petitions had been decided; the Tories during the session of 1722–3 to 169. Cf. Eveline G. Cruickshanks, 'The Tories and the Succession to the Crown in the 1714 Parliament', *Bulletin of the Institute of Historical Research*, xlvi, 1973, p. 176, and *The History of Parliament: The House of Commons 1715–1754*, ed. Romney Sedgwick (London, 1970), i, 34.
36. See p. 200 above.

mask was pulld off and the Tories might as well declare for the Pretender'. More directly, they manoeuvred two full-scale debates on 'the succession in danger' in April 1714, pressing Oxford's government close to defeat in the Lords, and securing eighty Tory desertions in the Commons, in 'the fullest [House] that ever was known in the memory of man.'[37] These moves culminated in a Junto motion in the Lords for a proclamation calling for the Pretender's capture 'dead or alive' – a phrase which made every Tory writhe – and a later vote in the Commons, promising £100,000 reward out of public funds to anyone who apprehended him. The address accompanying this vote (June 1714), assuring the Queen 'that this House will heartily concur with her Majesty in all other measures for extinguishing the hopes of the Pretender, and all his open *and secret* abetters', epitomizes the ruthless strategy of the late Stuart Whigs: a basically religious fear, exploited for over twenty years against opponents who could never fully live down their pre-Revolution past, now being made the final instrument of one of the most startling reversals of party political fortunes in British history.

And yet it was only four years before that the Whigs them-selves had suffered a comparable experience. They did so partly, it is true, because of disenchantment with the Spanish Succession War; but far more because in 1710 the Tories had seized an unexpected opportunity to alarm the political nation once again, but now to an unequalled pitch, with their proprietary spectre, the unholy alliance between the Whigs and the dissenters to undermine the Church of England, and thereby the monarchy too. The opportunity came in December 1709 when the Whigs impeached that ranting parson, Henry Sacheverell, for another provocative sermon. This time he had reserved his thunder for St. Paul's Cathedral, choosing his text from chapter 11 of the Second Letter to the Corinthians, 'in peril among False Brethren' (it was a sermon preached, appropriately enough, on Gunpowder Day).

No-one could deny that Sacheverell had invited retribution. As one of an ever-growing number of 'concealed Jacobites' or 'nonjuring jurors' among the lower clergy, his purpose had

---

37. *The Lockhart Papers* (London, 1817), i, 467–70; Brit. Lib. Add. MSS. 470727, p. 193: Sir John to Philip Perceval, 17 Apr. 1714. In general on the Whigs' succession campaign, Holmes, *British Politics in the Age of Anne*, pp. 85–6.

undoubtedly been seditious. Before an audience consisting largely of Whiggish London businessmen, he had attacked both the Glorious Revolution, obliquely, and the Toleration outright, accusing the Whig 'false brothers' of treachery to the state as well as to the Church by cherishing what he called this 'brood of vipers' [the dissenters] in our bosom, with their 'Hellish principles of fanaticism, regicide and anarchy'. His impeachers clearly hoped that during his trial the stigma of Jacobitism and 'a brand of indelible infamy' would be attached for good both to 'the flag officer' himself and to all the clergy and laymen who rallied to his defence. What they failed to anticipate was that prosecuting him before the highest court in the land would persuade hundreds of thousands of English men and women that there was no smoke without fire, and that everything the highflying clergy and their Tory patrons had been saying for years, in proclaiming the Church's peril and parading the demon of Dissent, was very likely true. And so by the Tory propagandists in print and by the High Church divines from their pulpits this impeachment of an undistinguished, unsavoury young clergyman was skilfully represented as the most serious attack since the 1640s on the very foundations of the Anglican Church.

The excitement engendered by the trial itself in February and March 1710 surpassed all prediction. From one end of the country to another it set 'husband against wife, parent against child, male against female.'[38] Tickets for the 2,000 seats were cornered and touted in a manner worthy of a modern Cup Final. The London mob rose, and in its second-worst riot of the eighteenth century wrecked six nonconformist chapels and made huge bonfires of their contents from Drury Lane to Blackfriars. The greatest ladies in the land got up at six every morning and joined in an unladylike scramble for places when the doors of Westminster Hall opened at nine. Furthermore the duchess of Cleveland locked her husband in his bedroom to prevent him from voting against Sacheverell in the House of Lords, and he was only rescued at the eleventh hour by the duke of Richmond, with a ladder. The political leaders of the age and many of its greatest lawyers debated for three weeks

38. Scottish Record Office, Ogilvy of Innerquharity MSS. G.D. 205/4: John Pringle to Sir William Bennett, 21 March 1710.

5. The sacking of Daniel Burgess's Presbyterian meeting-house and the burning of its contents in Lincoln's Inn Fields during the Sacheverell riots of 1710.
From *Vulgus Britannicus*, London, 1711

the issues of the case, which indeed reached down to the very roots from which the parties had sprung: the right of resistance, and with it the fundamental question of whether civil government was religious or secular in its foundations, of whether it had a divine right or 'contract' basis (Article I); the right of the dissenters to their 'Toleration' (Article II); the present state and future security of the Church of England (Article III).

The immediate effects of the trial were spectacular. The Doctor was found guilty by the House of Lords; but with feeling running so high he was given a derisory sentence which was regarded as tantamount to an acquittal. In the summer he went on a triumphal tour through most of the midland and western counties of England and into Wales, combining junketing with electioneering for seven outrageous weeks. When the autumn came, and Parliament was dissolved by a new ministry headed by Robert Harley, the Tories were able to fight, and triumphantly win, the 1710 Election largely on the strength of the continuing hysteria released by the Sacheverell affair and the emotive tribal cry of 'The Church in Danger'. As the High Anglican parsons gave thanks for the victory, and the exultant Tory squires back at Westminster quaffed their ale round the tables of the October Club, all looked for the new regime to quash the dissenters for good, proscribe the Whig leaders, and usher in a new golden age for true Churchmen, more glorious even than the last years of Charles II.

But the outcome, even in the short run, was frustration. Leaving aside the statutory toleration secured for the Scottish episcopalians (1712), the only solid achievement the 'Church party' had to show for the first three years of the Harley ministry, and for a whole Parliament, was the 'Fifty New Churches Act', which aimed to rectify the alarming preponderance of chapels over churches in the London suburbs, and a watered-down Act against Occasional Conformity, passed at length in December 1711.* For the rest, the new prime minister, the most artful dodger of his generation, cunningly blocked

* The latter with the connivance of the Whigs, who at a time when Tory peace plans hung by a parliamentary thread had to make an unenviable choice between standing by their nonconformist allies and forging a compact with Lord Nottingham, which they hoped (wrongly as it transpired) would bring about the defeat of the government's peace preliminaries.

nearly all the extremists' plans until very shortly before his own fall in July 1714. In this Queen Anne was for the most part his willing accomplice, and not least over the question of Church preferments. Since the late 1690s bishoprics had been unashamedly regarded by the leaders of both parties as political spoils for their own ecclesiastical zealots. But Anne and Harley had always resisted this trend, not without some success (as the 'Bishoprics Crisis' of 1707–8 had shown);[39] and they continued to resist it down to 1714, denying Sacheverell a bishopric and Swift an English deanery, and succumbing only in the case of Atterbury. In June 1714, a month before Harley (now Lord Treasurer Oxford)'s dismissal, there passed the notorious Schism bill, aimed at cutting off the lifeblood of Dissent by abolishing the academies. It became law only after a struggle in the Lords where the Whigs, led with élan by Lord Wharton (who did not fail to point out that three of the present Cabinet ministers had been themselves educated at academies), again assumed their natural mantle of defenders of the Toleration. But the Queen died on the very day the Schism Act was due to come into force; and there died with her any chance that it would ever be effectively enforced.

As for the long run, the association of eighty per cent of the clergy with extreme Toryism, and inevitably in the last year or two of Anne's reign with suspected Jacobitism – this, and two decades of mounting Whig anti-clericalism in the face of all this uninhibited politicking by the clergy – proved fatal to the hopes of an Anglican revival when the Whigs returned to office under George I. For the ultimate Whig answer to the religious problems of post-Revolution England went further than simply repealing, in 1719, the Tory persecuting Acts of 1711 and 1714. It went further than suppressing Convocation, that refuge for malcontent and Jacobite clergy, in 1717; further even than using the Fifteen Rebellion, and later Bishop Atterbury's Plot, to brand every Tory without distinction as a Jacobite and unfit to bear office, high or low. Their long-term solution was to pacify the Anglican clergy by allaying their sharpest fears of Puritanism and Popery, but to subject them at the same time to that remorseless patronage system which

39. G. V. Bennett, 'Robert Harley, the Godolphin Ministry and the Bishoprics Crisis of 1707', *E.H.R.* lxxxii, 1967.

they found so effective in controlling the politicians and drawing the fangs of the lay Tories. In this way they succeeded not so much in *healing* the divisions in the Anglican Church, or the divisions between Church and Dissent, as in *stifling* those clergy who tried to perpetuate them or turn them to political ends. They thus reduced the Church, first to quiescence and Erastian dependence, then to a prolonged inertia; and they ensured that what Professor Plumb has called the age of political stability after 1725 would also be an age of ideological torpor, an age when any religious charge there was left in politics could be expertly defused by the greatest bomb-disposal expert English public life has known, Sir Robert Walpole.

BIBLIOGRAPHICAL NOTE

Reference was made early in the text (pp. 182-3 above) and in n. 1 to the major debate which has taken place in recent years over the nature of late Stuart politics and parties. Of the participants only R. R. Walcott, *English Politics in the Early Eighteenth Century* (Oxford, 1956) and D. Rubini, *Court and Country, 1688-1702* (London, 1968) have made a serious case against the view that the Whig–Tory dichotomy remained the basic political fact of the post-Revolution scene. Professor Walcott's arguments found no favour in J. H. Plumb, *The Growth of Political Stability 1675-1725* (London, 1967) and G. Holmes, *British Politics in the Age of Anne* (London, 1967); while Dr. Rubini's interpretation of the politics of William's reign was challenged in 1969 by H. Horwitz, 'The Structure of Parliamentary Politics' and E. L. Ellis, 'William III and the Politicians', two of the essays in *Britain after the Glorious Revolution 1689-1714*, ed. G. Holmes (London, 1969). The view that the years 1694 and 1701-2 were important landmarks in the progress towards the full-blooded Whig–Tory conflict of Anne's reign was put forward in *The Divided Society: Party Conflict in England, 1694-1716*, ed. G. Holmes and W. A. Speck (London, 1967); while I. F. Burton, P. W. J. Riley and E. Rowlands, by detailed analysis of three division-lists in the middle of William's reign singled out 1696, rather than 1694, as the point by which 'a fundamental shift in political structure had taken place' ('Political Parties in the Reigns of William III and Anne: The Evidence of Division Lists', *Bulletin of the Institute of Historical Research*, Special Supplement No. 7, Nov. 1968). More recently B. W. Hill has provided not only a useful synthesis but valuable interpretative commentary on the debate in the course of a wide-ranging essay, 'Executive Monarchy and the Challenge of Parties, 1689-1832', *Historical Journal*, 13, 1970, and H. L. Snyder has laid the coping stone on the 'traditionalist' case in 'Party Configurations in the early Eighteenth Century House of Commons', *Bull. Inst. Hist. Research*, 45, 1972. Dr. Speck's definitive work (see n. 2 above) has demonstrated the polarization of the constituencies in the early 18th century, and contains a case study of the 'Church in Danger' Election of 1705.

* * *

A helpful brief introduction to the religious history of the period is G. R. Cragg, *The Church and the Age of Reason 1648–1789* (revised edn. London, 1966), ch. 4, 5. Thereafter the following will all help to substantiate and develop the various general points about the Church of England made earlier in this pamphlet.

N. Sykes, *Church and State in England in the Eighteenth Century* (Cambridge, 1934)

N. Sykes, *From Sheldon to Secker* (Cambridge, 1959)

G. Every, *The High Church Party, 1688–1718* (London, 1956)

A. T. Hart, *The Life and Times of John Sharp, Archbishop of York* (London, 1949)

G. V. Bennett, 'Conflict in the Church', in *Britain after the Glorious Revolution, 1689–1714*, ed. G. Holmes (London, 1969)

G. Holmes, 'The Church', ch. 2 (pp. 21–47) of *The Trial of Doctor Sacheverell* (London, 1973)

R. Thomas, 'Comprehension and Indulgence' (1962, see n. 11)

The intellectual threat to the Church and to orthodox Christianity is discussed in G. R. Cragg, *Reason and Authority in the Eighteenth Century* (Cambridge, 1964) and H. J. McLachlan, *Socinianism in Seventeenth Century England* (Oxford, 1951).

The fear of Popery inherited from the period before the 1688 Revolution is admirably illuminated by J. P. Kenyon, *The Popish Plot* (London, 1972) and J. Miller, *Popery and Politics in England 1660–1688* (Cambridge, 1973). There is a crying need for a major, authoritative study of post-Revolution Dissent in the years 1689–*c*.1720. A lot of valuable periodical material is hidden away in local or sectarian journals. Important information relevant to our period and theme can be found in a number of denominational or institutional histories or in scholarly local studies of nonconformity covering a much larger time-span. Examples are C. G. Bolam, J. Goring, H. L. Short, R. Thomas, *The English Presbyterians* (London, 1968), the main interest of which is, however, theological; H. McLachlan, *English Education under the Test Acts* (Manchester, 1931); A. Brockett, *Nonconformity in Exeter, 1650–1875* (Manchester, 1962) and D. G. Hey, 'The Pattern of Non-conformity in South Yorkshire, 1660–1851', *Northern History*, 8, 1973.

Finally the interaction of politics and religion over specific issues, and over patronage and preferment, can be studied in

G. V. Bennett, 'King William III and the Episcopate', in *Essays in Modern English Church History*, eds. G. V. Bennett and J. D. Walsh (London, 1966)

——, 'Robert Harley, The Godolphin Ministry and the Bishoprics Crisis of 1707', *English Historical Review*, 82, 1967

N. Sykes, 'Queen Anne and the Episcopate', *Ibid.*, 50, 1935

H. L. Snyder, 'The Defeat of the Occasional Conformity Bill and the Tack', *Bull. Inst. Hist. R.*, 41, 1968

H. T. Dickinson, 'The Poor Palatines and the Parties', *Eng. Hist. Rev.*, 82, 1967

G. Holmes, *The Trial of Doctor Sacheverell* (London, 1973)
——, 'The Substance of Conflict: Principles and Power', ch. 3 of *British Politics in the Age of Anne* (London, 1967)
M. Ransome, 'Church and Dissent in the General Election of 1710', *Eng. Hist. Rev.*, 56, 1941
E. G. Cruickshanks, 'The Tories and the Succession to the Crown in the 1714 Parliament', *Bull. Inst. Hist. R.*, 46, 1973

Political biographies of relevance include H. Horwitz, *Revolution Politicks: The Career of Daniel Finch, Second Earl of Nottingham* (Cambridge, 1968), A. McInnes, *Robert Harley, Puritan Politician* (London, 1970) and H. T. Dickinson, *Bolingbroke* (London, 1970). There is, unfortunately, no successor as yet to D. R. Lacey, *Dissent and Parliamentary Politics in England, 1661–1689* (New Brunswick, New Jersey, 1969); but see *ibid.*, ch. 10, 'Dissent and the Revolution, 1688–1689', an important contribution to our knowledge of the Revolution religious settlement.

POSTSCRIPT

Two important works published subsequent to this Note are:
J. Redwood, *Reason, Ridicule and Religion: The Age of Enlightenment in England 1660-1750* (1976)
M.R. Watts, *The Dissenters: From Reformation to the French Revolution* (Oxford, 1978), chs. 3, 4.

CHRONOLOGY OF POLITICAL EVENTS

1689   Accession of William and Mary; Revolution settlement, including 'Toleration Act' and Bill of Rights; war with France (to 1697).

1690   Secession from the Church of the Nonjurors.

1690–3 Coalition ministry under nominal leadership of the Tory, Carmarthen (Danby).

1693   Dismissal of Nottingham, Tory Secretary of State and 'Minister for the Church'.

1694   Death of Mary; appointment of Low Church Primate (Tenison); Triennial Act.

1694–9 Whig Junto-dominated coalition government.

1695   End of press censorship; increase of anti-clerical, anti-Christian literature.

1696   Jacobite plot to assassinate William III; the Whig 'Association'.

1697–   Crystallization of High and Low Church parties; 'Church in
1701   danger' cry raised by High Churchmen and Tories.

1700   Rochester and the Tories back in favour; death of Princess Anne's son, duke of Gloucester.

1701   Act of Settlement in favour of Hanoverian succession; death of ex-King James II.

1702   Abjuration Act; accession of Anne; renewal of war; Sacheverell's 'bloody flag' sermon; Tory election victory.

1702–4 Largely High Tory ministry, under moderate management of Godolphin, Marlborough and Speaker Harley.

1703   Failure of 1st and 2nd bills against Occasional Conformity; resignation of Rochester.

1704   Resignation of Nottingham; Harleyite Tories brought into office; Blenheim; failure of 'the Tack' and 3rd Occasional Conformity bill.

1705   60 seats gained by Whigs at General Election; 'Church in danger' motions defeated in Parliament.

1705–8 Coalition of Whigs with Court and Harleyite Tories.

1706   Regency Act.

1707   Act of Union with Scotland.

1708   Resignation of the Harleyites; attempted Jacobite invasion; Whig election victory.

1708–10 '2nd Junto administration', in conjunction with Godolphin and Marlborough.

1709   Act naturalizing Foreign Protestants; Malplaquet; Sacheverell's St. Paul's sermon – 'In peril among False Brethren'.

1710   Sacheverell's trial; fall of Godolphin and the Whigs; formation of Harley's ministry; Tory election triumph.

1711   Death of Rochester; 4th Occasional Conformity bill passed; Nottingham allies with Whig Opposition.

1713   Peace of Utrecht; increased Tory majority at General Election.

1713–14 Split between Hanoverian and Jacobite Tories; struggle between Harley (Oxford) and Bolingbroke for the Tory leadership.

1714   Schism Act; fall of Oxford; death of Anne; return of the Whigs to office after George I's accession.

1715   Whig majority of 150 at last Election before Septennial Act; Jacobite rebellion; resignation of Nottingham's Hanover Tories.

1719   Repeal of Occasional Conformity and Schism Acts, but not of Test and Corporation Acts.

1721   Robert Walpole, First Lord of the Treasury.

6. Dr. Francis Atterbury, dean of Carlisle and Christ Church and bishop of Rochester.

High Church–Tory champion, author of the Schism Bill (1714), later Jacobite and plotter (p.211), his career personified the embroilment of religion with party, and ended in despair and disaster, with the discovery in 1722 that Tory commitment to the restoration of the House of Stuart was no more than 'a rope of sand' (p.264).

After Kneller. *National Portrait Gallery*

9

THE SACHEVERELL RIOTS: THE CHURCH AND THE CROWD IN EARLY-EIGHTEENTH-CENTURY LONDON*

THE TRAIL OF POPULAR DISORDER LEFT IN THE WAKE OF THE ILL-STARRED prosecution of Doctor Sacheverell in 1710 stretched in the end into many corners of England and Wales. The verdict of the House of Lords on 20th and 21st March, a moral victory for the Doctor over the Whigs who had impeached him, was violently celebrated by mobs as far apart as Wrexham, Barnstaple and Gainsborough.[1] Cathedral cities, clothing boroughs, even somnolent market towns erupted.[2] In midsummer, when the chaplain of St. Saviour's enjoyed for seven weeks a hero's progress, there were fresh outbreaks both in places on his route and in others far distant.[3] In the autumn, Sacheverell mobs rampaged round many a hustings in the most tumultuous general election of the eighteenth century.[4]

None of these riots, however, could remotely compare in scale or violence with those accompanying the trial itself in London. For eight hours during the night of 1st-2nd March the capital experienced its second worst disturbance of the century. Seventy years later the Gordon Riots were to dwarf it, and all else, by their protracted

* This essay is an expanded and modified version of a paper first read at the Newcastle Conference on Social Control in January 1973. The author is grateful for comments and suggestions made at the time, particularly by Dr. W. A. Speck, Mr. J. Stevenson and Mr. Edward Thompson, and for help at a later stage from Mr. Clyve Jones and Mr. J. R. Sewell.

[1] Public Rec. Off., State Papers Domestic (hereafter S.P.) 34/12/14: Sir Joseph Jekyll to Lord Sunderland, Wrexham, 4 Apr.; Brit. Lib., Loan 29/238, fo. 320: George Whichcote to duke of Newcastle, Gainsborough, 27 Mar. (I am grateful to the duke of Portland for permission to make use of his papers, on loan to the British Library [Loan 29]); anon., *A Vindication of the Last Parliament: in Four Dialogues between Sir Simon and Sir Peter* (London, 1711; copy in Brit. Lib., Madan Coll.), pp. 298-9.

[2] For the rioting in Oxford, Exeter, Hereford, Frome, Cirencester and Sherborne, see Geoffrey Holmes, *The Trial of Doctor Sacheverell* (London, 1973) (hereafter Holmes, *Trial*), pp. 234-6.

[3] Most notably, Bridgnorth and Ely: Lincs. Rec. Off., Monson MSS., 7/3/124; *The Flying-Post*, 13 and 22 July; Brit. Lib., Loan 29/321, Dyer's News-letter, 31 Aug.; S.P. 44/109 and 34/37, no. 157: Henry St. John to Attorney-General, 29 Sept. 1710, and enclosed depositions.

[4] See the eleven examples listed in M. Beloff, *Public Order and Popular Disturbances, 1660-1714* (Oxford, 1938), p. 55. To these may be added disorders at the county elections for Yorkshire, Kent, and Norfolk (where Walpole was roughly handled); and at the borough elections for Taunton — where William Coward (the Whig candidate) was "insulted and abused" — Northampton and Nottingham. W. A. Speck, *Tory and Whig: The Struggle in the Constituencies* (London, 1970), p. 42; W. Bisset, *The Modern Fanatick* (London, 1710); *The Observator*, 18-21 Oct.; *The Flying-Post*, 28 Oct., 2 and 4 Nov.

anarchy and horror.[5]   Other disorders were to cause more bloodshed than the Sacheverell riots, notably the so-called "massacre of St. George's Fields" in 1768.[6]   But none until 1780 were as destructive, or as frightening to the government or the property-owners of London, as the "detestable tumults"[7] of 1710.

Indeed it was miraculous that neither the great crowds on the streets nor the upholders of law and order suffered heavier casualties. Considering the danger, the toll of the Sacheverell riots was almost trivial: at most, two deaths;[8] some fifty rioters wounded,[9] several of them no more than cut by splintering glass; and a handful of soldiers bearing some marks of battle.   Things might have been very different but for the exemplary discipline of the small number of regular troops used to disperse the mobs: they came from three crack Guards units — Lord Arran's troop of Life Guards, the Coldstream Guards, and the Second Horse Grenadiers — and included a high proportion of soldiers seasoned in Marlborough's campaigns.   In this respect it was a mercy the City Trained Bands were not called out until the situation was under complete control; though it is arguable that if the militia had been put under arms twenty-four hours earlier there might have been no outbreak at all.[10]

Another blessing in disguise was the absence of any Riot Act on the statute-book.   Up to July 1715 professional troops and militiamen alike — and any civilians who came to their aid — had to be very chary of killing or maiming in dealing with civil disturbances, since they were not legally indemnified if a victim subsequently proved to have been innocent; and even if they killed a genuine rioter they could be charged with murder at Common Law if his death was deemed the

---

[5] For the Gordon Riots, which led to close on 300 fatal casualties among the mob, see G. Rudé, "The Gordon Riots: A Study of the Rioters and Their Victims", *Trans. Roy. Hist. Soc.*, 5th ser., vi (1956), pp. 93-114; J. P. De Castro, *The Gordon Riots* (London, 1926).

[6] G. Rudé, *Wilkes and Liberty* (London, 1962), pp. 49-52, notes eleven deaths.

[7] S.P. 34/12/14: John Clifford *et al.* to [Henry Boyle?], 9 Mar. 1710.

[8] For the first case, firmly authenticated, see A. Boyer, *History of the Life and Reign of Queen Anne* (London, 1722), p. 417; Blenheim MSS., Box VII, [bundle] 18: deposition of George Gosdin before Francis Negus, J.P., 6 Mar. (I am indebted to the duke of Marlborough for allowing me to use material from his family archive).   For the second, more dubious, case, see H. C. Foxcroft, *A Supplement to Burnet's History of My Own Time* (Oxford, 1902), p. 427; G. Burnet, *A History of My Own Time*, 6 vols. (Oxford, 1833 edn.), v, p. 444; Blenheim MSS., Box VII, 18.

[9] According to L'Hermitage in his report to the States-General: Brit. Lib., Add. MSS. 17677DDD, fo. 432.

[10] See Holmes, *Trial*, pp. 157-60, 175.   The Lord Mayor, a Sacheverellite, made no attempt to summon an emergency meeting of the Lieutenancy Commission until forced to do so by a direct government appeal to the Lieutenancy.   Corporation of London Rec. Off. (hereafter C.L.R.O.), Lieutenancy minute book, 1696/7-1714, p. 151 (despite the date, 1 Mar., on the official minute, there is strong evidence that the meeting took place after midnight, that is, six hours after the riots began).

result of an excessive, unnecessary use of force.[11]   In such circumstances the flat of the sabre or the butt of the musket, reinforced by the
size and muscular power of the cavalry charger, were likely to be
preferred to the blade and the musket-ball, and scores of Londoners
had good reason to be thankful for this in March 1710.   In more than
three hours of action after the troops first engaged the rioters in
Lincoln's Inn Fields and Drury Lane not a shot was fired,[12] and it
was only in dealing with stubborn pockets of resistance in the con-
gested area between the lower end of Holborn and Fleet Street, and
later in a fierce little engagement on and near the Fleet Bridge, that
blades were used in earnest.[13]   Admittedly, law and discipline were
not the sole inhibiting factors; for by the time the government
secured the Queen's authority to deploy the few units of Guards
available at St. James's and Whitehall, the situation was already so
serious that the Secretary of State, Lord Sunderland, had no time to
draft careful written orders specifying the degree of force to be used.
The senior officer on duty, who was given command of all detachments, was no more than a captain and was only too conscious that
"he ventured his neck by going upon verbal orders".   In fact,
Sunderland had frankly warned him that "he must use his judgement
and discretion, and forbear violent means, except in case of
necessity".[14]

But if the roll of dead and injured gives no true indication of the
seriousness of the Sacheverell riots in London, there are other pointers
which do.   The alarm of the Queen and of both Houses of Parliament;[15] the fact that the government on the following day called in
reinforcements from Argyll's Troop of Horse Guards and from the

[11] Even the indemnity clause (III) in the notorious Act for preventing Tumults
and Riotous Assemblies (1 Geo. I, stat. 2, *cap.* 5) did not remove a soldier's duty
at Common Law "to fire with all reasonable caution, so as to produce no further
injury than what is absolutely wanted for the purpose of protecting person or
property".   See, for example, Rudé, *Wilkes and Liberty*, pp. 54-6; C. Grant
Robertson (ed.), *Select Statutes, Cases and Documents . . . 1660-1832*, 8th edn.
(London, 1947), pp. 518-21, and p. 523 (extracts from the Bowen-Haldane-
Rollit report on the Featherstone riots, 1893, from which the quotation is taken).

[12] As the crowds were fleeing from Drury Lane, some were heard to shout
out, "Damn them, we will be even with them tomorrow night, they dare not
fire upon us": T. B. Howell (compiler), *A Complete Collection of State Trials*,
33 vols. (London, 1809-26) (hereafter *State Trials*), xv, [col.] 659: evidence of
Edward Orrell, Old Bailey, 20 Apr. 1710.   See *ibid.*, xv, 662, for the use of the
flats of swords.

[13] Blenheim MSS., Box VII, 18: deposition of Thomas Hill before George
Tilson, 8 Mar., and "The Information of Henry Purdon and Charles Collins
taken upon oath . . . 2nd March 1709-10, before divers Justices there".   For the
action "near Fleet Ditch" in which the Life Guards "cut and slashed some of the
most daring . . .", see Boyer, *Queen Anne*, p. 417.

[14] A. Boyer, *The History of the Reign of Queen Anne digested into Annals*,
11 vols. (London, 1702-11), viii, p. 266.   See also Boyer, *Queen Anne*, p. 417;
E. Calamy, *An Historical Account of My Own Life, 1671-1731*, ed. J. T. Rutt,
2nd edn., 2 vols. (London, 1830), ii, p. 228.

[15] Holmes, *Trial*, pp. 163 note, 176, 179.

First and Second Regiments of Foot Guards;[16] the presence on the streets for three weeks thereafter of substantial forces of militia, and the willingness of London and Westminster ratepayers, despite some token Tory grumbling, to foot a heavy bill for keeping the trained bands under arms:[17] all these reactions, together with the rigorous legal action taken at first against the rioters, testify to the deep impression which the events of 1 March 1710 made on both politicans and property-owners. It was an impression which was to leave its mark on many memories, not least on Robert Walpole's, for three decades and more. In any other country, the Prussian envoy cynically observed, men would have feared the onset of civil war; even in England, inured as she was to political instability, there were some who were reminded of "the beginning of the late troubles".[18]

An analysis of the Sacheverell riots, in as much depth as the surviving evidence permits, is thus long overdue:[19] not simply for their intrinsic interest but to facilitate comparisons with other major London disorders of the century, already investigated.[20]   Elsewhere I have told the story of London's "night of fire", following the third day of Sacheverell's trial; I have also briefly discussed the bearing on the outbreak of various material grievances, which by the autumn of 1709 had made the government highly unpopular with ordinary

[16] S.P. 44/108, fo. 223: Sunderland to Argyll, 2 Mar., and endorsement.
[17] Brit. Lib., Add. MSS. 47026, pp. 17-18.   The bill anticipated was £10,000. It is impossible to say what the operation did cost the City, since the Trophy Tax accounts of the Commissioners of Lieutenancy have not survived for 1710. Initially all six regiments were raised, and the commanders of each regiment received £80 per double duty to defray their expenses.   C.L.R.O., Lieutenancy minute book, 1696/7-1714, pp. 151-2, 206.   (For these and other references to material in the Corporation Record Office I am indebted to the assistance of Miss Betty Marsden, the Deputy Keeper of the Records, and of Mr. James R. Sewell.)
[18] Deutsches Zentral Archiv, Merseburg, Rep. XI England 35D, fo. 26; *The Wentworth Papers*, ed. J. J. Cartwright (London, 1833), p. 113.   See also C.L.R.O., Repertory of the Court of Aldermen, vol. 114, pp. 153-6, 160-1, and Misc. MSS. 210.7: entry for 8 Apr. 1710.
[19] Beloff, *Public Order and Popular Disturbances*, pp. 51-4, discussed the problem of whether the riots were spontaneous or organized, but had little to say about motivation and nothing about the social composition of the mob. The value of his interpretative comments and those of G. M. Trevelyan, *England under Queen Anne*, 3 vols. (London, 1932-4), iii, pp. 38, 55-7 (who did briefly discuss the motives of the rioters), is vitiated by the limitations of the evidence available to them.
[20] G. Rudé's pioneer investigations of the riots of 1736, 1768-9 and 1780, together with three later synoptic essays on the activities, motivation and composition of the London crowd, have been brought together in his *Paris and London in the Eighteenth Century* (London, 1971).   See also *idem*, "The City Riot of the Eighteenth Century", in his *The Crowd in History, 1730-1848* (New York and London, 1964).   N. Rogers, "Popular Disaffection in London during the Forty-Five", *The London Jl.*, i (1975), pp. 5-27, utilizes and refines Rudé's techniques, but is concerned with individuals rather than "the crowd".

Londoners.[21] The objects of the present essay, are threefold: to probe more searchingly the nature of the riots and the motivation of the rioters; to consider the social composition of the crowd; and to enquire to what extent this great popular protest was incited and organized. We shall approach these questions separately, but aware that each has important connections with the others.

The nature of the 1710 disorders and the reasons why many thousands of Londoners took part in them[22] are basic to all further inquiry. Eruptions of this magnitude were rare in the eighteenth century, despite the fearsome reputation the London mob had earned since 1641-2 and continued to enjoy. When they did take place, it is natural for historians to wonder why the normal controls and safety-valves of late Stuart and Hanoverian society failed to prevent them. And it is clear that in 1710 one must look primarily at the extraordinary identification — almost unique in London's history, except at election times — between violent popular feeling and the cause of the Established Church of England. London experienced her "Protestant" mobs, especially in 1680, 1688 and 1780; likewise her "Tory" or "Jacobite" mobs during the first half of the eighteenth century. But only once, in 1710, was a large area of the capital at the mercy of that strange contradiction in terms, a "Church" mob.

Why the Anglican Church became at this juncture the focus of their unruly loyalties we must presently discover. The Sacheverell rioters, however, demonstrated in support of a single clergyman, not just in defence of an institution. When John Pittkin, a carpenter, was seized by the Life Guards on the Fleet Bridge, he was carried off assuring friends and captors alike "that Sacheverell was much in the right of it". John Stevens, before taking to the streets, had told the patrons of the Lamb Inn in Clement Lane "that rather than Dr Sacheverell should suffer he himself would head a mob of ten thousand men to rescue him from the Parliament". John Taylor's zeal, under questioning in the Guard Room, carried him even further. After shouting "God bless the Queen and Sacheverell", he announced that Sacheverell was so worthy a man that he deserved to be made a king, "and that he would spend the best drop of blood in his body to put the crown in the right place".[23] Plainly, therefore, "the

[21] Holmes, *Trial*, pp. 156-76, and "Note on the Economic Background to the Sacheverell Riots", pp. 177-8.
[22] Exactly how many it is impossible to say with confidence. But the question of numbers is discussed briefly below, pp. 70-2.
[23] Blenheim MSS., Box VII, 18: "Copies of the Informations & Examinations of Several Persons concerned in the late Great Riotts and Tumults, etc", third entry (for Pittkin); deposition of John Austin of Coventry, Attorney at Law, before Charles Delafaye, 4 Mar.; deposition of John Kelson, Henry Glover, William Wilmott and William Dickenson before Owen Buckingham, 4 Mar.

Sacheverell riots" are not so labelled for nothing.   And a first step towards understanding their motivation must be to set them in their immediate context.   To ignore the remarkable series of events and the no less remarkable man with which they were associated would be perverse.   "Sacheverell and High Church" were as quintessential to the riots of 1710 as were "Wilkes and Liberty" to those of 1768-9.

It was at the end of February 1710 that Dr. Henry Sacheverell, Oxford don and High Anglican parson,[24] was brought to trial in front of two thousand spectators in Westminster Hall.   But the atmosphere of public hysteria enveloping the trial had been building up since the previous December, when at the instigation of the Godolphin-Junto administration the Whig majority in the Commons had impeached Sacheverell for "high crimes and misdemeanours" against the state. His offence was that in spite of an explicit ban from the Court of Aldermen he had published a seditious sermon, preached on Guy Fawkes's day before the City Fathers in St. Paul's Cathedral.   On the anniversary, sacred to the Whigs, of a double deliverance from the horrors of Popery,[25] the preacher had chosen to ignore the accepted significance of the day and to take as his text the words of St. Paul in chapter eleven of the Second Letter to the Corinthians, "in peril among False Brethren".   Then for an hour and a half he had run through his whole repertoire of exotic phraseology and theatrical gestures to embellish the theme that at that very time there were in high places, both in the government and in the hierarchy of the Church of England, notorious traitors to both.   Although these men affected to be members of the Church, they were actually bent on undermining and destroying it, not least by selling out to the Protestant dissenters.   By betraying the Church they were automatically subverting the State, of which the Church was the crucial prop.   And he had made no bones about it, they deserved to burn in hell for their sins.[26]

It is often said that Sacheverell was prosecuted for "preaching against the Revolution of 1688"; and so, up to a point, he was.   In itself, however, this misses the gravamen of the charge against him. It is quite true that like several thousand other parsons who had reluctantly taken the oaths to the post-Revolution government, he had never abandoned the traditional High Anglican concepts of divinely appointed authority, and of Passive Obedience and Non-Resistance. It is also true that he was charged with maligning the "Resistance" of

[24] As well as being Fellow, Tutor and Bursar of Magdalen College, Oxford, he had been since May 1709 chaplain of St. Saviour's, Southwark.
[25] 5 Nov. was also the date of William of Orange's landing at Torbay in 1688.
[26] See Holmes, *Trial*, pp. 64-9, for the content of the sermon.   The full printed version, as published by Henry Clements of London between 25 Nov. and 3 Dec. 1709, and in a series of pirated editions subsequently, was given the title, *The Perils of False Brethren both in Church and State*.

1688 in the St. Paul's sermon.[27]   But ironically the real menace of
Sacheverell, from the government's point of view, was that although
he preached Obedience, he failed to practise it.   The Doctor was
a born demagogue; he had been recognized as such since he had first
electrified Oxford with a savage attack on Occasional Conformity
from St. Mary's pulpit in 1702.   And being also a man of turbulent
character and fierce ambition, he was fully prepared by 1709 to
exploit both the pulpit, in which he excelled, and the popular passions,
which in theory he deplored, to attempt to undermine a political
régime and a religious toleration he loathed.

To anyone reading the St. Paul's sermon today the seditious
intentions of the preacher seem undisguised.   Certainly it is easy to
understand why the Whigs found them so, and why the listening
congregation on that November afternoon was, in the words of one
clergyman present, "shaken . . . at the terror of his inveterate
expressions".[28]   In his peroration, for example, he exhorted both his
several hundred auditors and his countless thousands of readers,[29]
in a string of martial metaphors, to confront the false brethren by
presenting "an army of banners to our enemies", by putting on "the
whole armour of God", and by wrestling "not only against flesh and
blood, but against principalities, against powers, against the rulers of
the darkness of this world, against spiritual wickedness in high places".
Dr. Sacheverell, to use his own words in the St. Paul's pulpit, was
"sounding a trumpet in Sion".   And he had reason to hope that the
blasts would provoke some response in ears already attuned, in some
measure, to their notes.   For in London in the winter of 1709-10
a growing disillusionment with the protraction of the War of the
Spanish Succession by a Whig government and Parliament went hand
in hand with a dislike and suspicion of dissenters.   The links between
these attitudes were more than tenuous; for many leading citizens,
habitués of conventicles, had all too visibly prospered since the start of
the war, and *post hoc* was naturally identified with *propter hoc*.

These interwoven antipathies were reinforced by strong threads of
xenophobia.   The development of public credit since the early 1690s,
and the ever-growing sophistication during two long wars of the
mechanisms of international finance, had led not only to the burgeoning of a novel "monied interest" among the City business community
but to the increasing prominence within this interest of men of
foreign extraction: Iberian Jews, Huguenots, Walloons and Dutch-
men.   Some of them, it is true, were third or even fourth generation

[27] In Article I: see Holmes, *Trial*, p. 99.
[28] *Remarks and Collections of Thomas Hearne*, ed. C. E. Doble, *et al.*, 11 vols.
(Oxf. Hist. Soc., 1885-1921), ii, pp. 304-5: Rev. David Evans to Hearne,
10 Nov. 1709.
[29] The printed sermon can hardly have sold many less than 100,000 copies,
and therefore reached an audience of between a quarter of and half a million.

immigrants, such as the Houblons, Desbouveries, Delmés and Lethieulliers. But far more were of the second or first generation: Sir Theodore Janssen, Sir James Bateman, Sir Justus Beck, Matthew Decker, Peter Fabrot and Jacob Jacobsen, among many others.[30] The Bank of England, the symbol of the recent financial revolution and therefore, for hostile propaganda, the symbol of war profiteering, numbered almost thirty immigrants among its leading stockholders in 1709, more than a third of its plutocratic élite, and several figured on its board of directors. And like hundreds of native-born London businessmen, most of the foreigners underlined their lack of conformity by keeping themselves and their families outside the pale of the Established Church. Leaving aside the Jewish, Dutch and Lutheran churches in the capital, there were by 1711 thirteen places of worship in the London suburbs alone catering for the needs of the Huguenots, from merchant princes to Spitalfields silk workers.[31] Only a few months before Sacheverell preached at St. Paul's, the whole question of foreign Protestants in England had been given new dimensions: first by the passing of a General Naturalization Act against strong opposition by High Church clergy and Tory politicians, and secondly by the arrival, at the government's invitation, of 10,000 destitute Calvinist refugees from the Palatinate, most of whom were temporarily settled in the London area.[32] Since it was an accepted popular, as well as Tory, assumption that one "scarce ever knew a foreigner settl'd in England . . . but became a Whig in a little time after his mixing with us",[33] this was all extra ammunition for those Highflying clergy in London who in 1709 were once again proclaiming from their pulpits that "the Church was in danger" under the present administration. It certainly helped to furnish the locker of "their chief gunner", Henry Sacheverell.[34]

But of all the threats to the Church which Sacheverell and his like discerned,[35] none was more tangible, more easily grasped by the popular mind than the alleged threat from *native* Protestant Dissent. Even in a sermon concerned primarily with renegade Anglicans, as the 5th November sermon was, Sacheverell returned to his chief bugbears

---

[30] See the invaluable section on "Public Creditors", in P. G. M. Dickson, *The Financial Revolution in England . . . 1688-1756* (London, 1967), pp. 257-65.

[31] See the report of the Select Committee of the House of Commons, 1711 (the "Fifty New Churches Committee"), in *House of Commons Journals*, xvi, pp. 582-3; C. E. Whiting, *Studies in English Puritanism from the Restoration to the Revolution* (London, 1931), ch. 7, esp. pp. 360-4.

[32] The Naturalization Act was repealed by the Tories in 1712. On this and the Palatines, see H. T. Dickinson, "The Poor Palatines and the Parties", *Eng. Hist. Rev.*, lxxxii (1967).

[33] Bishop Francis Atterbury, quoted in John Toland, *A State Anatomy of Great Britain* (London, 1717), p. 15.

[34] See Holmes, *Trial*, pp. 45-7, for the "Church in Danger" campaigns of 1697-1709.

[35] The catalogue was comprehensive: *ibid.*, pp. 24-7, 35-41, 51-6.

again and again. Those "monsters and vipours in our bosom", those "clamorous, insatiable and Church-devouring malignants", "miscreants begot in rebellion, born in sedition, and nurs'd up in faction", would need constant vigilance lest they "grow eccentrick, and like comets that burst their orb, threaten the ruin and downfall of our Church and State".[36]

To many their "orb" already seemed to have swelled visibly since the institution of "the Toleration" by the Act of 1689. And just as London dramatized so many other features of national development in the early eighteenth century, so it highlighted with exceptional clarity the problem of Dissent. Out of approximately half a million Nonconformists in England and Wales by the time of George I's accession — the number of congregations was some 30 per cent higher than in 1690 — it was believed (and, it now seems, rightly so) that at least 100,000 were living in London, Westminster, Southwark and their out-parishes.[37] In 1705, during a fierce debate on "the Church in Danger", the Tory Member of Parliament for Worcestershire declared that already, "If I am rightly inform'd, there are 100 conventicles or thereabouts in and about London".[38] But what irked him no less, and what surely struck the true Londoner at least as strongly as his visiting country cousins, was the fact that despite the civil disabilities which Dissent still legally incurred, especially in terms of office-holding and university entrance, there was no necessary correlation between religious conformity and privileged social status. Both the imposing structures which many London congregations were erecting for their worship and the social display at their doors offered abundant proof to the outsider that Dissent was thriving in more than mere numbers: "... the dissenters are still building more [meeting-houses]", Sir John Pakington complained, "and ... their conventicles

[36] H. Sacheverell, *The Perils of False Brethren* (London, 1709 octavo edn.), pp. 15, 19.

[37] The provenance of these statistics will be discussed in a separate paper which I hope eventually to publish on "The Strength of Protestant Dissent in Early Eighteenth-Century England". Their basis is (1) the official record of dissenters' places of worship licensed in the first year (1689-90) of the operation of the Toleration Act (cf. E. D. Bebb, *Nonconformity and Social and Economic Life* [London, 1935], App. I); (2) a collation of the results of two independent "censuses" of Nonconformist congregations and ministers, begun in 1715 and substantially completed by 1717 (Dr. Williams's Lib., London, MS. 34.4, 34.5); (3) the report of the Select Committee of 1711 (see above, note 31) on the strength of Dissent in the London suburbs and in Westminster. From these and other sources, estimates and adjustments can then be made for (a) London within the walls, (b) the several hundred unenumerated congregations of Presbyterians, Independents and Baptists in the provinces, (c) the Quakers, (d) the lesser sects, (e) the foreign Protestants.

[38] Sir John Pakington's speech on "the Church in danger" [8 Dec. 1705], printed as an Appendix to "An Anonymous Parliamentary Diary, 1705-6", ed. W. A. Speck, in *Camden Miscellany*, xxiii (Camden Soc., 4th ser., vii, 1969), p. 83.

are now fuller than any of our churches, *and more attendance of coaches about them*".[39]   Many of the "rich coaches, fine liveries, splendid equipages . . .", which another Tory member had earlier seen as the hallmark of the new breed of City financiers, were part of the "state and bravery"[40] kept up by known "fanatics".   Their generous contributions to the construction of new chapels were but another manifestation of the same socio-religious phenomenon.

So it is unlikely to have been fortuitous that when the Sacheverell mobs, after two days of simmering, finally poured on to the streets on 1 March 1710, their original objective was the opulent Presbyterian meeting-house south of Lincoln's Inn Fields, opened in 1705 for a leading preacher of the day, Daniel Burgess.[41]   Neither was it coincidental that as the disorders reached their climax many of the rioters saw the firing of the Bank of England as a natural extension of their attacks on conventicles.   Indeed, papers handed out among the crowd of several thousand in "the Fields" bore the slogan: "Down with the Bank of England and the Meeting-Houses; and God damn the Presbyterians and all that support them".[42]

The Sacheverell rioters were no undiscriminating rabble.   They had specific targets in mind as they warmed to their work.   Some they located and scourged, others they failed to reach; but all are revealing indicators of their prejudices and impulses.   Some factors they do conceal.   But on the whole their message is transparent and thoroughly consonant with the general context of the disorders which we have just examined.   Before it was finally dispersed, the crowd which took possession of much of London's west end on the night of 1st-2nd March, chanting "High Church and Sacheverell", accosting frightened citizens with shouts like "God damn you, are you for the Doctor", had sacked and partly demolished six of the best-known dissenting meeting-houses in the capital.   They had made huge bonfires of their contents from Drury Lane in the west to Clerkenwell in the north and Blackfriars in the east.   Earl's near the junction of Drury Lane and Long Acre, Bradbury's off Fetter Lane, Taylor's between Leather Lane and Hatton Garden, Hamilton's in Clerkenwell, and Wright's inside the city walls in Blackfriars, had all suffered in turn the fate of Burgess's; except that in the Meeting House Court in front of Samuel Wright's the pyre was never ignited.   "They

---

[39] *Ibid.*   My italics.

[40] Bodleian Lib., Oxford, MS. Carte 117, fos. 177-8: "The Speech of an Honourable Member of the House of Commons upon the Debate of the Malt Tax" [1702].

[41] Burgess had brought his congregation to the new site from a former chapel in Russell Court, off Drury Lane, the lease of which had expired: Walter Wilson, *The History and Antiquities of Dissenting Churches and Meeting Houses . . . in London*, 4 vols. (London, 1808-14), iii, p. 492.

[42] [John Toland?], *High Church Display'd* (London, 1711), p. 96.

burnt not only the joiners' work of those meeting-houses, which they destroyed", recorded John Dyer, writer of a best-selling Tory newsletter, "but also the fine clocks, brass-branches and chairs and cushions of the vestry rooms; and they seized the builder of that in Leather Lane and threatened to throw him into the fire, alledging his crime was very great, for by building such houses he drew people from the public worship of God in the National Church".[43]

However, this is only part of the story. The mobs (the original concourse round Carey Street and Lincoln's Inn Fields having begun to split and fan out between 9.00 and 9.30 p.m.) were overtaken by the military while still in full cry: in Drury Lane well before midnight, in Blackfriars an hour to ninety minutes later, in Clerkenwell about 2.00 a.m. In each case they had other game in view, of which they made no secret, and some of it they would have bagged if the forces of law and order had not caught up with them first. The Drury Lane rioters had already threatened to make short work of a nearby chapel in Great Wild Street, which had only been by-passed in favour of Earl's because it was a mere "hen-roost" in comparison. And before the Life Guards clattered down Great Queen Street and came upon them, some of their ringleaders were canvassing the priorities of three further targets: the private residences of two notorious Whigs, Lord Wharton and John Dolben, and both the house and church of the Reverend Benjamin Hoadly.[44] There was nothing accidental about the selection. The earl of Wharton, cabinet-minister and Junto lord, was rightly suspected of having been a prime instigator of the impeachment,[45] and John Hodges, one of the incendiaries of Lincoln's Inn Fields, had boasted to his friends that "if he saw the said Earle he would run his fist down his throat".[46] Jack Dolben, who had chaired the committee which framed the impeachment articles, and who had narrowly escaped lynching earlier that evening,[47] was a classic example, as the son of a former archbishop of York, of the "false brothers" Sacheverell had denounced. And so in his own sphere was Ben Hoadly, the arch-latitudinarian rector of St. Peter-le-Poor, whom "Sacheverell was known to have the greatest enmity and rancour of mind against . . .".[48]

[43] Brit. Lib., Loan 29/321, Dyer's Newsletter, 4 Mar.

[44] *State Trials*, xv, 554, 627, 657-8; Boyer, *Queen Anne*, p. 416; [Toland?], *High Church Display'd*, p. 96; J. Oldmixon, *The History of England during the Reigns of King William and Queen Mary, Queen Anne, King George I* (London, 1735), p. 434; Calamy, *An Historical Account of My Own Life*, ii, p. 228. See also Scottish Rec. Off., G.D. 205/4 (Ogilvie of Inverquhurity MSS.): John Pringle to Sir William Bennett, 2 Mar. 1710.

[45] See Holmes, *Trial*, pp. 79-80, 84-5, 97-8.

[46] Blenheim MSS., Box VII, 18: deposition of Anne Corbière before Sir Henry Dutton Colt, 5 Mar. 1710. See also Matthew Bunce's evidence before the Lords, 4 Mar.: House of Lords MSS. 2665.

[47] Historical Manuscripts Commission (hereafter H.M.C.), *Portland MSS.*, iv, p. 532.

[48] Oldmixon, *The History of England*, p. 434.

Some three hours after the engagement in Drury Lane the Clerkenwell rioters, who had just burnt in St. John's Square the fittings of Hamilton's chapel, were surprised by the Grenadiers when in the very act of scaling the garden walls of Sir Edmund Harrison, a wealthy merchant and a leading London Presbyterian.   Minutes earlier, likewise bent on destruction, they had been trying to locate the house of Gilbert Burnet, bishop of Salisbury, the most notorious Low Churchman on the bench.   Burnet, whom they denounced as a "Presbyterian bishop" and the "rogue [who] had dirt thrown in his coach comeing from Sacheverell's tryal", was bravely watching them from one of his windows which overlooked the square; it was as well for him that he was not identified before the troops arrived.[49]

The timeliest military intervention, however, was in Blackfriars. From there three parties were preparing to move on: the first to deal with Nesbitt's meeting-house in Aldersgate Street, the second with the familiar premises of John Shower in Old Jewry, and the third to loot and burn the Bank of England in Grocers' Hall.[50]   The mob's designs on the Bank had been known for several hours; the directors were in a state of panic; the Bank's offices had already been given a tiny garrison of Grenadier Guards.   And although it was clear enough by midnight that the threat to the conventicles had become a general one — Dyer thought it "certain there had not been one left standing in the City and suburbs by the morning if the Guards had not prevented" — it was towards Grocers' Hall that the main body of troops was swiftly moving, at the instance of their guide, Captain Orrell, when they were providentially diverted by news of the tumult in Blackfriars.   "Gentlemen", Orrell had urged as he led the party down Holborn, "it is better to have all the meeting-houses destroyed than the Bank.   Pray, let us go thither".   Not surprisingly, when further disorders were anticipated on the Queen's birthday, 8th March, the Lieutenancy posted detachments from two regiments of Trained Bands at Grocers' Hall, there to "keep guard for such time as the Governor or Deputy Governor of the Bank of England shall direct".[51]

[49] Brit. Lib., Lansdowne MSS. 1024, fo. 206; Scottish Rec. Off., G.D. 205/4: Pringle to Bennett, 2 Mar.; A. Cunningham, *The History of Great Britain from the Revolution in 1688 to the Accession of George I*, 2 vols. (London and Edinburgh, 1787), ii, p. 294; Calamy, *op. cit.*, ii, p. 228; Blenheim MSS., Box VII, 18: depositions of John Smith of Clerkenwell, vintner, before Robert Pringle, 4 Mar., and Joseph Bennett, lighterman, before Charles Delafaye, 4 Mar.; House of Lords MSS. 2665: MS. minute of Thomas Wilson's evidence before the Lords, 3 Mar.

[50] *State Trials*, xv, 556; [Toland?], *High Church Display'd*, p. 97; Brit. Lib., Loan 29/321, Dyer's Newsletter, 4 Mar.   Shower's Presbyterian meeting-house was in the next street to the Bank.

[51] Brit. Lib., Loan 29/321, Dyer's Newsletter, 4 Mar.; Boyer, *Queen Anne*, pp. 416-17; *State Trials*, xv, 554, 556; S.P. 44/108: Sunderland to the Lieutenancy of London, 7 Mar.; C.L.R.O., Lieutenancy Minute Book, p. 156, 8 Mar.

Here, then, are the manifestations of a great popular demonstration both positive and negative in its motivation: for a Church believed to be in peril; in violent sympathy with a clergyman thought to have been maliciously persecuted; against Whig politicians and their clerical champions; above all, against nonconformity to established patterns, religious or social. Yet almost as revealing as what the mobs attacked or proposed to attack is what they did *not* assault or damage. They were at such pains to avoid indiscriminate destruction that, with immense labour, they carried the heavy timber and metal work of some of the chapels a considerable distance in order to burn them with safety in open spaces or the broadest thoroughfares.[52] The demolition party at Christopher Taylor's, having chosen the fashionable Hatton Garden in preference to the more convenient but narrow Leather Lane, even made three small bonfires there instead of one large one to reduce the risk to adjoining houses.[53] Had the rioters in general shown less respect for shops and residential property they could have accounted for twice as many meeting-houses in the time available. As it was, even during the worst hours of the riots, there is no report of any serious damage to a private house.

Equally significant, I have found no evidence of a single rioter even contemplating such targets as corn factors' warehouses or manufacturers' workshops. The Spitalfields weavers, a notoriously unruly element in recent years, seem actually to have been prepared to march against the mob.[54] The absence of the cruder types of social protest may appear hard to explain, at first sight. There can be little question that earlier this winter, before soaring grain prices had been brought under control[55] and before the schemes for settling the Palatine immigrants had come to fruition,[56] discontents of a basically economic nature had helped to create in the capital an uneasy atmosphere, decidedly unsympathetic to the administration. There was also another major cause of popular disenchantment in 1709 in the continuance of the seemingly never-ending war with France, with its toll of manpower, its demands on the pockets even of the poorer wage-earners through high indirect taxation, and its depression of some industries to the benefit of others. And although hopes of peace had

[52] See the map of the riot area in Holmes, *Trial*, pp. 158-9.

[53] Blenheim MSS., Box VII, 18: deposition of Robert Culbridge before Samuel Blaikerby.

[54] Beloff, *Public Order and Popular Disturbances*, pp. 82-6; H.M.C., *Portland MSS.*, iv, p. 532.

[55] For example, by the Act of Dec. 1709, prohibiting corn exports for nine months: Beloff, *op. cit.*, p. 70.

[56] The 3,000 earmarked for Ireland were despatched from Chester between Sept. and Nov. 1709, and almost as many again had by then been settled at home, mostly in districts remote from London. Others had sailed for the West Indies or Carolina. But the final 3,000, intended for New York, were still at Plymouth awaiting ship when the Sacheverell brushwood caught fire in the New Year. Dickinson, "The Poor Palatines and the Parties", pp. 476-8.

revived shortly before Sacheverell's trial, so that there are no signs of any overt anti-war protest in the March disorders, one must assume it unlikely that every rioter on the streets made a clear distinction, for example, between Wharton the warmonger and Wharton the scourge of High Church.

On the other hand, the economic lot of London's poor had improved steadily over the second half of the winter. If widespread material grievances still persisted by March, it can only be said that they were extraordinarily muted. Nowhere among the scores of depositions taken by the magistrates after the riots, nowhere among the testimony of over fifty witnesses at the treason trials of Dammaree, Willis and Purchase, can one find so much as a solitary reference, however oblique, to the economic plight of the poorer citizens of London. It is an astonishing fact, but an inescapable one. Equally conclusive is the teeming literature of the Sacheverell affair. In roughly six hundred pamphlets, broadsheets and printed sermons appearing in 1710 which had some bearing on the Doctor and his case, there is only one which contains an allusion — and that of the briefest kind — to dear bread.[57] If the pamphleteers and the preachers were in no danger of confusing the real issues of the affair with questions of trade, taxation or the cost of living, neither was the crowd. In March 1710 it was, to all appearances, every bit as much a "Church crowd" as the Highflying preachers themselves had prayed for — and in some cases preached for.

The role of the Church of England itself, and more specifically of the London clergy, in the Sacheverell riots is both important and strange. The strangeness lies in its own contradictions. There was no doubt where the Church stood in theory on the issue of violent popular protest. Obedience to social superiors, based on religious obligation, was the keystone of the whole hierarchical, authoritarian view of society which had been championed with so much fervour by post-Restoration divines. As for popular protest against *political* authority, against the law of the land, which is what the fiery demonstrations of March 1710 essentially were, this should have been anathema to the parsons — and to the High Church parsons most of all. Were they not the natural heirs of the long Passive Obedience tradition of the Reformed Church of England? How, therefore,

----

[57] I owe this information to the researches of Dr. W. A. Speck, who kindly drew my attention to the solitary exception. In anon., *The World Bewitch'd, or the D . . l in the Times. With a Certain Prophecy When Twill Mend: In a Dialogue Between a Londoner and a Countryman,* printed possibly in mid-February 1710, the "Countryman" regrets that "Dr. Seacherwell" (*sic*) should have set the parish by the ears, when all he wanted was peace, three meals a day, and plum pudding for Sunday dinner:
London. No matter for that Clod, you'll see that Sacheverell will be soundly punished.
Country. I should be glad of it, if it will make bread ever the cheaper.

could they condone the seeking to deny by force to the dissenters a liberty granted by Act of Parliament, the "levying war against the Queen's Majesty" which was charged in the treason indictments? Yet, in the event, clergymen caught up like everyone else in the furious party conflict of their day, clergymen as convinced and fearful as Sacheverell himself of the spreading tentacles of Dissent, found it possible not merely to condone but positively to encourage such a protest.

One must appreciate that by 1709, the apogee of the Whigs in the reigns of William III and Anne, at least four-fifths of the parish clergy in England and Wales were convinced that the ruling party, given half a chance, would sell out the Anglican inheritance to dissenters and latitude-men, if not to the enemies of Christianity itself. Because of this conviction, and because they saw Sacheverell's case as palpable evidence that their Church was indeed in mortal danger in Whig hands, they closed ranks behind this unsavoury man from the moment of his impeachment. Naturally enough, it was the London clergy who were best placed to demonstrate their feelings. This they did, for one thing, by providing the Doctor with a black-gowned bodyguard, a hundred or more strong, on his various appearances before the Commons and the Lords between 14 December 1709 and 25 January 1710; and on the last occasion their presence played a calculated part in exciting the large crowd gathered in and round New Palace Yard to cheer the hero of the hour.[58] More provocatively, in their own church services, they embarked between mid-December and late February on a systematic, and frequently explicit, use of pulpit, prayer desk and psalms in Sacheverell's cause. This campaigning came to a remarkable climax between the services commemorating Charles I's martyrdom on 30th January, which touched new heights of frenzied emotion, and the opening of the trial on 27th February. For four Sundays in a row, not content with inflammatory sermons, the High Church priests of the capital publicly prayed for God's blessing on a man accused by the Commons of Great Britain of high crimes and misdemeanours, a man about to be tried by the supreme court of the nation.[59]

One can scarcely overstress the contribution these parsons made to the hysteria which had taken possession of London by the end of February: the mood which produced, to begin with, the wild scenes on the first two days of the trial, as Sacheverell rode in cavalcade from the Temple to Westminster Hall and back,[60] and on the third day the great riot itself. The very men who, according to their professions,

---

[58] Holmes, *Trial,* pp. 90-1, 108-9.
[59] *Ibid.,* pp. 96-7, 118-19.
[60] *Ibid.,* pp. 128, 133-4, 156-60.

should have been pouring cold douches of ecclesiastical water on to the flames of popular emotion were plying the bellows instead.

How many of those who made up the crowd on 1st March had actually listened to their prayers and sermons, or had sung such rousing psalm verses as "Break their teeth O God in their mouths; smite the jaw-bones of the lions, O Lord",[61] we can have no means of knowing. London's lower orders were not conspicuous for devoutness or church-going; and in any event there were far too few churches to hold them. But how "vulgar", in the eighteenth-century sense, were the Sacheverell rioters? The surviving evidence bearing on their social composition presents a curious mixture of scarcity and rich plenty. The wealth sufficiently outweighs the poverty to allow certain conclusions to be reached with a degree of confidence.[62] But it is as well to be aware from the start of the statistical limitations within which we must be content to work.

In the first place, it is impossible to estimate the size of the Sacheverell mobs of 1-2 March 1710. How, for that matter, does one define "the mob" in a disorder of this nature? Of the thousands who

[61] Psalm lviii. 6.

[62] On the debit side must be placed: (1) the disappointing yield of the Old Bailey Sessions records: Greater London Rec. Off., Middlesex (hereafter G.L.R.O., Midd.), S[essions] R[oll] 2151, 9 Anne, 24 May [1710]; *ibid.*, MJ/GDB/299: Gaol Delivery Book, May 1710. Only 16 out of well over 100 persons arrested after the disorders were eventually brought to trial, and even then the indictments against those charged are inexplicably missing from the sessions roll. (2) The absence of any cases of popular disorder from the Treasury Solicitor's Papers, Public Rec. Off. (3) The loss of most of the private papers of one of the two Secretaries of State at the time of the riots, Henry Boyle. On the credit side, however: (1) because the mob attacked meeting-houses their action could be construed by government lawyers as an attempt to change the constitution by force. Three of the alleged rioters (Dammaree, Willis and Purchase) therefore came to be charged not with "grand riot and *male gestura*" but with high treason; their trials at the Old Bailey spread over three days (20-22 Apr.), and there are verbatim reports in *State Trials*, xv, 522-690. (2) Two MS. volumes preserved at Blenheim Palace*(Box VII, 18) among the papers of Boyle's secretarial colleague, Sunderland, contain many, though clearly by no means all, of the "informations" and depositions taken after 1 Mar. by a dozen overworked Justices of the Peace in London and Westminster: i.e. the raw material, gathered together by the zealous Sunderland, for the government's later prosecutions. (3) Important evidence was taken before the House of Lords, 2-4 Mar. (House of Lords MSS. 2665 and Lords' Committee Books; *The Manuscripts of the House of Lords*, new ser., viii, 1708-10, pp. 367-8). (4) There are some letters and affidavits of relevance among the official papers of the Secretaries of State (S.P. 34/12 and 44/108: the former (in-letters) includes a few letters and affidavits of relevance to the character of the mob). Of the many miscellaneous minor sources a particularly lucky survival is a contemporary printed broadsheet, of which I have seen only one copy, listing 105 names: anon., *A True List of the Names of Those Persons Committed to the Several Goals [sic] In and About Westminster . . . on Account of the Tumult, March the 1st* (London, 1710; copy in Brit. Lib., Madan Coll.). This has particular value as a social document, in those cases in which status, profession or occupation is indicated.

*Now deposited in the British Library: see above p. vii.

took to the streets that night, how many were actively rioting, destroying and looting, how many were cheering and egging on the activists,
and how many were simply looking on from the fringes? Of course,
there is no hope of our knowing. Even round figures from contemporaries are hard to come by. Francis Morgan, a Southwark
pawnbroker, arrived in Lincoln's Inn Fields, as he thought between
10.30 p.m. and 11.00 p.m.; and though "it is almost impossible to be
exact to half an hour", as Lord Chief Justice Parker reminded the
jury on 20th April,[63] it is clear that Morgan arrived long after the first
major exodus, to Bradbury's meeting-house, had taken place. When
the Attorney-General asked him, "How many people do you think
might be there [in the Fields] at that time", Morgan cautiously
replied "I believe two thousand". But he later added that "the mob
was so large, as to extend from the meeting-house to the fire [almost
two hundred yards]; there were great numbers running to and again
[*sic*]".[64] Edward Orrell, acknowledged on all hands as a most
judicious witness, put the number of rioters in Drury Lane about
11.00 p.m. (many, though by no means all, of whom had come from the
Fields) at two to three thousand, and about midnight we hear of "near
500 persons" still "gathered about" the fires in Hatton Garden,
"stopping coaches and demanding money in a riotous manner".[65]
The difficulty of making any kind of worthwhile estimate at night in
such conditions, even by the glare of firelight, was underlined by the
Lord Chief Justice's cynical comment to the jury at Dammaree's
trial: "when they came to the fire, there was a great mob about it; and
as you have heard from others of the witnesses that there were some
thousands, you may imagine them some hundreds".[66]

A further problem is that while a substantial core of rioters was
itinerant, moving from site to site, at least as many and very likely
more confined their activities to one meeting-house and one fire. Few
mobsters had the stamina of William Watson, bricklayer's apprentice,
who began at Burgess's as a roof-stripper, moved on to Bradbury's to
demolish the chimneys, and finished the night as cheer-leader in
Drury Lane;[67] or of William Collyer, butcher, who "bloody on the
head and his knee very much cutt" from breaking windows at
Burgess's, claimed to have been "the person that pulled the hands
from the dyall in the riott . . . in Fetter Lane [Bradbury's]", and
certainly ended up in Hatton Garden.[68] By contrast, even the two
men ultimately convicted of treason, Dammaree and Purchase, could

[63] *State Trials*, xv, 602.
[64] *Ibid.*, 560-1.
[65] *Ibid.*, 555; Blenheim MSS., Box VII, 18: deposition of Barnett [or
Barnard] Simpson, junr., of Grays Inn Lane, before Justice Ireton, 8 Mar.
[66] *State Trials*, xv, 601.
[67] See Holmes, *Trial*, pp. 165, 169.
[68] Blenheim MSS., Box VII, 18: Simpson's deposition.

only be proved to have participated in one riot, the former in Lincoln's Inn Fields, the latter in Drury Lane.

Let us suppose, however, for the purposes of our present inquiry that between 6.30 p.m. on 1st March and 2.00-3.00 a.m. on 2nd March there were at least five thousand Londoners active in varying degrees in the disorders (as opposed to those who were essentially inquisitive spectators): it would seem that this is the most conservative estimate possible.   Of these it has proved possible to identify 182 by name[69] — a tally rather better than satisfactory, considering that the authorities incarcerated far fewer than this and instituted proceedings against little more than a sixth of the number.   Such is the anonymity of the great urban crowd!   With so few troops available for deployment, with the constables and the watch generally paralyzed until the final stages of the riot,[70] and the trained bands not under arms until the streets were already virtually clear, the overwhelming majority of rioters and prospective witnesses were able to melt away as swiftly as they had materialized, safe from recognition.   Even Purchase, who had tried to run through an officer with his sword and should have been "cut to pieces" on Captain Horsey's orders, managed to make good his escape down Long Acre and through the back alleys to his lodgings, and he was only brought to justice because he was unfortunate enough to be recognized by George Richardson, an ex-colleague in the Horse Guards.[71]

The vast majority of those identified, 156 out of 182, can be considered fully-fledged rioters.   But the total includes a group of eleven who, though claiming to be mere observers or at most constrained participants, were very probably actively involved, and a further fifteen who were known either to have incited the mob (though it could not be proved that they had openly participated in its work) or to have started as bystanders and come under suspicion of joining in, if only marginally.   In 76 of the whole 182 cases we either know the occupation or the social status of the men concerned.   Generally this information is precise; but in five instances[72] status is deduced from, rather than explicit in, the

[69] See below, note 104, summarizing the status and/or occupations of identified rioters.   Because of uncertainty over Christian names it is possible that the "Corbett" and "Read" listed there were the only two rioters of these names involved.   The true total in that case would be 180.

[70] On the role of the constables and the watch, see *State Trials*, xv, 554, 674-5. Thomas Cave gave evidence (Blenheim MSS., Box VII, 18) that on the night of 1 Mar. — it must in fact have been after midnight — "he went to the watch house [in Clerkenwell] and told them the mob was setting the chapel on fire at St. John's.   But they would not stir, for they had no orders".   At least three constables, however — James Douxsaint, "Mr. Bull" and Edward Jones, Constable of St. Martin's — bestirred themselves to make some arrests once the troops were there to stiffen their resolution.

[71] *State Trials*, xv, 659-63.

[72] Those of Killett, Peter Brand, John Hodges, Robert Marsh and John Stevens.

evidence. All the social analysis that has been undertaken of the eighteenth-century urban crowd has had to rely perforce on "sampling". And there can be no more certainty in the case of the Sacheverell riots than in those of the other major London disorders of the Hanoverian period that what has survived is information on a *representative* cross-section. One can only say in this case that there are no reasons for believing it to be glaringly unrepresentative, and add that its value can be slightly enhanced by pooling with the named list a further list of fifteen offenders who are identified in the post-riot testimony by occupation but not by name; so that the "sample" numbers ninety-one all told.

Unless it is freakishly misleading, this would seem to suggest quite strongly that, in social terms, the Sacheverell riots were probably the most respectable urban disorder of the century. Certainly this was no protest of the miserably poor and inarticulate. Professor Rudé's researches into the character of the Wilkite and Gordon rioters[73] have led us to expect a preponderance of "the respectable working class" in those eighteenth-century London mobs which had a political or religious, as opposed to a purely economic, motivation. A clear majority — two out of every three in the Gordon riots — were wage-earners: journeymen and apprentices, domestic servants and labourers. Most of the remainder were small employers, independent craftsmen or tradesmen. Of the unemployed, the vagrant element, the dregs of the slums or the criminal underworld — in so far as it existed[74] — there was little sign either in 1768 or in 1780.

There was even less in 1710. Only two of our sample of "working-class" rioters were apparently unemployed; only two of those who made depositions affixed marks to them instead of signatures.[75] Predictably, apprentices were very much in evidence; there was a good deal of high-spirited hooliganism during the Sacheverell riots and this the apprentices in particular found congenial. The fourteen apprentices who can be identified either by name or occupation were drawn from the widest possible variety of trades. There were two in the joinery trade and two in bricklaying, the latter[76] both employed by the same master and highly conspicuous among the "pullers-down".[77] The rest were bound respectively to a glass grinder, a basket maker, a brass worker, a cooper, a clockmaker, a carver, a sawyer, a linen draper, a butcher and a poulterer. Several were in the

[73] See above, note 20.
[74] Cf. Peter Linebaugh's argument that "the distinction between the criminal and the respectable working class is difficult if not impossible to locate" in the 18th century, in Report of the conference on "Eighteenth Century Crime, Popular Movements and Social Control", in *Bulletin of the Society for the Study of Labour History*, xxv (1972).
[75] *Viz.* John Burton, labourer, and John Foreman, seaman.
[76] William Watson and Edward Newton Hughes.
[77] See below, p. 244.

thick of things. The poulterer's apprentice, employed in Clare Market, was one of those who carried the great door of Burgess's chapel to the flames, and the sawyer's apprentice, a muscular young fellow named Henry Sanders, smashed down Earl's door with two or three blows of his pick-axe; while Thomas Hill, employed by John Clowes, a clockmaker in Russell Street, paid for his night out by being chased by two Life Guards from Holborn into Red Lion Court and slashed by a sabre on the head and the hands.[78] It is of particular interest that the one indisputable fatality of the riots, the young man killed by a falling casement outside Burgess's, was an apprentice of a very superior stamp — bound to a linen draper and, according to Abel Boyer, "heir to a good estate".[79]

Of the remaining employees and wage-earners, domestic servants (sixteen) make up by far the most numerous batch, with known journeymen (two) very much less prominent.[80] Among the servants, coachmen and footmen appear to have been well to the fore. Michael Caldwell and John Clements went on the rampage from the house of their employer, John Snell, in Clerkenwell and later buried their plunder in his garden.[81] The livery of a law-abiding master was clearly no guarantee of good behaviour on this night. The coachman of Mr. Serjeant Goodwin (Robert Pond) and both the coachman and the footman of one of the very Justices of the Peace taking the depositions after the riots, Whitlocke Bulstrode, were very active. Even the coachman of the Whig leader, Lord Halifax, was not above suspicion. As well as liveries there were uniforms in evidence. Among our sample of malefactors are two soldiers (plus a third, a busy plunderer at Earl's, who it was "suppose[d] was a soldier; he was in a looped waistcoat and white stockings"[82]); also two sailors, one of whom led the way into Burgess's by clambering up the door and smashing a gallery window;[83] and in addition to a Queen's Waterman, the unfortunate Dammaree, there was a Yeoman of the Guard for good measure.[84]

If the Sacheverell rioters had closely conformed to the social pattern of the great mobs of 1768 and 1780 one might reasonably have expected to find the employed — leaving aside servants of the Crown

---

[78] Blenheim MSS., Box VII, 18: Joseph Collyer's examination before Robert Pringle, 3 Mar., and depositions of John Clowes, 4 Mar., and Thomas Hill, 8 Mar., before George Tilson; *State Trials*, xv, 555; G.L.R.O., Midd., S.R. 2151: recognizance for Thomas Hill, 20 Apr. 1710.

[79] Boyer, *Queen Anne*, p. 417. See also above, note 8.

[80] It is very possible, however, that several more journeymen may be concealed by the rather vaguer information on the supplementary list of unnamed rioters, or even by loose description of occupations in one or two of the depositions.

[81] See Holmes, *Trial*, p. 164.

[82] *State Trials*, xv, 657.

[83] Holmes, *Trial*, p. 162.

[84] Though the bill against the latter was found *ignoramus* by Westminster Grand Jury: Brit. Lib., Loan 29/321, Dyer's Newsletter, 13 Apr.

— outnumbering the self-employed by roughly two to one. In point of fact the ratio between them is more nearly equal. A notable feature of the evidence bearing on the social structure of the mob is the unexpectedly high number of small masters, craftsmen, self-employed artisans and tradesmen who were involved. More strangely still there were shopkeepers: John Beale, for example, who kept a barber's shop in Chancery Lane and put up £100 for his own bail;[85] Martin Kneebone, a woollen draper, who seems later to have turned Queen's evidence; and Francis Morgan, a pawnbroker. If we include a handful who are described in various testimonies as the sons of men of this status, twenty-six of our ninety-one rioters fall into this broad grouping of the self-employed.

An odd man out among them is a yeoman from the village of Marylebone, who was probably in town visiting his brother and who is worthy of remark as one of only three identified rioters whom we positively know to have been domiciled outside urban London or Southwark. The more sophisticated craftsmen were represented by a clockmaker, a periwig-maker and a gunlock-maker. John Wells, a brickmaster with premises in St. Pancras parish, was apprehended by the Guards in Little Drury Lane and later bound over on bail of £40.[86] A Southwark cutler, the son of a dyer in Princess Street and a bedsteadmaker named Giles, "who keeps a shop in Maypole Alley where he is new sett up",[87] were but three of those with a respectable artisan background; while the presence of three carpenters and three shoemakers suggests that the humbler domestic trades were probably well represented. Not that their own connections were necessarily so very humble. Nicholas Munden, an unmarried shoemaker who lived with his parents in Gilbert Street, and who was "taken . . . in Dr. Burgess's meeting house, actually at work in demolishing the same", was able to bring as one of his sureties when he applied for bail a relative, Robert Munden "of the Penny Post Office".[88]

A far more striking token of social respectability in the Sacheverell mob is the participation of an appreciable "white-collar" or professional element. At the bottom of this particular social group were an attorney's clerk named Rainer (possibly the conspicuous figure "in the light coat and short hair" who later admitted having led an advance party into Burgess's),[89] and two bailiffs. The presence of the latter

[85] G.L.R.O., Midd., S.R. 2151, 14 May 1710. The amount is a little conjectural because of fading in the MS. It could be £300, though this seems excessive for a barber.

[86] Blenheim MSS., Box VII, 18: "Minutes of what was done at St. Martin's Vestry, 2d March 1709/10". It seems that the magistrate in this case had some doubts as to whether Wells had been anything more than a "looker-on".

[87] *Ibid.*, information of John Buckingham before Charles Delafaye, 3 Mar.

[88] *Ibid.*, "Minutes of what was done at St. Martin's Vestry"; G.L.R.O., Midd., S.R. 2151, "Memord. qd. 24 die May 1710".

[89] Blenheim MSS., Box VII, 18: information of James Haines of Coventry before Charles Delafaye, 9 Mar., and George Gosdin, basketmaker's apprentice, before Francis Negus, 6 Mar.

astonished another member of that fraternity, Jacob Broad, when at the Old Bailey he was called to give evidence bearing on the movements of George Purchase: "My Lord [he told the judge] . . . I am not a man that engage myself in mobs, for those of my employment generally suffer in mobs; I avoid them if I can; and if I meet them I give them all the good language I can".[90]   Another name to note is "Eliad Mitcalff", who was one of those temporarily committed to New Prison by Justice Ireton after the riots.   He might possibly be one and the same with the apothecary, "Mr. Metcalfe", mentioned in a statement from one of the rioters, Thomas Pomfret, footman to John Jermingham, Esquire.[91]   There was also the postmaster of Gosport in Hampshire, Richard Dennett, who found himself embarrassingly implicated in the riot at Blackfriars, from which he returned to his inn "in a great sweat, a little after two o'clock", and who procured an affidavit to his good character from his vicar and twenty-five more of his fellow townsmen.[92]

Higher up the professional scale, we find two lawyers, a former banker and a physician.   One of the lawyers, unfortunately anonymous, was described in the testimony of John Smith, a Clerkenwell vintner, as the "chief ringleader" of the crowd which attacked Hamilton's chapel in St. John's Square.   The other was a man called Tresley[93] who was most probably an inciter rather than active participant but who was, in any event, sufficiently involved to feel it necessary to leave his lodgings — and London — immediately after the riots.   Another gentleman who was seen in the early part of the evening furiously tearing up pews in Daniel Burgess's meeting-house was followed back to his house by an inquisitive witness, who found on inquiry that his name was Read, and that he was "formerly a banker in Lombard Street".   Equally interesting is the evidence of the periwig-maker, Thomas Talboys.   "He says that either Wednesday or Thursday morning last there came to his shop a footman belonging to Dr. Cooke, a Phisitian.   This servant told him that his master was with the mobb the night before when Mr. Burgess's windows were broke".   There is nothing directly to prove that the maverick doctor was actually on the streets during the great riot

[90] *State Trials*, xv, 671.   Bailiffs did, of course, differ somewhat in social standing, but it will be recalled that Purchase, who was described as "a very civil fellow" when sober, "but when he is drunk . . . quite mad", carried a sword: see above, p. 72.

[91] The statement, however, did not directly implicate the apothecary.   See Blenheim MSS., Box VII, 18: St. Martin's Vestry minutes.

[92] *Ibid.*, testimony of Charles Collins, gent., and Henry Pardon of the Inner Temple, gent; S.P. 34/12/14: John Clifford and 25 others to Thomas Jervoise, M.P. Hants, Gosport, 9 Mar.

[93] He was the "gentleman, well dressed and having a blue cloak", who figures so prominently in the vivid testimony of the widow Newth concerning the first attack on the New Court meeting-house.   See Holmes, *Trial*, p. 162.

itself; but it seems likely that at very least he had a voice in its planning.[94] Lastly, there is a possible addition to the "white-collar" group of rioters, though not in one of the major professions, in the person of Peter Brand. His occupation is unknown, but we do know that he was a Roman Catholic, that he owned a house in Barmley Street, and that he was the only one of the sixteen rioters eventually brought to trial who was sufficiently confident and well enough advised to plead not guilty and prepare a defence. It was said that he told his anxious wife, on arriving home at 3.00 a.m. on 2nd March, that "he did not fear, for there was a nobleman would stand by them".[95]

There are fourteen names on our identified list of seventy-six still unclassified, and thirteen of them[96] form a group no less remarkable than the one just examined. In it is included one rioter, Silvester Stone, committed by Justice Ireton to the New Prison, who is described in one source as "Esquire",[97] and no fewer than nine who are explicitly described by one source or more as "gentlemen". One of them, Leonard Sandford, was seen on the roof of Burgess's helping to demolish the chimney stack.[98] Another was the son of that same Mr. Serjeant Goodwin whose "coachman was wounded by the Guards".[99] Yet another, John Berkeley, apprehended by the Guards in Drury Lane, was a country gentleman staying temporarily in town.[100] To these men and their fellows we can possibly add three others. Robert Marsh of Great Queen Street — a fashionable address — was discharged from prison on 2nd March after producing a "certificate", so called, from Lord Rockingham's brother. Then there was the "Mr. John Stevens" we noticed earlier, who was heard by two witnesses at the Lamb Inn to swear "that . . . he himself would head a mobb of ten thousand men" ("out of his own country", one witness added) "to rescue" Sacheverell from Parliament. As with Henry Chivins, the son of Bartholomew Chivins of Duke Street, who privately admitted taking part in the demolition of Burgess's, there are grounds for believing him to be of good family.[101]

[94] On the "council of war" on the night of 28 Feb., followed immediately by the preliminary attack on Burgess's premises, see *ibid.*, p. 160. On Read and Cooke, Blenheim MSS., Box VII, 18: depositions of Martin Kneebone, 15 Mar., and Thomas Talboys, 4 Mar.

[95] G.L.R.O., Midd., MJ/GDB 299; Blenheim MSS., Box VII, 18: deposition of Hannah Wetherall before John Pringle, 5 Mar.

[96] The exception is the bailiff's follower, William Hedges.

[97] Anon., *Daniel Danery's (The Queen's Waterman) Letter to the Lord Treasurer: Concerning a Discovery of the Ring-Leaders of the Late Tumult* (London, 1710); cf. *A True List . . . of Those Persons Committed to the Several Goals.* [98] Blenheim MSS., Box VII, 18: Kneebone's deposition.

[99] House of Lords MSS. 2665: evidence of Henry Bendish.

[100] Described by Delafaye and John Wace in an Obligation of 4 Mar. 1710 as "de Spencely in Com. Wigern, Gen[t]": S.P. 29/12/7; S.P. 34/12/5: affidavit of Jacob Pullen before Robert Pringle, 3 Mar.

[101] Blenheim MSS., Box VII, 18: St. Martin's Vestry minutes, 2 Mar., depositions before Charles Delafaye of James Haines, 3 Mar., and John Austin, 4 Mar.; evidence of Joseph Paine, upholsterer's apprentice, n.d.

Out of the ten certain and three possible "gentlemen mobsters" whose names are known, two admittedly had disreputable connections. Walter Corbet was an Irish Catholic whose striking figure and dress were noticed by many onlookers in Hatton Garden and Clerkenwell (he is one of five identified Papists who lent their assistance to a "Church mob"[102] for the sake of embarrassing a Whig ministry and spiting — as one of them said — those "king-killing rogues", the Presbyterians). He was known to one witness only as "a very idle person in no manner of business", but others made it clear that he preserved the façade of gentility by an income from gambling. John Crump, the son of "Mr. Crump of the Herald's Office",[103] was also thought "a person of loose character". Elsewhere, however, there are no hints of shady circumstances, no pointers as to why in these particular cases the civilized veneer should have cracked.[104]

It goes without saying that the very presence of so marked a professional and leisured element even among the named rioters, those actually caught or known to the authorities, has more than social implications. It surely offers prima facie grounds for supposing that the events of 1st and 2nd March owed not a little to incitement from above (quite apart from the crucial preparatory role of the parish clergy, already discussed), and that they owed even more to advance

[102] The other four were Peter Brand, Henry Chivins, Thomas Pomfret and William Watson, who was server to a Catholic priest.

[103] Leonard Crump, Portcullis Pursuivant.

[104] The status and/or occupations of those rioters who have been identified *by name* can be summarized as follows (the sources are as listed above, note 62, with the exception of the contemporary broadsheet *Daniel Danery's (The Queen's Waterman) Letter to the Lord Treasurer*): *Esquires:* 1 (Silvester Stone). *"Gentlemen":* 8 (Richard Bembridge, of Red Lion Square; John Berkeley, "de Spencely in Com. Wigern"; Walter Corbett; John Crump, "near Doctors' Commons"; George Hawkins I [a second George Hawkins, "committed to the Compter by Sir Cha. Speares", appears to be a different person]; [—] Read, of Red Lion Square, former banker; John Sallow; Leonard Sandford). *Gentlemen's sons:* 2 (Henry Chivins of Duke Street [see above, p. 77]; [—] Goodwin, son of Thomas Goodwin, Serjeant-at-Law). *Possible gentlemen* [see above, p. 77]: 2 (Robert Marsh of Great Queen Street; "Mr. John Stevens"). *Physicians:* 1 (Dr. Cooke). *Lawyers:* 1 ([—] Tresley, "lodging at the Ball Inn, Rogue Lane"). *Possible Professional Men:* 2 (Peter Brand, householder of Barmley Street [see above, p. 77]; "Mr" Killett, "lodged in Shoe Lane" [the fact that he was lodging with a master carpenter is to be noted, however].

Also: an apothecary (see above, p. 76), postmaster, attorney's clerk, woollen draper, 2 bailiffs and a yeoman; a brickmaster, tallow chandler, pawnbroker, periwig-maker, barber, bedstead-maker, cutler, gunlock-maker, clockmaker, farrier and waterman; a dyer's son, joiner's son, pastry cook, butcher, 2 carpenters and 3 shoemakers; 2 journeymen (1 brickmaker, 1 trade unknown, employed by Jackson of Stanhope Street), a labourer, stocking-presser, private soldier and 2 seamen; a bailiff's follower; 3 coachmen (to John Snell, gent., Mr. Serjeant Goodwin and Lord Halifax), 2 footmen, a footboy, 7 other domestic servants (2 to gentlemen, one to an M.P.'s sister), 11 apprentices.

Occupation unknown: 105 (of whom John Anderson was bailed on the £50 surety of a button-seller, and Philip Gardner absconded after the riots — sometimes an indication of means).

planning and to on-the-ground organization. And there is indeed abundant supporting evidence from more than a score of informants, deponents and trial witnesses: evidence which, however miscellaneous and difficult to collate, is cumulatively too substantial to ignore. It becomes easy to see why the Whigs became firmly convinced within twenty-four hours of the riots that they had been the result of "a general design" (as the Attorney General put it) that was not "accidental"; and that behind those actively demolishing and burning stood many more "accomplices, adherents, abetters and advisors".[105]

For one thing, quite apart from rioters identified by name, statement after statement from eye-witnesses is studded with references to anonymous individuals or groups, "in the habit" or "with the mien" of gentlemen, wearing "long wigs", carrying swords, but concealing elegant garments under voluminous cloaks or "great coats"; men who were either seen exhorting from the wings, or supervising on the stage, or directly involved in the various actions. Doubtless the garish firelight and the general atmosphere of frenzy and confusion heightened some imaginations. But for every piece of evidence which might be dismissed as vague or impressionistic there is another which carries too much circumstantial detail to be lightly set aside. One might incline to be sceptical of the testimony of Jacob Pullen, who lived in a house adjoining Earl's meeting-house off Drury Lane, that he saw "several gentlemen" among the mob after eleven o'clock, and "a minister, as he believes, having a minister's habit on"; but scepticism even here must be considerably tempered by the discovery that Pullen was no ignorant witness but a silk-dyer and part-owner of the very meeting-house under attack. The evidence bearing on the Leather Lane-Hatton Garden riot, though it varies from the vague and cryptic to the solid and specific, and is not without some inconsistencies, leaves little room for doubt that the mob here had firm direction as well as some active help from men of degree. Charles Fairhills, a coachmaker whose yard was next to that in which Taylor's meeting-house stood, saw three gentlemen — one waving a sword — run into his yard while the chapel was under attack; while William Grove, a local baker, observed at the chapel itself "two persons in their waistcoats without their coats, with their hatts edged with silver and with swords by their sides, worke very hard and laboured extremely in exciteing the mob". John Lunt of Little Kirby Street remembered seeing only one person who "appeared to be a gentleman" closely involved in this attack — he had a sword in one hand and a piece of wood in the other; but then, Lunt prudently watched from the safety of his doorway and there must have been much that he missed. Far more explicit was Henry Bendish, a Treasury official who had all too

---

[105] *State Trials*, xv, 550-1; *London Gazette*, No. 4660: proclamation of 3 Mar. 1710.

clear a view from his front windows when the rioters poured into Hatton Garden with their fuel. "He observed among the mob some persons in good dress that had the mien of gent, and others with good clothes under old coats, and 2 or 3 with old red coats who seemed to direct and govern the rest and caused them to make three fires and to take some of the stuff from the first fire, and with that and other stuff made [an]other two, the middlemost of which was before the deponent's house. These persons after some time went off[106] and left the ordinary people to themselves".

If, however, the evidence of incitement and of some measure of organization in the riot at Taylor's is convincing enough (as indeed is that concerning the later riot in Clerkenwell),[107] that bearing on the original "tumult" in New Court and Lincoln's Inn Fields is overwhelming.[108] Those presumed friends of Dammaree who sought to secure his release on bail by printing an open letter to the Lord Treasurer claimed that the waterman could not only supply valuable information on several important persons already arrested on suspicion of complicity in the Fields' riot, including Timothy Andrews and George Hawkins, "gentlemen", and Silvester Stone, Esquire, but that he also knew "several persons concern'd that at present think themselves secure, and those none of the meanest rank". Lincoln's Inn Fields was particularly public, surrounded on three sides by fashionable houses and on the fourth by the Inn itself, and the efforts at disguise or concealment here were rather more serious, and at times theatrical. We hear, for example, of "several men with red coats, long wigs, and footmen attending them" who were "seen among the mob, and damn'd some boys that held candles and other lights, lest it should have discovered them". Benjamin Johnson saw "several persons, I believe 6 or 7, with swords in their hands" outside Burgess's, cultivating anonymity under "shaby wigs". And Ward Gray Ashenhurst told a cloak-and-dagger story to the House of Lords about a mysterious coach "with the windows drawn up" which stood by the edge of the Fields, its liveried coachman huzzaing for High Church and Sacheverell. "And it being moved to go to Fetter Lane he took a hackney coachman into the box with him to drive to Fetter Lane",[109] and later on drove on to the fire in Holborn. Other testimony differs in detail, but conveys the same general message.

[106] Tipped off, it would seem, that the troops were out and already in action further west.

[107] For this, see Holmes, *Trial*, p. 174.

[108] See Blenheim MSS., Box VII, 18: depositions of John Lunt, Joseph Collyer, Sarah Sawery, William Grove, Arlidge, Thomas Mason, Charles Fairhills, Jacob Pullen; *State Trials*, xv, 554: Orrell's evidence; *Daniel Danery's (The Queen's Waterman) Letter*; House of Lords MSS. 2665: testimony of Henry Bendish, Ward Gray Ashenhurst, Benjamin Johnson and Matthew Bunce; [Toland?], *High Church Display'd*, p. 96.

[109] Presumably to be sure of not losing the way.

Proof that some of these men, with others, had actually hatched a conspiracy to "pull down the meeting-houses", as the government's lawyers alleged, was naturally more difficult to pin down. What was to prove the crucial testimony on the Crown side, by Thomas Talboys, who almost certainly turned Queen's evidence, tells of a "council of war" outside Doctor Sacheverell's lodgings in the Temple on the evening before the "grand rebellion", a council "composed of some reputable men, they appearing as such to me by their dress". In retrospect it seems insecure, even suspect testimony, at some points, although it is hardly to be doubted that some discussion did take place there.[110] Other evidence, however, from a rather more detached source, points to the likelihood that some of the ringleaders, among them Richard Bembridge and other "disaffected" gentlemen, had used the Rose and Crown tavern at Temple Bar as a headquarters and may have planned at least some part of the operation from there. One wonders whether Tresley, the lawyer, was one of this group, for when he received the news hard by, in Sheer Lane, that the advance party had broken into Burgess's and were pulling the pulpit down, he was heard to exult, "snapping his fingers", "*Then . . . we have done it*".[111] But in any event the Rose and Crown conspirators were unlikely to have been the only ones making plans, for apart from the debate in the Temple court on the evening of the 28th, Joseph Paine, an employee of Rawsey, an upholsterer in Bath Street, overheard a knot of twelve people gathered near Burgess's meeting-house about 9 o'clock the following morning talking of "pulling it down".[112]

However, the certain conviction that there was — indeed that there had to be — a considerable measure of organization in the early stages, at least, of the riot, stems not so much from evidence of this kind, nor even from the known involvement of so many men of affluence and status. It is rooted in the sheer logic of the problem which faced the rioters. After all, the internal demolition, and partial external demolition, of buildings as large and as well-appointed as most of these meeting-houses were (Burgess's and Bradbury's each had three spacious galleries, and they were probably not exceptional in this) was a major operation involving an exceptional labour problem. To strip out and carry away, in some cases a distance of several hundred yards, dozens of pews and hundreds of floorboards, together with doors, gallery rails, casements, wainscoting, pulpit, candle branches and clocks, not to mention tearing off tiles or slates and pulling down chimneys, needed not only gangs of men working

[110] *State Trials*, xv, 552-3, 655; Blenheim MSS., Box VII, 18: Thomas Gray's evidence before Robert Pringle, 4 Mar. (that Talboys had himself been in the "Council"); S.P. 34/12/14: Talboys to Henry Boyle, endorsed 7 Mar. 1710.

[111] Blenheim MSS., Box VII, 18: evidence of Peter Varnier, gentleman trooper of the Horse Guards, and Ann Newth.

[112] *Ibid.*, Paine's deposition.

methodically as well as furiously at every point,[113] but also men *with the proper tools.*

Perhaps the most significant fact to emerge from the mass of evidence provided by deponents and trial witnesses is that right from the start these tools were forthcoming. Many of the apprentices, journeymen and tradesmen who started from the Temple Bar up Sheer Lane early that Wednesday evening had arrived on the scene bringing their own tools with them: crow-bars, pick-axes, smiths' hammers, woodmen's axes and carpenters' tools. It is hard to believe that many of these men had no idea what they were about until they were spontaneously swept along. For that matter, we know that some of them — the two bricklayer's apprentices, Hughes and Watson, for instance — admitted receiving money for their night's work.[114] And the accounts of their subsequent activities at Burgess's, and even at Bradbury's, make it absolutely clear that many must have been allocated specific roles. William Watson explained proudly to his friends the following day "that there were pullers down and carriers, meaning those who pulled down the pews and those who carried the wood to the fire". And indeed in the first part of the evening the proceedings had such an air of a drilled operation about them that no-one could fail to be struck by it. Captain Orrell told the court at the Old Bailey that he was staggered at what had been achieved at Bradbury's in the three-quarters of an hour or so before he arrived ("Lord have mercy upon mee, said I, it is all down"). Indeed, when the Queen herself heard from her physician "of the order in which the mob moved in pulling down the meeting-houses, each acting their proper part, some pulling down, others carrying away, and some burning, and all this so quickly as an argument of its being designed beforehand, she seemed greatly concerned".[115]

But one must be careful not to stretch the evidence too far. Beyond the sacking and burning of the meeting-houses in New Court and off Fetter Lane few if any firm plans seem to have been made beforehand; and from 10.00 o'clock or so, as the narrative is pieced together in all its marvellous detail, the overriding impression conveyed is of an increasingly improvised undertaking. There are still some curious facts to be accounted for. Where, for example, did both Arlidge, the carpenter, and William Grove, the baker, get their advance "information that the meeting-house in Leather Lane", as well as that in

[113] At Taylor's alone, not by any means the largest of the chapels, we are told that there were 150 men, "as hard at work as they could be".

[114] "Doe your work well", Joseph Burgess heard Watson call out to a working party in one of the galleries of the New Court chapel, "or else you shall not be paid": Blenheim MSS., Box VII, 18: information of Burgess, journeyman brickmaker, before Charles Delafaye, 18 Mar.

[115] *Ibid.*, Sarah Sawery's evidence; *State Trials*, xv, 656; Herts. Rec. Off., Panshanger MSS., Diary of Sir David Hamilton, *sub* 27 Feb.

Fetter Lane, "was likely to be attacked", so that Arlidge was able to send his servant, Tomlin, well beforehand "to see if the mob had come there" and Grove managed to give Mr. Bishop, Clerk of the Leather Lane meeting, half an hour's warning "to remove what he could out of the said meeting-house"?[116] On the other hand, as the original core of rioters doubled, trebled and quadrupled its numbers, it was quite impossible that the early cohesion should last. And certainly a succession of incidents in the Fields, in Great Queen Street and in Drury Lane from 10.30 p.m. or so, onwards, illustrates most forcibly the tendency to fragment and to improvise. The apprentice Joseph Collyer told revealingly how in Lincoln's Inn Fields "about eleven of the clock" two gentlemen who had "encouraged the mobb in these their proceedings and gave them money to goe on with their work" persuaded a party "to goe thence to the Meeting House near Fetter Lane"; but on discovering *en route* that it had already been accounted for by another party they led the way back westwards to Drury Lane. On Edward Orrell's evidence, however, Drury Lane must already have been reached by this time by another large squadron which went directly from the Fields, a move preceded by the famous running debate before Powis House and in Great Queen Street, presided over by Dammaree, which Orrell described so vividly in court.[117] He also told on a later occasion, during Purchase's trial,[118] how this vanguard had some difficulty locating Earl's meeting-house, and several times threatened to break down the wrong door, a circumstance which speaks for itself no less than the clamorous arguments we noticed earlier, about what the next targets should be.[119]

The decline of organization had one perfectly natural corollary. As the element of improvisation increased, so too did the level of looting, hooliganism and sheer drunken revelry. Whatever the solider citizens felt about High Church and Sacheverell, it is quite apparent that the scores of taverns in the riot area provided as the night went on a multitude of muddle-headed reinforcements.[120] It is equally clear that many of the younger sparks, especially the apprentices — even some of those who had been organized — went along most of all for the pure devil of it. The final word could most appropriately be spoken by the ubiquitous William Watson, who arrived in Drury Lane just before eleven, having already spent four hours that evening, first stripping many of the tiles off Burgess's roof, then personally demolishing every chimney at Bradbury's with an

[116] Blenheim MSS., Box VII, 18: depositions of Tomlin and Grove before Bulstrode and Blaikerby, 2 and 3 Mar.
[117] Holmes, *Trial*, p. 168.
[118] *State Trials*, xv, 657.
[119] See above, p. 227.
[120] Dammaree had been drinking half the evening before he came on the scene at Burgess's, and Purchase had literally been drinking all day and could barely stand.

iron crow-bar. When he reached the site of Earl's bonfire (as he related next day with no little pride) he "was so tyred with what he had done before that he could not meddle with nothing [there], but was forced to content himself with being a looker on; but he hollowed and laught with them, for there was such havock, he never saw such pastime in his life".[121]

To the questions posed early in this essay, therefore, certain answers can be suggested with confidence. The great London crowd of March 1710 was indeed a *Church* mob, moved to riotous protest in defence both of the "establishment", in a corporate sense, and of its flamboyant individual champion of the hour. This fact is as evident from the nature of the mob's carefully-selected targets, most notably the meeting-houses, as from its patent lack of economic motivation and the insistent cries of "High Church and Sacheverell" which stimulated it in its destructive work. That it was also a *party* mob, a Tory mob, is demonstrable, in part, by its identification of Whig and immigrant Bank directors, along with dissenting preachers, as symbols of a hated nonconformity. It may also be reflected in its social composition: in the fact that, of all the London crowds of the eighteenth century, this was the nearest to a "white-collar" crowd (at least, it would seem that a significant proportion of the Sacheverell rioters were men more accustomed to the desk and the counter, or even to the coffee-houses of the leisured, than to menial toil). But most of all is the party element reflected in the incontrovertible evidence of incitement and *malice prépense* in the riots. The first three and a half hours of the disorders on the night of 1st March went more or less according to a plan — a plan which showed every sign of having been hatched by London Tories, men of some rank or local standing, with the deliberate object of exploiting, to the government's embarrassment, the great popular shibboleth of "the Church in danger".

That the subsequent cost of their mischief-making — in blood if not in money — was so low was due to some extent to the nature of their undertaking; but in the main (since the riots inevitably developed their own momentum, beyond the control of their organisers) it was owing to the marvellous disciplined efficiency of the troops belatedly deployed against the crowd. Authority learned its lesson, however, from "the night of fire" of 1-2 March 1710. At the next hint of serious trouble in the capital, in November 1711,[122] Oxford's ministry moved with

---

[121] Blenheim MSS., Box VII, 18: Sarah Sawery's evidence.

[122] The Whig leaders planned to raise an anti-peace and No-Popery mob on 17 Nov., the anniversary of Queen Elizabeth's birthday. Among the effigies due to be burned, but seized by government messengers on the 16th, was one of Doctor Sacheverell. Boyer, *Queen Anne*, p. 524; H.M.C., *Dartmouth MSS.*, i, pp. 307-8; Berks. Rec. Off., Trumbull MSS., vol. LI: T. Bateman to Sir W. Trumbull, 19 Nov. 1711.

decisive alacrity to nip it in the bud.   In 1715 came the Riot Act, in the wake of High-Church/Jacobite election disorders early in George I's reign.* Not until there emerged another charismatic hero-figure, championing a cause as popular as Sacheverell's, if very different, was London to experience again a storm approaching in intensity that of 1710.   And two generations of politicians, and of Londoners, had come and gone by then.

* See Nicholas Rogers, 'Popular Protest in Early Hanoverian London', *Past and Present*, 79 (1978).

10

THE ACHIEVEMENT OF STABILITY: THE SOCIAL CONTEXT

OF POLITICS FROM THE 1680s TO THE AGE OF WALPOLE

(with Colloquy, edited by H.T. Dickinson)

Few periods of domestic politics have been as comprehensively researched and reinterpreted over the past 25 years as the years between the accession of James II and the high summer of Walpole. Yet, by a strange paradox, no other tract of English political history has been surveyed with so little regard to its social and economic climate. For much of the 1950s and 60s research on England's economy and her pre-industrial society in the late seventeenth and early eighteenth centuries failed to keep pace with the surge of new interest in the politics of the age, and political historians were chary of attempting ambitious social perspectives from a rickety platform. Today we can offer no such excuse. The days of pioneer building by such scholars as J. D. Chambers, Edward Hughes and Ralph Davis are now well in the past, and where Laslett beckoned many have followed. Some admirable textbooks have become available, synthesizing much important work; so that the 'student of 1979 must wonder why the politics of England from the 1680s to the 1730s and the structure, mobility and wealth (or poverty) of her population should still have to be studied in compartments with so few points of contact.

There are, of course, exceptions. Close attention has been given, for instance, to the political ramifications of the hostility between the landed and 'monied' interests after the Revolution and Edward Thompson has made an enterprising foray into the territory of Walpolean Whiggery through his study of the Waltham Blacks.[1] Small beginnings are better than none; but this paper has been written in the conviction that it is high time we went much further. In a single essay I can only take one of the problems with which political historians have been concerned in recent years and discuss it within its social context. It is, however, an important problem and remains as intriguing today as when it was first posed by Dr J. H. Plumb in the Ford Lectures of 1965.[2] Why was it that the political stability which had deserted England for most of the seventeenth century, and which for at least four decades after the early 1680s continued to elude the determined search of her monarchs and statesmen, was at length restored under a Whig ascen-

1 E. P. Thompson, *Whigs and Hunters* (1975), Pt. 3, esp. Ch. 9.
2 J. H. Plumb, *The Growth of Political Stability in England, 1675–1725* (1967).

dancy during the 20 years in which Sir Robert Walpole dominated the arena?

On the theme which Plumb so skilfully developed certain variations have since been composed. Some have suggested that instability was not as chronic a condition, even in Anne's reign, as the banshee howls of the party men tend to suggest; nor was stability an entirely hopeless dream as early as the 1680s, despite the scarring of that decade's politics by plot, rising and revolution. Others would argue that the stability of the Whig oligarchy was neither so unshakeable, nor so 'profoundly inert' as Plumb suggests. But whatever their differences of emphasis, few historians have challenged the three essentials of the original thesis: that some of the raw materials of stability, for example the great resources of patronage at the Crown's disposal, had already become available under the later Stuarts; that until Anne's death there were crucial vitiating factors – major political and religious problems still unresolved – which made it exceptionally difficult in an age of party strife to put these materials to good use; and that the Whig achievement after 1714 was and remains a notable one, whether or not we are content to personalize it as much as Plumb does.

Walpole's rôle apart, attempts to explain the ultimate achievement of stability have concentrated heavily on two factors, the functional and the ideological. Much has been made, and rightly so, of the subjugation of the early Hanoverian electorate by manipulative and corruptive techniques, and of the scientific application of patronage to the control of parliament. It has also been shown how most of the toxic party issues which had kept both the electorate and parliament in a state of fever lost their potency between 1715 and 1725, and how the whole temperature of politics fell sharply in consequence.[3] Admittedly, it has also been argued that in the years which followed the end of the wars with France in 1713, and especially after the South Sea storm had abated in 1721, the marked easing of the so-called 'conflict of interests' did something to tranquillize both parties, and that Walpole's policies in the 1720s made no small contribution to the process.[4] But with this sole exception it would be true to say that in social or economic terms the subject of the achievement of political stability in England has never been seriously

3 Plumb, *Political Stability*, ch. 3; J. Cannon, *Parliamentary Reform 1640– 1832* (1973), pp. 33–41; W. A. Speck, *Stability and Strife: England 1714– 1760* (1978), pp. 146–52, 160–3; G. Holmes, *The Electorate and the National Will in the First Age of Party* (1976) and *The Trial of Doctor Sacheverell* (1973), pp. 276–83; J. P. Kenyon, *Revolution Principles*, pp. 170–208.

4 H. T. Dickinson, *Walpole and the Whig Supremacy* (1973) pp. 93–101; W. A. Speck, *Stability and Strife*, pp. 155–8; P. G. M. Dickson, *The Financial Revolution in England . . . 1688–1756* (1967), pp. 199–204.

debated. It is an omission which may well seem strange to anyone carefully re-reading the 1965 Ford Lectures, since they offered us a number
of significant leads in that very direction.[5]

In this essay I am concerned with two questions that were not raised
by Plumb's original thesis and with one question that was. The two
former concern aspects of the restoration of stability which have been
almost entirely neglected. In the first place, why did England manage to
confine her bitter political feuds after 1688 by and large within strictly
constitutional channels, that is to say, within the framework of parliamentary elections and regular meetings of parliament? Why, indeed,
neither from 1681 down to the summer of 1688 nor from 1689 down to
the 1720s – not even in 1715 – was there any significant support in
England from any section of the higher orders of society for any resort
to desperate or violent political solutions? (It was symbolic that the
one successful revolutionary *coup* of the whole period, that of 1688
itself, was so profoundly respectable that it made the election of a
'free parliament' – in which political divisions could be legitimized –
its main agreed objective.) In the second place, why was it that at no
stage after 1681, not excluding 1688, was there any serious pressure
from below, from the sub-political nation,[6] to exploit the troubled
conditions created, first by the Stuart reaction, then by the prolonged
'rage of party'? Why, in other words, did the great issues of the day,
while sometimes arousing popular interest, so singularly lack any
intrinsic popular dimension, by complete contrast with the divisive
political issues of the mid seventeenth century and the late eighteenth?
I suspect it is mainly because they can only be satisfactorily understood
in the light of what was taking place in English society between the
1680s and the 1730s that these two questions have so often been begged.
It is always easier to discuss what did happen in the past rather than
what did not happen. And yet in both cases what did not occur plainly
had the most vital bearing on the country's prospects of achieving political stability. Whatever contrivances, electoral or parliamentary,
were devised to stabilize the political nation, they could easily have
been rendered ineffective by forces determined to by-pass their conventions.

Our third questions concerns that part of English society which
formed 'the political nation' of the day. Historians have not demurred
from J. H. Plumb's view that by the end of George I's reign these groups

5 See *The Growth of Political Stability*, pp. xvi, xviii, 3, 4–9, 83, 86–92, 188.
6 I make a distinction here between this and the 'other' or 'alternative political nation' which John Brewer has illuminated in the mid-eighteenth
century. Down to the 1720s at least the latter was still able to find an adequate and frequent outlet through the old electoral process.

had achieved a measure of fusion, through a recognition of common interests and 'common identity', which they had not experienced since before the seventeenth century. But we know surprisingly little about this process. What can social or economic development themselves tell us about why, and when, it came about?

A paper concerned with the achievement of stability inevitably sets out to identify and emphasize those elements which tended towards fusion rather than schism in society and politics. This in no way implies that the *Divided Society* which Dr Speck and I portrayed in the late 1960s was a chimera.[7] A society riven by the animosities of Whig and Tory unquestionably existed in England after the 1688 Revolution, especially in the reign of Anne. As I now see it, however, the reality was less stark than we then depicted it. Even between the mid 1690s and the early years of George I – when party strife was at its most acute – there were softer contours on the social terrain, among them features which few scholars a decade ago were aware of. These contours, which began as early as the 1680s continued even through the volcanic eruptions of 1701–15, to hold out sure promise of a very different political landscape ahead.

*   *   *

Of all the 'social interpretations' of England's acute political instability between the 1620s and the 1650s, two have always struck me as inherently plausible. One relates to the popular, radical dimension which politics acquired after 1640: namely the fact that for long before the outbreak of the Civil War far too many of the rapidly multiplying 'poorer sort' in England had been pressing on economic resources inadequate to sustain them, above all on food supplies. Equally credible is the argument that the politically active families in the country had for some decades before 1641 been producing more younger sons than could be settled independently on the land. For in a pre-industrial society, even a relatively mobile society, where inheritance within the élite was largely governed by primogeniture, where the traditional occupation, fighting, had become an archaism, but neither professional life nor the political system had yet developed sufficiently to provide an adequate alternative to it, an over-supply of educated but frustrated younger sons was a recipe for serious disturbance. However, when we look ahead to the situation between James II's reign and George I's a difference of the

7   See G. Holmes and W. A. Speck, editors, *The Divided Society* (1967); Holmes, *British Politics in the Age of Anne* (1967), ch. 1; Speck, 'Conflict in Society' in G. Holmes, editor, *Britain after the Glorious Revolution, 1689–1714* (1969), pp. 135–54.

utmost importance emerges. England still experienced acute constitutional and political problems; but they were no longer subject to aggravation from either of those two quarters formerly so dangerous. This was essentially because a basic socio-economic equation which had defied solution in the first half of the seventeenth century had at last been worked out. The three crucial elements in this equation were population, economic resources and opportunities for respectable employment. In late Tudor and early Stuart England these elements had been irreconcilable. I shall argue, however, that between, roughly, 1680 and 1714 they were brought into balance, and that this balance was then maintained well into the Hanoverian period.

The first two major questions posed in this essay can only be adequately answered in the light of this remarkable achievement. A decisive check to population growth, together with the expansion of the country's economic resources (in particular her food supplies) and an eleventh-hour victory of wages over prices, had major implications for popular politics, and above all for the disappearance of popular radicalism. The same demographic trend interacted both with an upsurge in the economy and with a dramatic expansion of the employment opportunities available to the gentry's sons to inhibit violent reactions from politically alienated sections of the governing class, either from 1680–87 or after 1714. In each part of the equation supply and demand were brought into a comfortable balance which had been unattainable before 1660. And without such balances, I would contend, the resolution of the complex political problems of the late seventeenth century would have been far more difficult and the achievement of stability longer delayed.

The most important key to the whole situation is population: yet it is one which political historians investigating the years 1660–1760 have left almost entirely unused. So much uncertainty persisted for so long about the demographic trends of this century that ambitious speculation about their political consequences was naturally discouraged. With the mists now beginning to clear, however, it is profitable for us to ponder the situation that is being revealed and its implications for the achievement of stability.

England's population had grown with great rapidity for much of the sixteenth century, to reach a figure that was probably very close to four million by 1600; and recent years of patient analysis of parish register evidence[8] has confirmed contemporary impressions that this upward

8 Most systematically by the Cambridge Group for the History of Population and Social Structure, which has studied 404 'sample' parishes from the sixteenth to the eighteenth centuries, using sophisticated techniques, and more than 150 others. This paragraph could not have been written

trend continued into the Stuart age, so that between 1600 and 1640 a population rise of a further 25 per cent or thereabouts took place. Although it is well nigh certain that the brakes then went on, the registration of baptisms, burials and marriages was so severely disrupted by the mid-century traumas of the Church of England that their evidence for the period of the Civil Wars and the Interregnum can never be wholly satisfactory. By 1662, however, a settled Anglican ministry had been re-established, keeping for the most part reliable records; and their message sharply suggests that over the country as a whole, for at least 50 of the next 80 years down to 1742 – the year of Walpole's fall – Englishmen at best little more than reproduced themselves. Only in the last decade of the seventeenth century and during the first two decades of the new century did a slow recovery set in. There is evidence of a rising birth-rate in certain regions;[9] of some relief by the 1690s from the very high basic levels of mortality experienced since the late 1650s; and of a remarkable intermission in those waves of epidemics which had regularly broken over England from 1658 to 1686, and which returned to fill the churchyards up and down the land between 1719 and 1742, with an especially massive slaughter in 1728–29. But for the loss of young men in the wars of 1689–1713 and for the persistence of endemic diseases such as smallpox, the recovery of 1690–1720 would have added more than a modest 300,000–400,000 to England's inhabitants. As it was, the population of England and Wales together, at around 5.8 million in 1736, had crept up by no more than four, and probably as little as three, per cent over the previous 80 years.[10]

Even in isolation so significant a check to the population growth of Tudor and early Stuart England must have been a powerful stabilizing factor. What was politically crucial was that in the context of a population which remained so stable, and actually declined slightly between 1660 and 1688, the other two elements that concern us, economic resources and employment opportunities, both increased. Moreover

without the kindness of Dr Anne Whiteman of Lady Margaret Hall and Professor E. A. Wrigley of the Cambridge Group in making some of the Group's population estimates available to me. It owes a particular debt to Professor Wrigley, who read and commented on the first draft.

9   See, e.g., J. D. Chambers, *Population, Economy and Society in Pre-Industrial England* (1972), pp. 136–49 *passim*.

10 Even with renewed acceleration after 1736, the 6 million mark may not have been reached until the mid 1740s. The population curve described here corresponds closely with that depicted graphically in D. C. Coleman, *The Economy of England 1450–1750* (1977), p. 16, and to some extent with that presented in similar form in J. D. Chambers, *op. cit.* p. 19; although Chambers now seems to have overestimated the scale of the recovery from 1690 to 1720.

this increase was maintained, variably in the case of the economy, otherwise substantially, during the next 50 years, thereby guaranteeing that the moderate population growth which did take place between 1690 and 1720 could be accommodated with minimal social dislocation. The force of this argument can be appreciated by glancing next at the economic resources of England in our period and their political implications. And keeping in mind, to begin with, the popular threat to the achievement of stability, it is primarily to the changing face of agrarian England and to a standard of living which, with a few setbacks, rose steadily in the late seventeenth and early eighteenth centuries that we must look.

Although not every economic historian would agree with it, a very convincing case has been made of late for advancing the effective beginning of England's 'agricultural revolution' by something like a hundred years before its traditional starting-point in the middle of the eighteenth century. It is a simple enough matter, of course, to demonstrate that agrarian improvement after 1660 was uneven and often slow, and that innovations often had to struggle painfully up a mountain of caution and ignorance. Yet so many unassailable facts have now been established that historians interested in the ordinary Englishman's standard of living can no longer ignore them. It is plain, for instance, that agricultural prices remained remarkably low for the greater part of the years 1660–1750; and quite apart from the benefit to consumers, it is hard to credit that this price depression did not provide farmers and go-ahead landowners with a strong and sustained incentive to 'improve'. Certainly improved pasturage and winter feeding had enabled England by 1700 to become a country of meat-eaters to a degree that had not been possible a hundred years earlier. In 1722 the author of a best-selling contemporary description of England was to write:

> What Don Pedro de Ronquillo, the Spanish Ambassador, said of Leadenhall Market in London, that there was more meat sold in it in one week than in all Spain in a year, I believe to be perfectly true; for there are few tradesmen in London, *but have a hot joint every day.*[11]

Another firmly established fact is that England became a grain-exporting country from the 1670s and a heavy exporter after 1715.[12] Of course, all was not plain sailing with the harvest. There was a worrying

---

11 J. Macky, *A Journey through England* II (1722), p. 239. Except in the 1690s meat prices remained remarkably stable throughout our period and those of the 1730s were the lowest for a century.

12 See A. H. John, 'English Agricultural Improvements, 1660–1765', in D. C. Coleman and A. H. John, editors, *Trade, Government and Economy in pre-Industrial England* (1976), pp. 48–9.

run of meagre wheat yields in the period 1693–1700 and a 'pinching time' for the poor after the dismally wet summers of 1708 and 1709.[13] And yet it is now clear that at no time between 1679 and 1742 was England in any danger of a genuine famine of the kind that struck Scotland with terrible force in the 1690s, or France in 1693 and 1709. A true 'famine', by definition, must cause heavy mortality, either directly or indirectly; and the parish registers tell us that the application of this emotive word even to 1709, when bread was dearer in southern England than in any year except one in the whole century from 1660 to 1760, is totally unjustifiable.

Although parish relief must have played its part in averting disasters, the main explanation must lie in the growth of agricultural productivity in most regions of England since 1650, to the point at which a population of little more than five million was not only guaranteed a comfortable surplus in an average year but at least a bare sufficiency in a bad one. English farmers were especially successful during the seventeenth century in extending the acreage given over to the lesser grains. Obsessed with the well known indices of wheat prices, historians have too often overlooked the fact that a failure of the winter-sown wheat crop did not mean the automatic failure of spring-sown barley and oats, and that rye, though winter-sown, was hardier than wheat.[14] It is surely no coincidence that only three times between 1670 and 1741

13 In just four of the thirty years from 1711 to 1740 less spectacular crop failures pushed the average price of a quartern loaf in London slightly above 6d. – a figure reached approximately every other year in the much lower-wage economy of the years 1629–61. For prices see Lord Ernle, *English Farming Past and Present* (1912), p. 440; M. Beloff, *Public Order and Popular Disturbances, 1660–1714*, table, p. 159; W. G. Hoskins, 'Harvest Fluctuations and English Economic History, 1620–1759', *Agricultural History Review XVI* (1968), p. 19.

14 As late as 1766 Charles Smith calculated that even in times of relative plenty only about 60 per cent of the population at large normally ate wheaten bread. Even so, it has been estimated that this represented a 20 per cent increase since the 1690s. Charles Smith, *Three Tracts on the Corn Trade and Corn Laws* (1766), cited in P. Deane and W. A. Cole, *British Economic Growth 1688–1959* (2nd edn., 1967), p. 63; T. S. Ashton, *Changes in Standards of Comfort in Eighteenth Century England* (Raleigh Lecture), *Proceedings of the British Academy* (1954–5), p. 173. The ratios of wheat prices to the prices of barley, rye and oats in a string of towns, published in the weekly tables of John Houghton, *A Collection for the Improvement of Husbandry and Trade* (20 vols, 1692–1703, repr. 4 vols, 1969) are often highly revealing. Cf., for example, those for 2 Feb. 1694, at the height of a serious wheat shortage, with those for 27 Feb. 1702, in a time of plenty. *Ibid.* iv, no. 79; xvii, no. 501.

did English governments, sensitive though they were to any possible threat to public order, feel it necessary to exert their discretionary power under statute to place a temporary embargo on the export of grain. It is equally instructive that food riots in the reigns of William III and Anne appear to have been remarkably infrequent. They were predominantly Midlands or East Anglian phenomena, and even there concentrated mainly in the years 1693–95 and 1709.[15]

Agricultural progress was not alone in affecting the standard of living of ordinary Englishmen during the half-century after 1680. The rapidly cheapening prices of some colonial and East Indian goods, imported in great quantities during and after the trade boom of Charles II's later years, also contributed; refined sugar and tobacco had ceased to be luxuries by 1700, and tea by 1730.[16] Thirdly, there was an ample supply by the early eighteenth century of inexpensive clothing, especially the new calicoes and 'prints' of the Orient and Lancashire,[17] and also of household furniture and hardware produced for a large consumer market. Most important of all was the fact that before the end of the seventeenth century wages were at last winning the battle with food prices and the prices of consumer goods, for in an era of largely static population and exceptional wartime demands for manpower, labour had become a scarce commodity. In fact, some leading authorities are now convinced that in decades of especially good harvests and cheap food, most notably the 1680s and the 1730s, circumstances yielded the steady wage-earner an exceptional surplus spending capacity. The shrewd contemporary judgement of Defoe in the 1720s would seem to bear them out:

> As the people get greater wages [he wrote], so they, I mean the same poorer part of the people, clothe better and furnish better; and this increases the consumption of the very manufactures they make.

And it was 'the working *manufacturing* people of England' whom he considered to be the most favoured of all the wage-earners, spending more of their growing earnings 'upon their backs and bellies than in any other country'.[18]

15 Hoskins, 'Harvest Fluctuations', *loc. cit.* p. 21; M. Beloff, *Public Order and Popular Disturbances*, map opposite p. 68.
16 D. Defoe, *The Complete English Tradesman* (1745 edn.) I, p. 76; A. H. John, 'Aspects of English Economic Growth in the first half of the Eighteenth Century', repr. in E. M. Carus-Wilson, editor, *Essays in Economic History* II (1962), p. 366.
17 A. P. Wadsworth and J. de L. Mann, *The Cotton Trade and Industrial Lancashire* (1931), pp. 124–40.
18 *Complete English Tradesman*, I, p. 252.

Of course, there was much seasonal and some permanent unemployment in the England of 1680–1730, and for the late seventeenth century, at least, Hearth Tax returns and Poor Rate contributions have revealed considerable poverty. But for the political historian this should not obscure the other side of the coin. Population growth that was never more, and frequently far less, than steady; rising wages in many industries, involving in some cases increases of up to 25 per cent between 1680 and 1720; food that was in general cheaper, more plentiful and more varied than earlier in the seventeenth century, and at no time dangerously scarce: these elements together constituted an integral part of the fabric of political stability. More than anything else, they account for the almost total quiescence of genuinely radical politics between 1689 and the age of Walpole and Newcastle.

Although popular passions could often be inflamed by political or politico-religious issues, it is remarkable to what extent their expression was confined within conventional bounds. When popular feeling spilled over on any major scale it did so almost always into moulds already shaped by the feuds of the governing classes and of the electorate – an electorate overwhelmingly composed of men with some stake, however small, in property. It is surely valid to ask why it was that the Protestant mobs, the Whig and Tory mobs, the Church and Jacobite mobs, and the 'No Excise' mobs of 1688–1734 continually voiced the slogans of their masters, rather than articulating any distinctive grievances of their own? Or why it was that even when most powerfully stirred, and even in overcrowded, combustible London, the English lower orders showed no apparent interest in popular liberties, in rectifying some of the grosser inequalities in their society, or even in securing electoral recognition? There were, after all, radical, extra-parliamentary forces clearly identifiable in English politics as late as 1685. They were conjured into life in 1680–81 by the first Earl of Shaftesbury, desperate to keep up the momentum of his Exclusion campaign, and in 1683 government intelligence uncovered disturbing links between well-organized London republicans and radical groups in Dorset and the West Country. A recent scholarly study of the Monmouth rebels of 1685 suggests that some of them, at least, had imbibed the heady democratic wine of the Interregnum.[19]

Yet in general it would be true to say that for over a century between Venner's 1661 Rising and the late 1760s such popular forces, where (or if) they existed, were astonishingly inert. The brave words uttered on the scaffold in 1686 by Richard Rumbold, former proprietor of the Rye House, that 'there was no man born marked of God above another; for none comes into the world with a saddle on his back, neither any booted

19   P. Earle, *Monmouth's Rebels* (1977), pp. 4–5, 13, 16.

or spurred to ride him'[20] was a voice from the past, not a clarion call to the present or to the foreseeable future. Although Tory propaganda in Anne's reign did its best to wring what capital it could out of the supposed existence of 'Calve's-Head clubs' – cells of republican dissenters – in London, it is clear that from the 1690s onwards 'Commonwealth' ideas became, for the most part, the preserve of a handful of intellectuals or idiosyncratic political independents. Nothing illustrates more strikingly this change of custody than John Toland's legerdemain in 1698, when he re-wrote the *Memoirs* of Edmund Ludlow in such a way as to portray that old Cromwellian warhorse as a respectable Country Whig gentlemen.[21] Meanwhile *popular* radicalism came increasingly to resemble not so much an inactive volcano as a burnt-out crater. The fact was of crucial importance to the chances of building a politically stable state. With a constitution under considerable stress, from the 1680s at least to King William's death, with an uncertain succession thereafter, and with a political world violently embroiled until well into the 1720s in party and faction strife, even a mild eruption could have proved highly dangerous. Yet in 1688–89 there was scarcely so much as a warning puff of smoke, and in 1710, in 1715–16 and in 1733 it was impossible to detect even that.

It is an extraordinary fact that while a *jure divino* king was being turned off the throne in 1688, with no parliament sitting and for seven weeks no legally constituted government in England, the popular rôle in the revolution was limited to a short burst of ritual anti-Catholic rioting and game-poaching from 'Popish' landlords.[22] Scarcely less revealing is the political crisis of 1710, coming as it did at the fag end of a war of which the bulk of the nation had more than had its fill, after 18 months of exceptionally scarce and dear wheat, and when indirect taxation had begun to bite hard on 'necessaries' such as salt and meat. It was accompanied from March to October by a 'mobbish time' which most discomfited the Whigs. Yet no one in authority, either before or after the

20 T. B. Howell, editor, *A Complete Collection of State Trials* (1809–14), XI, p. 881.
21 An operation brilliantly detected by the researches of Dr Blair Worden. See B. Worden, intro. to Edmund Ludlow, *A Voyce from the Watch Tower*, Camden Society 4th series, 21, 1978, p. 19. For 'Calves-Head' republicans, see *ibid.* p. 19; *The Secret History of the Calves-Head Club; or, the Republican Unmasked* (1703). For the Commonwealthmen, H. T. Dickinson, *Liberty and Property* (1977), pp. 105–6, 111–12, 164–6; Mark Goldie, 'The roots of true Whiggism, 1688–94', *History of Political Thought*, I (1980), pp. 195–236.
22 Beloff, *Public Order*, pp. 25, 41–3; W. L. Sachse, 'The Mob in the Revolution of 1688', *Journal of British Studies* IV (1964).

change of ministry, appears to have genuinely feared sedition, still less revolution; no one even called for the suspension of Habeas Corpus. The attempt of the London mob in March 1710 to pull down the Bank of England was not an act of egalitarian subversion: it had exactly the same basic motive as the more successful attempts at the same time to sack dissenting meeting-houses.[23] 'High Church and Sacheverell', 'God save the Queeen and the Doctor', the commonest utterances of the crowd all over England in 1710, were also the toasts of every Tory squire and parson. They were slogans that would sweep one party out of power and another in; but they signified no threat to either the social or political order in which these parties flourished.

The absence of a popular and spontaneous dimension to politics has not gone completely unnoticed, of course. Credit has been given to the Junto for swiftly weaning the Whig party after the Revolution from its uneasy association with its former plebeian, crypto-republican allies. It has also been suggested that any radical movements of a socially sub-versive nature were inhibited by the hierarchical emphases of Anglican teaching under the later Stuarts, combined with the still powerful Puritan legacy of providentialism.[24] It is clear, however, that among a proletariat increasingly untouched by organized religion, ingrained notions of social deference could not be taken for granted: the case of the Waltham Blacks underlined this in the 1720s, as did the growing suspicion that the new SPCK charity schools, by making children 'impatient of the condition they were born to', might undermine the very social assumptions their syllabuses were designed to endorse.[25] On a different tack, it has been argued that frequent General Elections during the lifetime of the Triennial Act from 1694 to 1716 provided a politically overcharged society with a safety valve; and this may well have been of importance in London and some of the most populous pro-vincial towns where electoral disorders, involving both voters and non-voters, were endemic.[26] The electorate itself is now known to have been

23 G. Holmes, 'The Sacheverell Riots: The Crowd and the Church in Early Eighteenth-Century London', above, pp. 223-6.
24 Plumb, *Political Stability*, pp. 134−5; A. McInnes, 'The Revolution and the People' in G. Holmes, editor, *Britain after the Glorious Revolution*, pp. 84−90.
25 John Trenchard, in *The London Journal*, 15 June 1723. See H. T. Dickinson, *Politics and Literature in the Eighteenth Century* (1974), pp. 64−6.
26 McInnes, *loc. cit.* p. 91; Holmes and Speck, *The Divided Society*, pp. 2, 77−8. London itself was contested no fewer than 14 times between 1689 and 1715, Westminster 11 times, Southwark 12, Bristol 9 and Coventry 9. For these and many other examples see H. Horwitz, *Parliament, Policy and Politics in the Reign of William III* (1977), Appx. A; W. A. Speck, *Tory and Whig: The Struggle in the Constituencies, 1701−1715* (1970), Appx. E.

both larger and socially humbler in the late seventeenth and early eighteenth centuries than we had imagined, and the fact that it was growing at a faster rate than the population, and was still capable of giving a rough-and-ready representation to the opinions of the man in the street, may have been a far more effective antidote to political radicalism than historians have generally realized.[27]

All these hypotheses, especially the last, have something to offer us. Yet none of them should be strained. Only one of the conditions they emphasize (the element of Anglican social control) applied for most of the 1680s, and only one (Whig dissociation) was operative after 1720. More to the point, they all leave out of the reckoning the most pervading and persistent condition of all. It is difficult to believe that popular radicalism would not have found some outlet in the years between Exclusion and the fall of Walpole, despite all discouragements or distractions, had there been any *sustained* popular grievances that could have been appealed to. Transitory or sectional grievances there were, of course, as there always had been; but none that were sustained. And the reasons must be sought not primarily in politics, or in religion, but in an exceptionally favourable long-term conjunction of economic and social circumstances. Of the variety of explanations posited to account for the 'respectability' of the Glorious Revolution, how many touch on the most vital fact of all, that the 1680s had seen year after year of 'marvellous bounty' from the land and the most important period of commercial expansion and prosperity in living memory?[28] The mid and late 1690s were hard years by comparison; yet by far the most important cause of popular unrest – the Recoinage of 1696 – was nonpolitical. 'Country' campaigns in parliament in those years evoked no popular response, except in the 1698 Election. So too with the 1710 crisis. It is true that it burst upon a country which in many parts of the south had just suffered the two most appalling wheat harvests for half a century. Yet the barley and rye harvests of 1708–9 were more resilient and the food situation never got out of control. What is more, these were freak years: from 1700 to 1707 bread in many parts of England had been slightly cheaper on average even than in the plenteous 1680s.[29]

Only in the years 1715–16, when there were frequent disorderly demonstrations by Londoners in sympathy with the Jacobite cause, did a post-Revolution government half persuade itself that some threat existed to the established political and social order. But in this the

---

27 G. Holmes, *The Electorate and the National Will in the First Age of Party* (1976). See above, pp. 1-33 *passim*.
28 Hoskins, 'Harvest Fluctuations', pp. 22, 30.
29 *Ibid.* p. 29.

Whig ministers of George I were utterly mistaken. True, there was much economic dislocation in the southeast in 1715 to lend a sharper edge to expressions of popular hostility to the new dynasty and to the Whigs. Nevertheless, after a most thorough analysis of this unrest, Nicholas Rogers has concluded that although 'the London plebeians were a more formidable and less malleable force than recent historians have taken them to be', theirs was no radical groundswell. Their main battlecry, of 'High Church and Ormonde', was no more than a variant on the theme of 1710: 'their political notions were basically derivative, ... defined within terms of the existing political structure which allowed them a vicarious birthright.'[30] In this they were typical of their time. A fundamental conservatism stamps virtually every out-break of popular disorder in England from 1688 to 1716, from the full-scale London riot to the smallest local protest against enclosure, 'forestalling' or impressment, and it can only be fully understood within the context of economic and demographic trends which placed no intolerable stress on the lower or lower-middling storeys of the social structure. The same goes for the continuing quiescence not merely of popular but also of petty-bourgeois radicalism long after the much-exercised electorate of 1689–1715 had succumbed to atrophy. Can it be coincidence that radical politics, linked to popu-lar unrest, ultimately revived in the years 1768–70, at the end of a decade when a rapidly rising population suffered both hunger and industrial troubles infinitely more serious than anything England's population had experienced from the 1680s to the 1730s?

*   *   *

The basic demographic conditions which are so important in elucidat-ing the first of the questions posed in this paper are equally relevant to the second. In the generation before the Revolution fewer children were produced, and crucially fewer survived to teenage and manhood, than in the generation before the Civil War; in the two generations following 1688 their number only moderately increased. This was not peculiar to the lower social strata. So far as we know it was common to every level of English society. Dr Hollingsworth has demonstrated that aristocratic families followed the same trend;[31] and there are no rational grounds for supposing that the gentry constituted a special case if the peerage did not. The political relevance of this has been completely overlooked. Yet

30 N. Rogers, 'Popular Protest in Early Hanoverian London', *Past and Present* 79 (1978), pp. 90, 100. See also pp. 92–3, 96–8.
31 T. H. Hollingsworth, *The Demography of the British Peerage*, supplement to *Population Studies* XVIII (1964), ch. 3–4.

it points directly to a further link of prime importance between political and social stability, annealed once again by economic prosperity.

There were in England in the 1680s hundreds of Whig gentry families, and, after 1714, several thousand families of Tory gentry, who found themselves confronted with the bleak prospect of prolonged official disfavour. To both these groups there seemed little doubt that the doors of government patronage and even of local honour had crashed to in their faces for good. For most Tories under the first two Hanoverians this proved only too true. And for the post-Exclusion Whigs there could have been no reprieve if Charles II had not obligingly died in February 1685. Had such massive proscriptions taken place in the very different social and economic context of the early seventeenth century they would have spelt disaster in terms of political stability. The frustrated cadets of the squirearchy, especially of those lesser gentry whose prospects of providing an 'independence' for their younger sons out of landed patrimony were virtually nil, were for two centuries after 1550 the likeliest material from which reckless men could hope to fashion a dangerous political *coup* in England.

Why was such a *coup* not attempted after the dissolution of the Oxford Parliament in 1681? Why was it ill-planned and bungled in 1683? Why did the rebellion which did materialize in 1685 fail so abysmally to attract 'true gentry' (as opposed to 'pseudo-gentry') support, even in the old Puritan strongholds of the west?[32] Do not these events, or non-events, suggest that a ready supply of martial material, primed by economic stringency or by an acute sense of social grievance, was no longer forthcoming? Admittedly, several years of repression had either removed or frightened off many potential leaders and subalterns of Monmouth's army by 1685. But the same cannot be said of the events of 1715. The unwillingness of the English Tory gentry to commit themselves openly to the Pretender's cause should be pondered, not taken for granted: for after 1688, 1715 was the year of all years that could have changed the political future of Britain, had the political desperation felt by many Tory gentlemen been matched by desperation of a more material kind. But it was precisely this material desperation – the kind of desperation that drives men beyond mere pot-valour – which was lacking; and the fact that it was lacking, despite all the rhetoric the Tories had expended during the recent wars on the wretched plight of the landed interest, gives us more insight into the real foundations of stability in early eighteenth-century England than we can get from the manipulation of places, pensions or boroughs. The same factor may be equally relevant to the surprising frailty of the Jacobite conspiratorial base in England between 1716 and 1727, to the total inertia of the

32 P. Earle, *Monmouth's Rebels*, pp. 17, 28–33, 202-3.

English Jacobites, for example, at moments of opportunity such as the Atterbury Plot or the sudden death abroad of George I. With every year that passed after the Septennial Act of 1716, and especially after the decisive Tory election failure of 1722, the chances that the stability of oligarchic Whiggery would be disturbed at the polling booths steadily diminished. Yet Tory squires overwhelmingly chose to take their cue from their own shrinking body of representatives on the back benches of the Commons, who as Atterbury wrote despairingly in 1722 were 'a rope of sand', men whose 'thoughts both within doors and without are employed about nothing but securing their approaching elections.'[33]

The unwillingness of politically alienated gentry – even when they constituted a clear majority of their class – to attempt the overthrow of an inimical régime by force must not, of course, be simplistically interpreted. It would be absurd to seek the clues to it simply in the demography of the Augustan ruling class or purely in an economic context. We know that the psychological pressure exerted by the memories of 1642 – 60, shared by virtually all men of property in late Stuart England, had an important restraining effect on the embittered Whigs in 1681 and in 1685. The avoidance of another civil war in 1688, miraculous as it seemed to all concerned at the time, strengthened the determination of the next generation not to tempt Providence again. Such sentiments pervade the arguments on both sides during the Sacheverell debate in 1709 – 10, but above all on the Tory side where the influence of the passive obedience school of Anglican clergy had recently revived and touched new heights.

Nevertheless, even instincts as deep as these could have been overcome (as they had been in 1688) had things become too much to bear. This is why it was the ambivalent position of so many landed families which held the key and to the prospects of political stability. For however bleak the position must have seemed *politically* for the Tory gentry after 1714 (as with the Whigs in the 1680s), *socially* it was tolerable. Between 1680 and 1740 an exceptionally favourable combination of circumstances conspired to cosset England's governing classes, making not merely political frustrations but the trials of two burdensome wars and the resentments aroused by novel social groups more supportable. It was a combination made up, on the one hand, of a lower birth-rate than that of their Tudor and early Stuart forebears and a high rate of child mortality; and, on the other hand, of the fresh channels of

33   Anon. letter, 12 Feb. 1722, quoted in G. V. Bennett, *The Tory Crisis in Church and State: The Career of Francis Atterbury, Bishop of Rochester* (1975) p. 240. *ibid*, chs. 11 – 12 and pp. 285 – 94 for Jacobite inertia. See also P. S. Fritz, *The English Ministers and Jacobitism between the Rebellions of 1715 and 1745* (1975).

social mobility and the unprecedented range of respectable employment opportunities that were now open to their younger sons. In the very decades that gentry families began to shrink significantly in size and so bring the responsibilities of family heads within more manageable compass, the first phase of the great 'Commercial Revolution' of the seventeenth century was unfolding. Of even greater importance in the long run was the redoubling of demand, at the very same period, for a range of professional services unthought of two generations earlier. Together these developments guaranteed that few younger sons of gentle birth who survived to manhood need be inadequately provided for, and that the aspirations of the majority could be satisfied with little loss of status. This is not to say the landed interest was without its problems, particularly in the war years. But historians have taken too little account of the fact that, though the Lord took away with one hand from many country gentlemen, He often gave with the other.

In 1694 Edward Chamberlayne remarked of the younger brothers of the gentry that, with 'small estates in land', they were commonly 'bred up to divinity, the law, physic, to court and military employment; but of late [he added, with marked distaste] too many of them to shopkeeping.'[34] Because in the long run it was the expansion of the professions which offered the stoutest lifeline to the gentry, it is easy to overlook the significance for them, and ultimately for politics, of the spectacular burgeoning of England's foreign and colonial trade in the 1670s and 1680s. This undoubtedly increased the options of the lesser gentry, in particular, as the case of the Heathcote brothers – who came of stock uncharacteristically prolific for its time – perfectly illustrates. 'Gilbert Heathcote, gentleman', who died in 1690, belonged to the younger branch of a minor Derbyshire landed gentry family and owned properties at Monyash and Tapton, and at Barnsley in Yorkshire, as well as houses and tenements in Chesterfield, where he resided. To lay out premiums for the apprenticeship of seven sons, mostly in London, between 1667 and 1683, and then to find £500 to launch each into the world, was not easy for him. But the sons almost all served their apprenticeships in the expanding trade branches of Charles II's later years and the eldest – the great Sir Gilbert, wine merchant and Bank of England tycoon – was later able to thank God, not only for 'one of the best of fathers' but for having 'so particularly blessed his care in our education as to let him live to see his seven sons all merchants in good esteem, a thing scarce to be paralleled.'[35] The Heathcote brothers differed only in

34 *Angliae Notitia* (1694 edn.) pp. 442–3.
35 E. D. Heathcote, *An Account of the Heathcote Family* (1899), pp. 47, 63–7, 69, 75, 103, 105; 'A Paper signed by Sir Gilbert Heathcote', printed in *ibid.* appx. VI, pp. 238–9.

number and breadth of achievement from many other young men from comparable backgrounds, or better, who followed similar tracks in the years between the Restoration and the Revolution. The Heysham brothers of north Lancashire and the Scawens of Buckinghamshire provide four examples among many. And like Sir Gilbert Heathcote, the two Scawens were able to graduate after the Revolution from overseas trade to positions of great influence in the Bank and the attainment of enormous wealth.[36]

However, the benefits of the 'Commercial Revolution' were not limited to London. In the thirty years after the Restoration many outports cashed in on the new trading opportunities in northern Europe, Iberia, the Mediterranean lands and the New World, and the long years of war thereafter enabled them to consolidate their gains and continue their slow erosion of London's mercantile dominance. At the same time domestic industries which grew in response to these commercial stimuli brought new vitality and wealth to the manufacturing and commercial classes in those towns which were their chief foci. These changes were important to the rank-and-file gentry of Lancashire and Yorkshire, of the north and west midlands, of East Anglia and the southwest. Nor were some of their better-off county neighbours too proud to benefit from them. Provincial apprenticeships, to merchants, tradesmen or manufacturers, now pointed to viable careers for gentlemen's younger sons;[37] they were cheaper than London apprenticeships[38] and there is

36 For Thomas and Sir William Scawen, see R. Sedgwick, editor, *The History of Parliament: The House of Commons, 1715–1754* (1970) II, 410–11; for Sir William, D. Defoe, *A Tour through England and Wales* (Everyman edn.), I, 158–9.

37 R. Grassby, 'Social Mobility and Business Enterprise in Seventeenth-century England', in D. Pennington and K. Thomas, editors, *Puritans and Revolutionaries* (1978), p. 357, confirms this–noting especially the increase 1650–90.

38 *Ibid.* pp. 364–5. Defoe protested in the 1720s against the 'unaccountable' rise in London premiums of relatively recent vintage; that the 'thirty or forty pounds' which was once 'sufficient to a very good merchant' was 'now run up to five hundred, nay to a thousand pounds with an apprentice'. *Complete English Tradesman* I, 112–13. His complaints are to some extent borne out by the Stamp Office records for London from 1711 onwards. Yet It is possible to find examples of London merchants taking on gentlemen's sons for little more than £100, and in July 1712 Sir Herbert Croft, bart., of Herefordshire, indentured his son William to Jacob Hollidge, London merchant, for £215. P.R.O. I.R. 1/1/9, 1/1/120. Professor Hughes thought, on the basis of that evidence, that £130 in Liverpool was the highest provincial premium recorded *c.* 1718; but it has since been shown that a few exclusive 'gentlemen merchants' of Leeds were demanding premiums of from £150 to £300 for taking on the sons of

evidence to suggest that between 1680 and 1740 they were becoming more popular. They must surely have been balm to the politically frustrated. The wealthy merchant clothiers of Leeds between William III's reign and George I's were taking apprentices even from major families, like the Kayes of Woodsome, Tory knights of the shire, as well as from such lesser gentry as the Micklethwaites of Terrington and the Oateses of Chickenley. Merchant houses were not the sole attraction to gentle families: Manchester and Bolton linen drapers had begun to recruit from the squirearchy, outside as well as inside Lancashire, as early as 1680, and we hear of John Anderson, born into 'as considerable a family as any in Lincolnshire', serving his apprenticeship with a linen draper around the turn of the century. But merchants did enjoy a special cachet, and just as Leeds and Hull became magnets for the Yorkshire gentry so did Liverpool for those of Lancashire. Among the prospering traders who laid the foundations of the town's greatness in the years from 1690 to 1720 were younger sons of the Norrises of Speke and the Claytons of Fulwood, along with William Cleveland who was a transplant from a Leicestershire family.[39]

The case of the Norrises is instructive in more ways than one. Like Heathcotes they were an unusually fecund stock. Thomas Norris, who inherited the encumbered Speke estates in the 1680s, had five younger brothers in 1685. Two of them went into trade; but of the three others, one went to sea in the merchant service, another trained in Oxford for the Church, and the third qualified as a physician and practised in Cheshire. It would be difficult to exaggerate the importance of the unprecedented expansion of the English professions after 1660 in satisfying both the economic needs and the social aspirations of the great majority of country gentlemen who had younger sons, or brothers, to establish creditably. The Church of England did not share significantly

baronets, knights and gentlemen for 7 years between 1712 and 1721. In the ports I have found gentlemen's sons bound to merchants for as little as £15 (Bideford, 1712) and as much as £200 (Hull, 1730). E. Hughes, *North Country Life in the 18th Century: the North-East* (1954), pp. 106–7; R. G. Wilson, *Gentlemen Merchants: the Merchant Community in Leeds 1700–1830* (1971), p. 24; P.R.O. I.R. 1/42/49, 1/12/75.

39   Wilson, *op. cit.* pp. 24, 246; G. Jackson, *Hull in the Eighteenth Century* (1972), pp. 104–6; T. Heywood, editor, *The Norris Papers* (Chetham Society, 1846), pp. xx–xxi and *passim*; F. E. Hyde, *Liverpool and the Mersey* (1971), pp. 13–14, 16; Hist. MSS. Comm. *Portland MSS.* IV, p. 623 for Anderson. See Wilson, *op. cit.* p. 25, Wadsworth and Mann, *Cotton Trade*, pp. 73–4, 94, P.R.O. I.R. 1/42/7 (2 Nov. 1711), for linen-drapers' and woollen-drapers' premiums in Leeds, Manchester and Bolton, much lower than those of merchants.

in the physical expansion; yet it did achieve higher prestige than it had ever done before 1642, and began to attract a greater proportion of recruits from armigerous families. Medicine was able to maintain its status as a suitable profession for gentlemen under the later Stuarts, owing not a little success in attracting their sons into 'physic' to the fact that by 1700 a Continental training could be had more speedily, more efficiently and more cheaply than one at home.[40] Its attractions could never compete, however, with those of the law. With demands for legal services heavier even than in the litigious early seventeenth century, calls to the bar maintained record levels throughout the 1670s and 1680s; and it is striking how often from now on barristers from provincial gentry stock chose to make their base not in London, where the competition was ferocious, but in the towns of their native heaths. At the same time, the rising profits of the 'lesser degrees' of the law began to tempt more of the gentry, especially those in straitened circumstances, into the more economical course of apprenticing their younger sons to attorneys or solicitors as articled clerks.[41] Despite the presence of too many black sheep in the profession, the properly qualified and registered attorney had already begun even before 1688 to establish his claim to the status of 'gentleman', and by 1730, this transmutation was complete for *bona fide* solicitors as well as for attorneys.[42]

For the gentry one of the most promising achievements of the Restoration monarchy was the success of Charles II and Pepys in making the new naval profession more attractive to young men of good breeding. Significantly, a narrow majority of the men who earned distinction as admirals during the wars of 1689–1713 were of gentle birth and had taken up 'the sea-service' as a career before the Revolution.[43] Such officers had been far less prominent in the 1650s. Once these wars began it was new professions rather than old ones which surged ahead, making it easier than ever before for the appetites of the gentry to be assuaged. The Royal Navy had become by far the most imposing force of its kind in the world by the beginning of the eighteenth century. Even so, during the 20 years after the Revolution it offered fewer career opportunities than the army; for land warfare on an entirely new scale raised the

40 T. W. Innes Smith, *English-Speaking Students of Medicine at the University of Leyden* (1932); E. A. Underwood, *Boerhaave's Men* (1978).

41 See my *Augustan England: Professions, State and Society, 1680-1730* (1982), chapter 5, and my Raleigh Lecture, 'The Professions and Social Change in England, 1680-1730', below, pp. 309-50.

42 See, e.g., *Lists of Attorneys and Solicitors admitted in pursuance of the Late Act for the Better Regulation of Attorneys and Solicitors* (by the Speaker's Order, London, 1729), pp. 3–5 and *passim*.

43 Five examples are Edward Russell, George Rooke, John Jennings, George Byng and Matthew Aylmer.

number of commissioned officers in the army by the later years of Anne to at least 4,000, well over six times their number at the end of Charles II's reign. The purchase system guaranteed that men of some birth and connection would enjoy most of the pickings, but the fact that its demands were not excessive in wartime, so far as the ordinary foot regiments were concerned, proved a boon to many poorer gentry families. In addition to the purchase system there was also by Anne's reign a half-pay system for 'military men', a system institutionalized for the peacetime army in 1713;[44] and this guaranteed that the massive contraction of the army from 1712 onwards was not accompanied by a proportional contraction of the profession.

Between 1680 and 1725 the bureaucracy of the Crown grew out of all recognition, and many of its largest departments achieved a new professionalism. Most of all was this true of the revenue service. The London offices of the Exchequer, the Treasury, the Customs and the Excise, the Post Office, and the large new revenue offices of the war years all teemed with gentlemen's sons. Many of their fathers had been well content to secure them clerkships of as little as £50 to £60 a year initially, in the hope that they would lead to better things in a civil service which now offered far greater career security, as well as hundreds more London jobs, than had been the case before 1680: indeed in many offices clerkships were the only way to promotion. Little is known as yet about recruitment to the local posts in the revenue departments which accounted for almost half the new bureaucracy: there were over 6,000 of them by the 1720s. But there are indications that to landed families still scratching along on rental incomes of £80–£200 a year in the early eighteenth century, the prospects of placing a younger son in, say, one of the 2,900 local gaugerships in the Excise, at £50 a year, was not a horrifying one. The route that could lead to Supervisorships, worth £90 a year by 1715, or to Collectorships of £120 a year, posts of considerable local status, was not to be lightly ignored.

The growth of the professions was one of the essential elements from which the fabric of political stability was created in the years from the 1680s to the 1730s. It was of great moment, both at the time and for the future, that in the course of this half century the English gentry acquired a gilt-edged investment, commonly (though not always) regardless of political affiliation, in this major social change. And to the achievement of stability not least important was the acquisition before 1714 by so many gentry families of a vital stake in those new professions, now firmly wedded to the service of the state through pen or sword.

*   *   *

44   R. E. Scouller, *The Armies of Queen Anne* (1966), p. 327.

Trends that with hindsight can be recognized by historians were not all equally plain at the time. To many contemporaries that 'sense of common identity in those who wielded economic, social and political power' which, as J. H. Plumb reminds us,[45] was so essential a prerequisite of stability, still seemed far from realization as late as the second half of Anne's reign. And in the eyes of some thousands of country gentlemen, especially, at least two of the major changes taking place in recent years in the fields of commerce and the professions caused unease: so far from relieving social stresses they appeared to be creating unhealthy new tensions and thereby aggravating party-political animosities. War had led to the diversion of much London capital investment from overseas trade either into the new funded loans, at enticing rates of interest, or into the stocks of the big City corporations, three of them post-1689 creations; and in the process a financial élite of startling wealth and influence had emerged. War had also provided another ladder to unacceptably rapid social advancement by necessitating armed forces of unprecedented size. Looking at these developments with a jaundiced eye, and fearful of their further extension, many country gentlemen in Queen Anne's England – especially Tory squires who were readily convinced that the Whigs were scooping the pool – would have been hard to persuade that the governing class of their day was moving towards fusion rather than towards greater fission. Sir John Pakington voiced their fears when he spoke in 1709 of the danger of 'the moneyed and military men becoming lords of us who have the lands'; and in the winter of 1710–11 the fire of Swift's *Examiner* was turned against this same unholy, socially disruptive alliance.[46]

It is with the reality behind these fears, and the light which recent work on society and the economy can throw upon it, that the third and final question in this essay is concerned. Were the assimilation of novel social groups, the forging of links of mutual interest running through the governing class and across the lines of party loyalty and in the end the removal of social conflict from the causes of political dissension, achieved with great suddenness in the 1720s, and then only because a prolonged period of peace had removed the worst element of friction? Or were these processes far more gradual, and far earlier in their beginnings, than most political historians have assumed – or indeed than the noisy battle-cries of the early eighteenth-century 'conflict of interests' would seem to suggest?

Some points are certainly clearer today than they were a decade ago. They do not alter the fact that after its eruption in the 1690s the 'conflict

45 *Growth of Political Stability,* p. xviii.
46 *The Examiner,* No. 13, 2 Nov. 1710; Pakington's speech on the Bewdley election, quoted in G. Holmes, *British Politics in the Age of Anne,* p. 149.

of interests' did put the achievement of political stability in greater jeopardy. Neither do they relegate to the level of a phoney emotion the alarm expressed about it, at a time when war and party fury were wracking the nation. The rise of a 'new interest' in the City, incorporating 'a sort of property which was not known' in 1688,[47] was no figment of Tory imaginations. It was a blazing comet across the London sky, and in its garish light a few emotive incidents, such as the Bank's ill-considered deputation to the queen in June 1710, not unnaturally took on a sinister significance. But one can also understand how Westminster politicians, dazzled at the time by the comet's light, became blind during Anne's reign to those reassuring signs which can now be distinguished. They were loth to recognize that the 'conflict of interests' was primarily a metropolitan phenomenon: a source of genuine stress in London and the heavily taxed southeast, but of less account to the many counties where the Land Tax was lightly assessed and no 'new interest' had intruded into economic life. They either did not realize, or chose not to see, that the numbers of 'monied men' pure and simple – those 'retailers of money' whom Swift denounced as a threat to the constitution – were very few; that fundholders or company directors were more catholic in function, and often more traditional in background and more assimilable socially than hostile propaganda allowed. While noting with apprehension the cautious attitude of London businessmen towards land purchase, interpreting it as a device for evading a just contribution 'to the public charge', country gentlemen rarely observed that this trend pre-dated the financial revolution and even the war, and did not anticipate that it would be reversed once a saner balance was achieved between land values and rents and profits from trade or paper investment.[48] The years that immediately followed the Peace of Utrecht did much to prove the pessimists wrong, while the South Sea Bubble and its aftermath completed their re-education. Not merely did the 1720 crisis bring land back into a degree of favour with the City investor it had not known since the 1650s; it also killed for good the dangerous myth that all the 'knavery and cousenage' which the country gentlemen had been

47 Henry St John to Charles Boyle, Earl of Orrery, 9 July 1709, printed in H. T. Dickinson, editor, *The Letters of Henry St John to the Earl of Orrery, 1709–1711, Camden Miscellany* xxvi (1975), p. 146.

48 *The Examiner*, No. 37, 19 April 1711; Lord Bolingbroke, *A Letter to Sir William Wyndham* (1753 [written 1717]), p. 28; E. Chamberlayne, *Angliae Notitia* (1694), p. 583; P. G. M. Dickson, *The Financial Revolution in England . . . 1688–1756* (1967), p. 495; *The Supplement* No. 427, 6–9 Oct. 1710 (manifesto of the four Tory candidates for the city of London); D. W. Jones, 'London Merchants and the Crisis of the 1690s', in P. Clark and P. Slack, editors, *Crisis and Order in English Towns, 1500–1700*, p. 336.

coached into attributing to the monied men was purely the monopoly of the Whig side in the City.

The 'military men' had always been rather more of a paper tiger than the 'monied men', because even at the height of the wars they were readier to translate their professional profits into landed security and assume the social and fiscal obligations of 'men of estates'. And in any case, the quintessential military men of the quarter of a century after the wars were no longer those ogres of Swift's *Examiner*, that favoured minority of 'generals and colonels' who were accused of jostling honest squires out of their borough seats in 1710 and jamming London's streets with their coaches. Far more typical of the early Georgian social scene were the hundreds of half-pay army officers, who spun out precarious genteel existences round the card tables of Tunbridge Wells or Bath, the coffee houses of Stamford, or the assembly rooms of York or Winchester.[49] They were men whose stereotype social peccadillo – hanging out for a well endowed wife from the county society from which most of them originally sprang – was a subject rather for mild satire than for deep social or political unease.

The chief beneficiaries of the army's expansion between 1685 and 1712 were the younger sons of the country gentry. But they were not the sole beneficiaries. In the years of ample opportunity and rapid promotion under William and Anne the new officer corps absorbed both scions of the aristocracy and representatives of the urban bourgeoisie.[50] As well as the great economic advantages it conferred on the gentry, the growth of the professions did bring wider benefits to political society in Augustan England. Indeed, in the context of the long haul towards stability it was important that the gentry, while richly participating in the profits, as in the army, did not monopolize them. For the professions were the most active vehicle of social mobility in this period; and as such they had a crucial contribution to make to that burgeoning 'sense of common identity' within the political nation which concerns us. Most professions recruited widely – far more widely, indeed, than did the army. They were consequently able to provide invaluable milieux in which thousands of men of landed and often armigerous families could find common ground with thousands more from very different backgrounds. Here a community of interest could genuinely be experienced, based on mutual concerns and respect. Professional status itself became a bond that served more tightly to integrate many units of local society. Mutual professional interests even helped to heal the

49 *The Examiner*, No. 13, 2 Nov. 1710; John Macky, *A Journey through England* II (1722), pp. 41–2, 205; Defoe, *Tour* I, pp. 126–7.
50 For the latter, see *Complete English Tradesman* I, p. 247; R. Sedgwick, *op. cit.* I, pp. 479–80.

breach between Anglicans and Dissenters.

We may take this line of argument, in conclusion, one stage further. Professional men, almost by definition, were a predominantly urban breed. And the towns of Augustan England had an important contribution to make to the achievement of stability. The new social and cultural attraction of the provincial urban community proved a remarkably successful solvent of both social and political distinctions within educated society, in both its upper and middling ranks, as our period unfolded. By 1730 contemporaries were far more alive than their predecessors of early Restoration England to the social advantages of the growing town. They had become aware of it as a place where the gentleman's son (or daughter) living on an annuity or on investment income, the lawyer or doctor, the army officer awaiting re-employment, the retired or even still practising merchant, the smart innkeeper, and not least the squire for whom the country life had lost its charm, could live together in a habitat that was congenial, increasingly well appointed and relatively cultivated. Furthermore, these revivified towns were being recognized as places where the genteel could by and large live more cheaply than elsewhere: no negligible consideration in an age of high taxation. Not even the presence of trade or developing industry was yet seen as a deterrent by neighbouring gentry: Shrewsbury, Chester, Derby and Nottingham seemed scarcely less attractive than Bury St Edmunds, Warwick, York and Beverley. The early eighteenth-century provincial town had, in fact, become a social welder of exceptional importance.[51] In London, with its profusion of coffee houses, taverns, mug-houses and clubs, there persisted a good deal of both social and political segregation. But the social commerce of provincial towns and cities between the 1680s and the age of Walpole, as typified by, say, the race meeting, the public concert, or that supreme symbol of the new provincial 'culture', the assembly room, was not the exclusive preserve of the families of the town gentry, the clergy and other professional men, and the neighbouring squires. The assemblies of Sheffield and Birmingham catered alike for merchants, wealthy 'hardwaremen', ironmongers and goldsmiths, for parsons, medical men and attorneys, and for the squires who came in from their grand houses outside the towns. And in Leeds R. G. Wilson has shown us vividly how, in the first half of the eighteenth century 'not only did the close association between gentry and merchants . . . create a society that was far more open than on the Continent, but also there was

51 C. Morris, editor, *The Journeys of Celia Fiennes* (1949 ed.), p. 72; Hist. MSS. Comm. *Portland MSS.* II, p. 308. IV, p. 429; Defoe, *Tour* I, pp. 46, 222, 231, II, pp. 156, 268; Macky, *Journey* II, pp. 153–4, 172, 205.

a perfect mutual understanding of each other's world.'[52] I know of no parallel in any growing or prospering late seventeenth or early eighteenth-century town to the social segregation which the new manufacturers of the 1770s and 1780s were to experience.

Without social stability, as J. H. Plumb has argued, there could have been no political stability. And it has been the contention of this essay that outside London and the southeast the fabric of social stability in England from the 1680s onwards was basically strong and growing steadily more secure. This fabric was woven not from artificial fibres but from natural ones: from the necessary 'sense of common identity' within the political nation itself, and the necessary measure of acquiescence from those who stood outside and below it. They were fibres that owed their toughness and resilience to organic growths, rooted in the social and economic evolution of England since the Civil Wars. Walpole's consensus policies of the 1720s and 1730s possibly made the growths still healthier; but they did not produce them.

Naturally it is impossible to quantify, and difficult even to pinpoint with concrete examples, the precise contribution of demographic stasis or the growing real wages of labour to the process whereby social stability was finally translated by 1730 into political stability. Still more is this true of such intangibles as the expansion of the professions and 'the urban renaissance'. But that such factors made their contributions we can be sure. Of course, provincial party politics delayed the completion of the work, particularly in towns which experienced frequent and often rancorous elections. But the altogether slower pulse-rate of political life after the passing of the Septennial Act in 1716 ensured that even in such parliamentary boroughs the logic of social change could not be resisted. When John Macky visited York soon after George I's accession, the city's 'polite' society was still embarrassed by the convention, established in the acrimonious atmosphere of the previous reign, of holding two weekly assemblies: Monday being a Tory day, Thursday reserved for the Whigs. Such anti-social doings could not however be tolerated in more tranquil times. Lord Carlisle, staunch Whig though he was, took the initiative by 'carrying mixed company' to both assemblies; and Macky learned that 'the officers of the army'

52 See M. Walton, *Sheffield* (4th edn, Sheffield and Wakefield, 1968), pp. 104, 97-106 *passim*, 125-7, 142; C. Gill, *History of Birmingham* I (1952), pp. 60-9 *passim*; M. Rowlands, *Masters and Men in the West Midland Metalware Trades before the Industrial Revolution* (1975), pp. 114-18, for the social 'mix' in these two metal working towns in the early eighteenth century; R. G. Wilson, *Gentlemen Merchants*, pp. 208, 230, 231-2, for Leeds. For the mingling of substantial shopkeepers with professional men and prominent local landed families in the small cathedral city of Wells, see E. Hobhouse, editor, *The Diary of a West Country Physician* (1934).

had subsequently played their part in the healing process by themselves 'making no distinction'. Although the rival gatherings had merged harmoniously long before it, the appropriate epilogue was played out in 1730 when work began on the building of Lord Burlington's splendid assembly rooms, one of the urban showpieces of the north.[53] Of a thousand bricks such as these, small though each may have been, was much of the solid edifice of early Georgian political stability constructed.

53 Macky, *Journey* (1722) II, p. 211; *V.C.H. Yorkshire: The City of York* (1961), p. 531; P. Borsay, 'The English urban renaissance: the development of provincial urban culture *c.* 1680 – *c.* 1760', *Social History* V (1977), p. 582.

POSTSCRIPT

Reference was made above (pp. 253-4 and n. 8; cf. below, p. 277, n. 2) to the work of the Cambridge Group for the History of Population and Social Structure. In 1981, E.A. Wrigley and R.S. Schofield, in *The Population History of England, 1541-1871: A Reconstruction*, made the fruits of the Cambridge Group's massive demographic labours accessible in print. Of many critiques to appear subsequently, the most helpful, as well as the most intelligible, to the semi-numerate layman, is that by M.W. Flinn, in *Economic History Review*, 35, 1982, pp. 443-57.

(Edited by H.T. Dickinson)

*The other scholars engaged in the discussion that follows were Professors
J. Cannon, W.A. Speck and N. McCord, and Drs F. O'Gorman and J. Derry.*

Discussion on this paper focused on three issues: the achievement of
political stability, the economic and social foundations of Holmes's
thesis, and the reasons for the absence of popular radicalism in an age of
intense party rivalry.

Cannon wondered whether Holmes was retreating from the position
which he had taken up in earlier works when he had been at pains to
stress the intensity of party rivalry during Anne's reign.[1] Holmes saw no
reason to retract his earlier claim that Whigs and Tories had then been
sharply divided on a whole range of issues, but was prepared to tone
down his previously unqualified emphasis on how divided English
society had been. In looking at the period from a different vantage and
with different priorities in mind he had become more aware of the long-
term social and economic factors which helped to promote stability.
Neither the rage of party nor the 'Divided Society' of which he and
Speck had written in 1967 were illusory; but it was possible that in the
past he had overstressed Whig—Tory disputes as a *cause* of political
instability, whereas he would now concede that they were rather a
symptom. Some progress towards political stability had clearly been
made before 1714. There was much greater ministerial stability during
the last decade of Anne's reign than in the 1690s. The queen's ministers
only lost one Commons division in the period 1708 to 1714 and the relations between Crown and parliament had been put on a fairly even keel
before 1714.

O'Gorman was not convinced that there was a divided society in the
reigns of William III and Queen Anne when there were so many signs of
social and economic stability. In his view the similarities and continui-
ties between the periods before and after 1714 were more significant
than the contrasts. Holmes, supported by Speck, was not prepared to go
so far. Both saw a marked change in the political situation between
Anne's reign and the 1720s. Party divisions before 1714 ran very deep
on a number of issues – on religion, the war, and the succession to the
throne in particular. While politicians had made some progress in
adapting to post-1688 circumstances, they were not in agreement on
these crucial issues. Holmes suggested that the governmental instability

1 Particularly in *The Divided Society: Party Conflict in England 1694–1716*
(1967, with W. A. Speck) and *British Politics in the Age of Anne* (1967).

of Anne's reign was due in part to the refusal of the queen and her leading political managers, Godolphin and Harley, to submit to one-party rule. St John and the high Tories might well have instituted a one-party oligarchy after 1710 as ruthlessly as the Whigs had done after 1714 had Harley and the queen not frustrated their ambitions.

The discussions on the social and economic evidence presented by Holmes were more central to the thesis of his paper. Speck questioned whether the demographic evidence was as firm as Holmes supposed. (pp. 253-5) Population statistics for this period were not entirely reliable; estimates for the population of England and Wales in 1688 varied between 5,200,000 and 5,800,000; 'this is so large a discrepancy that we cannot say there is a firm base to start from'. Holmes accepted that population figures were only estimates and for this reason he had preferred to base his case on the general trends of demographic change. His figures were largely gathered from Anne Whiteman and the group of Cambridge scholars engaged in research on population.[2] They had proved that the population of England and Wales was larger in 1660 than historians had previously thought, that the population was fairly stable in the period 1660 to 1690, grew moderately in the years from 1690 to 1720, and then levelled off again during the following 20 years. Speck feared that Holmes was asking his readers to accept the Cambridge estimates prematurely as a new orthodoxy.

Speck went on to ask whether it was significant that demographic growth reached a plateau in the period of political stability whereas a faster rate of growth had occurred during the era of political instability. Dickinson added that commercial and financial growth were also slower in the years of political stability than they had been in the previous decades. Holmes admitted the superficial attractions of these arguments but he would not like to draw any sharp distinction between the social and economic developments before and after 1714. Although he accepted that the financial revolution of the 1690s had caused most trouble in the reigns of William III and Queen Anne, he preferred in general to consider the period from 1680 to 1740 as a whole when examining social and economic developments. He also disputed any suggestion that the economy was stagnant between 1720 and 1740;

2 There is an extensive note on the work of the Cambridge Group for the History of Population and Social Structure in P. Laslett, *The World We Have Lost* (2nd edn, paperback, 1971), pp. 254–7. An important article by Dr Anne Whiteman of Lady Margaret Hall, Oxford is in *Statesmen, Scholars and Merchants: Essays in Eighteenth-Century History Presented to Dame Lucy Sutherland* (1973) under the title 'The Census that Never Was: a Problem in Authorship and Dating.' For a summary of recent findings, see D. C. Coleman, *The Economy of England, 1450–1750* (1977).

Little's thesis was far too extreme.[3] Growth was slower, but in almost all sectors of the economy it was continuous during these decades: 'The general trend was inexorably upwards'. He accepted Dickinson's point that slower economic growth might have been a factor in promoting political stability in the age of Walpole, but was not convinced that faster economic growth in the earlier decades had been a significant cause of political instability. On the whole, Holmes believed that the results of the commercial revolution had been beneficial for society at large.

McCord thought that Holmes's case could actually be strengthened by showing that there was not necessarily any conflict of interest between those involved in agriculture, manufacturing and mining. Indeed, it was often landed men who developed all three sectors of the economy. Most towns, even those experiencing significant growth, were still quite small and were closely involved with the social and economic life of their rural hinterland. Holmes agreed with these observations. In most areas there were close social and economic links between the urban merchant oligarchy and the local landed gentry. While several towns such as Liverpool and Birmingham did grow significantly, no town, except London, had a population larger than 35,000 to 40,000 in 1730.

Cannon wondered how significant the growth of the professions was by 1720, and how great were the opportunities for profitable employment for the younger sons of the gentry. (pp. 265-9)   Some professions —medicine, teaching, even the law for example—were not very palatable for the gentry because of their long training and uncertain financial rewards. Holmes replied that the slowing down of the growth in the professions by the 1720s had to be seen against the background of a relatively static population. Certainly after 1713 there were fewer opportunities in the army and navy while opportunities for a career in the Church did not grow significantly. There were, however, more opportunities in teaching. Tutors employed by rich families could be rewarded quite handsomely.

There was considerable discussion of the absence of popular radicalism in the period 1680 to 1740 (pp. 258-62). It was agreed that there had certainly been many disturbances of a bread-and-butter kind, such as turnpike riots, press gang riots and industrial disorders. While these could be regarded as expressions of dissatisfaction with social and economic developments, they were not overtly political and offered no serious challenge to the governing élite. O'Gorman drew attention to Hayter's work which showed that most riots and demonstrations at that period were short-lived: 'we are talking about popular unrest rather

3   A. J. Little, *Deceleration in the Eighteenth-Century British Economy* (1976).

than radicalism, which presupposes some ideological objective.'[4] McCord stressed that the forces of law and order generally handled the disturbances with considerable skill. Speck objected that the Riot Act of 1715 had certainly been a panic measure. Holmes accepted this, but argued that the act put the military firmly under the control of the civil magistrates. The troops were less likely to resort to violent measures to suppress riots after 1715 but, once ordered to use force, were inclined to act more firmly than before.

Dickinson remarked that popular radicalism in the earlier seventeenth century had not been led by men drawn from the lower orders but by men who possessed some property, enjoyed some education and resented being excluded from political, social and economic advancement. After 1688 opportunities for upward mobility did exist and these syphoned off the potential leaders of popular radicalism. O'Gorman, Cannon and Derry agreed with Dickinson that the governing élite was determined that its own internal political disagreements must not be pushed so far as to give the lower orders a chance to make political mischief: it had clearly learned the political lesson of the 1640s.

Holmes accepted this line of reasoning. He conceded that, in retrospect, it was the most serious deficiency in his whole argument and that it was the single most important modification that he would wish to make. The bulk of the gentry, even when shut out of power, were not willing to whip up popular support in order to challenge the political system and to undermine social and economic stability. He had argued that economic prosperity meant that the gentry did not wish to encourage popular unrest, while this same prosperity meant that both the lower and 'middling' orders lacked the serious and sustained grievances which might have provoked them into radical political action. It was significant that there were far fewer riots, especially food riots, in this period than in the later eighteenth century.[5]

Dickinson also pointed out that the political radicalism of the 1640s had been stimulated and influenced by the religious radicalism of the period. In the decades covered by Holmes's paper there was little religious radicalism of this type. The High-Church clergy were certainly prepared to stir up popular hostility to Dissenters and to Methodists, but they did not preach political radicalism or social revolution. Holmes agreed. His own research on the Sacheverell disturbances of 1710 convinced him that the clergy and gentry, who had helped to foment the disorder, were confident that the trouble could be contained: 'they kept popular emotions on a fairly tight chain and it was their chain'.

4 Tony Hayter, *The Army and the Crowd in mid-Georgian England* (1978).
5 J. Stevenson, *Popular Disturbances in England, 1700–1870* (1979).

The Right Honble Sr Thomas Parker
K.^t Lord Chief Justice of the Court of Queens Bench.

7. Social Mobility through the Law:

Sir Thomas Parker, son of a small-town Staffordshire attorney, after his appointment as Lord Chief Justice of the Queen's Bench, 1710. One of his first tasks was to preside over the treason trial of the three Sacheverell rioters (pp.232n., 233 et seq.). Formerly the leading Commons manager at Sacheverell's trial, the eloquent Parker was later created Baron (1716) and 1st Earl of Macclesfield (1721) and became George I's Lord Chancellor (1718-25).

Engraving by J. Simon from the painting by Thomas Murray.
The Ashmolean Museum

11

GREGORY KING AND THE SOCIAL STRUCTURE
OF PRE-INDUSTRIAL ENGLAND [1]

DESPITE the rich and exciting work of recent years, the social history of England between the Restoration and the Industrial Revolution still bears something of a hangdog look, scarcely warranting, as yet, the cosmic conclusions and ferocious controversies to which students of early Stuart and early nineteenth-century society have grown accustomed. Yet, thanks to the work of one remarkable Englishman, who was born in 1648 and died in 1712, there is one aspect of this pre-industrial period—its social structure—on which we are all happy to pontificate. Gregory King's table of ranks and degrees, on which in the last resort so much of this confidence rests, has now acquired a unique cachet. The continual reproduction in post-war textbooks of this famous document,[2] which we think of as King's 'social table' but which he described as his 'Scheme of the Income and Expense of the Several Famillies of England', is just the most obvious symptom of its dominant historiographical influence.

It is my belief, however, that this trust has been misplaced; that King has been responsible for much complacency and confusion about the pre-industrial social structure; indeed that, historiographically speaking, one of the worst things that could have happened for the study of that society was that in 1696 one of the cleverest, most original men of his day should have chosen to write down, on one page of a celebrated manuscript work, what *seems* to be a cameo of the social structure of his day.

A few amber lights, admittedly, have flashed on the table from

[1] A preliminary version of this paper was delivered to the Cambridge Social and Economic History seminar in February 1976. I am grateful for the suggestions made on that occasion by Professor D. C. Coleman and Mr Peter Laslett. I am also indebted to Professors C. D. Chandaman and Henry Horwitz, Mr Clyve Jones, Mr Alan Downie and Drs J. V. Beckett, M. B. Rowlands and W. A. Speck for helping in various ways to further my understanding of King and his work.

[2] In whole or in part. The sequence runs to at least a dozen, beginning with G. M. Trevelyan, *English Social History* (2nd edn., London, 1946) and G. N. Clark, *The Wealth of England* (London, 1946), and ending with P. Mathias, *The First Industrial Nation* (London, 1970) and J. D. Chambers, *Population, Economy and Society in pre-Industrial England* (Oxford, 1972).

time to time: Mingay's against the incomes of the aristocracy, for instance, and Mathias's against the concealment of important occupational groups within King's 'families' and blanket categories.[3] In 1967, J. P. Cooper iconoclastically suggested that the 'evident uncertainty' in King's mind, revealed by his working papers, about the numbers of paupers, farmers and freeholders raised some queries against his methods as a social analyst.[4] But we have been reluctant to take these hints: inhibited, no doubt, by the manifest admiration for King's achievement which even his cautious scrutineers display. Mathias, for instance, can still describe the table as 'the most precise picture of the British economy and social structure just before the industrial revolution'.[5] And more recently Mr Laslett has paid glowing tribute to 'the first man to study the structure of a pre-industrial society . . . on lines at all similar to the social scientific procedures of our own day', compelling respect by the official status of his sources as well as the solidity of his methods, and producing findings of 'the highest authority'.[6]

Why should dependence on King have remained so total? It is true that his work as a social analyst towers over an extended plain mid-way between two peaks: Thomas Wilson's *State of England*, written in 1600, and Patrick Colquhoun's *A State of Indigence*, in 1806.[7] Scattered over this plain are occasional small hills,[8] but only one mountain. But a more insidious cause of the veneration bestowed on King's table is that he speaks the language of our own

[3] G. E. Mingay, *English Landed Society in the Eighteenth Century* (London, 1963), pp. 20–22; P. Mathias, *op. cit.*, pp. 25, 29, pointing especially to the concealment of servants and manufacturers (*cf. idem*, 'The Social Structure in the Eighteenth Century: a Calculation by Joseph Massie', *Econ. Hist. Rev.*, 2nd ser., x, 1957). See also P. Laslett, *The World we have Lost* (2nd edn., London, 1971), p. 270, n. 38 —an aside which expresses some uneasiness at the danger that 'our view of pre-industrial social structure as a whole', being too King-centred, may prove to 'be true of the 1690s only'; and the general caution against 'the frankly uncertain statistical foundations' of much of King's political arithmetic in Colin Brooks, 'Taxation, Finance and Public Opinion, 1688–1714' (Cambridge Univ. Ph.D. thesis, 1971), p. 276, n. 1.

[4] J. P. Cooper, 'The Social Distribution of Land and Men in England, 1436–1700', *Econ. Hist. Rev.* 2nd ser., xx, 1967, pp. 432–34.

[5] *First Industrial Nation*, p. 23 (my italics).

[6] Introduction to *The Earliest Classics: John Graunt and Gregory King* (Pioneers of Demography series, London, 1973), pp. [2], [6]–[8]. Mr Laslett adds: 'He seems to have been commissioned by the Government, and, within certain limits, he was undoubtedly believed by the Government'.

[7] For Wilson's work see Camden Society, 3rd ser., lii, 1936, ed. F. J. Fisher. Colquhoun's treatise (1806) provided for the year 1803 a structural and statistical breakdown of the society of his day as ambitious as King's and evidently influenced by the latter's approach.

[8] Notably those of Edward Chamberlayne (social estimates included in the numerous edns. of *Angliae Notitia*, 1669–1702), and Joseph Massie (see above, n. 3).

generation. He speaks not with the tongues of men but with the symbols of mathematicians. Is it not this that makes us so peculiarly receptive today to King: that he chose to adopt in the 1690s the quantitative approach to social analysis? On to that one celebrated page of manuscript King crammed no fewer than 285 lovely, hard figures, comprising *in toto* 1,015 digits. In an age which deifies the statistic and grovels before the graph, King can hardly miss.

To reinforce our confidence, his credentials as a demographer have now been most impressively endorsed;[9] and the consequent temptation to attach the same weight to his skeletal picture of society as we do to his painstaking calculations of population size and trends is bound to be a hard one to resist. And so, we permit ourselves the usual token laughs at his leverets and his medieval history; we may even admit that the frailty of his commercial and comparative statistics has been exposed;[10] yet we take it as read that when Gregory King told posterity about the social structure of late seventeenth-century England, he knew what he was talking about.

But did he? What were his sources of information? And how scientifically did he use them? Can we be sure that he even intended his 'ranks, degrees, titles and qualifications' to be a realistic representation of the framework of his own society? And if not this, then what was the table's purpose, in the context of the whole work—the *Natural and Political Observations*—of which it is such a small part? Would it not have alarmed King deeply (adamant as he was against personally publishing anything of his major work in his own lifetime)[11] to know that these columns of figures, with their cryptic categories, would serve a generation eleven times removed from his own as a model? And can we conceivably justify any King-based models of today which are applied not simply to a once-for-all situation but to an essentially static pre-industrial social pattern?

[9] Notably by D. V. Glass, 'Two papers on Gregory King', in D. V. Glass and D. E. C. Eversley, *Population in History* (London, 1965). See T. H. Hollingsworth, *Historical Demography* (London, 1969), pp. 81–88, esp. 85–87 for the only serious recent attempt to blacken King's demographic reputation; Anne Whiteman, 'The Census that Never Was', in A. Whiteman, J. S. Bromley and P. G. M. Dickson (eds.), *Statesmen, Scholars and Merchants* (Oxford, 1973), for a refined but devastating scholarly demolition of Hollingsworth's case.

[10] See R. Davis, 'English Foreign Trade, 1660–1700', *Econ. Hist. Rev.* 2nd ser., vii, 1954, p. 155, n. 6; E. Le Roy Ladurie, 'Les comptes fantastiques de Gregory King', *Annales E.S.C.* 23, 1968, pp. 1086–1102 (Professor D. C. Coleman kindly drew my attention to the latter article).

[11] Charles Davenant, *An Essay upon the Probable Methods of making the People Gainers in the Balance of Trade*, 1st edn. (London, 1699), pp. 23–24; British Library, (B.L.), Harl. MS. 6944, fo 117: Leibniz to Samuel Stebbing, Hanover, 4 September 1708 (postscript: 'je vous prie Monsieur de faire mes complimens... à Mons. King qui obligeroit le public s'il publiois ses calculs politiques').

These are some of the questions to be considered in this paper. An indispensable key to virtually all of them is the problem of King's intentions: of what were the general impulses which drove him to the study of political arithmetic, his specific objectives in writing the *Observations*, and above all his reason for including in it a 'social table'. Our *point d'appui* throughout, in fact, will be the man himself. Although biographical material is patchy[12] there are four things of particular relevance to our questions which his papers do disclose: his frustrated ambition; his deep conservatism; his obsessive, ensnaring passion for figures; and yet with all this, a certain underlying humility. These personal facets will provide the framework of much of my argument.

In the first place, why in 1695 did King quite suddenly develop, at the age of 46, an absorbing interest in 'political arithmetic'?[13] The clue lies in his frustrated professional ambitions. Although late in life he became a public servant,[14] his principal professional career was centred from 1677 on the College of Heralds,[15] where in 1688 he became Lancaster Herald. Dugdale apart, Gregory King was arguably the most accomplished and authoritative herald of the seventeenth century. Yet twice in his career he had to suffer the most bruising setbacks to his just professional aspirations and pride. It is the first of these occasions which is crucial for us. During 1694 and in the winter of 1694–95 King twice fell foul of the Earl Marshall.

---

[12] Brief sketches of his life and professional career have been written in this century by Thompson Cooper (*D.N.B.*) and G. E. Barnett (introduction to *Two Tracts by Gregory King*, Baltimore, 1936). More illuminating and very carefully researched is the account by D. V. Glass (see 'Two papers', n. 9 above). All owe a good deal to King's first and still fullest biographer, Sir George Chalmers (1802). The greater part of King's surviving correspondence is in B.L. Harl. MS. 6815, 6821, 6837, 6944 and 7525. There are also some items of biographical interest in P.R.O., T.64/302 (King Papers) and T.1/130; in the unpublished papers of Robert Harley (B.L. Loan 29); in one of King's business letter books for the years 1704–07 (B.L. Loan 57/73, Bathurst Papers); and in his 'Staffordshire Notebook', 1679–80 (*Collections for a History of Staffordshire*, ed. by G. P. Mander for William Salt Arch. Soc., 1919, London, 1920). King's autobiography (Bodleian Library, MS. Rawlinson C.514, printed in J. Dallaway, *Inquiries into the Origin and Progress of the Science of Heraldry*, Gloucester, 1793) unfortunately stops in 1694.

[13] There is not a hint of such an interest in his autobiography, down to 1694; though his 'Staffordshire Notebook' (see n. 12 above) reveals an early awareness of the size and social composition of communities.

[14] He was by then 54. See p. 290 below.

[15] Having earlier spent five years in the 1660s as clerk-assistant to Sir William Dugdale, he was appointed Rouge Dragon Poursuivant in 1677 and Registrar of the College in 1684. King was also a man of many other parts, as his epitaph properly records: an expert map-maker and surveyor; something of a property developer; a most polished etcher and engraver; and a mathematician (his father's occupation).

As a result, he found himself not merely anchored to the position of Lancaster Herald, but removed from the Registrarship of the College; and when, shortly afterwards, a charge of embezzlement was brought against him in connection with royal funeral fees, King's disillusionment with the heraldic career reached an extremity.[16] It is no coincidence that it was in that year, 1695, that he sat down and wrote his autobiographical essay.[17] It was a watershed in his life: a time for stocktaking, then for forging boldly ahead to deploy, in a completely fresh field, those remarkable talents he well knew he possessed.

But if the personal impulse was powerful, the intellectual and political climate of 1695 was singularly appropriate for its accommodation. In Britain 'the art of reasoning by figures, upon things relating to government', as a contemporary described political arithmetic,[18] was a novel science. Its founding father was generally held at the time to be Sir William Petty,[19] and as late as 1688 its distinguished practitioners had been few. However, over the next six or seven years what had started as a largely academic study received the stamp of deadly earnestness from the War of the League of Augsburg. And in 1695, exactly at the time when King was ripe for a new intellectual challenge, this war had reached its climax. The cost in blood, taxation and commerce had already far surpassed that of any war in living memory. A national bank had been created, and a funded National Debt inaugurated. And amid all the prevailing fever and uncertainty, an increasingly Whiggish ministry was besieged by platoons of optimistic 'projectors', hatching and peddling a variety of new money-raising schemes.

What government fiscal policy needed at this juncture, above all else, was a rational foundation of reliable information. Thus far William III's ministers had been heavily dependent on Petty's work for their estimates of the size of the population and the total wealth of the nation, and the results had not been reassuring.[20] In any case,

[16] Dallaway, App. p. xlvi *et seq.*; G. P. Mander, intro. to 'Staffs Notebook', *loc. cit.*, p. 193.

[17] See n. 12 above. The essay parades past achievements as a backcloth for present discontents.

[18] *The Political and Commercial Works of . . . Charles D'Avenant, LL.D.*, ed. Sir C. Whitworth (London, 1771), i, 127 [hereafter Davenant, *Works*].

[19] King himself would not have agreed. He looked to John Graunt as his mentor. See Glass, 'Two papers', *loc. cit.*, pp. 162–63.

[20] Petty's *Verbum Sapienti*, in which his original population estimate for England and Wales of 6 mns appeared, was written in 1666 but not published until 1691. Meanwhile he had produced in the 1680s at least three revised estimates, based on Hearth Tax returns, ranging from 7.0 mn to around 7.4 mn. The figure of 7 mn was most widely entertained. Greater London Council Library, the 'Burns Journal' of Gregory King, hereafter cited as B.J., pp. 120, 121(3), 275. (The Burns Journal

a current tendency for the Commons to resort regularly to graduated poll taxes and to excises made it desirable that the government should also have clearer insight into how numbers and wealth were distributed between different sectors of society.[21] In this social territory, however, just as in the demographic field, the working politicians were still groping around in a fog of uncertainty and confusion.[22]

The advance signal of relief came during 1695 when a former Excise official, Dr Charles Davenant, lifted the whole debate on fiscal policy on to a new plane by publishing his *Essay on Ways and Means of Supplying the War*. This marked the beginning of a spate of constructive writing, and not least of a further stream from Davenant's own fluent pen. His 'Memoriall concerning the Coyn of England' and 'Memoriall concerning Creditt', for instance, followed rapidly in November 1695 and July 1696, and were privately submitted to leading ministers.[23] But the most crucial significance of the *Essays on Ways and Means* lay in its effect on Gregory King. Quite probably he was already friendly with Davenant; and they certainly remained on the closest terms from now until King's death.[24] Over the next few years the two men were to exchange ideas and information freely, and during that time Davenant frequently picked King's brains without much shame.[25] Yet at the outset it was King who

---

is photographically reproduced in *The Earliest Classics*—see n. 6 above); C. Brooks, *op. cit.*, pp. 312–13. In the early 1690s two members of the Royal Society, John Houghton and Thomas Neale, had supplied Parliament with fresh data, but in the latter's population calculations, at least, little confidence could be reposed. See H. Horwitz (ed.), *Parliamentary Diary of Narcissus Luttrell* (Oxford, 1972), pp. 112, 123, 141; W. Cobbett, *The Parliamentary History of England*, v, App. x, for Houghton's *Account of the Acres and Houses* (London, 1693).

[21] 'In these sort of speculations not only the quantity but the quality of the inhabitants must be duly pondered. They must be divided into their several ranks and classes'. Davenant, *Works*, ii, 173.

[22] See *Luttrell's Parl. Diary*, pp. 144, 160, for the Commons' finance debates of January 1692 during which Paul Foley and Sir Edward Seymour differed by an incredible 100,000 in their estimates of the number of gentlemen in England.

[23] The first was addressed to Godolphin, First Lord of the Treasury, 'in obedience to your Lordshipp's commands', and the second to the Treasury Commissioners in general. There are copies in London Univ. Library, MS. 60, Davenant's MS. tracts, 1695–96; also in B.L. Harl. MS. 1223, fos 71–95, 115–56, which suggests they either came into Robert Harley's possession directly, in the 1690s, or were acquired by him later, *via* Gregory King (Harley acquired many of King's papers after the latter's death in 1712).

[24] See, e.g., a letter from Davenant to King, dated 'Nov. 17th, 1710. My birthday', and signed 'Your most affectionate servant', in P.R.O. T.64/302.

[25] The full extent of Davenant's indebtedness is revealed by comparing his unpublished tracts—for example, the two cited above (n. 23) and the 'Essay on Publick Virtue' (London, 1696: submitted to Godolphin and Shrewsbury)—with

was the chief debtor. Quite apart from the general stimulus it afforded him in directing his pent-up energies and frustrations into the exciting channel of political arithmetic, the Lancaster Herald owed specifically to the *Essay on Ways and Means* the base figure, culled by Davenant from the very last set of Hearth Tax records, of the number of houses in England and Wales in the year 1690. This figure, of just over 1,300,000 houses, was to be the point of departure for all King's own subsequent researches, even into social structure.[26]

As he worked away with consuming energy at the groundwork for his masterpiece, for much of 1695 and on into 1696, he did so with two overriding objectives in mind. He lays them down in the very first sentence of the *Observations*: 'to be well appriz'd of the true state and condition' of England, '*in the two main articles, of its people, and wealth*'. These he considered the twin foundations of sound government at any time; but as imperative necessities 'at a time when a long and very expensive war against a potent Monarch . . . seems to be at its crisis'. On these foundations—an accurate calculation of the population and as close an estimate as he could reach of the national wealth and expenditure over the first seven years of the war —he proposed to build all else: his forecasts of future trends, if the war continued; his fiscal recommendations, the chief *raison d'être* of his work; his careful comparisons between England's position and that of France and Holland.

What is more, King approached his main objectives with a very clear order of priorities in mind. Top priority went to cracking the toughest nut of all, the population nut. Next, he probed towards various general conclusions about the national income and wealth, in peace and war.[27] Only then did he attempt an anatomy of the

---

King's notebooks and *Observations*. In the 'Essay on Publick Virtue' wholesale borrowings which had started out purportedly as a common endeavour, or as what 'upon a nice & strict inquiry *wee* find very strong reason to believe' (see London Univ. MS. 60, pp. 113, 114) ended, rather disgracefully, as 'these observations [which] *I* have gathered by long enquiry and study in these matters . . .' *Ibid.*, p. 270.

[26] King began the first chapter of his *Natural and Political Observations* with the statement, taken directly from Davenant, that 'the number of houses in the kingdom, as charged in the books of the hearth office, at Lady-day, 1690, were . . . 1,319,215'. G. Chalmers, *An Estimate of the Comparative Strength of Great Britain* (London, 1804), App., p. 33. (All references to the *Observations* hereafter are to the Chalmers version, 1804 edn., cited: Chalmers, App.) That King never checked this figure personally (see p.298 and n. 81 below) is a truly extraordinary fact in view of John Houghton's conflicting evidence on the same point, published in 1693 (see n. 20 above).

[27] Under three heads: (a) the rental and capital value of its lands and property (calculated at 18 years' purchase), (b) the annual produce of its trade, (c) the

nation's income and expenditure, in details that could be roughly related to various points of the social scale and set alongside a corresponding social breakdown of his population total. His analysis of the social structure was at no time envisaged as an end in itself. Rather he saw this 'scheme' of income and expenditure as an ambitious top crust to be superimposed on the foundations already laid: something that might enable a more sophisticated superstructure of proposals to be erected above them. That this was the way King thought, and worked, is beyond doubt. The evidence contained in Davenant's 'Memoriall concerning Creditt', submitted to the Treasury lords in July 1696,[28] is in itself convincing; and it is supported to the hilt by the two major survivals from King's own working notebooks of the years 1695 to 1700.

From the 'Memoriall' it is obvious that, while King had completed his demographic calculations long before the midsummer of 1696 and had communicated much of their detail to his friend (as he had to others),[29] Davenant had only had the benefit of the herald's unfinished work and very tentative conclusions in dealing with the annual income and outgoings of the nation—even in general terms.[30] In view of this it is no surprise to discover that the notebook embodying some of King's first explorations into political arithmetic, early in 1695, contains only two oblique and speculative ventures into the social structure: to call them ranging shots would be complimentary.[31] Much more revealing is that the same experimental pattern, and the very same order of priorities, is repeated in King's later and far more compendious journal, now known as the Burns Journal, in which the first entries were made in the summer of 1695.[32]

This journal must have been the immediate predecessor of another (now, alas, lost) in which the very last weeks of preparation for the writing of the *Observations* were recorded. Even so, the Journal's 295 pages[33] cover almost every inch of the ground brought within the

---

'stock of the Kingdom' in a variety of commodities, from coin and plate to livestock and industrial products.

[28] Though much of it was probably drafted a month or two earlier. See B.J., p. 221 *et seq.*

[29] *E.g.* to George Stepney in April 1696, and (in an earlier and somewhat different version) to a prominent peer in the government, probably Lord Godolphin, late in 1695. B.J., pp. 171, 269, 271, 275.

[30] *Cf.* London Univ. MS. 60, pp. 113–19 *passim* with Chalmers, App., pp. 47, 49, 61 and B.J., pp. 247, 261, 270–71.

[31] P.R.O., T.64/302: '[Com]putations of the Numbe[r] of People, etc. by Greg^y. King 1695', pp. 14, 18v. (hereafter P.R.O., T.64/302: notebook).

[32] See n. 20 above. The journal continues into 1696, with some entries added as late as 1700.

[33] The pagination runs from 1 to 291, but the unnumbered page opposite p. 1

compass of the end-product; and only 15 bear in any way on the social structure.[34] In some of them the social material is fragmentary and incidental; even the most extended piece of social analysis in the journal was plainly regarded by its author as no more than a preparatory exercise.[35] In the latter part of the journal there is, significantly, a batch of truly definitive material which, having passed through at least a year of refining fires, was communicated by King to Davenant in July 1696[36]—just too late to be incorporated into the 'Memoriall'. It supplemented at great length the demographic data which Davenant had received long before, with what was, in effect, the substance of at least six further chapters of the *Observations*. But it included no social table, nor anything remotely resembling one. Indeed the Burns Journal must leave any careful student convinced that it was only after the midsummer of 1696 that Gregory King (almost as an afterthought?) decided to put the icing on the otherwise almost-finished cake of his great creation, by drawing up the full 'Scheme of the Income and Expense of the Several Families', as we now know it; and having made the decision, proceeded to re-order these calculations, by taking them back from the year 1695, to which (up to now) he had invariably made them relevant, *to the year 1688*.

Something which has attracted only spasmodic notice is that although the bulk of the factual and statistical data contained in the *Observations* is related in one way or another to the mid 1690s, the famous social table itself is, as we are explicitly told, 'calculated for the Year 1688'. Why was this? The answer has the closest bearing on the value of King's table to us as a social document; for it is intimately connected with the second major facet of the man himself which I suggested deserves our attention, namely, his conservatism.

Gregory King was a deeply conservative man, in two senses. In the first place, he was politically conservative. Bluntly, he was a thorough, divine right Tory; and it is really very odd that this point has never appeared to be of much significance to historians. As his

---

is utilized and three sets of 'pages 120–21' are included, only one of the four supernumerary pages being a blank.

[34] B.J., pp. 65–67, 70–75, 209, 246, 265, 270, 280–81.

[35] B.J., pp. 280–81. It occurs among a long series of 'Conclusions or Aphorisms' drawn up in the last 2–3 months of 1695 (the statistical conclusions concerning England relate explicitly to Michaelmas 1695). Although in many respects fuller in information than the 'social table' of the *Observations* it omits such crucial occupational groups as freeholders and farmers, army and navy officers, soldiers and seamen.

[36] Or perhaps in June—King does not seem quite certain which month, on recollection. See B.J., pp. 221–30, inclusive: indexed on p. 285 'Observations upon the People of England in a kind of Treatise as given to Dr. Davt.'.

autobiography shows, King was a warm admirer of Charles II in that monarch's closing years, and was distressed by his death; and although, as a good professional, he was to conform to the post-Revolution regime in 1689 and officiate at the coronation of William and Mary, he admitted to having had some sympathy with James II.[37] It was not entirely coincidental that both the major setbacks of his heraldic career occurred at periods of Whig ascendancy;[38] still less was it coincidence that, despite his obvious inclination in the mid-nineties to serve the government,[39] he had to wait until the Tory resurgence following Queen Anne's accession for his first mark of official favour, the secretaryship of the Commission of Public Accounts.[40] Almost certainly he owed it to the rising star of Robert Harley, who had shown distinct interest in King's major work in 1696–97, after its completion.[41] Thus King's career shows marked parallels with that of his friend Davenant, another unabashed Tory.[42]

[37] Dallaway, xxxvi, xxxviii–ix; *cf.* Chalmers, *op. cit.*, App. 'Notices of the Life of Gregory King', pp. 16, 18.

[38] Especially striking was the second, in 1709–10, when his claims to the plum vacancy of Clarenceux King of Arms were rejected in favour of Sir John Vanbrugh, the Marlboroughs' architect at Blenheim and the darling of the politically-influential Kit-Cat Club. See Chalmers, App., pp. 25–26; B.L. Harl. MS. 7525, fos 40–41: King to Harley, 2 January 1710[–11]; 'Staffs Notebook', *loc. cit.*, p. 197, for King's 1679 estimate of Clarenceux's total emoluments as second only to those of Garter King, viz. at £230 p.a. 'clear', plus lodgings and visitation fees, and a Herald's income, 'clear', at only £50 p.a., plus lodgings valued at £20 p.a.

[39] See his draft letter to Sir Stephen Fox, 19 December 1695, in B.J. p. 241.

[40] The Commission's first Secretary in the 1690s was George Tollet. King's appointment, worth £100 p.a., was made in April 1702. (See J. A. Downie, 'The Commission of Public Accounts and the formation of the Country Party', *Eng. Hist. Rev.*, xci, 1976, p. 38, n. 3; N. Luttrell, *A Brief Historical Relation of State Affairs*, Oxford, 1857, v, 160; B.L. Add. MS. 29568, fo. 89: King to Hatton, 18 August 1702.) He held the post in both periods of this Tory-dominated body's operation in Anne's reign, 1702–04 and 1711–12. In between times he served in a £300-a-year job as Secretary to the Commissioners of Army Accounts, and in 1708 was appointed one of three commissioners to state the debts of King William III. (Bodl. MS. Rawlinson A.289, for his official correspondence 1705–06; Luttrell, *Brief Hist. Rel.* vi, 314.)

[41] See letters from King to Harley, 1697 and 1711, in B.L. Loan 29/298M, especially that of 8 December 1697; B.L. Harl. MS. 7575: King to Harley (copy), 2 January 1711; National Lib. of Australia, Kashnor MSS: copy of the *Natural and Political Observations*, 1697, bearing Harley's 'Queries and Observations' and King's replies to them. This latter document has been consulted on microfilm, hereafter cited, Kashnor MSS., *N.P.O.*

[42] For all his furious activity with the pen in the 1690s, Davenant did not re-enter government service, as Inspector General of Imports, until 1705. He had, however, refused Godolphin's offer of a post in the Excise in November 1702. H.M.C. *Portland MSS.* iv, 52: Godolphin to Harley, 21 November, 24 November 1702. In general see D. A. G. Waddell's biographical essay in *Econ. Hist. Rev.* 2nd ser., xi, 1958–59, pp. 279–88.

However, he and Davenant shared something more than the ups and downs of the political see-saw. They nursed a mutual suspicion of Continental entanglements. Above all, they shared an instinctive conviction that no protracted war could possibly have other than ill effects for England: ill effects on her wealth, on her economy, on her social well-being and even on her population growth. In chapter 10 of the *Natural and Political Observations*—the great statistical *tour de force* entitled 'The State of the Nation, Anno 1695'—King charted year by year what he implicitly believed had been England's descent down the slippery slope towards penury since 1688. His conclusion was stark: 'That, after the year 1695, the taxes actually raised will fall short every year, more and more, to that degree, that *the war cannot well be sustained beyond the year 1698 upon the foot it now stands...*'[43] Davenant, in his 1696 'Memoriall', had made precisely the same prediction as to when the point of utter exhaustion would be reached. Their words echo like some funereal duet. And since William III, by making peace at Ryswick, deprived the country this time round of the chance to disprove their case, Davenant had not changed his tune by 1699, as the mournful dirge on 'the wounds of the late war' in his *Balance of Trade* essay bears witness.[44]

Such an outlook, admittedly, was not freakish in the 1690s; and in 1695 there was still *prima facie* evidence—heavy shipping losses and trade dislocation, especially—which seemed to many to justify it. What is truly instructive, however, is that this fundamentally pessimistic, Tory-'Country' view of England's incapacity to bear for long the burdens of large-scale warfare was so ingrained in Gregory King that right at the end of his life, despite all the triumphs of the Spanish Succession War, he was quite unconverted. In an eloquent memorandum which he sent to Davenant in December 1710, he argued that in fighting for seventeen years 'so potent an enemy as the French King', with his unparalleled resources, it had been folly 'in the beginning of the last warr, *when the kingdom was at the heighest pitch of wealth*', to embark on a policy of accumulating a great funded debt.[45] And in the maestro's final, fascinating exercise in political arithmetic, a detailed draft letter endorsed 'Upon Mr. Scobel's proposition for raysing a considerable sum by a Tax on Traders and

[43] Chalmers, App., pp. 61–62 (my italics). King firmly believed that the war had caused a decline in population to set in. See *ibid.*, pp. 42–43; Kashnor MSS. *N.P.O.*, in which King elaborates his reasons for this conviction, for Harley's benefit.

[44] See n. 11 above and *Works*, i, 135.

[45] By 'long mortgages and anticipations of the flower of the revenue'. P.R.O. T.1/130/15E, endorsed 'Observations on the Two Lotteries of 1694 and 1710— Sent to Dr Davenant circ. 8 Dec. 1710'.

Retailers, aº 1710–11',[46] he contended that the nation was decidedly poorer now than it had been even in 1695, let alone in 1688; and, as ever, he was prepared to get down to figures to drive home his point.[47] He had calculated in the *Observations* that at the time of the Revolution 511,586 families were 'increasing the wealth of the Kingdom' and 849,000 families 'decreasing' it. But he now attested, early in 1711, that 'in all probability the increasers are not at this time above 400,000 families and the decreasers, and not increasers, 900,000 families.'[48]

Here, then, is our clue to why King determined some time in the summer of 1696 to relate all his calculations about the nation's wealth and taxable capacity—and therefore his social table too—to the year 1688. For him 1688 marked the line between normality and grave aberration; and such it remained until the day of his death.[49] If I seem to have somewhat laboured this point, it is because it has something of fundamental importance to tell us about King's limitations as a social analyst. It indicates why, even in his own day, his famous table was never a strictly contemporary social document. And it heavily underlines the dangers of using a 'Scheme of the Income and Expense of the several Families' for the year 1688 as a model for interpreting the social structure of England during much, or all, of the subsequent pre-industrial period. For not only was King's resort to social categorization entirely subordinate to a deeper purpose—a fiscal purpose; his whole thinking about society was retrospective. Despite the veneer of modernity which overlays his work King's attitudes were, up to a point, the anachronistic social attitudes of a herald who had made his last provincial visitation in 1684:[50] at a time when visitations themselves had become a hopeless anachronism.

The fact is, the English society of 1695–96 was already in a state of flux: it was already beginning to witness important changes in

[46] P.R.O., T.64/302. Francis Scobell, the experienced High Tory M.P. for Launceston, had made his proposal to the Commons' Committee of Ways and Means.

[47] *E.g.* he claimed the general national income was in 1711 only 39 mns, 4½ mns less than he had believed it to be at the Revolution. Such evidence as that in 1709 it had taken a mere four hours to attract £2 mn in subscriptions to a new Bank loan to the government—more than Charles II's ministers could normally expect from the produce of two years' ordinary revenue—apparently left him unimpressed.

[48] He appears to have calculated that the population had fallen by 1711 close to 5,300,000.

[49] Davenant's attitude was much the same: see *Works*, i, 132 (written October 1697).

[50] Of Cambridge and Huntingdon. He later attended Clarenceux on the final London Visitation of 1687. Chalmers, App., pp. 16–17.

the landowning sector, the rise of a new 'monied interest' in the City, the rapid expansion of the civil service and of the armed forces, vital new stimuli to certain branches of industry and distributing trades, and the inauguration of a period of steady urban growth in some parts of the provinces; not to mention many subtler transmutations. King was in a position to have recorded the first phase of these changes, had he had any desire to do so; for, like many of his contemporaries, he cannot have been entirely unaware that something was stirring. But for him the only true society, the only firm base to which all must return if there was to be any future health for England, was the *societas ante bellum*.

By itself this is a misfortune for historians. What makes it a dangerous snare into the bargain is that the fossilizing effects of his socio-political outlook were magnified by a second aspect of Gregory King's intense conservatism. So far from having any vision of England's potential greatness—though he wrote at the very moment of time when she was taking the first strides along the road to first-class European status—he was on the contrary obsessed by her vulnerability, by the fragility of the foundations on which even her pre-war prosperity had rested. By the end of 1695 his demographic work had convinced him that all previous political arithmeticians had seriously exaggerated the size of the country's population.[51] This, he thought (and with justice) had had in turn a damaging effect on fiscal policy: '. . . the calculations of Sr. Wm. Petty, & others, of the number of People obtaining too much credit with the House of Commons, makes all our Poll Bills and other Taxes which depend upon that Article, to fall so very short'.[52] And these convictions led him to the far more sweeping conclusion that Petty, through misplaced national pride, had inflated almost all his reckonings, notably those concerning the wealth of the nation relative to its neighbours. In an early draft of his manuscript King roundly deplored 'the vanity of over-valuing our own strength [which] is so natural to our Nation . . .'[53]

It was his stern determination not to fall in the same trap as Petty, linked with his resolve to provide the Treasury and the Commons with more realistic data from which to estimate tax yields, which has posed the gravest problems for the social historian. For King's highly conservative over-reaction against the more euphoric assumptions of recent years frequently led him into contrary error whenever he left firm demographic ground. To be more specific: it produced in his social table serious distortions of two vital sets of statistics, in a

[51] See especially B.J., p. 275.
[52] *Ibid.*, p. 241: draft to Sir Stephen Fox, 19 December 1695.
[53] *Ibid.*, pp. 1, 240.

downward direction. It beguiled him (1) into underestimating the number of families in some of the wealthiest, and fiscally most productive classes; and (2) into underestimating (sometimes quite grossly) income levels at many rungs above the poverty line.

In the brief time available I can offer but a handful of examples from each of these two broad tracks of error. I will begin with incomes; since I am convinced that King took as one of his two salient points of reference in the table a total income figure for the whole nation which was unquestionably too low and that this critically affected his judgment of both incomes and numbers at many individual social levels: *because the way he worked made it imperative that both columns should add up in the end to his pre-calculated totals.*[54]

The case of the peers' incomes has attracted attention: and it is important enough to deserve re-emphasizing. Lawrence Stone has estimated the mean gross income, from all sources, of 121 peers in 1641 at £6,060.[55] Since then, the English peerage had acquired a net increase of roughly forty new members, many of whom were, to put it mildly, plump in the pocket. King's £2,800 for the peers' gross income in 1688 is as ludicrous as the somewhat earlier figure in his notebook of £2,000 for their annual rental income.[56] No doubt the peerage was a wealthier body a generation after 1688 than at the time of the Revolution: by 1710 three giants were topping £30,000 a year,[57] at least four other peers were amassing between £20,000 and £30,000;[58] over £10,000 a year had become perfectly commonplace above baron's rank. But the change inside a mere twenty years can hardly have been a massive one. In the significantly revised version of his table which Gregory King supplied to Davenant in 1698[59] he cautiously pushed up the average gross income of his peers

[54] For my hypothesis about King's methods, and further comments on his total income figure, see below pp. 300-2 and n. 90.

[55] *The Crisis of Aristocracy* (1st edn., Oxford, 1965), p. 762.

[56] P.R.O., T.64/302: notebook, p. 14. Office-holding alone was a major element in aristocratic wealth. In 1714 at least 42 English peers held office (civil or military) or pension: the emoluments were very rarely less than £1,000 p.a. (the minimum pension for a nobleman). In many cases the rewards amounted to £3,000–4,000 p.a. G. Holmes, *British Politics in the Age of Anne* (London, 1967), pp. 436–39.

[57] Dukes of Newcastle, Bedford and Beaufort.

[58] Dukes of Ormonde, Somerset and Devonshire (the latter with the aid of the Lord Steward's office) and Lord Brooke.

[59] This was the version printed as 'Scheme D' in Davenant's *Essay on the Probable Methods of making the People Gainers in the Balance of Trade* (London, 1699). The table is omitted from the Whitworth edition of Davenant's works. The differences between this revised version and the original version (in the form reproduced by G. E. Barnett, from B.L. Harl. MS. 1898 in *Two Tracts by Gregory King*, Baltimore, 1936) are laid out below in an appendix to this paper.

at the time of the Revolution from £2,800 to £3,200. If he had doubled that sum he would still have been too conservative.

King had no second thoughts in 1698 about the baronets' income. Yet at £880 a year it was almost as unrealistic as his figure for the peers. His contemporary, Chamberlayne, confidently declared that the baronets were 'possest, one with another, of about 1200[l] a year', and further specified that this was '*in lands*'.[60] But even this may have been decidedly too low an average for 1688. Professor Aylmer has suggested that the mean income of all English baronets in the early 1630s was roughly £1,500;[61] and among those promoted to the rank between the Restoration and the Revolution not many lean kine can be identified. Recent work[62] has shown that even in the notoriously poor counties of Cumberland and Westmorland £1,000 a year was a low income for a baronet by the first half of the eighteenth century. Moving down the ladder, King's figures for landed esquires[63] could well be a 25 per cent underestimate; and the implications for the total landed wealth of the esquires of an error of even £100 per family are manifest.[64] As for the income of the knights, King's figure of £650 a year will scarcely bear examination: quite apart from what is known of the position in the early seventeenth century,[65] one must take account here of the great accretions of wealth to the dozens of 'City knights' during the commercial boom of the 1670s and 1680s.[66] King's view of the knighthood in 1688 was detached from late seventeenth-century reality.

[60] Edward Chamberlayne, *Angliae Notitia* (18th edn., London 1694), p. 442.

[61] G. E. Aylmer, *The King's Servants* (1st edn., London, 1961), p. 331. This estimate is for 1633. It is amply borne out by local studies: *e.g.* the 31 baronets of Kent, *c.* 1640, had average incomes of £1,405 p.a. and the 28 baronets of Yorkshire £1,536 p.a. A. Everitt, *Change in the Provinces: The Seventeenth Century* (Leicester, 1969), p. 55, drawing on his own work on Kent and that of J. T. Cliffe on Yorkshire. *Cf.* J. T. Cliffe, *The Yorkshire Gentry* (London, 1969), chs. 2, 5, *passim*.

[62] J. V. Beckett, 'Landownership in Cumbria, *c.* 1680 – *c.* 1750' (Lancaster Univ. Ph.D. thesis, 1975).

[63] £450 p.a.

[64] This margin may be conservative. It is based partly on early seventeenth-century evidence (*e.g.* Aylmer's estimate for 1633, *op. cit.*, p. 331, is £500 p.a.), partly on my own awareness of the sizeable flock of esquires in the 'great commoner' class of the county *élites* (£2,000–£15,000 p.a.) by *c.* 1700. I hope to develop this point in a forthcoming essay on the early eighteenth-century gentry.

[65] *Cf.* Aylmer and Everitt, *loc. cit.*

[66] Among the tycoons of the 1690s who had been knighted before the Revolution were Henry Johnson, William Ashurst, John Eyles, John Parsons, Benjamin Newland, John Bludworth, John Lethieullier, Robert Clayton, Patience Ward and Basil Firebrace. Even for the *landed* knights Chamberlayne estimated an average of £800 p.a. (*Angliae Notitia*, London, 1694, p. 442). A Norwich brewer was thought to have earned a knighthood in 1711 when he had achieved £2,000 p.a. H.M.C. *Portland MSS.* v, 29.

But elsewhere, too, he seems to be in an income world of his own. The case of the lawyers is not the most aggravated; but even so the incomes of several thousand provincial attorneys and court officials would have had to be microscopic to explain a mean of £140 a year, considering the princely incomes of the judicial *élite* of late seventeenth-century England, in which annual pickings of £2,000 were modest for a successful barrister. In many cases, those humbler incomes were not microscopic.[67] As for his 'shopkeepers and tradesmen'—surely the craziest of all King's categories—we need only reflect that it included many innkeepers who we now know could vie in wealth and standard of living with the lesser gentry;[68] literally thousands of master manufacturers who have no other home in the table;[69] and not least astonishing, all the great wholesalers and factors in England. We then get the £45 a year for this 'class' in something like its true perspective.

When it comes to enumeration of families, it is more difficult to corner King, if only because many of his categories are so ill-defined, or outmoded, or both. If Massie,[70] who aped King in numerous respects, found it necessary to include in his calculations in 1760 four income groups of master manufacturers and five of tradesmen, what was so radically different about the situation seventy years earlier? King's inclusion of scriveners among the lawyers,[71] instead of in the business sector, is another instance of smudgy, antiquated thinking. But the smokescreen is nowhere thick enough to obscure the fact that guesswork abounds in King's enumeration; or that there are in columns 1 and 2 the strangest anomalies and confusions, even where one might least expect them. Harley criticized King for underestimating the numbers of clergy, and King's defence is unconvincing.[72] In 1698 he himself conceded that he had put too low a number, by 10,000, on the shopkeepers and tradesmen. His 1711 estimate,

[67] *Cf.* the life-style of the attorneys, notaries, proctors and other officials who served the duchy court at Preston, of the local lawyers who handled most of the business of the assize towns, such as Leicester, and 'the rich attorneys in great practice' who clustered round the Cornish Stannary towns. On the other hand King presumably omitted *knighted* lawyers—most of them, by definition, successful—from this category.

[68] A. Everitt, 'The English Urban Inn, 1560–1760', in A. Everitt (ed.), *Perspectives in English Urban History* (London, 1973).

[69] The category of 'merchants and traders by land' which occurs in the frequently-quoted version of the table printed by Chalmers, App., pp. 48–49, is a copyist's freak peculiar to the manuscript version of the *Observations* which Chalmers used.

[70] See note 3 above.

[71] B.J., p. 280.

[72] Especially as he admitted including householding dissenting ministers in his 10,000 clergymen. See Kashnor MSS., *N.P.O.*, ch. 6, reply to Harley's 'Clergymen 10,000. These too few . . .'

in response to Scobell, reveals that by then he recognized the gross inadequacy even of his revised figure of 50,000.[73]

With the 'freeholders' and 'farmers' King was for a long time utterly at sea, his estimates for their combined total oscillating wildly, in a series of entries from the spring of 1695 to the summer of 1696, between 240,000 and 780,000.[74] It is with the table's 12,000 'Gentlemen', however, that the problem of definition, and therefore of enumeration, takes on its most baffling form. Did King have in mind only armigerous gentlemen at this point of his table? Almost certainly not. The Burns Journal establishes that in some of his early social explorations he was happily accepting the pragmatic approach of recent Poll Taxes, which imposed the lowest gentry rate on those 'owning themselves gentlemen' and recognized as such by their neighbours—'reputed gentlemen', King calls them.[75] With them in mind he played around at one time with figures as high as 20,000 or even 23,000. Why he settled for 12,000 is, on the face of it, inexplicable. That he was perfectly aware of the phenomenon of the urban gentry, as well as taking account of non-armigerous country gentry, some of his notes again make clear.[76] If he left them out of the final scheme, where did he put them? Urban gentlemen alone were to be numbered in many thousands by 1700. Only a fraction were government office-holders, and the proportion actively engaged in a profession at any one time cannot have been large. Two statistics help to put this problem of the gentry in context and underline its gravity. Professor Aylmer suggests a figure for the esquires and 'gents' together in the 1630s, before the most startling proliferation of pseudo-gentry had begun, of between 17,000 and 23,000.[77] In the Land Tax Act of 1702 there were roughly 32,000 commissioners named, and only a tiny proportion were below the rank of gentle-

---

[73] P.R.O., T.64/302: 'Upon Mr. Scobel's Proposition . . .' In this paper he postulates for fiscal purposes no fewer than 151,000 'traders' (including overseas merchants), vintners, brewers and public-house keepers, and it is inconceivable that only a third of them were deemed heads of households. About a year earlier King had calculated that there were then some 24,500 merchants, tradesmen and artificers in London, who were householders and who also kept apprentices. P.R.O. T.1/130/15F: paper endorsed '1709/10. Computation of the amount of the money taken with apprentices'.

[74] P.R.O., T.64/302: notebook, pp. 14, 18v.; B.J., pp. 65, 209; *ibid.*, p. 270, where the figures eradicated and the alternatives inserted are equally revealing. It seems highly likely that King's final choice of 330,000 (amended in 1698 to 310,000) was reached by a process of elimination, working downwards from a total number of solvent householders; though his figure of 40,000 for the 'freeholders of the better sort' was fixed at an earlier stage.

[75] The 'pseudo-gentry' of modern historians' usage. See B.J., pp. 67, 70.

[76] *E.g.* B.J., pp. 59, 64, 91.

[77] G. E. Aylmer, *The King's Servants*, p. 331.

man. Yet King's combined total for the whole 'mere' gentry in 1688 is but 15,000.

Why was such opacity and confusion possible? Why was so much guesswork seemingly unavoidable? Why was King so error-prone that he even contrived to underenumerate the peers by almost a sixth?[78] These questions direct attention inexorably to the sources and the methods to which he resorted in compiling the 'social table'. Most critically, we need to know whence he derived the first four columns—the most important for the student of the social structure —and also the cardinal dividing line, that grimly fascinating horizontal line between those 'increasing' and those 'decreasing' 'the wealth of the kingdom'.

A common illusion is that King's social statistics were based, in the main, on a study of the Hearth Tax returns. This statement appears to originate with Dorothy George in 1931.[79] Though often repeated, it is wholly erroneous, stemming from Mrs George's misunderstanding of a passage of Davenant's.[80] Indeed it is virtually certain that King never went back *in person*, in the 1690s, to the general records of the Hearth Office, not even to check his population figures.[81] On the other hand, plausible contemporary support can be mustered for the theory that King used Poll Tax material in constructing his table. Four Poll Taxes had been imposed between 1689 and 1694;[82] and when the revised version of Gregory King's table was printed in 1699, by Davenant, the Doctor made impressive claims on his friend's behalf:

> This skilful and laborious gentleman has taken the right course to form his several schemes about the numbers of the people; for besides many different ways of working, he has very carefully inspected the poll books, and the distinctions made by those acts,

[78] There were in 1688 approximately 30 holders of Scottish and Irish peerages whose main estates and normal residences were in England. Their numbers, and wealth, increased during William III's reign. In one of his early tables, dating from autumn 1695, King rightly included these peers, bringing his total for the lay nobility to a realistic 200. (B.J., pp. 280.) Subsequently, however, they slip out of the reckoning into some undiscoverable limbo.

[79] D. George, *England in Transition* (Pelican edn., London, 1953), pp. 10, 16.

[80] *Cf. ibid.*, p. 16, with Davenant, *Works*, ii, 203–04.

[81] No other deduction seems possible from King's replies to two of Harley's queries and objections in 1697: viz. 'Are these [King's figures for inhabited houses in provincial towns] estimated or numbred from the Hearth Books?', and 'It is to be doubted these Assessments [on Births, Marriages and Burials] are of no very g[ood] foundation'. Kashnor MSS., *N.P.O.*, ch. 1.

[82] These were the Single Polls of 1689 and 1690 and the Quarterly Polls of 1692 and 1694.

and the produce in money of the respective polls, going everywhere by reasonable and discreet mediums; besides which pains,
he has made observations of the very facts in particular towns and
places, from which he has been able to judge and conclude more
safely of others. So that he seems to have looked further into this
mystery than any other person.[83]

Does this mean that King had at his disposal for social analysis
official material as susceptible to scientific 'sampling' techniques as
that which underpinned his demographic work? Although it is a
fallacy to suppose he was employed by the government in the 1690s,
it is hard to escape the deduction that he did have some friends in
official places,[84] in view of the limited access he managed to acquire,
while working on the *Observations*, to certain government records.
What could be more natural, one might think, than that King should
use these contacts to 'carefully inspect the poll books'? Unfortunately, a careful combing both of King's papers and the Exchequer
records compels a very different, and quite unexpected conclusion. We
now know from his notebooks that he probably had the first inklings
of the importance of the poll tax returns as social documents as early
as September 1695. Once aware of this, it becomes terribly hard to
credit that only at the eleventh hour—at the point, in fact, where
the preparatory work in the Burns Journal stops, almost a year later
—did he suddenly secure access to a marvellous seam of this material,
which is nowhere revealed in those voluminous notes. In that case
it must surely have taken something like a further year to complete
his labours, instead of a few weeks.

Strong suspicion turns to certainty on examining King's meticulous replies, in April 1697, to the comments of Robert Harley on his
conclusions and his methods. Nowhere in these answers did King
claim to have seen the original poll tax records, central or local. On
the contrary, he confirms that even for the bare total yield of those
two Polls which he did make some use of, he had relied on the figures
printed in Davenant's *Ways and Means* essay and not on any civil
servant's goodwill.[85] His transparent eagerness elsewhere in his

83 *Essay upon . . . the Balance of Trade.* See Davenant, *Works*, ii, 175.

84 One or two contacts in the Exchequer can surely be assumed; one 'good
friend' we know of (Sansom) in the Customs, and another (George Stepney) in the
diplomatic service. Also King himself was named a commissioner for London (one
of over 300) in the 1694 Act for levying new duties on births, marriages and
burials. B.L. Loan 57/73, fo 83; B.J., p. 171; Chalmers, App., pp. 23–24;
London Inhabitants within the Walls (London Record Society, 1966), intro. (by D. V.
Glass), p. xvii.

85 This was more than strongly hinted in the earlier Burns Journal. *Cf.* J. Thirsk
and J. P. Cooper (eds.), *Seventeenth-Century Economic Documents* (Oxford, 1972),

'Reply' to reveal his sources of information, and (in merciless detail) his methods of deduction from them, make it inconceivable he would not have displayed a first-hand acquaintance with 'the poll books', if only he had been in a position to do so. He was not; and the truth is that, even if he had been so remarkably favoured as to be allowed a free run of the Exchequer's poll tax returns, he would have found there precious few, if any, *assessments* (the key social documents) for William's reign, and not many even dating from Charles II's time.[86]

Assuming, therefore, as we must, that Davenant misunderstood the devious intricacy of his friend's methods, and in consequence deceived himself about the *bona fides* of the social table's foundations, what hypothesis is it reasonable to advance about King's sources and methods on the evidence that survives?

In the first place it can be either demonstrated or deduced that he was able to draw on four sources of some official standing. They were: (1) The actual provisions of the first three Poll Acts, those of 1689, 1690 and 1692;[87] (2), as already noted, the total yields of the 1689 and 1692 Polls (these totals he culled from Davenant and they were inaccurate, though not seriously so); (3) some of the assessments (mostly London assessments) for the 1695 duties on Births, Marriages and Burials—those same duties which proved such a boon to King's demographic studies;[88] and (4) the total number of houses

---

pp. 770 n. 1, 785–86, 798, 802–03. Harley proceeded to make corrections in King's (*i.e.* Davenant's) figures, adding for good measure the yield of the two remaining Polls; and King significantly began his reply: 'In the consideration of the Poll bills (the true produce whereof you having favour'd me with, requires my particular acknowledgments) those two which I examined [i.e. the statutes themselves] were the first Twelve penny Poll and the first Quarterly Poll'. Kashnor MSS., *N.P.O.*, ch. 9.

[86] The pattern for William's reign was established by the first Poll Act of 1689 (1 Gul. and Mar., sess. 1, c. 13) which required the Exchequer to receive, in addition to the proceeds of the Poll, and the Receivers' accounts, (a) (from the Commissioners) 'a true duplicate of the whole summe charged within every hundred, lath, wapentake, parish [or] ward . . . *without naming the persons*', and (b) (from the Receivers-General) full schedules of defaulters, drawn up by the Collectors. The accounts are now in P.R.O., E.181, the duplicates and defaulters' schedules mostly in E.182. It is clear that the detailed assessments of individuals and families were intended to remain in the counties, and almost invariably did so. Under the vast umbrella of P.R.O., E.179 there are a fair number of detailed assessments relating to the first post-Restoration Poll Tax, 12 Chas. II (*e.g.* for parts of Devon, Cornwall, Lancs. Glos. etc.) and distinctly fewer relating to the levies of 18 and 29 Chas. II (*e.g.* for Hunts.); but by the 1690s the cupboard is almost totally bare.

[87] For 1689 and 1692, see King to Harley in n. 85 above. For 1690, B.J., pp. 71–72.

[88] B.J., pp. 59, 64 and *passim*: *cf.* Chalmers, App., p. 59; Glass, 'Two papers', *loc. cit.* King saw the assessments for 18 London parishes and 7 'outparishes'; some of them listed occupations, one (for St. Mary Le Bow) being a superb social document. *London Inhabitants within the Walls 1695*, pp. xvii–xix.

officially excused from paying the window tax in 1696.[89] These, I believe, were the only solid official bricks which Gregory King used in the creation of that amazing framework on to which historians have hung so many conclusions and hypotheses about pre-industrial society. And, cleverly as he manipulated them, these bricks made up a very, very small pile. In the second place—and of more importance to him—he made use of two pre-cast pillars to hold up the whole construction. These were the two vital totals which King had arrived at quite independently of any Poll Tax material: namely, the total number of households in the land, clearly derived from his base figure for inhabited houses of close to 1,300,000; and the total annual income of the whole population, calculated at £43.5 millions, a figure he arrived at by the most convoluted and questionable means, which he later explained, in mind-boggling detail, to Harley. And I would argue that it was because King was too conservative in arriving at this *national* income figure, and not least because he badly undervalued the total for landed rents (misled by the yield of the Land Tax) that he got so many of his specific income figures, later, seriously wrong.[90]

For the rest, King drew to some extent (though a great deal less than has sometimes been assumed) on his heraldic experience; he drew on smatterings of literary evidence, which happened to lie conveniently to hand.[91] But above all, he drew on his own resources of mind—those mathematical gymnastics which mark almost all his work, but which were nowhere more severely stretched than in compiling his 'Scheme of the Income and Expense of the several Families of England'.

How much help did he get altogether from his fiscal sources?

---

[89] See Chalmers, App., pp. 59–60; Kashnor MSS., *N.P.O.*: King's replies to Harley's queries on ch. 9, 'A Calculation of the Poll-Bills and some other taxes . . .'. *Cf.* B.J., pp. 156–57.

[90] For King's curious calculations on national wealth, see Kashnor MSS., *N.P.O.*, ch. 6. Much of this long passage is conveniently reprinted, with some textual corruptions, in Thirsk and Cooper, pp. 791–95, but a key section on the land tax yield, including King's euphoric, unwarrantable deduction that 'the omissions, the fraud, the favours and the great underrating complained of in the North West is nothing so considerable as we are apt to believe', is omitted.

Modern economic historians would do well to look again at King's £43.5 mns, bearing in mind not only the dubiety of his methods but later figures for *c.* 1800 (both contemporary and otherwise), *e.g.* Deane and Cole's estimate for the total national income in 1801 at £232 mn. Even an error in the region of 3 mns was crucial for King's purposes, since it would be reflected overwhelmingly in his estimates for the *higher* income groups in his table.

[91] *E.g.* he told Harley that he had based the number of 'common seamen' [50,000] on Sir Francis Brewster's estimate of merchant seamen in 1687. King's notes on Brewster's *Essay on Trade* (London, 1696), pp. 75–80, are in B.J., p. 209.

Relatively little, it seems; and only in one area that was fundamental. It was what he could glean about tax exemptions, in conjunction with a national Poor Rate figure of £665,000 per annum for 1685 (borrowed from Davenant, again)[92] which led him to a fairly certain belief that the number of insolvent persons in England in 1690 had been about 2.8 millions. By translating this figure into households,[93] and by keeping as the basis of all his social calculations thereafter— since it was his firmest ground—the *heads of households*,[94] he established the limits of his two major construction sites, the numbers of solvent and insolvent families. Thereafter, those samples of the 1695 assessments for the births, marriages and burial duties which King managed to see, and analyse, yielded him solidly-based information about household size at different social levels;[95] and this clearly played its part in the drawing up of the valuable 'heads per family' column. Yet so too did his personal surveys, such as the scrupulously detailed one he made of Sevenoaks parish, Kent, in June 1695,[96] bearing out Davenant's claim that, for sampling purposes, he had 'made observations of the very facts in particular towns and places'. In the end, one can only conclude that the direct harvest of the Poll Tax, garnered into the final table, was in statistical terms a meagre one.

On the other hand, it was in the Poll Acts themselves that he distinguished both those social groups which Parliament deemed particularly suitable for fiscal milking and those groups which were officially considered too poor to pay; and these gleanings helped to determine the social categories which King eventually chose to include in column 2 of his table. Thus an earlier list of social groupings, compiled about Michaelmas 1695, is headed 'According to their Degrees, Titles & qualities, as they are generally distinguisht in Poll Bills & other Taxes'.[97] And frustratingly for the historian, King

[92] 'That the Poors rate exhibited by the Author of Wayes and Means p. 77 and 79 being at the latter end of K. Cha. 2d reign abt. £665,000, we may estimate the same anno 88 at £680,000 and anno 95 at £740,000 . . .' King to Harley, comments on ch. 9, Kashnor MSS., *N.P.O.*

[93] By applying a ratio appropriate to 'poorer houses'. *Ibid.*

[94] This was a point he was at great pains to emphasize to Harley: *e.g.*, on the clergy, 'I state them only with respect to "Heads of Families"'; on the common seamen, 'so as to denominate them Masters of Families, in wch respect only they are here inserted'.

[95] See. *e.g.*, P.R.O., T.64/302, notebook, p. 17v: 21, 24 June 1695. The same sources, the Burns Journal suggests, may also have led him to make suppositions about the relative proportions of knights and baronets to esquires and of both to 'gentlemen'.

[96] *Ibid.*, pp. 15v–17. He surveyed 395 households, including 206 in Sevenoaks town on 10–11 June.

[97] B.J., pp. 280–81.

demonstrates in the Burns Journal that, working within these guide-
lines, he was well able to attempt a far more sophisticated breakdown of some of the general professional and business groups than
actually appears at the end of the line. No-one interested primarily
in conveying as full a picture as possible of the social structure could
have resisted the inclusion of such precise data as that, for example,
there were among the lawyers 500 clerks in Chancery and Exchequer,
among the clergy 200 pluralists in parish livings worth at least £120
a year, or among the tradesmen 5,000 substantial innkeepers. But,
as I have stressed, detailed social analysis was not King's purpose.
With his overriding fiscal interest he concentrated austerely on just
those basic divisions which, he believed, helped to illuminate in bold
outlines his scheme of incomes and expenses.[98] He even excluded his
intriguing estimate, made at a late stage of his work in 1696, that of
the 364,000 'Day Labourers & Outservants' inserted in the final
table some 300,000 were in rural employment.[99]

Yet this last figure, which does not appear in the table, typifies so
many that do. For it is patently far more the product of strained
deduction, of mathematical juggling, or even plain guesswork, than
of firmly-grounded information. Words such as 'I compute', 'I
estimate', occur again and again in King's notes, with no source
given or hinted at. That he was uncomfortably aware that chapter 6
of his work, of which the 'Scheme' forms the centrepiece, was one of
the most vulnerable parts of the whole exercise is all too evident from
the distinctly frenetic tone of his defences against Harley's thrusts at
this Achilles heel in 1697, as compared with the absolute conviction
of some of his earlier replies to that rigorous examiner. And when,
in 1698, he supplied Davenant with the second version of the table,
we may assume he took as much account as *amour propre* allowed of
reactions to the first;[100] for numerous manuscript copies of the
Observations had been circulated in the past two years.

Gregory King was enormously proud of his *Observations*, taken by
and large. But he was realist enough, and in the end had enough
basic humility, to appreciate that in some areas of knowledge there
were severe limits to what any political arithmetician, even the most
brilliant and resourceful, could achieve with the evidence currently
available to him. The social structure was one such area. Even

---

[98] Among the detail jettisoned as superfluous or subsumed elsewhere in the table
were such titbits as that King believed there to be 500 dissenting preachers in
England, 800 goldsmiths (300 in London) and 200 London doctors. For these
estimates, those cited in the text above, and others, see B.J., pp. 70–73, 265, 280–81.

[99] B.J., p. 209.

[100] On this point *cf.* David Cressy, 'Describing the Social Order of Elizabethan
and Stuart England', *Literature and History*, no. 3 (March 1976), p. 32.

supposing most government financial records to be accurate—and King was not ingenuous enough to make such a supposition—no-one could reasonably expect unrestricted access to them, certainly no-one concerned to advance basic premises critical of current government policy. Davenant later voiced bitter resentment at the many rubs which he, a former member of the bureaucratic brotherhood, had been forced to endure from officialdom in the course of his own research and writing.[101] As for King himself, he made his commonsense pragmatism perfectly plain in the preface to the *Observations*. To know the 'true state' of a nation—this was the highest ideal: 'but since the attaining thereof (how necessary and desirable soever) is next to impossible, we must content ourselves with such near approaches to it, as the grounds we have to go upon will enable us to make'.[102] And inscribed philosophically on the second leaf of the Burns Journal, standing alone on an otherwise blank page, is this aphorism:

> Pour bien savoir les choses, il en faut savoir le détail: et comme il est presque infiny, nos connoissances sont toujours superficielles et imparfaites.

This could well have served as King's own epitaph on his 'social table'. But what should be ours? Whatever our reservations, it would be rank injustice to regard it as anything less than an extraordinary pioneering feat, a creation of awesome scale and of the boldest originality. Even when stripped of many of its dubious statistical embellishments, its ravaged grandeur will always retain features of lasting value to the historian. Sparse as King's official sources were, they were enough to allow him a more penetrating and dramatic insight into the frightening extent of the problem of poverty in late Stuart England than any previous economist or political arithmetician had achieved.[103] As for his social categories, and the seemingly deliberate status-order in which they are arranged: although we ought to recognize them for what they are—a monument to a static, and in some ways anachronistic view of a pre-war society, an *ancien régime*—they remain a legacy of permanent value, in the sense that they reflect how the pre-industrial Englishman of a traditionalist cast of mind preferred to think his social order was constituted. Seen in this light, Gregory King's table is in direct line of descent from

---

[101] See Davenant, *Works*, i, 149; ii, 168—two very important, and largely unnoticed passages written in 1697 and 1699, in the second of which he speaks for his fellow political arithmeticians as well as for himself.

[102] Chalmers, App., p. 31.

[103] As Davenant recognized at the time, this was the table's most important message for contemporaries. *Works*, ii, 198.

the sumptuary laws of the late fifteenth century, through Sir Thomas Smith, Wilson and Chamberlayne, to Massie, and perhaps even to Colquhoun.[104]

Far more vital to the historian, however, is to keep in mind at all times that King's great 'Scheme' was the work of flesh and blood and not the creation of some wholly objective and impersonal genius. In it we should recognize the brainchild of a brilliant yet uneasy man: a man who had been cruelly frustrated in his profession and who was almost too anxious to prove himself in a novel sphere of activity; a man who knew his way to truth but could not rest content when he found it barred; a man who at times allowed his hyperactive mind to fall victim to his greatest obsession, bemused and entrapped by the web of figures he had spun for himself. Not least, we must never impose upon his scheme far greater strains than he himself meant it to bear. So it need not surprise us that what had never been designed as an exact mirror of England's social structure even in 1688 was producing grave distortions already by the time of King's own death in 1712.

The social structure of pre-industrial England was a thing of infinite subtlety. It deserves to be studied intensively, not least at local level,[105] and in its own right; and studied as the structure of a society which was never static and was capable, certainly during periods of prolonged warfare, of positive dynamism. There is so much yet to be done; and such a wealth of material still to be fully worked.[106] However great our admiration for the work of 'G. K. Esqr Lancaster Herald', Davenant's 'wonderful genius, and master of the art of computing', is it not time that as students of a past society we determined no longer to be suffocated by his pervasive presence?

[104] Professor Donald Coleman first drew my attention to the significance of this continuity. Cressy argues, however (see n. 100 above), that 'King's is the first ranking of the social order which combines reference to economic circumstances with a system of esteem'.

[105] For example, we need many more social anatomies of provincial communities, following the admirable models of G. H. Kenyon's work on Petworth and J. D. Marshall's on Kendal. See *Sussex Arch. Collections*, xcvi (1958), xcviii (1960); *Trans. Cumberland and Westmorland Antiq. and Arch. Soc.*, lxxv, New Series (1975).

[106] The surviving poll tax assessments of 1661–98 warrant a sustained assault. So do the lists of Land Tax commissioners incorporated in successive Aids and Land Tax bills from 1689: by 1700 they represent a nearly complete roll-call of the upper and middling gentry of every shire. Freemen's registers; jurors' lists; poll books for some of the large boroughs (e.g. Norwich, Bristol, Liverpool, Newcastle) which supply voters' occupations as well as names; poor rate books; the militia muster rolls of the Seven Years' War—all await the systematic scrutiny of the social historian.

Gregory King's 'Scheme of the Income and Expense of the several Families of England, . . . for the Year 1688'

(The 'Barnett version', 1936, from B.L. Harleian MS. 1898; amendments in square brackets from the revised, 'Davenant version', 1698[9]. N.B. The first five columns of figures and the last (9th) column only are reproduced below. Column 7, 'Annual expenditure per family', has been reconstituted from King's *per capita* figures.

Number of Families	Ranks, Degrees, Titles, and Qualifications	Heads per Family	Number of Persons	Yearly Income per Family £	Total Yearly Income £	Annual Expenditure per Family £	Total Increase of Wealth Yearly £
160	Temporal Lords	40	6,400	2,800 [3,200]	448,000 [512,000]	2,400 [2,800]	64,000
26	Spiritual Lords	20	520	1,300	33,800	1,100 [900]	5,200 [10,400]
800	Baronets	16	12,800	880	704,000	816 [784]	51,200 [76,800]
600	Knights	13	13,800	650	390,000	598 [585]	31,200 [39,000]
3,000	Esquires	10	30,000	450	1,200,000	420 [410]	90,000 [120,000]
12,000	Gentlemen	8	96,000	280	2,880,000	260 [256]	240,000 [288,000]
5,000	Persons in [greater] offices [and places]	8	40,000	240	1,200,000	216 [208]	120,000 [160,000]
5,000	Persons in [lesser] offices [and places]	6	30,000	120	600,000	108 [102]	60,000 [90,000]
2,000	[Eminent] Merchants and Traders by Sea	8	16,000	400	800,000	320 [296]	160,000 [208,000]

8,000	[Lesser] Merchants and Traders by Sea	6	48,000	200 [198]	1,600,000 [1,584,000]*	168 [162]	240,000 [288,000]
10,000	Persons in the Law	7	70,000	140 [154]	1,400,000 [1,540,000]	119 [91]	210,000 [280,000]
2,000	[Eminent] Clergymen	6	12,000	60 [72]	120,000 [144,000]	54 [60]	12,000 [24,000]
8,000	[Lesser] Clergymen	5	40,000	45 [50]	360,000 [400,000]	40 [47]	40,000 [32,000]
40,000	Freeholders [of the better sort]	7	280,000	84 [91]	3,360,000 [3,640,000]	77	280,000 [350,000]
140,000 [120,000]	Freeholders [of the lesser sort]	5 [5½]	700,000 [660,000]	50 [55]	7,000,000 [6,600,000]	82-5	350,000 [339,000]
150,000	Farmers	5	750,000	44 [42-10]	6,600,000	47-10	187,000 [187,500]
16,000 [15,000]	Persons in Sciences and Liberal Arts	5	80,000 [75,000]	60	960,000 [900,000]	42-10 [41-5]	40,000 [75,000]
40,000 [50,000]	Shopkeepers and Tradesmen	4½	180,000 [225,000]	45	1,800,000 [2,250,000]	57-10 [55]	90,000 [225,000]
60,000	Artisans and Handicrafts	4	240,000	40 [38]	2,400,000 [2,280,000]	42-15 [40-10]	120,000
5,000	Naval Officers	4	20,000	80	400,000	38 [36]	40,000
4,000	Military Officers	4	16,000	60	240,000	72	16,000
						56	
511,586 [500,586]		5¼ [5⅓]	2,675,520 [2,675,520]	67 [68-18]	34,495,800 [34,488,800]	63 [62-15]	2,447,100 [3,023,700]

*This *should* be the revised figure. In fact it stays as 1,600,000

Number of Families	Ranks, Degrees, Titles, and Qualifications	Heads per Family	Number of Persons	Yearly Income per Family £	Total Yearly Income £	Annual Expenditure per Family £	Total Increase of Wealth Yearly £
							Decrease
50,000	Common Seamen	3	150,000	20	1,000,000	22–10	75,000
364,000	Labouring People and Outservants	3½	1,275,000	15	5,460,000	16–2	127,500
400,000	Cottagers and Paupers	3¼	1,300,000	6–10	2,000,000	7–6–3	325,000
35,000	Common Soldiers	2	70,000	14	490,000	15	35,000
849,000		3¼	2,795,000	10–10	8,950,000	11–4–3	562,500
	Vagrants as Gipsies, Thieves, Beggars. etc.		30,000	2	60,000	3	60,000
	So the General Account is				—	—	
511,586 [500,586]	Increasing the Wealth of the Kingdom	5¼ [5⅓]	2,675,520	67 [68–18]	34,495,800 [34,488,800]	63 [62–15]	2,447,100 [3,023,700]
849,000	Decreasing the Wealth of the Kingdom	3¾	2,825,000	10–10	9,101,000	10–19–4	622,500
1,360,586 [1,349,586]	NEAT TOTALS	4 1/420 [4 1/13]	5,500,520	32–0 [32–5]	43,505,800 [43,491,800]	30–12–7 [30–8–6]	1,825,100 [2,401,200]

THE PROFESSIONS AND SOCIAL CHANGE IN ENGLAND,
1680-1730

IN the summer of 1698 a visitor to Bury St. Edmunds was struck by one particular house, built in 'the new mode' that set it apart from those 'great old houses of timber' in which the well-to-do of the neighbourhood still lived. This 'high house' standing some sixty steps up from the ground and crowned with a lantern tower belonged, she found, to an apothecary. Since the visitor was that intrepid sightseer Celia Fiennes, who could no more pass a paper mill than a mansion without an incurable itch to get inside it, she was soon being shown round by the affable owner; and the costly furnishings, the fine china and the plate she saw within amply bore out the local opinion that he was 'esteemed a very rich man'.[1] Over thirty years later the earl of Oxford was to go to Bury and find that by then, with modern buildings palpably gaining ground on the old, it was lawyers—judges and barristers—who were in the van of progress.[2]

Few who journeyed through England between the 1690s and the 1730s and obligingly left accounts of their travels failed to remark on the physical and social presence of members of the professions. Lawyers perhaps attracted more notice than any.[3] The first fine house to greet Fiennes as she rode from the south into Preston was a lawyer's house, newly built in the London suburban style. Perhaps the sight did not surprise her unduly, for Preston was the seat of the courts palatine of Lancaster as

---

[1] Christopher Morris (ed.), *The Journeys of Celia Fiennes* (revised edn. 1949), pp. 151–2.

[2] This was in 1732. Hist. MSS Comm., *Portland MSS*, vi. 150.

[3] What was said of the English traveller at the beginning of George III's reign—that 'his eyes are constantly caught by the appearance of a smart house, prefaced with white rails and prologu'd by a red door with a brass knocker', and that he was 'always told that it belongs to lawyer such a one'— could have been appropriately written thirty years earlier. Samuel Foote, *The Orators* (1762), pp. 21–2.

well as being the mecca of the Lancashire landed gentry; and before 1731 the number of attorneys and solicitors alone living and practising there was to rise to at least 28.[1] But the Revd. Timothy Thomas was clearly astonished in 1725 to find in grimy Sheffield a north side 'rebuilt within these few years . . . [which] now makes no mean figure in brick', where Mr Sherburn, the duke of Norfolk's agent, had a house with apartments fit to entertain his grace himself when he toured his south Yorkshire estates. And 'a short stop' some miles to the south 'at a new-built little box, very pleasantly situated in a grove . . . [which] belongs to a gentleman of the law, Mr. Wright'[2] further reminded Thomas of that clutch of attorneys now thriving among the forges, the cutlers' wheels, and the coal pits of Hallamshire.[3]

Since the Restoration a growing number of barristers had chosen to settle in the provinces, where the rewards were far less glittering than those enjoyed by the bar elite but generally more secure.[4] The business of the London courts was becoming ferociously competitive: three parts in four, said Addison, of those 'ingenious gentlemen' who were 'carried down in coachfuls to Westminster Hall, every morning in term time', spoiling for a fight, were fated to remain 'only quarrelsome in their hearts'.[5] So by the early eighteenth century hundreds had preferred a more comfortable berth in the provinces, where they could often cut a fine figure, like Roger Comberbach the Recorder of Chester or Robert Raikes, who lived a country gentleman's life in Northallerton, 'a famous jockey' (it was reported) and 'some say more conversant with ladies than law books'. At very least the local barrister could expect to prosper quietly in

[1] *Journeys of Celia Fiennes*, p. 187 and n. 5; John Macky, *A Journey through England*, ii (1722), 153–4; *Lists of Attornies and Solicitors admitted in pursuance of the late Act for the better Regulation of Attorneys and Solicitors: presented to the House of Commons*—(London, 1729[-30]), p. 27; *Additional Lists of Attornies and Solicitors admitted in pursuance of the late Act*—(London, 1731), pp. 3–109 *passim*, 258–60. [Hereafter cited as *Lists* (1730) and *Additional Lists* (1731)].

[2] For Thomas Wright, attorney of the King's Bench, see *Additional Lists* (1731), p. 30; PRO, I.R. 1/4, p. 193; Robert Robson, *The Attorney in Eighteenth-Century England* (Cambridge, 1959), pp. 71, 155.

[3] 'A Journey through Hertfordshire, Lincolnshire and Notts to the Northern Counties and Scotland', begun 10 April 1725: Hist. MSS Comm., *Portland MSS*, vi. 145–6.

[4] For the example of one county early in our period, see P. Styles, 'The Heralds' Visitation of Warwickshire, 1682–3', *Birmingham Archaeological Soc. Trans.* 71 (1953), pp. 121, 127–8, 132.

[5] *The Spectator*, No. 21, Saturday, 24 March 1711.

the manner of Edmund Blundell of Prescot, advising south Lancashire attorneys on many thorny problems.[1] But of course, such men were far outnumbered in any local community by the attorneys and solicitors themselves. Concern had been widely expressed between the 1680s and Queen Anne's reign over their startling increase in every county since the early seventeenth century: phrases such as 'swarm like locusts' and 'exorbitant proportions' are not uncommon then.[2] But there was considerably more to come, and papers laid before the House of Commons in 1730 and 1731 were to reveal just how impressive even the strictly legitimate element of the profession had become, far away from the capital. Leeds by then had twelve registered attorneys and solicitors, not counting Robert Lepton in Hunslet Lane and six more who practised in nearby Birstall, Elland, and Kippax. Manchester linen-drapers could take their business to no fewer than 19 attorneys in the town itself, to three in Salford, or to two members of the ancient Mosley family practising in Stretford; while among the fashionable resort centres of the north, Beverley could boast ten resident lawyers, rejoicing in such exotic names as Randolphus Hewitt and Suckling Spendlove, and York had 23.[3] Travellers in farthest Cornwall in 1730 must have been even more astonished to come across eleven attorneys with practices and houses in the most westerly market town in England, Penzance.[4]

But lawyers were not the only professionals to catch the traveller's eye. Closer to London, and particularly on its outskirts,

[1] W. R. Williams, *The History of the Great Sessions in Wales 1542–1830* (Brecknock, 1899), pp. 71, 113–14, for Comberbach and his contemporary, Hugh Foulkes, also of Chester; Hist. MSS Comm., *Portland MSS*, iv. 641: John Durden to [R. Harley], Scarborough, 5 Dec. 1710; R. Stewart-Brown, *Isaac Greene: A Lancashire Lawyer of the Eighteenth Century* (Liverpool, 1921), pp. 8–9.

[2] e.g. John Aubrey, *The Natural History of Wiltshire* (ed. J. Britton, 1847), pt. ii, chap. xvi (unpaginated); E. S. de Beer (ed.), *The Diary of John Evelyn* (Oxford Standard Authors edn. 1959), p. 1049, 4 Feb. 1700.

[3] Numbers calculated from *Lists* (1730) and *Additional Lists* (1731), *passim*. *Additional Lists*, p. 74 for Lepton; p. 80, for Francis Mosley of Turfemoss; pp. 64, 98, for Hewitt and Spendlove.

[4] Similarly with Helston in the same county, where (assuming a roughly stable population between 1715 and 1730) there was one lawyer to approximately every 170 inhabitants in a place of 'no particular manufacture [as a local clergyman described it] but a medley of all sorts of trades, just enough to supply the town and the neighbourhood with all the necessaries and comforts of life'. Bodleian Lib. MS Willis 48, f. 127: John Jago to Michael Peach, Helston, 24 July 1715; for Penzance, Helston, and other Cornish attorneys (99 in all) see *Lists* (1730) and *Additional Lists* (1731), *passim*.

the scene was a more varied one. Visitors to Greenwich by George I's reign found that this sprouting town of 4,000 inhabitants and the fringes of Blackheath behind it had become a high-class professional ghetto, a retreat not just for city lawyers but for retired generals and many other officers of the army and navy, and as Defoe observed, for working civil servants too—ordnance officials and dockyard executives.[1] Most long-serving officials of the central government now preferred to settle within easy commuting distance of their offices: Adam de Cardonnel lived unflamboyantly in a house at Chiswick and Josiah Burchett, that indispensable factotum of the Admiralty, among the Jewish businessmen at Hampstead.[2] But some had moved a little further afield and bought land. Travellers through Sussex between 1694 and 1717, for example, found two manor houses cheek by jowl, Cuckfield and Wakehurst Place, occupied by colleagues and close friends at the Navy Office, Charles Sergison, Clerk of the Acts, and Dennis Lyddell.[3]

Even the clergy were able here and there to reassure the English traveller, through brick and stone, that the good things of this world had not entirely passed by the most ancient of the learned professions. But outside the closes of cathedral cities, where the amount of new and elegant building since the late seventeenth century caused some remark,[4] it was often medical

[1] Daniel Defoe, *A Tour through the Whole Island of Great Britain* (Everyman edn.), i. 95; Macky, *Journey*, i (1714), 80. Cf. C. W. Chalkin, *Seventeenth-Century Kent* (1965), p. 258.

[2] *DNB* on Cardonell; G. F. James, 'Josiah Burchett, Seceretary to the Lords Commissioners of the Admiralty, 1695-1742', *Mariner's Mirror*, xxiii (1937), 492-3.

[3] T. W. Horsfield, *History, Antiquities and Topography of the County of Sussex* (Lewes, 1835), i. 253, 259; M. A. Lower, 'Some Notices of Charles Sergison, Esq., one of the Commissioners of the Royal Navy temp. William III and Queen Anne', *Sussex Arch. Soc. Collns.* xxv (1873), 62-3, 79-80; R. D. Merriman (ed.), *The Sergison Papers* (Navy Record Soc. 1949), p. 2. Lyddell, who died in 1717, was Comptroller of the Treasurer's Accounts. See also *VCH Sussex* vii. 156 for the Cuckfield estate.

[4] For example, the splendour of the houses of the cathedral clergy in Salisbury, Durham, and Lichfield greatly impressed Defoe and Macky: *Tour*, i. 189, ii. 248; *Journey*, ii. 156-7. In 1725 Lord Oxford's chaplain noted with approval the number of fine new parsonage houses along his route through north Yorkshire (Hist. MSS. Comm., *Portland MSS*, vi. 97, 99) and had he passed earlier through Hemsworth he would have found another there (*Journeys of Celia Fiennes*, p. 95). The parish clergy of Oxfordshire, among others, were building too: see, e.g., Jennifer Sherwood and N. Pevsner (eds.), *The Buildings of England: Oxfordshire* (1974), pp. 519, 526 for Burford rectory and Chalgrove parsonage (c.1700-2).

men who vied most with provincial lawyers in flaunting their prosperity. In Wells even the dean and prebends were outshone by the city's only physician in the early years of the eighteenth century, Dr Claver Morris. Morris lived in one of the handsomest houses in the city, built between 1699 and 1702 at a cost of £807, with every convenience a man of his interests and conviviality could desire—from a private laboratory down to a splendid cellar, normally well stocked (as befitted that of a good Tory) with smuggled French clarets.[1] When the centre of Warwick was rebuilt after being largely destroyed by fire in 1694 the most richly ornamented of the four largest and tallest new houses was tenanted by the town's leading apothecary-doctor, John Bradshaw.[2] Indeed, wealthy apothecaries at this time seem to have had a passion for tall houses. John Pemberton, Liverpool's leading apothecary for much of the period 1660–1703, was thus an odd man out when, during the building of Moor Street, he turned down repeated requests to add a fourth storey to his house, the first to go up on one side of the road. He could well have afforded to comply, for he died a rich man. But he preferred to puff off his self-consequence instead by defying his gentry landlord, Sir Edward Moore, and telling him flatly 'he would not have it built an inch higher'; and since Moor Street had a marked fall of ground and all the other tenants on his side had 'engaged to build uniform with him', his next-door neighbour had to bend double to get into his own upper rooms and the street as a whole, thought Sir Edward, was 'wronged . . . five hundred pounds'. Moore found Pemberton's perverse combination of *nouveau* wealth and pride peculiarly hard to stomach—'a base, ill-contrived fellow', he called him.[3] Bury

[1] E. Hobhouse (ed.), *The Diary of a West Country Physician*, A.D. *1684–1726* (1934), pp. 12–14, 18, 22–3, 63–4. Perhaps Morris was a special case, in that he had already married and lost two wives before he began building his house at the age of forty, both his first two wives had brought him property, and he made a third advantageous marriage in 1703. But physicians' houses at least as impressive as his were more than isolated freaks in the Augustan provinces: Landor House in Warwick, rebuilt for Dr Johnson early in William III's reign, Dr John Castle's 'Great House' in Burford (*c.*1700) and the grandiloquent town mansion in Pontefract later dubbed 'Doctor Burgess's folly' are three examples. Sherwood and Pevsner, *Oxfordshire*, pp. 519–20; *Journeys of Celia Fiennes*, p. 94; information on Landor House kindly supplied by Mr Peter Borsay.

[2] I am indebted to Mr Borsay for this information and also for that in p. 321 n. 4 below.

[3] *Liverpool in King Charles the Second's Time*: 'by Sir Edward Moore, Bart. of Bank Hall, Liverpool, written in the year 1667–8' (ed. W. F. Irvine,

St. Edmunds thought a good deal better of Thomas Macro, the apothecary whose 'high house' Fiennes had so admired. Yet Macro's career, too, could well be considered a prime example of social mobility through the profession of medicine, if an unusual one. He started in business as a small grocer, and though he developed a deep interest in herbal remedies I am not certain that he ever had any formal training as an apothecary; yet after building the best new house in the town in his forties, he educated his son at Cambridge and Leyden as a fine gentleman, bibliophile, and scholar, and before he died in 1737 owned a landed estate.[1] Several I have already mentioned in other professions had clambered at least as far up the social ladder as Macro, among them three of the civil servants. Burchett—possibly the son of a tradesman in Sandwich—Sergison, and Lyddell all began their working careers as clerical drudges, the two latter in the obscurity of the dockyards.[2]

The years when the Macros, Sergisons and Burchetts were building up their fortunes, between the 1670s and the 1730s, are not usually associated with profound social change;[3] and in a spacious and fertile essay published in 1966 Professor Lawrence Stone[4] developed the hypothesis that after a century, from 1540 to 1640, in which English society 'experienced a seismic upheaval of unprecedented magnitude', with opportunities for individual upward mobility that were wholly exceptional, 'an increasingly immobile society' [as he put it] evolved be-

---

Liverpool, 1899), pp. 119–20. Pemberton died in 1703 owning extensive property in the town, and having seen his son become a wealthy merchant and his daughters prosperously married to local men. Ibid., p. 119 n.

[1] *Journeys of Celia Fiennes*, pp. 151–2; *DNB* article on Cox Macro (though the author fails to mention that Macro senior turned from grocery to medicine); E. Ashworth Underwood, *Boerhaave's Men at Leyden and After* (Edinburgh, 1977), pp. 11, 187.

[2] G. Jackson and G. F. Duckett, *Naval Commissioners . . . 1660–1760* ([Lewes], 1889), p. 92 for Lyddell; M. A. Lower, 'Some Notices of Charles Sergison', loc. cit., p. 75. Burchett's precise social origins remain cloudy, but they were unimpressive; when he was dismissed by Pepys in 1687 from the clerkship to which the Admiralty Secretary had appointed him (aged 14) in 1680, Burchett described himself as 'a poor young man who is entirely at a loss to keep himself'. Burchett to Pepys, 28 Aug. 1687, quoted in G. F. James, loc. cit., p. 478.

[3] But for recent qualifications of this orthodoxy see, for example, W. A. Speck, *Stability and Strife: England 1714–1760* (1977), ch. 3, 'Social Change'; Geoffrey Holmes, 'Gregory King and the Social Structure of pre-industrial England', *Trans. Royal Hist. Soc.* 5th series, 27 (1977): see above, pp. 292-305.

[4] 'Social Mobility in England, 1500–1700', *Past and Present*, 33 (1966).

tween 1660 and 1700, setting a pattern of development which lasted from then until the Industrial Revolution. Once the base of the pre-Reformation social oligarchy had been broadened to accommodate the rise of the gentry and the bestowing of greater social recognition on certain non-landed elements, including leading members of the old professions, a greatly restricted land-market and a deliberate reduction of educational opportunities after 1660 enabled the new élite to close ranks again almost as effectively as the old. Thus Stone postulated for the years after 1688 an oligarchic rather than an 'open' society, one to which the avenues of entrance were severely limited and controlled: a society in which young men from, in particular, the classes of yeomanry, small tradesmen, craftsmen, and artisans who had had so many opportunities to rise before 1640 now had precious few.[1]

Hypotheses are put forward to be tested; and Professor Stone, who delights in providing matter for argument, would probably have been disappointed as well as surprised if his 'social mobility' edifice had survived unscathed at every point since 1966. It has already taken something of a battering from students of the land market and from a number of historians of education as well. But I believe the most serious weakness in the elaborate model he constructed for the society of the pre-industrial century is its failure to take account of a crucial period in the development of the English professions. Of course Stone was right to draw attention to the importance in this respect of the years 1580–1640, which saw a remarkable professional advance by the common lawyers and significant changes both in the practice of medicine and in the growth of a professional consciousness among clergy and royal officials; and this appears to fit neatly into his hypothesis. But one of my two main objects in this paper will be to argue that there was a much more far-reaching transformation of the professions later, in a period that can be very roughly demarcated at the one end by the introduction of a formal examination for a naval commission in 1677/8 and the creation in 1683 of England's first really large professional government department, the Excise, and at the other end by, for example, the foundation of the great Edinburgh medical school in 1726 and the passing of the Lawyer's Bill in 1729; and that these late seventeenth- and early eighteenth-century developments produced social changes

---

[1] Ibid., especially pp. 33 (and n. 42), 34, 39, 44–5, 51, 54–5.

which, so far from clogging the channels of upward mobility, kept some of the old ones wide open and created others that were essentially new.

First, however, I hope to explain how the connections between the professions and social change at this period went far beyond the problem of mobility, vital though that was. For this is a problem which should ideally be seen in a very broad social context; one in which rapidly rising standards of material prosperity and comfort, economic demands that were growing steadily more complex, a period of fruitful urban development, and not least the needs of the post-Revolution state throughout eighteen years of relentless warfare, were all basic ingredients. All are inseparable from the rapid evolution and innovation in the professional sector which took place between Charles II's reign and the early years of George II, either because of the impetus they received from the professions or the response they evoked from them. I have already referred in the introduction to this lecture to an obvious link between urbanization and the professions. But I have chosen to concentrate here on the one ingredient in the situation which seems to me central to almost everything else, namely, the growth of prosperity in our period and with it the improvement in the quality of life. Many students of pre-industrial England now agree that, thanks partly to the so-called financial and commercial 'revolutions' of the later seventeenth century, and partly to the astonishing improvement in the fiscal resources of the state between 1683 and 1712, an enormous amount of both private and public spending power was produced and released. The result of this, and also of fifty years of uneven but still significant agrarian progress after 1680, was a society which over five to six decades from the mid 1670s grew strikingly in material prosperity (a benefit far more widely shared than was once thought), and a society which, in part consequence, became more sophisticated, probably more status-conscious, certainly more comfort- and amenity-conscious, and also more cultivated than any which had preceded it in England.

Several of the consequences of this burgeoning of wealth and social sophistication have recently attracted attention. Professor Plumb has written persuasively of the 'commercialisation of leisure' from the end of the seventeenth century onwards; Mr Machin has argued that 'the Great Rebuilding' of England reached its peak not in 1600 but around 1700; and Peter Borsay has pointed to what he calls an 'urban renaissance' in the

English provinces between 1680 and 1760.[1] The place of the professions in this many-hued, subtly changing scene has never been adequately assessed, but it is not, I hope, difficult to appreciate.

On the one hand, the professions obviously helped to create a good deal of the new spending power in a consumer society; and as their own numbers and rewards rose, so they bought land, stocks, and securities;[2] they built houses (especially town houses, as we have seen); they patronized a host of tradesmen, craftsmen, and other professionals.[3] Not least, they developed the keenest interest in improving the amenities of the places they lived in. Professional men are to be found interesting themselves, and often taking the lead in, for example, town planning;[4] the improvement of water supplies;[5] the promotion of river navigation schemes;[6] the founding of charity schools.[7]

[1] J. H. Plumb, *The Commercialisation of Leisure in Eighteenth-century England* (Stenton Lecture, Reading, 1973); R. Machin, 'The Great Rebuilding: A Reassessment', *Past and Present*, 77 (1977); Peter N. Borsay, 'The English Urban Renaissance, 1680–1760', *Social History*, 5 (1977).

[2] P. G. M. Dickson, *The Financial Revolution in England: A Study in the Development of Public Credit, 1688–1756* (1967), chs. 11 and 17, *passim*, contains much interesting information on the latter, especially in respect of doctors and lawyers. On investments by physicians, for instance, see pp. 267, 278–9, 426. See also Sir Zachary Cope, *William Cheselden* (1953), p. 11, for a leading surgeon's investment in South Sea Stock in 1714.

[3] To give one example, among many. They often spent heavily on fitting their children for suitable careers, and among the fellow professionals to profit from this were the growing number of schoolmasters in private educational establishments.

[4] e.g. Thomas Newsham, barrister-at-law, Town Clerk of Warwick, was a dominant figure on the Fire Court which carefully planned the rebuilding of the town in the 1690's (cf. above, p. 317).

[5] As with Lawrence Carter, senior, Leicester's leading solicitor in the late 17th century. Carter lived—like his son, a prominent barrister and politician —in one of the 'severall good houses, some of stone and brick' which Celia Fiennes found in 'the Newark', one of the few enclaves of good private building in Augustan Leicester. *Journeys*, p. 163; J. Simmons, *Leicester Past and Present*, i (1974), p. 100.

[6] For Isaac Greene's services to the corporation of Liverpool in connection with the river Weaver navigation (1719), see Stewart-Brown, op. cit., p. 21; for Alexander Leigh, the wealthy Wigan attorney, and his active promotion and financing of the river Douglas navigation, see M. Cox, 'Sir Roger Bradshaigh and the Electoral Management of Wigan, 1695–1747', *Bulletin of the John Rylands Library*, 37 (1954–5), p. 138 and n. 3.

[7] Clergymen, such as White Kennett, minister of St. Botolph's, Aldgate, and rector of St. Mary Aldermary, Thomas Bray, his successor at Aldgate, Thomas Bennet, rector of St. James's, Colchester, William Stubbs, archdeacon

But at the same time we also find them patronizing local music societies and assemblies;[1] by their own private leisure interests making their neighbourhood a place to be sought out by visiting antiquarians, virtuosi, bibliophiles and collectors;[2] and either delivering, organizing, or subscribing to all manner of those courses of public lectures to which the educated Englishman of the early eighteenth century was growing so addicted— lectures on natural philosophy, on trigonometry, mechanics or hydrostatics, on geography, on anatomy (a particular source of fascination), and so on.[3] The lawyers frequently exercised far-

of St. Albans, and Richard Willis, dean of Lincoln, naturally played the most prominent roles with their fund-raising sermons and tracts and pastoral oversight [for the above see G. V. Bennett, *White Kennett, 1660-1728, Bishop of Peterborough* (1957), pp. 187–90; J. Hunter (ed.), *The Diary of Ralph Thoresby, F.R.S.* (1830), ii. 380–1; Thomas Bennet, MA, *Charity-Schools Recommended, in a Sermon preach'd at St. James's Church in Colchester, on Sunday March 26*, 1710 (London and Cambridge, 1710); M. G. Jones, *The Charity School Movement* (Cambridge, 1938), p. 73; John Strype, *A Survey of the cities of London and Westminster* (1720 revision of John Stow's *Survey* of 1598), Book V, p. 43]. But among other professional men identified with the charity school movement from 1699 onwards were, e.g., Dr Gideon Harvey, senr., the physician, and John Hooke (d. 1712), serjeant-at-law. Jones, op. cit., pp. 39, 40, 73.

[1] E. Hobhouse (ed.), *The Diary of a West Country Physician*, pp. 51-3,. 56, 58–134 *passim;* Defoe, *Tour*, ii. 231; Macky, *Journey*, ii. 41–2, 211.

[2] Defoe, *Tour*, i. 47 (for Dr Beeston and Mr White, physician and surgeon of Ipswich); Hist. MSS Comm., *Portland MSS*, vi. 76–9 (for Dr Thorpe, physician of Rochester, and Mr Martin, the bibliophile attorney of Diss, Norfolk); William Munk, *The Roll of the Royal College of Physicians of London*, i (1878), 453–4 (for Nathaniel Johnston, MD [d. 1705], who in the end ruined a flourishing practice at Pontefract through his obsession with Yorkshire antiquities and natural history); G. F. James, 'Josiah Burchett', loc. cit., pp. 493–4, for the collection of 392 paintings which Burchett had built up at Hampstead by the time of his death. See also E. A. Underwood, *Boerhaave's Men*, pp. 178–81 for the extraordinary west-country physician, John Huxham (1692–1768), and his meteorological investigations at Plymouth, 1724–35, which attracted the interest of the Royal Society.

[3] e.g. E. R. G. Taylor, *The Mathematical Practitioners of Tudor and Stuart England* (Cambridge, 1954), p. 284, for John Harris's public lectures on applied mathematics, 1698–1707, one of a score of London schoolmasters and academy tutors active in this field; Underwood, op. cit., p. 128, for James Jurin's celebrated public lectures on experimental philosophy, 1710–15, when he was headmaster of Newcastle-on-Tyne grammar school; G. C. Peachey, *A Memoir of William & John Hunter* (Plymouth, 1924), pp. 18–19, and Z. Cope, *William Cheselden*, p. 5, for Cheselden's and Francis Hauksbee's courses of public anatomy and zoology lectures in Fleet Street, 1721–2, 'being chiefly intended for gentlemen', in which 'care will be taken to have nothing offensive'; W. Brockbank and F. Kenworthy (eds.), *The Diary of Richard Kay, 1716-51 . . . A Lancashire Doctor* (Chetham Soc., Man-

reaching local influence in their role as Town Clerks, and the civic importance of both them and medical men was occasionally signalized by their election as mayors.[1]

However, it is a different side of the relationship of the professions to a more prosperous and socially demanding England that I want to explore most carefully, namely their response to that prosperity and to those demands. For it is here I see the main clue both to the transformation of the professions themselves and thereby to their emergence as the most active and capacious vehicle of social mobility under the later Stuarts and the first two Georges. Professional men, by definition, provide certain specialized services for their fellow citizens and for the state. So it should not really surprise us to find that in response to a society and a state which increasingly required new services, or a greater volume and variety of existing services, on a scale without precedent—and (a vital point) had the capacity as never before to pay for those services—the professions did expand; that they did prosper; that they adapted their methods of training and to some extent of organization to meet the requirements of the changing world about them; and that in addition they acquired new offshoots, tiny to start with but destined in time to become large branches.

To begin with, between the 1680s and 1713 the English state needed a far larger civil service, army, and navy then ever before, far larger even than Cromwell's; and so far as the bureaucracy was concerned, the determination of all early Hanoverian administrations to keep the land tax as low as possible and their heavy dependence in consequence on indirect taxation, in much the same multiplicity of forms devised during the French wars, guaranteed that the need would, in effect, be just as great after the Peace of Utrecht as before it. But the state could not have had these services, with all their professional implications, had not first the monarchy in the 1680s and then the Parliaments of post-Revolution England been able, and

chester, 1968), pp. 63–5, for the Revd. Caleb Rotherham's Manchester subscription lectures on magnetism, electricity, hydrostatics and pneumatics; ibid., pp. 26, 42, 47–8, 97–8, for other south Lancashire lecture courses, 1738–45, patronized by local physicians, surgeons, attorneys, and clergy, including Dr Hamer's lectures on trigonometry, logarithms, and natural philosophy.

[1] Among lawyers, surgeons, and apothecary-doctors who served as mayors in this period were John Bradshaw (Warwick), Thomas Macro (Bury St Edmunds), James Yonge (Plymouth), Philip Potter (Torrington) and Alexander Leigh (Wigan).

prepared, to foot the bills. The result by 1710, at the climax of the struggle with Louis XIV, was a civil service (excluding household officers, officials of the law courts, and political appointees in the government)[1] of well over 11,000, some 4,000 commissioned officers in the army, and in the royal navy perhaps 1,000 officers of lieutenant's rank and above, plus a much larger number of warrant or 'petty' officers, some of whom would in due course achieve commissions.[2]

Once this great edifice of state-employed professionals had been erected it proved extremely difficult to dismantle: for reasons already suggested the 'army of civil officers', as a prominent member of the Commons apprehended early in George I's reign, had come to stay,[3] and so had the 'military men' and the naval profession, essentially because of the half-pay system, which was institutionalized for both armed forces in 1713. And thus it was that three professions which had been no more than nascent in the 1670s (indeed, in the case of the army and the bureaucracy so tiny and insecure that, considered as lifelong occupations, they barely merited the description), had all become long before the 1720s fully-fledged and well-fleshed

[1] Because of these numerous exclusions my estimate of the number of 'civil servants' (a conservative one, which also leaves out of account several thousand auxiliaries, part-timers, and trainees) is not measurable against Gregory King's optimistic guess of 10,000 'persons in greater and lesser offices' for the year 1688. It does, however, include dockyard officers, clerks, and craftsmen, and that basic core of dockyard workers not laid off in time of peace, who together with a part of the Ordnance Office establishment may legitimately be seen as the forerunners of the 'technical civil service'.

[2] The above figures will be fleshed out in my book *Augustan England: Professions, State and Society, 1680-1730*, to be published [in 1982] by Allen and Unwin. Of the many sources drawn on, the most important are *The Calendars of Treasury Books* for Queen Anne's reign; John Chamberlayne's *Magnae Britanniae Notitia* (1708, 1710, and 1716 editions); five volumes (I–IV and VII) in the series *Office-Holders in Modern Britain*, compiled by J. C. Sainty and J. M. Collinge (University of London, 1972–8); John Ehrman, *The Navy in the War of William III 1689-1697* (Cambridge, 1953), appendix on dockyards; D. A. Baugh, *British Naval Administration in the Age of Walpole* (Princeton, 1965); R. D. Merriman (ed.), *Queen Anne's Navy* (Navy Records Soc. 1961); R. E. Scouller, *The Armies of Queen Anne* (Oxford 1966); E. Hughes, *Studies in Administration and Finance, 1558-1825* (Manchester, 1934); an establishment list of the Treasury in 1711 in Brit. Lib. Loan 29/45B/12; and *A List of the Principal Officers, Civil and Military, in Great Britain in the year 1710* (printed for Abel Roper by John Morphew, London, 1710).

[3] See the speech of Archibald Hutcheson, MP for Hastings, a former member of the Board of Trade, in the debate on the Septennial bill, April 1716. *Cobbett's Parliamentary History of England* (1806-20), vii. 356-7.

professions. In the meantime, in the course of twenty years of major warfare the élite of these professions—three or four hundred men, to put the figure at its lowest—had made fortunes. The army, for instance, had no fewer than 68 generals by 1710; the 'non-political' civil service contained close on a hundred officials whose income from salaries alone or from ascertainable fees[1] was worth anything from £500 to £2,500 a year.

But what of the senior professions in our period—the law, medicine, and the Church—and another profession well-established though still unorganized by 1660, schoolteaching, whose rapid expansion since Tudor times had, of course, drawn very heavily on clerical manpower? Here again, with the qualified exception of the clergy, we find the same three elements interacting: demand, supply, and the resources necessary to sustain and increase supply. The law provides the most obvious illustration. More young men trained for the bar in the late seventeenth century, and many more young men went into attorneys' and solicitors' offices as articled clerks then and in the early eighteenth century than at any previous time. Between 1660 and 1689, 1,996 young men were called to the bar at one or other of the four inns of court, 623 more than in the thirty years before 1640, customarily considered the common law's most dynamic and productive period before the nineteenth century.[2] And although the output of the inns fell away to some extent during the reigns of William III and Anne, recovering again in the 1720s, it remained more than enough to maintain the strength of the bar at the unprecedented level it had reached by the early 1690s. I have alluded already to the proliferation of attorneys and solicitors in particular local communities. To convey some idea of what this meant nationally, we know that

[1] Very probably this figure is an underestimate, because in some parts of the executive, notably the Exchequer where fees remained the basis of remuneration, their level in most individual cases is not ascertainable without detailed departmental studies on the admirable model of H. C. Tomlinson's *Guns and Government: the Ordnance Office under the later Stuarts* (1979) [see especially pp. 83–102, 'The Rewards of Office']. See also Kenneth Ellis, *The Post Office in the Eighteenth Century* (1958), Part One.

[2] The figures for 1610–39 are taken from W. R. Prest, *The Inns of Court . . . 1590–1640* (1972), Table 8. Those for 1670–89 are distilled from H. A. C. Sturgess (ed.), *Register of Admissions to the Honourable Society of the Middle Temple*, i (1949); F. A. Inderwick (ed.), *Calendar of Inner Temple Records*, iii (1901); R. J. Fletcher (ed.), *The Pension Book of Gray's Inn*, ii (1910); *The Records of the Honourable Society of Lincoln's Inn: The Black Books*, iii, iv (1899–1902). I am grateful to Mr Richard W. Pearce of St. John's College, Cambridge, for the figure of 714 calls for the years 1660–9.

the *bona fide* attorneys alone—those formally sworn and registered by the Courts of Common Pleas and King's Bench—rose from 1,725 in 1633 to 3,129 in 1729-30,[1] plus another 418 accredited attorneys who chose to register under the provisions of the 1729 Act with one of the provincial courts of record;[2] and this over a century when the population was increasing very very little; when solicitors (on whom for technical reasons it is almost impossible to pin any precise numbers) and entering clerks are known to have been spawning at least as actively as attorneys;[3] and when notaries and scriveners were still fairly numerous on their own account.[4]

All this can only have happened, in the first place, because there was a greater demand for lawyers' services by the second half of the seventeenth century than prior to 1640, and above all a demand for a greater range and variety of such services than ever before. By the years 1680-1730 the call was not only for practisers who could handle the mounting volume of litigation in the courts.[5] There was a pressing need for experts 'of a clear,

[1] M. Birks, *Gentlemen of the Law* (1960), p. 99; R. Robson, *The Attorney in Eighteenth-Century England* (Cambridge, 1959), p. 166.

[2] Between May 1729 and March 1731. *Lists* (1730), pp. 27-35; *Additional Lists* (1731), pp. 111-18, 255-60.

[3] See Birks, op. cit.; the report of the Strickland Committee to the House of Commons, delivered 14 Mar. 1729, which showed, for example, roughly 1,000 entering clerks on the books of the Court of Commons Pleas alone by that time (evidence of Sir George Cooke, Prothonotary, *Commons' Journals*, xxi. 267). William Tully told the Committee (ibid.) he believed there were 'some thousands of entering clerks' practising in the country at large.

[4] By 1700 their narrower specialisms were already in danger of being absorbed in the general competence of the 'ministerial persons' of the law. Nevertheless, a study of lawyers in Halifax, for example, has detected 7 scriveners as well as 33 attorneys and solicitors practising in that parish in the period 1668-1730. C. D. Webster, 'Halifax Attorneys', *Trans. of Halifax Antiquarian Soc.* (1968-9), pp. 80-7, 117-19. For notaries and scriveners see also John Patten, *English Towns 1500-1700* (1978), pp. 283, 288; R. Robson, op. cit., pp. 26-8; W. Holdsworth, *A History of English Law*, vi (2nd edn. 1937), 447. Campbell allocated a short chapter to each in his survey of the London professions in 1747 and recommended the notary's, in particular, as 'a very reputable employ'. R. Campbell, *The London Tradesman: being a Compendious View of all the Trades, Professions, Arts, both Liberal and Mechanic, now practised in the Cities of London and Westminster* (London, 1747), pp. 79-80, 82-4, esp. p. 83.

[5] For the general increase of Common Pleas business in the early decades of the 18th century, see *Commons' Journals*, xxi. 267. Edward Hughes (*North Country Life in the Eighteenth Century: The North East 1700-1750*, p. 77) describes this as 'a great age of litigation in the north', and cites as one example the 21 suits in which William Cotesworth was involved during ten years as lord of the manor of Gateshead.

solid and unclouded understanding'[1] who could both draft and execute increasingly complicated property and marriage settlements or comprehend, in developing commercial and manufacturing centres, the mysteries of international exchange; for men who could negotiate mortgages, collect rents on commission, and keep accounts for local land- or property-owners; who could act as investment consultants, and quite frequently—before the arrival of the provincial private banker—serve as money-lenders. But what is equally clear is that along with this ever-rising tide of demand for both litigious and non-litigious services, there must also have been an ability and a willingness to pay for them, and meet in the process the substantially higher fees which were generally being charged to clients by the years 1680–1730.[2]

Another professional sphere in which by the late seventeenth century the changing expectations of the consumer were beginning to have a profound effect was education. The desire of parents, from the aristocracy down to the urban tradesman and the ambitious yeoman, for the best education—or at any rate the most fitting education—for their sons, rather than being content with the most convenient, traditional local education for them, had three main consequences. It encouraged the habit of employing private tutors in the families of the nobility and wealthy gentry and so afforded a new career-opportunity to the ordained clergy of the Church of England. It stimulated a remarkable growth in demand, partly private and partly generated by the needs of the armed forces, for schoolmasters who specialized in subjects other than the basic three Rs, Latin, and Greek: for experts in mathematics; in commercial and career-orientated subjects such as book-keeping, surveying, even excise-gauging; for teachers of navigation, of calligraphy, and to a lesser degree modern languages.[3] Some of them could be accommodated within the existing or new endowed foundations,[4] but most taught in a rich new crop of private schools

[1] R. Campbell, op. cit., p. 70.

[2] Lawyers' fees are a major theme developed in the essay 'The Lawyers and Society in Augustan England' in my *Augustan England* (1982), pp. 130-2, 156-9.

[3] Foster Watson, *The Beginning of the Teaching of Modern Subjects in England* (1909); E. G. R. Taylor, *The Mathematical Practitioners of Tudor and Stuart England* (Cambridge, 1954); id. *The Mathematical Practitioners of Hanoverian England* (Cambridge, 1966); A. Heal, *The English Writing Masters and their Copy Books* (1931); R. S. Tompson, *Classics or Charity? The Dilemma of the Eighteenth Century Grammar School* (Manchester, 1971); M. Seaborne, *The English School: its Architecture and Organization, 1370–1870* (1971).

[4] For example, in Manchester, Birmingham, Hull, Newcastle upon Tyne,

and academies.[1] Finally, parental ambitions made the taking in of boarders and fee-paying day boys, as much by the best of the old grammar schools as by the most progressive of the new 'modern' schools, a commonplace in late Stuart England. And so profitable did this enterprise become after 1680 that, what with this and his increasingly technical or non-classical specialisms, the secondary schoolmaster and academy tutor of George I's reign was in many places almost unrecognizable as the successor of the miserably paid drudge so familiar in the mid seventeenth century. The financial incentives for able men, either with or without taking orders, to take up schoolmastering as a life profession were transformed by the early eighteenth century;[2] though among those who did so, there remained of course very many, especially among the ushers, who could only watch disconsolately as the gravy train passed by.

However, the reaction of the professions to Augustan society involved much more than supplying governmental or largely economic demands, or simply responding to that society's growing wealth. We should also see it as a reaction to the greater sophistication I emphasized earlier and to the Englishman's rising and widening expectations. These, for one thing, generated certain demands which the existing professions could not meet; so that this period sees the birth of a number of small professions which are truly novel, in that they are by 1730 minor occupational groups, whereas in 1660 only isolated individuals had foreshadowed them. The age of baroque and Palladian

and Holt grammar schools; and in many endowed 'secondary' foundations of the years 1660–1720, including Christ's Hospital; Tuxford School, Notts; Sir John Moore's school, Appleby Magna; Brigg Grammar School; Pierrepoint's, Lucton; Williamson's School, Rochester; Sir Thomas Parkyn's School, Bunny; and Saunders' School, Rye.

[1] The works of Taylor and Heal (above, p. 323 n. 3) teem with examples. Twenty-eight private writing schools were advertised in the pages of John Houghton's periodical *A Collection for the Improvement of Industry and Trade* in the eleven and a half years from March 1692 to September 1703. Bret's Academy at Tottenham Cross in Charles II's reign provided a staff of seven to teach a comprehensive 'modern' syllabus, and Watts's Academy in Little Tower Street, which began by teaching accountancy and book-keeping only, was employing in the 1720s four masters or 'professors', a resident French tutor, and several more part-time tutors. W. A. L. Vincent, *The Grammar Schools: their Continuing Tradition, 1660–1714* (1979), p. 200; N. Hans, *New Trends in Education in the Eighteenth Century* (1951), pp. 83–6; Taylor, *Mathematical Practitioners* (1966), pp. 113, 164.

[2] The argument is developed at length in my essay 'Schools and the Schoolmaster', in *Augustan England*, ch. 3, especially pp. 57-70.

mansion-building, together with the careful, symmetrical planning which so much new urban development required by 1700, called for a new breed of specialist architects.[1] Again, while a more scientific approach to agrarian improvement and the maximization of rents among the big landowners gave birth to the full-time estate steward or agent,[2] it was a more grandiose approach to the planning and even mapping of their grounds that encouraged the training of surveyors. And of course one of the most interesting occupational offshoots of a society more leisured and cultivated than that of two generations before was the emergence of musicians as a minor profession, reputable enough to be considered suitable, in some quarters, for the scions of good families; though there were those who professed a certain social uneasiness at the development.

If a parent cannot make his son a gentleman, and finds that he has got an itch of music [wrote R. Campell Esq. in his guide to trades and professions in George II's reign], it is much the best way to allot him entirely to that study. The present general taste of music in the gentry may find him better bread than what this art deserves. The Gardens in the summer time employ a great number of hands; where they are allowed a guinea a week and upwards, according to their merit. The Opera, the play-houses, masquerades, ridottoes, and the several music-clubs employ them in the winter. But I cannot help thinking that any other mechanic trade is much more useful to the society than the whole tribe of singers and scrapers: and should think it much more reputable to bring my son up a blacksmith (who was said to be the father of music) than bind him apprentice to the best master of music in England.

The writer was willing to admit, however, that 'this . . . must be reckoned an unfashionable declaration in this musical age'.[3]

However, the professional response after 1680 to essentially non-economic social expectations can be seen writ largest of all

---

[1] H. M. Colvin, *A Biographical Dictionary of English Architects, 1660–1840* (1954), especially the valuable introductory essay on 'The Architectural Profession' (pp. 10–25). James Lees Milne, *English Country Houses: Baroque, 1685–1715* (1970) and John Summerson, *Architecture in Britain, 1530–1830* (4th edn. 1963), pp. 119–243, also contain many individual examples, as of course do the numerous county surveys in N. Pevsner, *The Buildings of England* (1951–).

[2] E. Hughes, 'The Eighteenth Century Estate Agent', in H. A. Crowne, T. W. Moody and D. B. Quinn (eds.), *Essays in British and Irish History in honour of James Eadie Todd* (1949).

[3] Campbell, op. cit., p. 93. See also E. D. MacKerness, *A Social History of English Music* (1964), especially pp. 83–4, 88, 103–4; John Harley, *Music in Purcell's London: The Social Background* (1968), the introduction to which touches on the pre-Restoration background of professional music-making.

in the case of a major ancient profession, that of medicine. By the later decades of the seventeenth century a less philosophical attitude to illness and pain, an attitude that was a natural consequence of a more comfort-conscious society, and also a less devout one, led to a rising pressure on both the drugs and the diagnostic advice of the apothecary and at the same time stimulated the most important advances yet seen in England in the art of surgery. The science of *materia medica* made significant strides during the seventeenth century; and it was the now formidable array of medicines which any well-appointed apothecary could stock and dispense by 1700, and above all the variety of opiates and other 'exotic' drugs now on the bill of lading of almost every East Indiaman sailing into London,[1] which were decisive in translating the status of the apothecaries in the course of the half-century after 1680 from that of a superior trade to that of a profession, most of whose members were engaged in some measure in general medical practice by 1730.[2] Their chance would naturally have been more difficult to seize had it not been for the small numbers and the high fees of the *pukka* doctors, the university-trained physicians, in later Stuart England. The abandonment of the London field to them by the physicians during the Great Plague and the decision of the House of Lords in 1704 to uphold the legality of their right to prescribe for patients as well as dispense, gave the apothecaries two powerful shoves along the way. But in the end, as their sourer critics in the Royal College of Physicians, like Robert Pitt, were not slow to observe, they were floated into the ranks of the professionals and 'this new dignity of *Doctor*' on a sea of pills, boluses, decoctions, electuaries, and juleps for which there now seemed a limitless market.[3] An estimated

[1] By 1665 a standard pharmaceutical guide was listing some 240 exotics, and it has been estimated that the import of drugs into England was at least 25 times greater in 1700 than in 1600. See R. S. Roberts, 'The Early History of the Import of Drugs into Britain', in F. N. L. Poynter (ed.), *The Evolution of Pharmacy in Britain* (1965), pp. 171–2.

[2] In general see C. Wall, H. C. Cameron, and E. A. Underwood, *A History of the Worshipful Society of Apothecaries of London* (1963), vol. I; Bernice Hamilton, 'The Medical Professions in the Eighteenth Century', *Economic Hist. Rev.* 2nd ser. iv (1951), esp. pp. 141, 159–66; R. S. Roberts, 'The Personnel and Practice of Medicine in Tudor and Stuart England', Part I. The Provinces, *Medical History*, vi (1962), Part II. London, *Medical History*, viii (1964). Cf. J. F. Kett, 'Provincial Medical Practice in England, 1730–1815', *Journal of the History of Medicine*, xix (1964), pp. 17–18, 20, 28.

[3] R[obert] Pitt, MD, *The Antidote: or the Preservation of Health and Life, and the Restorative of Physick to its Sincerity and Perfection* (London, 1704), Preface.

1,000 apothecaries' shops in London and its suburbs by Queen Anne's reign, compared with 104 (or, by one account, 114) in 1617;[1] the fact that apothecaries have been located by Dr Patten in 21 out of the 47 East Anglian market towns in the second half of the seventeenth century, compared with only five at any time in the century before 1600; the 29 apothecaries who made up the largest single element in the medical fraternity in Bristol by 1754[2]—such figures, and many more, speak for themselves about the new physical dimensions which the old profession of medicine acquired in the process.

The rise of the surgeon to a place of some honour among medical men—marked by the great gulf which existed by 1730 between the leading practisers of 'chirurgery' in London and the provinces, men of now unchallenged professional status, and those who still plied the old trade of 'barber-surgery'— was achieved more rapidly than that of the apothecaries, and with fewer advance signals over the first sixty to seventy years of the seventeenth century. All the same, it owned much to the same root factor—a greater willingness of patients to submit to their ministrations, a greater confidence in their developing skills, and of course the fact that dread of the knife was now dulled to some extent by the use of laudanum and other partial anaesthetics. Even among the surgeons proper, it is true, there was a recognized hierarchy. It embraced a numerous rank and file of workaday practitioners who still confined themselves in the main (and mercifully so) to bloodletting, blistering, mending fractured bones, minor external surgery, and increasingly to the highly profitable business of treating venereal disease with mercury—'upon [which] alone', one

There is ample confirmation from contemporary sources of the growing convention of patients addressing apothecaries as 'doctor'. See, e.g., Roberts, *Med. Hist.* vi (1962), 375–6; *A Dialogue concerning the Practice of Physic* (London, 1735); Extracts from the Town Wardens' Accounts of Torrington for 1696 and 1714, printed in J. J. Alexander and W. R. Hooper, *The History of Great Torrington in the County of Devon* (1948), p. 133; Hist. MSS Comm., *Kenyon MSS*, p. 311.

[1] R. Pitt, loc. cit.; *The Case of the Apothecaries* (London [1727]), conceding that the 'apothecaries' shops within London and seven miles thereof... upon a fair computation will appear to be upwards of a thousand'; [Samuel Foart Simmons], *The Medical Register for the Year 1783*, p. 25. Cf. Wall, Cameron, and Underwood, *op. cit.*, p. 51.

[2] John Patten, *English Towns, 1500–1700*, pp. 254, 283; W. H. Harsant, 'Medical Bristol in the Eighteenth Century', *Bristol Medico-Chirurgical Journal*, xvii (1899), 301.

Londoner wrote in the 1740s, 'the subsistence of three parts in four of all the surgeons in the town depends'.[1] At the top of the profession, on the other hand, were now several hundred men who could boast an arduous and careful training[2] and often quite remarkable manual dexterity. And though there were many fine surgeons in England between the 1660s and the 1690s, the turning-point probably came around 1700 with London's rapid emergence as a surgical teaching centre of un-questioned stature. In this, the revived prestige of the anatomy teaching at Surgeons' Hall and the well-advertised and well-patronized private lecture courses and demonstrations mounted by leading London surgeons from Anne's reign onwards were both important.[3] But probably more so was the instruction available by the early eighteenth century in the London hos-pitals, not only from the salaried surgeons of St. Barts and St. Thomas's, but informally in the three new hospitals, the West-minster, Guy's, and St. George's, whose foundation between 1719 and 1733 was no coincidence in the medical context of the period.[4] It is not surprising, therefore, that the most pro-

[1] R. Campbell, *The London Tradesman*, p. 52. See also below, p. 334; A. Clark (ed.), *The Life and Times of Anthony Wood, antiquary, of Oxford . . . described by himself* (Oxford, 1891–1900), iii. 202 (on the work accruing to surgeons from the increase in brothels, 1686); Alexander and Hooper, *History of Great Torrington*, p. 133 (extract from the Wardens' Accounts for 1731); A. G. Debus (ed.), *Medicine in Seventeenth Century England* (Berkeley and Los Angeles, 1974), pp. 138, 263.

[2] A seven-year apprenticeship to a master surgeon was the basis—but increasingly not the limit—of all training, in the provinces as well as in London, and for trainees in the capital there was a stiff examination to be passed before final qualification.

[3] G. C. Peachey discovered 'no definite evidence of the regular delivery of any lectures on anatomy in London, outside the medical corporations and the Royal Society', until the opening of the eighteenth century. But between 1701, when George Rolfe began to lecture both in London and Cambridge, and 1729 he found 19 private teachers of anatomy in England, 16 of them giving courses of lectures or demonstrations in London. *A Memoir of William and John Hunter*, pp. 8–33 *passim*.

[4] There is a good modern account of the foundation of these new hospitals, together with the London Hospital (1740) and the Middlesex (1745) in E. A. Underwood, *Boerhaave's Men*, pp. 159–64. For an 18th-century account see [S. F. Simmons,] *Medical Register for 1783*, pp. 32–3. In the case of the older hospitals the year 1702, when the regulations of St. Thomas's were amended to permit its house surgeons to take in pupils as 'dressers'—on condition that 'none shall have more than three cubs at one time'—was an important landmark. J. F. South, *Memorials of the Craft of Surgery in England* (ed. D'Arcy Power, 1886), p. 249.

gressive provincial surgeons by 1730 were trying to give their sons or their star apprentices a period in London to complete their training; it was for this that Robert Kay of Bury sent his son as a pupil to Mr Steade of Guy's in 1743, where he spent an invaluable year (beautifully documented in his diary) observing operations and attending endless lectures and demonstrations.[1] Surgical instruments themselves were being perfected, and new ones devised. The first surgical instrument-makers began to appear in a few leading provincial centres at the end of the seventeenth century, having hitherto been confined to London. But young Richard Kay was nevertheless at pains to equip himself on the best advice with a brand new case of instruments just before leaving Town and coming back to Lancashire to join his father's practice.[2]

In this atmosphere the surgeon's 'art' flourished as never before; and what is more became socially estimable. Two different new techniques of 'cutting for the stone' were perfected in London between 1719 and 1727, the first by John Douglas, the second by William Cheselden, and Cheselden became so adept that he was soon able to perform his 'lateral' operation in 54 seconds, and later reduced the time much further—and therefore the risk to the patient to minimal proportions.[3] Claver Morris sent a patient from Wells to Robert Gay of Hatton Gardens for the removal of a breast cancer. Ophthalmic surgery, especially the couching of cataracts, made a notable advance. Thomas Rentone received the staggering sum of £5,000 from the Secret Service money in the 1720s 'for making known his art, skill and mystery in cutting

[1] *Diary of Richard Kay*, pp. 66–88 *passim*. 'Seldom a day but something remarkable happens', he wrote at one point; '. . . I believe being here is being at the fountain head for improvement.' Ibid., p. 70.

[2] Patten, op. cit., p. 288; *Diary of Richard Kay*, pp. 88–9. The instruments used by the great Cheselden in his lateral lithotomy operation were drawn by G. Vander Gucht and the illustration included in James Douglas, *An Appendix to the History of the Lateral Operation for the Stone* (1731). It is reproduced in Cope, *Cheselden*, p. 25.

[3] Peachey, *Memoir*, p. 23; *DNB* on Cheselden. According to Dr James Douglas (the brother of John, the surgeon) Cheselden later improved so far on his record that in straightforward cases 'he performs this operation with so much dexterity and quickness that he seldom exceeds half a minute'; and Cheselden himself stated in print that of the first hundred patients he operated on at St. Thomas's with the new method, he lost only six. James Douglas, *The History of the Lateral Operation for the Stone* (1731) and William Cheselden, *The Anatomy of the Human body* (1730 edn., with appendix), quoted by Cope, op. cit., pp. 29–30.

ruptures'.[1] And many ambitious operations and treatments were performed in the provinces, too.[2] The great rewards which the best surgeons could by now expect and their ability to maintain the style of living of wealthy gentlemen—certainly vying with many of the leading physicians in this respect—inevitably helped to raise still further the status of their branch of the profession and to make it so attractive to prospective entrants that it was said by 1747 that 'there are none of the liberal arts more likely to procure a livelihood than this. An ingenious surgeon, let him be cast on any corner of the earth, with but his case of instruments in his pocket, he may live where most other professions would starve'.[3] Cheselden was able to charge £500 an operation to his wealthier patients at the height of his fame (between £9 and £20 a second when cutting for the stone) and Charles Maitland got double that sum for inoculating Prince Frederick against the smallpox in the later years of George I.[4] Equally impressive in its own way is the fact that when Edward Greene, senior surgeon of St. Barts, sat for his portrait he had both the social panache and the money to employ the leading French court painter of his day, Rigaud, the same artist whose portrait of Louis XIV, designed as a present for Philip V of Spain, the King had liked so much he could not bear to part with it.[5]

At the same time there were some fine pickings to be had in the provinces, especially for the dexterous surgeon able to attract a county clientele, or build up the best practice in a growing town. The same man who, quite early in his career, was able to write with something akin to enthusiasm of the pox, 'by this one disease I got this year above £120' was subsequently able to charge from 25 to 30 guineas apiece for 'tapping' rich patients, and in one year between £30 and £70 each for successfully treating nine cases of piles.[6] For country surgeons

[1] *The Diary of a West Country Physician*, p. 29; Cope, op. cit., pp. 75–81; Brit. Lib. Add. MSS 40843, f. 9.

[2] See, e.g., L. M. Zimmerman, 'Surgery', in A. G. Debus, op. cit., pp. 61–2; F. N. L. Poynter (ed.), *The Journal of James Yonge [1647–1721]*, *Plymouth Surgeon* (1965), p. 208; *Diary of a West Country Physician*, p. 99 (22 Aug. 1723); *Diary of Richard Kay*, pp. 91 ff., esp. pp. 134, 141–2, 147.

[3] R. Campbell, *The London Tradesman*, p. 57. It is interesting that one of Cheselden's apprentices, John Belchier, (born *c*.1706) was educated at Eton. William Wadd, *Nugae Chirurgicae* (1824), p. 17.

[4] *DNB* on Cheselden; Brit. Lib. Add. MSS 40843, f. 11.

[5] I owe this information to Dr Robert Beddard of Oriel College, Oxford. The portrait of Greene, Master of the London Barber Surgeons' Company in 1711, now hangs in the College's Champneys Common Room.

[6] *Journal of James Yonge*, pp. 162, 207, 208.

of high reputation there was certainly every incentive to use
their years of accumulated experience to keep their wealthier
patients alive. 'January 30th', wrote James Yonge of Plymouth
in his journal, 'died Mr W. Addie, another good friend and
profitable patient; he had an ulcer in the bladder 4 years, in
which time I had of him near £200'. Yonge's comfort was that
in the following two years, 1703 and 1704, he still had 444
patients on his books, 'a pretty good estate' (as he modestly put
it) and 'more business than I was desirous of'.¹ It may be that
for every James Yonge, or even for every country surgeon of
comfortable means in the early eighteenth century, like the
senior Kay of Baldingstone or William Barman of Wilmington,
Kent, there was another more akin to George Wakeman, a
struggling practitioner at Cople, Suffolk, who in February
1712 could afford to lay out only £5 to train his son Richard as
a glazier in Bedford.² All the same, by the 1730s the status gap
even in the provincial town between the well-esteemed surgeon
and the physician, who only sixty years before had been on a
very different social and professional plane, had shrunk so much
that some very distinguished physicians, such as Thomas White
of Manchester (1696–1778), did not hesitate now to train their
only sons as surgeons. In fact there were many close family links
by this time spanning the two branches of the profession.³

It is this whole question of professional status-changes, and
their catalytic effects, which brings me back to the other major
theme of this lecture which I anticipated earlier, the relationship between the professions and social mobility. There are
three keys, I would suggest, to the supreme importance of the
Augustan professions, old and new, in maintaining a far more
mobile society than the Stone thesis allows for and also a stabler
and better integrated society than the cruder vehicles of 1540–
1640, with their more violent motion, had produced.⁴ One key

¹ Ibid., pp. 209, 226, 227.
² See *Diary of Richard Kay*, pp. 91, 112, for the size and profitability of his
father's practice; PRO IR 1/1/121 (for Barman), IR 1/42/44 (for Wakeman).
³ e.g. Nathaniel Smith, whom Boyer described on his death in 1723 as 'a
celebrated anatomist and one of the surgeons to St. Bartholomew's Hospital'
(*Political State of Great Britain*, xxv, 356) had a brother, Lawrence, who was a
physician. Richard Kay's first cousin, Samuel, was a physician in Manchester
and played a vital part in furthering his career as a surgeon (*Diary*, p. 61).
See also above, p. 333 n. 3 for the case of the Douglas brothers.
⁴ The sudden, explosive progress of the new 'monied interest' did of
course cause some disturbance to the social structure for some three decades

is that very rise already noticed in the prestige of auxiliary branches of old professions (hitherto of dubious standing, with the exception of registered attorneys); and at the same time, the transition of those three youthful professions, the army, the navy, and the civil service, into now permanent reservoirs of employment, acceptable to the members of the existing professional and landed classes, and desirable in the eyes of other groups as yet outside their ranks. We have observed what occurred within the medical profession, with the apothecaries and surgeons. A rough parallel can be detected within the teaching fraternity, with the emergence of a small élite in the most successful of the post-primary schools. And there was a much closer parallel within the law. By 1729-30 the clerks of the House of Commons unhesitatingly added the designation 'gentleman' to the name of every duly qualified solicitor as well as attorney reported to their office by the judges' clerks; and it was not many years after the foundation in the late 1730s of their first joint professional association, legitimately called the 'Society of Gentlemen Practisers', that Hume Campbell, the barrister, told a gathering of attorneys and solicitors from the Home Counties that 'he considered the worthy part of the profession, whether attorneys, solicitors, or counsel, as one body'.[1]

By then, moreover, the amount of social aspiration invested in those newer professions wedded to the service of the state had increased vastly since Charles II's reign; and in particular was this true of the navy and the bureaucracy. The transformed status of the non-political civil service by the 1730s depended not just on the great expansion in numbers noted earlier and the rewards it held out to its top executives, but to the infinitely greater prospect of permanency the Crown's service now offered. This was a direct result of the determination of three great Treasury ministers, Rochester in the 1680s and Godolphin and Harley from 1702 to 1714, to fight for the concept of the bureaucracy as a profession—latterly a stern battle waged against the piratical raids of the party bosses, who were ready enough to plunder it so as to reward their adherents. The fact

after the early 1690s. But even this was more localized than we are often tempted to think. See the comments on this question in 'The Achievement of Stability: The Social Context of Politics from the 1680s to the Age of Walpole', my contribution to John Cannon (ed.), *The Whig Ascendancy: Colloquies on Hanoverian England*, (1981): see above, pp. 270-2.

[1] *Records of the Society of Gentlemen Practisers in the courts of Law and equity called the Law society* (introduction by Edwin Freshfield, 1897), p. 33.

that half the jobs in the civil service were superannuable by 1713,[1] and the evidence in London alone of hundreds of men, starting their careers between the 1680s and the 1720s, who managed to serve for twenty, thirty, or even forty years in the same or in cognate departments,[2] are measures of the Treasury's success. Possibly more significant still in terms of social mobility and integration was what happened to the navy. In the late 1670s the status of its officers was not high; they were plagued by dilettantes of what Pepys called 'the bastard breed';[3] and it was by no means clear that the Admiralty Secretary would realize his great objective of making theirs a profession suitable for the sons of gentlemen, without any loss of efficiency and yet without closing the door on promotion from the lower decks. By the end of the wars of 1689–1713, demonstrably and triumph- antly, his dream had become reality. The navy of Queen Anne and George I was one whose quarter-decks were, by and large, stocked with gentlemen's sons who had proved their seamanship, and with seamen whose hard-won commissions were now (as they had not been with the old 'tarpaulin' officers of Charles II's reign) a passport to gentility. It was a proud service and the competition to enter it and succeed in it was fierce.

If status changes both among and within professions provide one of our three keys, they also point the way, together with the physical expansion that almost everywhere accompanied them, to the second. The professions of 1680–1730 could provide a unique vehicle of upward mobility not least because of sheer carrying capacity. A rough estimate—and in the nature of our information it can only be extremely rough—would put the number of permanent jobs in the professions by 1730[4] at

[1] Between 1687 and 1713 graduated contributory pension schemes were adopted by the Excise Office, the Salt Office, and the London establishment of the Customs. *Calendar of Treasury Books*, viii. 1173; E. Hughes, *Studies in Administration and Finance*, p. 211; E. E. Hoon, *The Organization of the English Customs Service 1696–1786* (2nd edn. Newton Abbott, 1968), pp. 105–6.

[2] See especially the lists of office-holders printed in successive editions of Edward Chamberlayne's *Angliae Notitia* and John Chamberlayne's *Magnae Britanniae Notitia* from the 1680s to the 38th edn. of 1755, and the compila- tions of J. C. Sainty and J. M. Collinge, cited above, p. 320 n. 2. See also Brit. Lib. Loan 29/128: Whitelocke Bulstrode to Lord Oxford, 21 Aug. 1714, for a warm tribute to Harley from a senior Excise official.

[3] J. R. Tanner (ed.), *A Descriptive Catalogue of the Naval Manuscripts in the Pepysian Library*, i (1903), 205: 29 Mar. 1678.

[4] I have attempted to calculate how many professional jobs were filled by men who were fully qualified—not mere trainees—and who had a reasonable

between 55,000 and 60,000. My guess is that this represented an increase since *c.*1680 of very little short of seventy per cent. An expansion of respectable employment opportunities of this order would have been notable in any circumstances. But when we consider supply in relation to demand; when we take account of the minimal increase of population between the 1650s and the late 1720s—no more than a few per cent in England and Wales; when we bear in mind that the size of the nuclear family in all strata of society was smaller than it had been before 1640—that there were, in other words, fewer sons to be provided for; that the business world had increased its attractions[1] and that there was therefore far less need than before for the landed gentry to seek a monopoly, or even a lion's share, of professional jobs; then it manifestly becomes a factor of prime social importance.

But what made it possible for social classes and groups other than the gentry, including groups far below the ranks of the governing élite, to take up the large surplus thus created between the 1680s and the 1730s (and indeed long after), and to profit to an extent that must otherwise have been impracticable from the development of the professions? To answer this question we need one more key—the master key—to the relationship between this development and social mobility. And it is to be found in the ways in which men trained for the professions in late Stuart and early Georgian England and in the cost of their training.

Many of the most thrusting professional groups of the years 1680–1730 had one thing in common: they demanded an apprenticeship of their recruits, and usually, though not in all cases, a lengthy one. Such was the case with surgeons, apothecaries, attorneys and solicitors, and proctors in the civil law courts;[2] with naval officers and increasingly, as time went by,

prospect of permanency. The estimate includes half-pay officers of the armed forces but excludes officers in the merchant navy, on whom I have been unable to come by even approximate information, officials of the Household and the permanent staff, including craftsmen, of the royal dockyards.

[1] Richard Grassby, 'Social Mobility and Business Enterprise in Seventeenth-century England', in D. Pennington and K. Thomas (eds.), *Puritans and Revolutionaries* (Oxford, 1978), pp. 357, 364–5. See also G. Holmes, 'The Achievement of Stability: the Social Context of Politics from the 1680s to the Age of Walpole', above, pp. 265-7.

[2] For instance, in Sept. 1711 Darby Stapleton, a victualler's son from Newington Butts, was articled for 7 years to Thomas Newman of Doctor's

with officers in the merchant marine.[1] The same condition applied to a number of the budding professions too: to musicians, to quite a large proportion of the architects, to many of the surveyors. It even came gradually to determine entry to a segment of the teaching profession, notably writing-masters.[2] In general the apprenticeship was formal, as to a trade or a craft. It involved the drawing up of indentures or articles and the payment of a premium by the young man's parent, guardian, or patron. In London the standard period of apprenticeship for intending surgeons was seven years, and for apothecaries eight. Outside London a seven-year training was normal for both.[3] The overwhelming majority of attorneys' and solicitors' clerks in both the capital and the provinces were articled for five years. For the very new professions conditions were doubtless much more flexible, but I have come across examples of a seven-year indentured training with a London musician, with several writing-masters, and a Norfolk surveyor.[4] On the other hand, those who sought a commission in the Royal Navy by learning the ropes either as 'volunteers per order' or as captain's 'servants' (and after 1715 those who followed these routes were

Commons, one of the Proctors-General of the Arches Court of Canterbury; in Dec. 1719 John Pearce, nephew to the London bookseller Awnsham Churchill, was similarly articled to William Chapman, Procurator General of the same court. PRO IR 1/1/12, IR 1/7/71.

[1] Although I have not included them in my counts (see above, p. 333 and n. 4), the merchant navy officers were by the late 17th and early 18th centuries a numerous group (England had the largest merchant marine in the world by the 1720s), and quite often men of substance. Already gentry families such as the Norrises of Speke were beginning to send younger sons into the service. *Journeys of Celia Fiennes*, p. 128; Macky, *Journeys*, i. 62; T. Heywood (ed.), *The Norris Papers* (Chetham Soc. 1846), pp. xx–xxi. In general see Ralph Davis, *The Rise of the English Shipping Industry* (1962), pp. 117–18.

[2] The music and dancing masters employed in private academies also took apprentices frequently, and so did some of the 'mathematical practitioners', especially those who were trained, as many were, to give instruction in commercial and technical subjects.

[3] Some country apothecaries would take a boy for less and the apprenticeship period of a surgeon might very occasionally be reduced by a year. Apart from the surviving records of guilds and companies, the indispensable source of information on early 18th-century apprenticeships are the Stamp Office registers in the Public Record Office. 19 vols. (IR 1/1–12 and 1/42–9) cover the years 1711–31.

[4] PRO IR 1/1/98; 1/4/4; 1/4/10; 1/4/191; 1/12/1. On the other hand, a London painter took an apprentice for 5 years 5 months in 1718, and a dancing master accepted one for six years in 1715. PRO IR 1/7/1, 1/4/57.

in a majority) were serving not a formal but certainly a *de facto* apprenticeship, and one which became more rigorous and protracted in the light of experience as time went by: Pepy's original three-year minimum length of qualifying service at sea before a 'volunteer' could take his lieutenant's examination was raised by the Admiralty to four years in 1703 and eventually to six in 1730.[1]

Thus it was that in the period covered by this lecture the whole traditional concept of the English professions as 'learned' occupations—vocations for which youths prepared themselves by attendance not just at a grammar school but at a university and/or one of the inns of court—was fundamentally modified. Dr Charles Goodall had recognized the writing on the wall in his own field in 1684, when in the preface to his treatise on *The Royal College of Physicians* he wrote distastefully (in this context of the apothecaries), 'we have to deal with a sort of men not of academical but mechanic education'. I would estimate that no more than a third of the qualified men in professional occupations by 1730 had been trained in the time-honoured way. Even the new bureaucracy recruited only a tiny proportion of graduates and was to a very marked degree in practice an apprentice-based profession: informally so, for the most part, so far as the London civil service was concerned, though with the 'supernumerary' system in the Excise and the system of 'preferable men' adopted in the Customs coming very close to formality.[2] The social repercussions of this re-orientation of professional training were immense. For although apprenticeship, formal or informal, could very reasonably be regarded as the equivalent of the vocational training of the ancient 'learned

[1] Admiralty Order, 1 May 1703, printed in R. D. Merriman (ed.), *Queen Anne's Navy: Documents, 1702–1714*, pp. 319–20; Admiralty Memorial to the King in Council, 30 Jan. 1729–30, printed in D. A. Baugh (ed.), *Naval Administration, 1715–1750* (Navy Records Soc. 120, 1977), pp. 60–1; D. A. Baugh, *British Naval Administration in the Age of Walpole*, pp. 100–1.

[2] The majority of government officials, whatever their social background, learned their business to begin with in subordinate clerkships. For the 'supernumeraries' and 'preferable men', see John Owens, *Plain Papers relating to the Excise Branch of the Inland Revenue Department from 1621 to 1878* (Linlithgow, 1879), pp. 116–19; E. Hughes, *Studies in Administration and Finance*, pp. 161–2; *Rules of the Water-side* (London, 1715), pp. 88–9; E. E. Hoon, op. cit., pp. 144–5, 205–6. There was a certain amount of formal apprenticeship in the Exchequer and associated offices, and likewise in the dockyard service: e.g. in June 1716 the son of Robert Maidstone, gent. of St. Andrews', Holborn, was articled for 5 years to Phillip Tullie, one of the Clerks of the Pipe Office. PRO IR 1/4/197.

professions', and in terms of professional efficiency was often superior to it, it was on the whole *much less expensive* than such a training.

The contrast was especially vivid in the cases of the law and medicine. Reading for the bar by George I's reign could cost a keen young man, availing himself of the best tuition at the Inns and living as well as most of his peers, upwards of £200 a year:[1] which meant that by the time they were called many law students of the 1720s must have drained their families of as much as £1,200 or even £1,400. This represented a big change since the 1620s when a young man could study in comfort and live luxuriously on £80 a year, and even since the early 1670s when Roger North scraped along for five years at the Middle Temple on a total allowance of around £240, though admitting that 'without the [further] aid I had from my brother [Sir Francis], I could not have subsisted and must have fallen'.[2] The expense of an orthodox physician's training at Oxford or Cambridge varied considerably: but it, too, was certainly rising quite steeply between the late seventeenth century and the mid-eighteenth, and two contemporary estimates to which some credence can be given put the poles for the man who went the full course, from matriculation, through the arts degree to the final doctorate in medicine, at between £1,000 in the 1690s and as much as £1,500 in the 1740s. After all, even to go up from Wells for a few days to take his Oxford doctorate in 1691 cost Claver Morris £89. 15s. 2d., with fees alone accounting for over £56.[3]

What of the junior branches of these same professions? In 1697 Thomas Brown, physician turned playwright, claimed that a good surgeon's education could be had in London by then for £120—in other words, £17 a year—though it might cost more (presumably if the trainee served his term with one

[1] E. Hughes, 'The Professions in the Eighteenth Century', *Durham University Journal*, xliv (1952), 48. One estimate for a year at the Middle Temple in 1720 was £178. 17s. 0d.—and that included a mere £5 on books! E. Hughes, *North Country Life in the Eighteenth Century: the North East 1700–1750* (Oxford, 1952), p. 82.

[2] W. R. Prest, *The Inns of Court, 1590–1640*, p. 28; North's Autobiography, in A. Jessopp (ed.), *The Lives of the Norths* (1890), iii. 18.

[3] Thomas Brown, MD, 1697, cited in B. Hamilton, 'The Medical Professions in the Eighteenth Century', *Econ. Hist. Rev.* 2nd ser. iv (1951), 163 n. 1; Munk, *Roll of the Royal College of Physicians*, ii. 64–5; pamphlet of 1749, cited in Sir George Clark, *A History of the Royal College of Physicians of London*, ii (Oxford, 1966), 545–6; *Diary of a West Country Physician*, pp. 147–8.

of the top hospital surgeons).[1] The registers of the Stamp office, dating from 1711 when apprenticeship premiums first became dutiable, suggest that the facts were a good deal less simple than this, but on balance even more favourable to families of limited means. In 1711 and 1712, for instance, not one apprenticeship in ten to a member of the London Company of Barber Surgeons (to which even the crack surgeons continued to belong until 1745) involved a premium of £100 or more.[2] Only surgeons in good practice like George Dottin, John Dobyns, or Peter Lamarque asked as much, and Dobyn's price of £139. 15s. was unusually stiff.[3] Lamarque is known to have been a gifted teacher; and yet even in the years from 1720-7 he trained Abraham Chovet, the son of a wine merchant who after 1730 was to become one of the best-known surgical demonstrators in London, for a premium of £105.[4] Of course, some of the crack operators valued themselves more highly than this. William Cheselden is known to have received £200 when he took on his own eighteen-year-old brother in September 1714,[5] and over the next fifteen years or so sums of £150 and £200 are dotted with greater frequency through the voluminous pages of the London registers. In the summer of 1716 a Cheapside druggist, Joseph Webb, paid Robert Gay of Hatton Garden no less than £250 for initiating his son in the 'art',[6] and when Thomas Reynolds of Wellingborough was sent to George Coldham of Covent Garden in July 1730 to add the finishing touches to his training, he was charged £52. 10s. 0d. for a single year.[7] Yet even by now a sound seven-year surgical grounding could still be had in the capital for around £100 down, though naturally one would pay extra for private courses of lectures or for a

[1] B. Hamilton, loc. cit.

[2] The entries are hard to interpret because more of the masters involved were barber-surgeons than true surgeons, and there is no foolproof way of identifying the occupation of each one with certainty, though most of the former charged only minimal premiums of £5 to £20.

[3] PRO IR 1/1/9. See also IR 1/1/1, 1/1/121 for Dottin (£107) and Lamarque (£100).   [4] Peachey, *Memoirs of William and John Hunter*, p. 31.

[5] Cope, *Cheselden*, pp. 10-11.

[6] PRO IR 1/4/196. In April of the same year Cheselden's own master, James Ferne, senior surgeon of St. Thomas's, took £215 with a pupil, and in 1719 three surgeons, John Bamber, Alexander Small, and Joseph Browne, charged premiums of £200. IR 1/4/153; IR 1/7/10, 1/7/36, 1/7/52.

[7] PRO IR 1/12/68. Cf. [R. Kay, ed.,] *A Lancashire Doctor's Diary, 1737-1750* (1895), p. 12 for the 24 guineas, irrespective of board and lodging and the fees for a private midwifery course, paid by Richard Kay's father to Guy's in 1743 for his son's one-year course in instruction.

hospital training. In the provinces the average cost of apprenticeship for potential surgeons, as opposed to the old-style barbersurgeons, also rose between 1680 and 1730; but even at the end of the period the investment involved, considering the length and rigour of the training, was still very reasonable. Between 1673 and 1684 James Yonge, then consolidating his reputation as one of the outstanding surgeons in the West Country, took a series of apprentices into his flourishing Devonshire practice, and very rarely asked more then £50 of their parents.[1] Premiums in the range between £30 and £60 remained the provincial norm into the early years of the eighteenth century; but by the mid and late 1720s, as the status of the provincial surgeon became more assured and his techniques more advanced, £60 to £90 had become much commoner, and here and there a practitioner of note, like Samuel Pye of Bristol and Jonathan Lippeatt of Newbury, would ask £100, or slightly more.[2]

An apothecary's training was unquestionably cheaper than that of a surgeon in the first half of our period: the going rate for entering the average London apothecary's shop from the 1690s to the later years of Anne was around £50—just over £6 a year[3]—while in the country £30 to £40 was common form, although the price could occasionally be as much as doubled for sons of gentlemen or pseudo-gentlemen.[4] As late as 1716 one of London's most well-to-do and fashionable apothecaries, James St. Amand, asked no more than £70 to take the son of an Isleworth gentleman into his shop.[5] By 1720–30 the loftier status of the doctor-apothecary was at last being more clearly reflected in the higher premiums he required. Even so, while a London training now quite often cost between £80 and £120,

[1] *Yonge's Journal*, pp. 143–90 *passim*. On a solitary occasion, in 1675, he did go as high as £90, but agreed to clothe the apprentice himself.

[2] In Aug. 1723 Pye invited Dr Claver Morris and a Wells surgeon, Mr Lucas, to watch him cut for the stone by the supra-pubic method and he shortly afterwards published *Some Observations on the Several Methods of Lithotomy*. Yet in Jan. 1723 he had asked no more than £100 with an apprentice. Lippeatt took on the son of William Hayward of Appleford, gent., in June 1730 for £105, and even fifteen years earlier it had cost a Suffolk gentleman £107. 10s. to place his son with Habakkuk Layman of Diss, Norfolk. *Diary of a West Country Physician*, p. 99 and n. 2; PRO IR 1/48/29; IR 1/12/75; IR 1/4/102.

[3] B. Hamilton, loc, cit., p. 163 n. 1. For typical London examples in 1711–12 see PRO IR 1/1/14, 1/1/24, 1/1/106, 1/1/109.

[4] For the former see, e.g., IR 1/1/98, 1/1/120, 1/42/2, 1/42/6, 1/42/66, 1/42/68; for the latter, 1/42/44, 1/42/72, 1/1/148.

[5] IR 1/4/135.

and on a seller's market in the provinces there was a comparable rise above the old very modest levels, even as late as this it was perfectly feasible to get the first toehold on the professional ladder for £40 or less, and at the end of eight years' training to fit out one's shop and invest in a small medical library, even in London, for another £20 or £30.[1]

An education for the 'practick part' of the law could only rarely be as cheaply acquired as this; and after qualification, if the hope was to proceed beyond mere clerkship, it was desirable to have some capital in reserve. As early as 1683 John Aubrey had observed that many attorneys of his day 'will take a hundred pounds with a clerk'.[2] By Anne's reign, according to his own reputation and the purse of an applicant's father, a top-flight London attorney-at-law might charge as much as £200, even £220,[3] and a Chancery solicitor up to £250 for taking a youth into his office for five years;[4] while just occasionally a really prestigious and well-connected local practiser (such as James Long of Wootton Bassett, attorney of the Queen's Bench, and most probably a member of a wealthy and well-connected Wiltshire family) was able to put his price a trifle above the normal £100 to £105 ceiling which held firm in the provinces right through to 1730.[5] But these were very definitely

---

[1] 'Fitting out' could of course cost a great deal more, if means allowed it and self-consequence or ambition prompted it—as Dudley Ryder discovered in the case of his apothecary cousin, Watkins. W. Matthew (ed.), *The Diary of Dudley Ryder 1715-1716* (1939), p. 30. A more general contemporary verdict, however, was that 'there is no branch of business in which a man requires less money to set him up . . .; ten or twenty pounds, judiciously applied, will buy gallipots and counters and as many drugs to fill them with as might poison the whole island'. R. Campbell, *The London Tradesman* (1747), p. 64.

[2] John Aubrey, *Collections for the Natural and Topographical History of Wiltshire* (ed. John Britton, 1847), pt. ii, ch. cxi (unpaginated).

[3] e.g. Samuel Mason, attorney of the Queen's Bench, June 1712; Charles Bernard, attorney of the Common Pleas, Mar. 1715; Nathaniel Hickman, attorney of the King's Bench, May 1716; Thomas Dugdale of Tokenhouse Yard, Feb. 1730; James Cock of Dowgate Hill, Apr. 1730. PRO IR 1/1/105, 1/4/42, 1/4/188, 1/12/4, 1/12/17.

[4] Twice in one month in 1712 leading Chancery solicitors, Thomas Paratt and William Bedford, took sums as high as this, as did John Mills of the Six Clerks Office in Chancery in 1713. IR 1/1/103, 1/1/112, 1/4/14. Paratt took £250 with the son-in-law of a London surgeon, William Timme: an interesting commentary on the means of the surgeon, as well as one of many illustrations of cross-fertilization between the professions, and not least between the newer professions.

[5] In his case, £110 in Feb. 1712 (IR 1/42/62). Sir James Long, 5th bart. of Draycot, nr. Chippenham, was MP for Wootton Bassett, 1715-22. John

the upper limits. As Dr Robson has said, most London articled clerkships by the early decades of the eighteenth century involved an outlay of between £50 and around £160,[1] on average less than the cost of a single year at the inns of court; while in the provinces £60 was not a freakishly low sum even for a gentleman to pay for establishing his son in a lawyer's office in the last years of Queen Anne. In the north it is striking to find so outstandingly successful a local figure as Isaac Greene of Prescot and Liverpool asking only £80 of a county squire's son in 1712,[2] and even in the late 1720s, north of Trent, in Wales and in the south-west beyond Wiltshire, the £60–£90 premium remained the convention for a five-year training.

The point at the heart of all these figures is I hope obvious enough, though it has rarely been grasped. They mean that the vast majority of young men between 1710 and 1730 who were trained for the junior, but now socially acceptable branches of these two 'great professions' did so for an investment of from £5 to £15 a year in the case of medicine and of from £8 to just over £20 a year in the case of the law. We are thinking, in fact, of sums that were within the horizons of families of many different social backgrounds above the massed ranks of the wage-labourers. Not even the clergy (although the Church remained easily the most accessible of the traditional professions for families of modest means) could hope—except in the most exceptional circumstances—to scrape a training on less than £30 a year by the early eighteenth century. It cost a fairly poor Lancashire parson £278 to keep his son at Oxford from his matriculation in 1687 until 1695, shortly before he was ordained deacon.[3]

Cox of Great Coggeshall, Essex—an *esquire*, and therefore a very rare bird among provincial attorneys—asked £107. 10s. in July 1715 for only four years of articled clerkship, the same terms as those required by John Read, a Plymouth lawyer, in June 1712. The most expensive country attorney I have come across in the two decades before 1730 was another Wiltshire practiser, Anthony Martyn of Chippenham. He received £120 when he took Richard Wastfield, a local gentleman's son, into his office in June 1715. For the above cases see IR 1/4/49; 1/42/129; 1/4/44.

[1] Robert Robson, *The Attorney in Eighteenth-Century England*, pp. 56–7.

[2] IR 1/42/64. Across the Pennines William Buck of Rotherham, a member of a very solid and reputable family of south Yorkshire attorneys and solicitors which handled plenty of London as well as local business, was content to take only £65 from the father of James Burnett of Lofthouse in Dec. 1711, IR 1/1/130.

[3] R. Trappes-Lomax, *The Diary and Letter Book of Thomas Brockbank, 1671–1709* (Chetham Society, 89, 1930), p. vii. The yearly amounts varied

I shall not labour the implications of all this for the maintenance, from the Restoration through to the very eve of indus-
trialization, of an 'open' yet an integrated social order. But I
have analysed one sample of 50 persons who were articled to
attorneys or solicitors in London and the provinces between
April 1711 and October 1712; and of the 45 whose background
is firmly documented, fractionally over half had fathers who
were styled either esquires or gentlemen, three of the five
esquires being of county families and including a Wiltshire
Ernle.[1] Of the rest, eight were widows' sons, two had a clerical
and three a medical background,[2] while the other identifiable
parents were a goldsmith, a yeoman, a mariner, two London
mercers, a bookseller, an innkeeper, a London joiner who put
up £45. 7s. 6d., and a Norwich baker who found an attorney
willing to take his boy for £40. How many of the 'gents' were
themselves lawyers it is impossible to say; but since the amount of
professional in-breeding going on in the law by this time was
already considerable there must have been some. Otherwise
the only really untypical feature of the sample may be the rather
low proportion of clergymen's sons in it: for it has been established that ten per cent of all the 610 children of the cloth
apprenticed between 1710 and 1720 were, in fact, articled to
lawyers.[3] The Augustan attorney was not in general a man of
lowly origin; it is the variety of his social background, not its
humbleness, which is striking. Quite often he was only one step
away from the tradesman's counter or the craftsman's workshop;
but the trades tended on the whole to be substantial ones, like

from £40 in the first year to £19 in 1690-1 and averaged just over £33 a
year for nearly 8 years. For a commoner with *any* sort of appearance to keep
up £30 a year was cutting it extremely fine at Oxford or Cambridge back in
the 1620s. J. T. Cliffe, *The Yorkshire Gentry from the Reformation to the Civil War*
(1969), p. 76.

    [1] The Ernles were one of the leading families in Wiltshire, and it is clear
that by the early 18th century a very small but significant element among
trainees for the 'lesser degrees' of the law was now being drawn from the
élite of the squirearchy. For example, John Borlase of Pendeen, Cornwall,
MP for St. Ives 1710-15, articled a son to a St. Austell attorney in 1715;
and in 1716 one of the knights of the shire for Gloucestershire, Thomas
Stephens of Upper Lypiatt (MP 1713-20) paid a £200 premium to have
his son, George, trained in London by a successful King's Bench attorney:
IR 1/4/33, 1/4/188.

    [2] The sons of a surgeon, an apothecary, and a druggist, respectively.

    [3] Robson, op. cit., p. 55 n., citing P. A. Bezodis, unpublished Fellowship
dissertation (Trinity Coll. Cambridge), 'The English Parish Clergy, 1600-
1800', p. 483.

mercers and victuallers, and the crafts superior ones like watchmakers.[1] Similarly, there was a steady trickle of recruits from the respectable yeomanry into lawyers' offices throughout the years 1711–30,[2] but virtually nothing from landed society below that level. Nevertheless, there was no lack of comets in the sky to inspire them all: the Bensons of York and Bramham—the father, according to Reresby, 'one of no birth, and that had raised himself from being clerk to a country attorney', the son, a peer of the realm by 1711; or Isaac Greene, son of a bankrupt merchant, who bought his first south Lancashire manor (and by no means his last) at the age of 34; or Thomas Brereton, whose father was an alehouse keeper, but who used an articled clerkship in Chester as the first rung on a ladder that led to marriage to a brigadier's daughter, an estate at Shotwood Park, and 26 years as MP for Liverpool.[3]

For the junior branches of the medical profession the starters contained fewer pedigree specimens than those bound for lawyers' offices and more mongrels of dubious ancestry. I have taken at random intervals from the Stamp Office records of 1711–12 and 1730 a sample of 66 men of ascertainable background who entered the profession as trainees through apprenticeship either to apothecaries or to surgeons. In one respect it is an untypical sample; only a tiny three per cent of the entrants in it came from families with an existing connection with medicine, and there is plenty of other evidence to suggest that internal recruitment was at a higher level than this.[4] Otherwise the message is clear and convincing enough. No parent was higher in rank than 'gentleman'; but it was this elastic category which supplied the largest proportion of recruits, 27 per cent, with a slight bias in favour of surgery.[5] It is very evident that the other profession

---

[1] A further small group of entrants I have looked at for 1730 contains no one with a father lower down the social scale than a saddler from Chippenham.

[2] Some of them picked up bargains: e.g. John Marsh of Hampstead, yeoman, placed his son in April 1713 with Henry Courthorpe of London, an attorney of the Court of Common Pleas, for a £50 premium. Moreover, the articles were for the unusually long period of 7 years: IR 1/4/50.

[3] A. Browning (ed.), *Memoirs of Sir John Reresby* (Glasgow, 1936), p. 90; Stewart-Brown, Isaac Greene, p. 6; *VCH Lancs* iii, 110; Hist. MSS Comm., *Egmont Diary*, i. 87; [R.] Sedgwick [(ed.), *The History of Parliament: The House of Commons 1715–1754* (1970)], i. 484–5.

[4] e.g., a second sample, taken from a more limited period—the years 1715, 1716 and 1719—shows 6 apprentices with a medical family background (the fathers being a druggist, 2 surgeons, and 3 apothecaries) out of 42 entrants.

[5] Ten out of 42 in the second sample, but this group contained at least one esquire and possibly two.

which benefited most from the rising status of the apothecaries and surgeons was the Church. There are seven clergymen's sons among the 66 apprentices, the majority carrying premiums of between £50 and £61. 10s., though two were accommodated for as little as £25 and £30. The gentleman's town or country house and the parsonage apart, the farm was the commonest source of supply. A fifth of the whole group, in fact, came from vicarages or farms,[1] the father of one country lad being described as a plain 'husbandman'. Otherwise their backgrounds were astonishingly diverse. Their parents ranged on the one hand from Norwich and Whitehaven merchants, two master mariners, a Ripon mercer and a Norwich brewer, through a group of superior craftsmen (a London tinplate worker, a clockmaker, and a herald-painter from Exeter) to textile workers, a small innkeeper, three bakers (one a man of means), two blacksmiths, a carpenter, a gardener, and a cook.[2]

It was at this very time, too, that the composition of the English medical profession was being reshaped at a higher level still, that of the physicians. From 1700 to 1740 Oxford and Cambridge suffered a dramatic loss of ground at the hands, first, of a number of continental universities, whose medical faculties were enjoying a golden period at this time, above all Boerhaave's Leyden, and then as a result of the establishment between 1720 and 1726 of what was soon to become the great Edinburgh medical school. Leyden, Rheims, Utrecht, and Edinburgh attracted many dissenters' sons debarred from Oxford and Cambridge;[3] but also, because they offered a much more

---

[1] Much the same is the case with the recruits of 1715-16 and 1719 sampled (8 out of the 42)—though the proportion of 6 clerical to 2 yeomen parents was more heavily weighted in favour of the cloth.

[2] It is interesting that in neither of the two samples examined, 108 cases in all, was there a single explicit instance of a lawyer's son going into medicine, despite the traffic the other way. Clergy and medical men apart, one writing-master is the only professional parent in the 1715-16 sample In the second sample, as in the first, trade, manufacture, and the crafts were well represented—by a Virginia merchant, 2 goldsmiths, a prosperous coachmaker, a small clothier, a linen draper, and a brazier. The lower end of the spectrum was made up of a butcher (paying £28), 2 cordwainers (one of whom paid only £10. 15s. to a surgeon), and a barber.

[3] e.g. John Oldfield and Robert Nesbitt, who graduated at Leyden in 1718 and 1721 respectively, were both the sons of Nonconformist ministers and their later success as London physicians and election to fellowships of the Royal College represent notable feats of social mobility. Among the early English-born graduates of the Edinburgh school were the Lancashire dissenter, Samuel Kay—the uncle of Richard Kay of Baldingstone (see

intensive, as well as a far better training (it has been recently shown that a hard-working young man with a classical grounding but without previous medical training often got a doctor's degree at Leyden and Rheims in 18 months or less) hundreds went to these universities, including many Anglicans, who could not have afforded the lengthy Oxbridge route to a practice in 'physic'.[1] The fact that 746 English-speaking students of medicine, 352 of them English nationals, trained at Leyden under Boerhaave from 1701 to 1738 gives some idea of the scale as well as the social character of the infusion that resulted.[2]

Although I have chosen to illustrate my argument about the professions and social mobility mainly from two of the old professions, perhaps I might reinforce it, in conclusion, by a briefer reference to two of the newer ones, the army and navy. At first sight they appear to present a complete contrast: the former the only one of the newer professions in which recruitment and training by apprenticeship played scarcely any part, and generally considered by historians of the eighteenth century a stronghold of social privilege, the latter more flexible in its attitude on both scores than any other contemporary profession. Yet if one digs down into the social amalgam of the two officer corps which took shape between the 1680s and the 1720s, the differences that come to light are less pronounced than one might expect. Not surprisingly the most numerous beneficiaries by far of the army's unexpected expansion between 1685 and 1712 were the younger sons of the country gentry. The purchase system was a built-in guarantee that men of good family, or at least influential connections, would benefit most. But one must not write off as ill-informed prejudice that obsession with the *nouveau* element in the army which characterizes so much Tory and Country Whig opinion during the Spanish Succession War.

above p. 333 n. 1) and a young Quaker from across the Pennines, John Fothergill, who was later to enjoy a London career of exceptional prosperity. E. A. Underwood, *Boerhaave's Men*, pp. 73, 131, 170–1; *Kay's Diary*, pp. 2, 18, and *passim*; Anon [MacMichael], *Leading British Physicians* [1830], pp. 183–4, 192.

[1] See the graphs and tables in Underwood, op. cit., pp. 37–9, 75.

[2] Ibid., p. 24. Leyden-trained physicians who returned to practise or teach medicine in early 18th-century England spanned a wide social range from the sons of well-to-do country squires, such as Dr Cromwell Mortimer and Dr Nathan Alcock, to the Devonshire butcher's son, John Huxham. There is much valuable biographical information in R. W. Innes Smith, *English-Speaking Students of Medicine at the University of Leyden* (Edinburgh, 1932).

It was not coincidence that in his first devastating issue of *The Examiner*, in the winter of 1710, Swift used not only the new, overweening 'monied interest' but also the army officers, the 'generals and colonels', as his classic examples of unhealthy social mobility: 'a species of men quite different from any that were ever known before the Revolution', whose coaches now choked the streets of London in the long winter hiatuses between campaigns.[1] Almost twenty years of warfare created avenues of opportunity which were rarely glimpsed in the stabler conditions of a small peacetime army. In wartime the initial demands of the purchase system were not excessive, so far as the ordinary foot regiments were concerned—especially when colonels were frequently having to raise new regiments hastily—and (as one MP reminded the House of Commons in 1709), 'promotions may be made every day in the old regiments', as junior officers stepped up without the usual payment into dead men's shoes.[2]

Such circumstances changed the social structure of the army in a way that some even thought reminiscent of the bad old days of the New Model. What was often overlooked was that the wars proved a particular boon to many poorer gentry families, who would have been ill equipped to compete before 1685 and were to be disadvantaged again not many years after 1720.[3] But at the same time the new officer corps absorbed not only the sprigs of the aristocracy, on the one hand, but parsons' sons and a surprising number of officers of bourgeois stock as well. It was a Staffordshire clergyman named Wood who, perhaps with the help of a relative, got his son Cornelius into Queen Catherine's Troop of Life Guards as a private in the 1680s: and it would certainly have cost him much less than the £100 price of a 'gentleman trooper's' place in the mid eighteenth century. The Irish and Flanders campaigns of 1689–95

[1] *The Examiner*, No. 13, 2 Nov. 1710. Cf. the comments of two Country Whigs. James Lowther and Edward Wortley Montagu, on a similar theme in Cumbria RO Carlisle, Lonsdale MSS: James Lowther to William Gilpin, 12 Feb. 1708; *Cobbett's Parliamentary History*, vi. 889, 4 Feb. 1709[-10].

[2] E. W. Montagu's speech, loc. cit.

[3] The Wightmans of Kent are a good case in point: hard hit by the land tax, and with at least 3 boys to provide for on a very straitened income. Their son Joseph in 18 years' service became a major-general, active in mopping up the Highlands after the Fifteen. Charles Dalton, *George the First's Army, 1714-1727*, i (1910), 48–9. More remarkably, if socially less acceptably, Charles Wills, the general who thwarted the Scots at Preston in 1715, was one of six sons of a debt-ridden Cornish yeoman. Ibid. 59–70.

gave Wood his chance and by 1704 he was a major-general.[1] By the reign of George I the most traditionally *un*military families could reflect with pride how

in the late wars between England and France . . . was our army full of excellent officers who went from the shop, and behind the counter, into the camp, and who distinguished themselves by their merits and gallant behaviour! as colonel Pierce, [Generals] Wood, Richards, and several others that may be named.[2]

The navy's very different history before 1689, the far more testing technical demands it made on its officers (one excepts the artillery and engineer officers of the army from the comparison), and above all its less uniform methods of recruitment made it inevitable that of the two professions it would display the greater variety of social origins. Eager as it was to attract the scions of good families, the Admiralty was taught by the harsh experiences of the Nine Years' War the folly, in a profession where experience and seamanship counted for so much, of developing a system of admission and promotion that seemed to offer 'a very great discouragement [as their Lordships put it in 1702] to such persons as have . . . served many years as mates and midshipmen, and in every respect qualified themselves to perform the duty of lieutenant'.[3] As a result, during the Spanish Succession War the 695 men newly commissioned as lieutenants included no fewer than 303 who had previously seen service in the merchant fleet and then transferred to the navy, usually as petty officers in the first place;[4] the rest being those drawn from the two streams of direct 'apprentice' entrants, the 'King's Letter Boys' and 'servants'. But one major difference between the situation and prospects of all these entrants and the rough 'old tarpaulin' officers of the 1670s was that by the early 1700s almost all shared a common aspiration to a secure social status, and increasingly to the manners and life-style of gentlemen. The other decisive difference was the facility with which promotion came in the wartime navy to the man of true merit—

[1] C. Dalton, *English Army Lists and Commission Registers, 1661–1714* (1892–1904), v. pt. ii, p. 3.

[2] Daniel Defoe, *The Complete English Tradesman* (1745 edn., but written 1726), i. 247. General Sabine's family had been in trade in Canterbury. Three of Marlborough's favourites, Maccartney, Cadogan, and Whetham, came of either mercantile or lawyer stock.

[3] Commissioners of the Admiralty to the Navy Board, 6 Jan. 1702, printed in Merriman, *Queen Anne's Navy: Documents 1702–1714*, p. 319.

[4] D. A. Baugh, *British Naval Administration in the Age of Walpole*, pp. 97, 98 (table 5).

a condition which did not by any means disappear even in the predominantly peaceful decades from 1719 to 1739, though the pace was obviously slower by then.

Two cases of spectacular social mobility via the late Stuart navy are often quoted: those of Cloudesley Shovell, who became a rear-admiral at 31 after being a cabin-boy at 14, and David Mitchell, whose road to a flag began in the merchant marine in Charles II's reign as ship's boy and later mate. But they were neither freakish exceptions nor stereotypes. The tally of those appointed admirals, to go no lower, between 1689 and 1713 includes a long list of men who were able by seamanship and leadership to transform their social prospects out of all recognition. John Baker, the stepson of a Deal carpenter, learned his skills, as Mitchell did, on a merchantman. Admiral Hopson, knighted in 1702, may not (as was once thought) have started his working life as a tailor's apprentice; but he certainly rose from the lower deck, as did Sir George Walton.[1] Almost total obscurity shrouds the parentage of Sir John Norris, who vaulted from lieutenant's to full admiral's rank between 1689 and 1709,[2] and of Admirals Thomas Swanton and Sir George Saunders, except that they are known to have been Londoners. In such company Sir Charles Wager, despite his unpretentious upbringing in Cornwall, did have a point when he explained to Walpole many years later that he was 'not altogether an up-start'.[3] Even senior officers of gentry stock, like two of Anne's most distinguished admirals, Jennings and Byng, sometimes reveal on closer examination struggling or impoverished back-grounds.[4] Without doubt there were still some extremely

[1] The bulk of the biographical information in this paragraph is drawn from J. Campbell, *The Lives of the Admirals and other eminent British Seamen* (4 vols., 1742-4); J. Charnock, *Biographia Navalis* [*from 1660*] (London, 1794-8), especially vol. ii; Sedgwick, vols. i and ii, on those officers who held parliamentary seats; and sundry articles in *DNB*.

[2] Norris's very slow promotion during his first 9 years in the Navy (he joined as a cabin-boy in 1680 and was still rated 'able seaman' in the books of the *James Galley* in 1686) suggests few if any social connections of value at that time. Dr Aldridge, who has thrown useful light on his early career, believes he was born and brought up in Ireland but his precise family background remains a matter for speculation. D. D. Aldridge, 'Admiral Sir John Norris 1670 (or 1671)-1749: His birth and early service . . .' *Mariner's Mirror*, 51 (1965), 173-5.

[3] Sedgwick, ii. 503. Cf. W. Coxe, *Memoirs of the Life and Administra of Sir Robert Walpole* (1798), iii. 116-17: Wager to Walpole, 12 July 1731, and enclosure, for Wager's own version of his origins and connections.

[4] To say, for instance, that Sir John Jennings was the younger son of a

rough diamonds in high posts in Queen Anne's navy along with some highly polished ones; and none rougher than John Benbow, the son of a Shrewsbury tanner, who in 1702 was appointed Commander-in-Chief of the West Indies fleet. But when Benbow died of his wounds in the Caribbean early in the Spanish Succession War, the days of the quintessential seventeenth-century 'tar' admiral—of the Hopsons, the Berrys,[1] and so forth—were almost over. Most successful officers even of Benbow's generation,[2] and not least those who had worked their way right up the ladder with the minimum of advantages, no longer doubted that captaincy of a first or second rate should give a man ingress into good society; or that a flag, if he so wished, should be his passport into county society.

Nevertheless, the fact that, say, Cloudesley Shovell became a big landowner in Kent and Mitchell a Shropshire squire at the height of their naval careers did not destroy those common interests which, as 'sea officers', they shared with the most junior lieutenant in the fleets under their command. And there is, surely, a general moral here which might be drawn in conclusion. Because of the way the professions recruited and trained their members in the years 1680–1730 they were able, as we have seen, to recruit remarkably widely. Not only for the reasons I have mentioned, but because also of the still relatively moderate expense of training for the Church and for school-teaching; because of the apparent indifference of the new revenue departments to social status when appointing their local officials at least; because even the bar, the highest rampart of social privilege in the professions, could be stormed by money and talent without birth: for all these reasons it was possible for men of the most diverse social backgrounds to enter the professions *and then be welded together*. Within bodies which, despite some internal tensions, tended by their very nature, their mutual concerns and respect, to foster community of interest and at times a very high degree of *esprit de corps*, social prejudice

Shropshire gentleman, is true; what it does not tell us is that he was Philip Jennings's fifteenth child!

[1] Sir John Berry (d. 1691), who rose to vice-admiral's rank from 'poor boatswain's boy' and whose widow later married an apothecary at Mile End, was a particularly unambiguous specimen of the old school. Sir G. Jackson and G. F. Duckett, *Naval Commissioners . . . 1660–1760* (Lewes, 1889), p. 62, quoting G. W. Marshall, *Le Neve's Pedigrees of Knights* [1660–1714], Harleian Soc., 1873.

[2] John Benbow was only just 36 when the war with France broke out in 1689: he was slightly younger, in fact, than Shovell and Mitchell.

would be defeated sooner or later by the pressure towards fusion. Professional status itself thus became a bond that helped more closely to integrate many units of local society as decade succeeded decade after 1680, and as English society in general left behind its seventeenth-century traumas and moved towards the relative calm of 1730.[1] In short, that same transformation of the professions which was so influential an agent of social change became, almost by the same token, a powerful tranquillizing force as well. When, therefore, Lord Chesterfield wrote to a friend in George II's reign, 'I entirely agree with you in your resolution of breeding up all your sons to some profession or other',[2] he was not simply advocating a well-trodden route to individual security or to social advancement; he was also (whether he recognized it or not) endorsing a recipe, tried and tested by then over many years, for maintaining social stability in pre-industrial England.

[1] For a fuller discussion see my essay 'The Achievement of Stability', above, pp. 272-5.

[2] Written in 1755. Quoted from the correspondence of the 4th earl of Chesterfield by E. Hughes, 'The Professions in the Eighteenth Century', loc. cit., p. 47.

INDEX